THE
BOER
WAR

THE BOER WAR

THE STRUGGLE FOR SOUTH AFRICA

BILL NASSON

Cover illustration: Royal Munster Fusiliers fighting from behind the redoubt at Honey Nest Kloof, South Africa. Feb. 16, 1900 (Library of Congress)

Copyright © Bill Nasson
(Originally published by Tafelberg, an imprint of NB PUBLISHERS, Cape Town, South Africa in 2010)

This edition published by Spellmount,
an imprint of The History Press, 2011

The History Press
The Mill, Brimscombe Port
Stroud, Gloucestershire, GL5 2QG
www.thehistorypress.co.uk

© Bill Nasson, 2010, 2011

British Library Cataloguing in Publication Data.
A catalogue record for this book is available from the British Library.

ISBN 978 0 7524 6022 2

Printed in Malta

This one is for Ann,
of gables more green than Dutch

The real point to be made good to South Africa is that we, not the Dutch, are boss. *British prime minister, Lord Salisbury, 27 July 1899*

Every sea in the world is being furrowed by the ships which are conveying British troops from every corner of the globe in order to smash this little handful of people.

A Century of Wrong, *issued by F. W. Reitz,*
state secretary of the South African Republic (London, 1900)

Dwindle, dwindle, little war,
How I wonder more and more,
As about the veld you hop,
When you really mean to stop.
'Saki' *(Hector Munro),* The Westminster Alice *(London, 1902)*

The war in South Africa has exceeded the limits of barbarism. I have fought against many barbarous Kaffir tribes in the course of my life; but they are not so barbarous as the English, who have burnt our farms and driven our children into destitution, without food or shelter.

The Memoirs of Paul Kruger, *vol. 2 (London, 1902)*

So how do we decide when and whether to intervene? I think we need to bear in mind five major considerations. First, are we sure of our case? War is an imperfect instrument for fighting humanitarian distress, but armed force is sometimes the only means of dealing with dictators. Second, have we exhausted all diplomatic options? We should always give peace every chance. Third, on the basis of a practical assessment of the situation, are there military operations we can sensibly and prudently undertake? Fourth, are we prepared for the long term? And, finally, do we have national interests involved?

British prime minister, Tony Blair,
on the invasion of Iraq, 3 November 2006

CONTENTS

LIST OF MAPS*

* Distance scale: 1 mile = 1.6 km

PREFACE

'THE BOER MUTINY HAS COMMENCED,' WROTE AN INDIAN NATIONALIST in Calcutta in October 1899. That cheeky sentence both described a war that had broken out in South Africa and conveyed a meaning for those who had brought it about – the British. India had had its mutiny, or rebellion, against their empire in 1857, which had been saved by its nerve or, rather, by its cannons. Now it was the turn of what some curious Asian observers called 'the Dutch peril' to rise up against imperial power. This time, would the British Raj again prevail?

In its war for South Africa it did, but it turned out to be hard going. The Anglo-Boer War of 1899–1902, or South African War, or Boer War, or Second Anglo-Boer War, or even Second War of Freedom, was a conflict which finally completed the British imperial conquest of Southern Africa. It was the biggest ever 'small war' of late-Victorian 'New Imperialism', and has a recognised significance in wider world history. This book provides a general account of how that war came to pass – how the political contest between Boer republicanism and British imperialism developed into a bitter and violent struggle; how the warring sides conducted their military operations; how adversaries saw each other; how hostilities affected belligerent societies and others which became party to the conflict; how the combatants finally turned to peace; and, finally, how the conflict has come to be remembered and how might it be viewed now.

In producing this volume I have incurred a number of debts. Its original version, *The South African War, 1899–1902*, was published over a decade ago in London by Hodder in the *Modern Wars* series of its Arnold imprint. I must record my thanks to the publishers for being able to re-use material in this new version.

That edition was written while I was in the Department of History at the University of Cape Town, and I would like to acknowledge colleagues and students there for intellectual stimulation, support and friendship over the years. A particular tribute is due to those undergraduates who took my War and Society course for the benefit of their bright and engaging class and individual company there and, sometimes, beyond.

At the University of Stellenbosch, I have especially to thank Albert Grundlingh and other colleagues of the Department of History, Sandra Swart, Anton Ehlers and Wessel Visser, for their exceptional welcoming generosity. I should also like to acknowledge Joan and Ian Dichmont, dear friends of my late parents, for kindly allowing me to read and to quote from Alan Corbett's unpublished Boer War letters to his family in England. Particular thanks are also due to Alexander Milner and Stefan Gerber of Natte Valleij, as well as to Jan Solms and Rohan Etsebeth of Fanakalo for kind permission to use their *Boer & Brit* wine bottle as an illustration. Leah, my usual target reader, made the usual suitable comments. Lastly, as nothing goes without saying, let me say that working with NB Publishers has been a treat. Erika Oosthuysen took the bait and has been enormously supportive and helpful. At Tafelberg, nothing has been too much bother for Annie Olivier, who has seen it all through with enthusiasm, encouragement and consummate professionalism. Besides my publishers, I am grateful to John Hall for making sense of the maps, and to Peter Joyce, Maria Chafetz, Wilhelm Snyman, Lauren van Vuuren, Tanya Barben and Belinda Botma for excellent professional assistance.

BILL NASSON
Professor of History,
University of Stellenbosch

THE LEGACY AND THE LESSONS

THE ANGLO-BOER WAR, FOUGHT MORE THAN A CENTURY AGO, HAS A FIXED place in modern historical memory. At the time, it was the most absorbing military drama on the world stage. Traces of this, the last and largest of Victorian Britain's imperial conflicts, are, of course, very much in evidence in modern South Africa, but they are also discernible in Europe and elsewhere.

In Britain's Merseyside, Liverpool football fans still crowd into a stand known as the 'Kop', after the January 1900 battle of Spioen Kop. The Netherlands acquired clusters of Transvaal neighbourhoods or *Transvaalbuurten,* with streets named after celebrated Boer generals like Louis Botha or Christiaan de Wet, although more recent Dutch political persuasions have seen the name of Paul Kruger obliterated in favour of heroic icons of the anti-apartheid struggle.

To some, the early Boer communities also served as something of an inspiration. In the former American Confederacy, for example, envious one-time rebels in the southern state of Georgia admired the wartime republics sufficiently to confer the name Pretoria on a local town. Popular Parisian folk art of the early twentieth century includes robust images of republican anti-British, French-Boer fraternity. In the First World War, German soldiers sang of how the Boers had bloodied the British. For their part, Russian soldiers on the Eastern Front took up a folk song, *Transvaal,* as a misty expression of their own sense of national suffering. For years, radical Quebecois nationalists would deface Montreal Anglo-Boer memorials to the empire patriotism of Canadian troops who had died in South Africa. More than one British and Antipodean town has its Pretoria Road or Mafeking Avenue, to say nothing of crops of civic and church memorials to distant soldiering sacrifice.

In South Africa, as remembrance and commemoration of the conflict have grown more inclusive with changed political conditions, there have been increasing calls for recognition of black involvement and of the war's long-neglected and still unknown number of black casualties. Meanwhile, the graves of combatants in military cemeteries and in more scattered, sometimes isolated, farm and other rural locations, as well as those of Boer civilians, continue to serve as silent sites of remembrance. But they are ever more in danger of dissolving, and not only through custodial neglect. A harsh African climate and nibbling hunger for fertile land continues to topple crosses and to smother resting places.

Then there are the more picaresque reminders. South African fruit stalls sometimes still sell a brand of orange-pink mango called 'Tommy Atkins', the generic nineteenth-century name for the common British soldier, celebrated in music hall and by Rudyard Kipling in his 1890s *Barrack Room Ballads*. For decades, the sports press used to greet British and Irish Lions rugby touring sides with warnings that an overwhelmingly Afrikaner Springbok team was waiting to avenge the Boer War. A smart commercial twist to this nationalist challenge occurred in 1999, the war's centenary and the year of a Springbok-British & Irish Lions test series – South African Airways advertised itself as 'Carrier to the Anglo-Boer War'.

Then there is the vintage reference to a British soldier as a sun-burned *rooinek* or 'redneck', an epithet that has been part of the gastric juice of Afrikaner masculine tradition for years, not least when the Anglo-Boer War has been replayed as some bruising college school rugby match, almost but not quite war. As vintage – if more perjorative – is the English anti-Afrikaner term, rockspider, coined during the war to describe the stealthiness of Boer commandos who avoided open combat and preferred instead to squirm down behind rocks as concealed marksmen. Still, nowadays, 'rockspider' and '*rooinek*' are stamped on a South African bottle, symbolizing a fraternity of a vinous kind. *Boer & Brit*, a beefy Stellenbosch red blend, has been made by youthful winemakers who are, respectively, the great, great descendants of Transvaal President Paul Kruger and Britain's General Sir John French.

At this pendulum level, the writer Robert Greig has recalled how white English-speaking liberal students were dubbed 'uitlanders' or foreigners by unfriendly Afrikaner peers in the 1970s. Some relished rubbing in old 'injuries', like the myth of genocidal British concentration camp administrators seasoning rations with 'ground glass'.[1] But it is conceivable that had the Boer republics won in 1902, twentieth-century Afrikaner society would have come off badly in Britain for some war transgression of its own creation.

At the same time, the place of the Anglo-Boer War in the making of South African history does not wholly explain the much wider historical fascination which its events continue to generate. Some part of that interest is certainly lingering popular nostalgia for a long-gone era, an imagined time before the advent of modern, industrial-scale mass slaughter, when men were supposed to have fought more honourably, or at least more politely. It is a romantic hankering after 'the last of the gentlemen's wars', in the memorable description of Major General J.F.C. Fuller, a notable military theorist of the twentieth century who had also fought in South Africa. Through this rosy filter glows an image in which plodding but hardy British regiments fought clean and courageous engagements with decent Boer citizen commandos. Those gripping symbols of an empire besieged – Mafeking, Kimberley and Ladysmith – were lodged deep in the national British psyche, the spirit of that flag-waving time revived many decades later in the 1982 Falklands War, when an expeditionary force – the modern equivalent of the Victorian gunboat – relieved South Atlantic Crown land from invading Argentinians.

Another element of the spell is thrown by a constantly rising stock of specialised historical reference, including encyclopaedias and handbooks, assessments of the art the war inspired and more recent studies of its military medicine.[2] There is also a fair portion that is arcane or even outlandish. Anyone curious about the merits of the Boer republicans' Krag-Jorgensen rifle now has a handbook with an imposing technical sweep. Equally, the pivotal role of Rudge, Raleigh or BSA in scouting and dispatch cycling has been documented. The unique use of dolomite and sandstone in British fort and blockhouse construction has not gone unnoticed, nor has the technical modification of Royal Navy guns for use as field artillery.[3]

We may not know yet how many ways there are of skinning a cat, but it is quite probably the same number of ways there are of writing a single-author history of the South African War. Between the end of the 1970s, when Thomas Pakenham produced his massive military history, and the centenary of the war, there have been several interpretative publications, including a couple of visually-driven texts and the original edition of the present volume.[4] Naturally, historians were unable to escape the post-1999 stimulus of centenary commemoration, and the past decade has brought a fresh set of perspectives. Still, these have been almost exclusively specialised works – each adding some minute new particulars to the sum – rather than general narratives. One purpose of this book, therefore, is to appeal to and to inform the ordinary reader seeking to understand what the 1899–1902 crisis added up to.

This book is also, in some sense, a response to the memorable plea from the novelist Kathy Lette's Australian anti-heroine, Maddy Wolfe, to 'go on, rewrite history then! . . . it's a time-honoured English tradition. The Boer War, Gallipoli, the Fall of Singapore.'[5]

Now, over a century since the end of hostilities, consideration of that Boer War remains timely, possibly in more ways than one – because it taught lessons that should have been learned, and which by and large have mostly not been.

In the first place, it was a classic war of irony or illusion, in that those who brought it about did not get the war that they had anticipated. It was hatched to demonstrate, in the words of Britain's prime minister, that in South Africa 'we, not the Dutch, are boss'.[6] It began, in the view of the acting Transvaal president, Schalk Burger, as a war of misjudgement. The more optimistic of the Boers hoped to wrap things up before heavy British forces arrived. For their part, many on the imperial side expected the colonial enemy to yield without too much of a struggle. Instead, hostilities produced a bitter total war of great waste and immense civilian suffering. It was also a political minefield, littered with controversy over cause, motivation and meaning and fired by questions of religious faith, moral conduct and the reputation of the British empire.

And, like many other colonial wars, it had an exasperating tendency to last longer than virtually everyone had initially envisaged. Moreover, its outcome was mutually deflating. The Boers lost their stubborn battle to hold on to republican independence from Britain. While the British won, gaining the Transvaal Colony and the Orange River Colony, it was not without hand-wringing in London over the economic and political costs of its campaign, over its less than gymnastic military efficiency, and over whether it had a reliable enough level of national fitness to secure the imperial future.

The South African War, a 'big' modern small war and the last of Queen Victoria's reign, tested the capacity of invading British forces to adapt to demanding local fieldcraft conditions. These brought the tactical headache of lengthy supply lines, long ranges, expansive fields of fire and the risks inherent in a great deal of clear light. Equally, just as the conflict put pressure on Britain's military and financial resources, so, too, it handed the Boers fatal strategic choices, dragging republican society close to the edges of social and political disintegration and ultimately changing the whole face of South Africa. As the first war of the twentieth century, its posture was transitional, an agrarian conflict with a distinctly industrial radiation. Indeed, as a war of the modern kind, its real meaning was industrial, with the gold mines of the Transvaal central to the issue and the future of South Africa as an industrialising country in the balance.

At the same time, the campaign belonged simultaneously to two different eras. While it was a traditional countryside war of movement, with cavalry and mounted infantry carrying the fight over enormous spaces, its operations were tied to modern firearms, railways, aerial observation, electric power, the early use of field telephone communication, the telegraph, censorship, and the cultivation of press influence. And to break its stubborn enemy and win a day which was so slow in dawning, a frustrated British empire did not hesitate to pick up the destructive implements of total war: laying waste to the land, interning women and children, and resorting to the exile and occasionally the execution of adversaries. It is not for nothing that even fairly conservative British historians of this period have found little credit in a war termed 'the British Empire's Vietnam'.[7]

To be sure, there were rules. In conventional battle both sides took and held prisoners and did not finish off wounded opponents on the field as something less than fellow human beings. To that extent, in an invariably ruthless African colonial context, the Anglo-Boer conflict was, ironically, 'not the "last" of the gentlemen's wars, but possibly the first'.[8] Yet, a victorious outcome would not be decided expeditiously on the battlefield. To achieve that, the British Army had learned from its recent experiences of colonial pacification in Afghanistan, in the Sudan and elsewhere how deeply to carry aggressive action into the body of opposing societies.

The accomplishment of colonial conquest went to the head of the more go-ahead imperial politicians, although not always its blunders, complications and costs. It is that which raises a second reason to consider the meaning of the South African War today, for it throws a ghostly shadow, prompting colonial parallels with the present. Although actual empires have been dismembered, the world has had to continue to live with sabre-rattling, invasion, conquest and occupation. The catastrophic present invasions of Afghanistan and Iraq remain proof, if it were still needed, that old imperial habits of imposing order, improvement and a preferred kind of government have not been lost altogether: they linger on in the more zealous sensibilities of Washington and London.

The twenty-first century wars for Iraq and Afghanistan, perhaps clothed in deception and justified by a humanitarian best-behaviour excuse for intervention, were launched under the familiar short-war illusion that it would all be over very soon. In the case of Britain's Labour prime minister, confidence that force was the morally right thing merely betrayed 'his invincible historical ignorance'[9] of an imperial past in which an invading British army in Afghanistan in the later nineteenth century and an invading Anglo-Indian army in Iraq (or Mesopotamia as it was then) in the earlier twentieth century had found themselves in a very messy strategic situation. 'An epic of inefficiency' describes very well the fortunes of that early British Expeditionary Force to Baghdad.[10] This was more or less the situation in South Africa from which the British had to recover.

There is also, possibly, one last thing to weigh up when considering the war for South Africa and the recent war for Iraq. It is, most obviously, the importance in both wars of key strategic resources, gold then and oil reserves now. But the story may also have other parts. Essentially, both wars erupted from an air of crisis and heightened tensions between upstart agrarian states suddenly enriched by mineral resources and seen by older industrial powers as getting away with too much. The actions forced by Britain in 1899 and the United States of America in 2003 were launched on the basis that they had been defensive interventions provoked by belligerence and immediate threats. Public support for expeditionary action was by no means assured, and opinion had to be massaged in ways that presented the South African Republic's president, Paul Kruger, and President Saddam Hussein of Iraq, as unequivocally the aggressors. Thus, peace feelers and compromising mediation were ignored or brushed aside for fear not that they would fail but that they might succeed.

Nor do the suggested similarities end there. Invading forces waded in under illusions that it would all be over swiftly, with enemy subjects making peace once their capital cities (Pretoria and Baghdad) had been taken. However, instead of a knock-out blow, occupation triggered draining irregular or guerrilla resistance. In the idea of humanitarian emancipation in Iraq, again, there is a resemblance to the 1890s. Then, propaganda represented war as having been motivated in part by lofty impulses to free the Transvaal's unfranchised Uitlanders or foreigners from Paul Kruger's oppressive and autocratic regime, and to ease the plight of Africans under its thumb. In the Middle East, it was the turn of Iraqis to be released from the merciless grip of Saddam Hussein.

Both presidents, too, were demonised. Paul Kruger was depicted as a kind of Victorian ogre, an obdurate and anti-modern autocrat, both stubborn and stupid. His bloodthirsty Arab equivalent of a later age, Saddam Hussein, was targeted as an ambitious rogue dictator of irredeemably evil intentions who had become an immediate and deadly threat to his neighbours and to the security of civilised democracies. Inevitably, something dangerous was impending. In both cases, the conclusion was more or less the same: there had been a build-up of mass arsenals, modern German and French armaments in the Transvaal and Iraq's later fearsome – and mythical – weapons of mass destruction.

For Alfred Milner, British high commissioner in South Africa, and his pushy 'forward' policy, time to settle the Transvaal problem was running out fast, just as it did for the George W. Bush administration in Washington and its London ally in the case of Iraq. A last common factor, then, was that war was to be provoked. The means chosen consisted of an overbearing ultimatum, containing demands that the belligerent who tabled it knew could not be accepted without the loss of independence, autonomy and face. So, at the very end of a mortally dangerous crisis, the sabres stopped rattling and the armies took to the battlefield.

What follows is an interpretation of the decisive war for South Africa, or what at times has also been called the Transvaal War, the Great Boer War or even – for Edwardian juveniles – the Grate Bore Wore. Any history of a major conflict is an attempt, using imperial measures, to squeeze quarts into pint pots. As pointers to further reading on topics or themes which have either been bypassed or just touched on fleetingly, this treatment includes a select bibliography of useful and more recent works on the war. As much as anything, they are a further reminder that there is nothing quite like war to make one conclude that what history amounts to is, ultimately, the story of human folly.

1

SEEDS OF MODERN CONFLICT

T HE DEEP ORIGINS OF THE SOUTH AFRICAN WAR LIE IN DEVELOP-
ments that occurred many decades before the outbreak of hostilities in
October 1899.

The flames of Boer-British antagonism, which began as soon as British troops
landed at the Dutch Cape in 1806, were fanned by the movement of Dutch-
speaking farmers into the interior and the creation of their small republics. These
flames then flared, both brightly and ominously, when diamonds and gold were
discovered on the region's high central plateau. At stake was immense wealth, but
also British imperial dominance on the one hand, and the independence and cultural identity of two fledgling states on the other. In these circumstances, conflict
was probably always on the cards.

By the end of the nineteenth century, the colonised African region that had
become known as South Africa had been moulded by over three centuries of
European imperial influence. To begin with, the Dutch mercantile empire moved
beyond seeing the tip of the subcontinent as a handy seaport between Amsterdam and Djakarta. It had decided on expansion and settlement. Unlike those of
Australia, the Southern African coastlines and hinterland looked worth breaking
into, while holding the Cape of Good Hope and Table Bay still gave the Dutch sure
command of the sea route to Asia.

Conquest and capitalist agricultural and commercial growth – processes which
proved ruinous for independent indigenous societies like the Khoikhoi and the
San (Bushmen) – produced a gradual melding and blending of settler cultures
and classes into a new social order. A distinctive, largely farming Dutch African
(or Boer) class had emerged as the dominant European presence. By the end of the

eighteenth century, these men and women had no doubt that they belonged to a quite new commercial and trading order with a developed race and status consciousness, although they were as yet in no sense a unified or ideologically coherent nation.

A free patriarchal society of town and countryside, this intensely Protestant *burgher* or citizen order was in possession of a good many chunks of the Cape colony that were obviously worth possessing, and even a few that were not. As the nineteenth century drew near, itchy frontier colonists were finding that expansion into land beyond the settled areas was still being checked by the density and defensive resilience of their African peasant inhabitants. Dutch interests were pushy, but something stronger was required if further European ambitions were to be fulfilled.

Imperial Britain provided that muscle. Up to the end of the eighteenth century, its port options on the key trade route between Western Europe and India and the Orient had been unsatisfactory, the choice lying between the island canteen of St Helena in the south Atlantic, and disagreeable dependence on the Dutch harbour at the Cape. The only British nibble at Southern Africa had been in 1785, when a parliamentary committee had suggested Das Voltas Bay, between Portuguese Angola and the Dutch Cape, as a bracing spot to which to exile convicts. In the event, things were settled by the decision to use Botany Bay for this purpose and South Africa lost the historic opportunity to become Australia.

But Britain was soon back, and with more ambitious intentions. By the 1790s, growing imperial rivalry and jostling for spheres of influence and strategic sites in the Indian Ocean were souring relations between Britain, France and the Netherlands. Some of these tensions were resolved by the Napoleonic wars, in which London exploited its decisive naval supremacy to attack the maritime stations of its continental adversaries.

Driven by the compulsions of war and the strategic imperatives imposed by trading interests, British forces invaded the Dutch-controlled Cape. The defences of an increasingly rocky Dutch East India Company crumbled at a touch and, by 1815, the permanence of Britain's colonial control of the Cape was finally sealed by treaty recognition.

The regional impact of the new nineteenth-century empire was huge. To its Cape colonial heartland it brought British culture, the ideological predominance of free-trade capitalism, and an immigration thrust which gave rise to a new

English-speaking settler community which was resolutely British in its circumstances and outlook. A sliver of the wealthier urban-rural Dutch élite was happy enough to get into bed with British administrators in a marriage of class convenience, but such 'anglicising' accommodation did not go far. In general, there was very little British assimilation with a continuously expanding rural Boer population.

But there was much more to growing British intervention than the implanting of an imperial order. South Africa's incorporation into an industrialising British empire enlarged the colonial capitalist system and greatly increased its dynamism. In the Cape, the market imperatives of efficiency and improvement cleared the way for free wage labour to supplant the bondage of the earlier Dutch slave-holding period. An inflow of mercantile capital provided reservoirs of credit for agricultural development and speculation, driving up land prices and closing doors to the poorer Boer pastoralists. And vigorous imperial-backed military expansionism delivered African land and labour to sweeten colonial inventories.

Yet, many ordinary Boers groaned under the burden of a predatory Britishness, of the loss of traditional tied labour through slave emancipation, of drought, and of a bruising struggle for land ownership and security. In a movement towards the end of the 1830s, thousands of pioneer migrants, or Voortrekkers, left the Cape Colony, together with their Coloured and African servants, in an exodus into the interior in what would become known as the Great Trek.

This Boer migration represented a rebellious escape from the arrogance of British rule and English economic ascendancy, for new emigrant tenure in the north. But in search of easier livings, land-hungry trekkers had a hard time of it. An initial enclave in the eastern coastal settlement of Natal was uprooted in the 1840s when the British annexed the area, locking up its valuable acres for speculative land and commercial exploitation. Having failed in Natal, many Boer trekkers rolled on to find better pickings in the interior. After much floundering and political squabbling among themselves and with creeping imperial authority, precarious truces and tributary relations with some African chiefdoms and warfare with others over land, the Boers founded two independent white republican states. The autonomy of these republics, the *Oranjevrijstaat* or Orange Free State and the *Zuid-Afrikaansche Republiek* or South African Republic (Transvaal), was formally recognised by London in the 1850s. For imperial interests, nothing very much hung on them.

The republican Boers, ensconced in their highveld territories, were fractious and their administration tottery. This was an impoverished hinterland, and the sparsely settled trekker communities, greatly outnumbered by the African inhabitants, battled to assert effective control over the expropriated land and labour to which they laid sweeping claim. While these early agricultural states established a solid ethnic and cultural identity, in other respects they struggled to assert their nominal independence from British trading and other influences. The free Boer diaspora was really just the unproductive edge of an expanding colonial market, and was recognised as such by many Cape and Natal Boers, for whom equal rights with British settlers and a stable colonial environment did quite nicely. As contented Crown subjects accepting the legitimacy and security of an imperial order, they were disinclined to pack up for the uncertainties of a rickety republicanism.

It is commonplace nowadays for historians to argue that nineteenth-century Boer expansion represents a tributary of the great world flood of European migration, colonial conquest and settlement, tugged along by long-distance hunters and traders, and powered by the bullock wagon, the horse and the musket. It is equally customary for scholars to emphasise that the Boer migration was one strand in a web of Southern African population upheavals and movements which created new African states and societies. In this, the demographic disruptions throughout the interior highveld plateau, as a result of warfare centred around the Zulu kingdom in the Natal lowveld, turned out to be favourable to the wants of Boer independence. It delivered land for appropriation by trekker republicanism and weakened the capacity of some African inhabitants to repel invaders.

Still, while all this helped the Boers to hold their ground and to assert their sovereignty, in many respects it was a tenuous business until well into the later nineteenth century.[11]

If British power in the region waxed and waned during this era, there was seldom any lack of exertion to fortify and defend its perceived economic, political and strategic interests. On the secure outer rim, colonial ports controlled external trade, while the Royal Navy commanded the coasts and seas. Inland, the inching conquest of independent African people for the extraction of tax and labour required fighting, and there was a good deal of that to be done by imperial troops. Through the increasingly violent closing decades of the nineteenth century,

British armies and settler colonial armed forces, sometimes in warrior alliances with shrewd African collaborators, inexorably rolled up African chiefdoms.

Behind the increasing momentum and coordination of British conquest and intervention lay the emergence, in the later nineteenth century, of diamond and then gold mining. As the interior flywheel of the Southern African economy, this unleashed massive demands for capital, transport, industrial infrastructure and labour for diggings, plantations and commercial farms. With the subcontinent suddenly emerging as a vital economic and strategic interest for Britain, any remaining polities sufficiently independent and powerful to hinder imperial economic and political paramountcy were an impediment to be removed. So, when the defiant Zulu declined to supply labour and taxes, their kingdom was destroyed and dismembered (in the 1879 Anglo-Zulu war).

That left one remaining major obstacle, the Transvaal Boers, now targeted by their immensely rich Witwatersrand gold holdings.

The South African Republic asked only to be left alone. But, from the 1870s onwards, the British lion began to paw at the young country. Its immense gold deposits were turning it into the economic hub of the entire Southern African region, putting at the centre of affairs a rather uncompliant settler state which not only showed no allegiance to British imperialism, but which was strengthening its republican nationalism in response to mounting external pressure. Without prevailing influence and control over the Transvaal, Britain's grand dominion over South Africa looked anything but assured.

At first no-one wanted war but, still, Anglo-Boer relations were rapidly deteriorating over issues which increasingly looked worth fighting over. At the beginning of the 1880s there had been a minor conflict between Britain and the Transvaal that ended in a surly peace. By the 1890s, amidst renewed tensions, there was an imprudent military attempt to try to deal with the Transvaal without paying the price of all-out confrontation. This was the 1895 plot by stealthy and well-connected British interests both to mount an insurrection within and to invade the republican state.

The ignominious failure of this hare-brained coup, which became known as the Jameson Raid, meant that four years later Britain's colonial secretary, Joseph Chamberlain, and its South African high commissioner, Alfred Milner, were confronted with the higher cost of a major war in order to get their way. As Chamberlain's junior minister, Lord Selborne, had emphasised in an important 1896 memorandum after the Jameson Raid, Britain would have to intervene directly to control the Transvaal because it had become the natural commercial centre of the entire South African region.[12]

As we have already noted, the war proved to be a far larger, longer and more costly undertaking than the British had envisaged. In one grisly calculation, by 1901 it was costing the Treasury £140 to knock out a single Boer combatant; put another way, that was the price of a ton of bullets.[13] Similarly, shattering defeats in the early months of hostilities induced a sense of crisis in imperial circles, and called into question national fighting efficiency and British 'racial' vitality, initiative and competence. At the other end of the scale, the well-armed Boers generally fought with equestrian agility, fieldcraft guile and defensive tenacity in what in many ways came to resemble a people's war, with many rural women servicing the republican war effort or, as distinctions between frontline and home front collapsed, becoming sucked into the hostilities themselves.

Myths about the war have also had their lengthy run. We have already touched on the idiosyncratic notion of a long line of chivalrous male encounters, making this the last of the gentlemen's wars, an antiquated hangover from the knightly Hundred Years War.[14] In reality, imperial methods of warfare, especially in the closing guerrilla stages of the contest, were shredding the agrarian basis of Boer society, threatening the very future of a way of life the war was being fought to defend. Imperial politicians were short on sops or kid gloves, remaining unrelenting until the republics caved in. There was little chivalry in their methods.

Equally, some Boer men and women *bittereinders* or die-hards were all for fighting to the end rather than accepting unconditional surrender. In that manner, the war was prolonged by hard-nosed elements on both sides. Yet, in finally making peace, Britain moved smartly from destroying the republicans to negotiating with them. Calculated magnanimity in victory ensured that while the Boers may have lost the war, their more reconciliating leadership nonetheless won a sizeable slice of the peace.

Moreover, like any war, the struggle developed a momentum of its own. And it drew in others. In what was wishfully termed a 'white man's war', black inhabitants were not always off-stage as curious spectators, and their reactions to the conflict and immersion in its flow were significant ingredients of the story. In a sense, this was a truly 'South African' war.

Arguably, the essential nature of the conflict may have been fashioned by its

Anglo-Boer, European character, lying in assumptions which were distinct from those of the region's traditional African societies. But the scale of auxiliary black involvement in military operations on both sides, the ways in which blacks intervened from the margins on their own account, and the bleak experience of African refugees in British concentration camps, undermines completely any idea of a war conducted on the basis of the exclusion or neutrality of a formally non-belligerent majority.[15]

What of the war's historical significance? Here, its importance is real, and not only in the South African context. Like the colonial American War of Independence, it represented a sharp test of arms and will between European adversaries overseas, a protracted contest marked by strategic and tactical difficulties and moral anxieties over war conduct.

On the issue of national independence against imperial gain, it can be seen as the most important colonial war of the early twentieth century and, as an example of modern African colonial warfare it ranks, perhaps, alongside the Italian wars of conquest for Libya and Ethiopia. At another level, as already suggested, the Iraq War more than a century later may carry echoes of a South African antecedent.

Moreover, in its range and complexity the conflict also went far beyond being a limited Victorian backyard operation. As a European war fought out in Africa it had a considerable international impact. In early twentieth-century Britain, issues of popular patriotism, relative imperial decline, and the efficiency of structures and institutions were brought into scrutiny by its troubling impact. For Australia, New Zealand and Canada, empire military involvement watered the ground for those Dominion myths of masculine sacrifice and national identity which would ripen later, in the Great War of 1914–1918.

And for ordinary Dutch, Belgian, French, German, Russian and other European peoples, as well as for many Americans, the distant conflict projected the inspiring image of a tiny white Christian nation's heroic challenge to bullying imperial power. Indeed, around the world the war became some mighty if symbolic anti-British cause, encouraging the foolish to make all manner of gestures, some bizarre. In one, Tsar Nicholas II considered withdrawing his fortune from the Bank of England, and dreamed of chancing a Russian invasion of British India while London was distracted by Pretoria.

There are other factors which made this conflict a war of modernity. Some of these involved scale, levels of technology, logistical organisation, advanced armaments, and ideological ardour. Moreover, it was also a war which fell squarely within one of the most belligerent phases of capitalist imperialism, and within an epoch of rapidly modernising industrialisation. While the most aggressive eruptions of the 'scramble for Africa' were over by then, the offensive impetus remained strong; a resort to war was always justifiable for the safeguarding of perceived interests, one of the instinctive assumptions in 'an age of victors and vanquished nations'.[16]

Then, too, there was the war's imaginative scope, or the powerful codes through which its harsh realities were expressed. The shadows cast by British corpses in the trenches of Spioen Kop, by the executions of rebel Boers under Cape martial law, by blackened farmlands, by sacked mission station lands, and by dead Boer infants in British internment camps, nudge the mind forward to the furrowed corpses, suffering and destruction associated with great industrial wars of the modern age. If this was not yet a truly total war for *both* sides it was, perhaps, a conflict waged well up that evolutionary scale.[17]

Culturally, it was also a war waged on the very edge of modern memory, inspiring a large contemporary imaginative literature on the 'truths' of 1899–1902, not only in Dutch/Afrikaans and in English, but also in other European languages. And in this context, new Afrikaans war fiction a century on has finally been breaking with ingrained myths of British bestiality and Boer purity, to explore a more universal perception of the horrors of the conflict and the rawness left in its wake.[18]

For white colonial protagonists, the hostilities were a chastening experience, at times unleashing an unsparing ferocity which had been reserved for African adversaries. Previously in the century, both British and Boers had been blooded separately in combat with Africans, except for in the swift first Anglo-Boer War or 'Transvaal Rising' of 1880-81. When these enemies now clashed wholesale, European affinities counted for something, but not for too much. Republican Boers found the British as bent on grinding them into submission as had earlier Xhosa or Zulu chiefdoms. Equally, as it crumpled, Boer society may have caught a whiff of what its own warriors had dished out in expeditions to throttle frontier San communities in the later eighteenth century. Here was a situation not without some tragic irony, even though hardly any republican contemporary seems to have been in the least aware of it. After all, the 'habit of treating trouble-some natives as "vermin" was bound to brutalise white men's treatment of one another when they fell out'.[19] To which it might well be added, and some men's treatment of some women.

Lastly, while the formal business of war involved only about one fifth of the region's population, with the combined white population of the Boer republics smaller than that of London, the 1899–1902 conflict was a crucial historical hinge. While it would be trite to call it a drama in which everyone took part, there could be no overlooking the importance of its outcome to the future not just of dominant English and Afrikaner societies, but of the colonised black majority as well.

In that respect, quite apart from what the war would teach the Edwardian War Office about reforming and improving the efficiency of military institutions, or its impact upon local agriculture and the labour market, it also helped to deter-mine the course of modern South African history. The peace which ended the war also defined and completed South Africa, bringing to an end more than a century of smaller wars of colonial conquest. It is, then, important to understand the anchoring role of the conflict, in laying the keel for a reconstructed and uni-fied capitalist society as the basis of a twentieth-century white segregationist state. As a formative episode, 'it was as important in the making of modern South Africa as the American Civil War was in the history of the United States'.[20]

Any historian who tries to depict the hostilities cannot but be aware of widely held popular understandings of the war in many imperial histories and general histories of South Africa. In these perspectives, novice Boer successes in the field provided evidence of high military talents despite meagre means; stumbling Brit-ish arms were at first overawed, and then later foiled by gifted and gritty repub-lican campaigning abilities. Britain prevailed over sparsely equipped, rough farm-ers, but only through merciless sacking, burning, and the herding of civilians.

There is an element to this of the farmer and amateur soldier as a kind of David, holding out against the lumbering regimental Goliath of the professional British army. Yet, at least at the outset, the Boer irregulars were not altogether short of means. And, if most were indeed farmers, they were not exactly the retiring colo-nial cousins of Welsh sheep drovers, Highland crofters or Herefordshire stud farmers, as some of the more romantic British pro-Boers fondly imagined them.

In masculine socialisation and a political culture which linked citizenship to armed service obligations, the Boers were a long way from the shires. African societies like the Ndebele and the Venda, who had earlier faced the guns and horses of a predatory and militarist Transvaal, knew well just how lethal an adversary they could be.

The obvious challenge for the British was in coming to terms with the imposing demands and difficulties of an expeditionary campaign fought at a great distance, in a very large country (bigger than France, Germany, Italy and the Low Countries combined), against a well-gunned, highly mobile, and increasingly dispersed enemy which was criss-crossing a terrain which it knew intimately. A feature of the war was the British achievement in gradually making good their initial blunders, in improving the professional running and direction of operations, and in eventually fighting a flexible and ruthlessly effective big-countryside war.

In that respect, the hardest phase for Britain was not the short period between October 1899 and June 1900, when its forces confronted assembled enemy armies. After several expensive defeats, the invaders recovered and skewered the republicans through concentrated pressure and organised thrusts.

What was more difficult was the ensuing longer and fluid guerrilla phase. This was the real nut to be cracked, for the key to eventual victory lay in adapting to a long-range campaign in which success depended on grinding down the enemy, and in which the most embittered foe was often not just what was left of the Boer commandos, but also of women and families, the civilian front, glued together by moral stiffening.

Ultimately, the Anglo-Boer contest provided an instance of a stretched imperialist power comprehensively winning a modern war against proficient colonial opponents. There are not too many instances of *that* during the past century, to say nothing of the present. Now, as then, it takes the press to see the writing on the wall. With its government stuck in another expeditionary Afghan war amid increasing public unease, Britain's liberal *The Guardian* concluded at the end of 2009 that the conflict was 'ill-conceived, unwinnable and counterproductive'.[21]

If the Boer struggle was an anti-imperialist people's war it was, perhaps, a more lukewarm version of the exemplary modern guerrilla wars of the past century. The republicans lacked the revolutionary zeal, sense of sustained common purpose, and crucial integration of military discipline and popular political unity which has made up for more conventional deficiencies in classic anti-colonial revolutionary armies. In that sense, an imposing single command eluded the largely undisciplined Boers, and they could not avoid going the way of their nineteenth-century African counterparts in military confrontations with superior imperial forces.

Against that, there is the question of how the Boers measured up to the initial and real possibility of winning, or of at least forcing an early, bargained peace. For this, they had the advantages of mobility, speed, surprise and a superiority in arms to bring decisive victory in the field. Undoubtedly, the pastoral republics and their imperial adversary were 'ill-matched',[22] but not necessarily from the start. Yet, despite a frisky advance, the Boers lacked the strategic vision and flexibility at the outset to keep things tilted their way.

Perhaps they ought to have embarked on a guerrilla war *before* hostilities took on an irregular character. For in time they would face, in the great distances of the South African interior, a remorseless campaign to defeat them step by step. Shrinking numbers and a crumbling stock of provisions produced what at best ended up as a war of running evasion. As time ran out, this became a glum guerrilla strategy to stave off defeat, while counting a fearfully steep social and political cost. It was never a realistic basis for winning against a powerful and committed industrial enemy.

For the Boers, there was also something else to worry about. For, once war broke out, the contested legacy of their own recent African conquests became the republicans' albatross. The problem for Pretoria and Bloemfontein was that there was always more than London with which to contend. It was not only the empire that had to be beaten back. The lines of authority and control had to be held against black people hostile to the Boer position and its claims. And when republican strategy required the invasion of British territory, the practice of establishing occupation authority was bound to antagonise many of these inhabitants.

For Britain, on the other hand, fighting the war did not entail open confrontation with black communities. If it involved inflicting hardship upon some, this was tempered by a judicious currying of favour with others. It worked. One need not necessarily accept the view that the Boers' defeat was due largely to 'their inability to garner any significant African support', or in their failure to draw Africans into an 'anti-imperial alliance'.[23] As it was the bedrock of their existence, they could not but hang on to their own colonial order. Ideally, what the Boers needed was black neutrality. What they got was an aggressive factor which eventually played its part in forcing their eventual surrender.

Like many such encounters, the war in which they finally surrendered was widely expected to be brief. As in August 1914, opinion in October 1899 was that hostilities 'would be all over by Christmas', with few observers having any realistic comprehension of what was to come. For the British, even though South African entanglements had recently administered the bitter pill of imperial military humiliation at Isandlwana (at the hands of the Zulu, in 1879) and Majuba (at the hands of the Boers, in 1881), too many still assumed that this would be another soft Egypt or the Sudan. Used to moving effortlessly against primitively equipped tribesmen, most officers and men had yet to run into a European enemy. Their guesses as to what to expect tended to be alarmingly uninspired.

As for the republicans, with an accommodating British Liberal prime minister, William Ewart Gladstone, no longer in Downing Street, but with an abundance of gold now on the Witwatersrand, this was not to be a re-run of the 1880–81 Transvaal affair. Then, Pretoria's citizen soldiers had seen off an outnumbered British expeditionary force in a campaign which lasted only three months, and which produced a negotiated outcome reasonably pleasing to the separatist aspirations of Boer society on the highveld. The war which now broke out would be fought for all of thirty-two months, and would leave a considerably more expensive balance sheet. For, following the American Civil War and the Franco-Prussian War, it would become the third major military conflict of the industrial age.

But, before we turn to the story of that tragic confrontation, we need first to consider why and how the British and the Boers were brought to war.

2

FOOLS RUSH IN

THE BOER WAR . . . BROUGHT FIRST THE CULMINATION AND THEN THE END of an arrogant, boastful epoch, in which British public opinion seemed to have abandoned principles for power – the political equivalent of that *fin-de-siècle* spirit in art and literature which produced decadence and Oscar Wilde.'

So wrote A.J.P. Taylor in the *Manchester Guardian* on the fiftieth anniversary of the outbreak of the Anglo-Boer War. For Britain's best-known historian of his time, an appalling litany of miscalculation, blunder and sheer folly had forced the pace of events in South Africa.

On the face of things, the long-term guarantee of a British South Africa lay in policies of gradual persuasion, moderation and conciliation, cosseted by 'wise economic planning' and rising living standards for the black majority.

This was the ideal. In the event, matters were handled quite differently, with disastrous results. The ground was clear for impatient men with a liking for impetuous action. The Jameson Raid had not only failed to net Britain the Transvaal. It had also destroyed the position of compromising Boer moderates, blackened the colonial secretary, Joseph Chamberlain, and ensured that Britain's South African high commissioner, Alfred Milner, a man of 'German dogmatism', would be pitted against a crop of Boer leaders 'as violent and as obstinate as himself'.

In the view of the historian, Alan Taylor, the Raid rendered war inevitable. But personal motivation was also a powerful part of the equation – the British prime minister, Salisbury, 'was dragged into war by Chamberlain; and Chamberlain was dragged into war by Milner'. Perpetually in search of a handy expedient, it was Milner who wanted to rush in at the end of the 1890s, unwilling to wait for the incremental establishment of a British dominion through 'the passage

SOUTH AFRICA AT THE OUTBREAK OF THE WAR

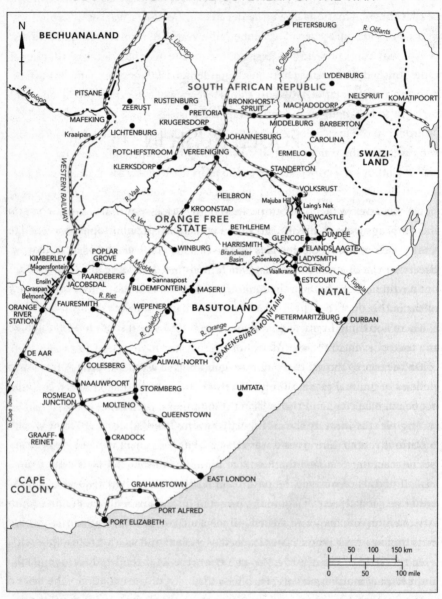

of time'.[24] Would that this were the only ink spilt on the cause of this conflict, or that the explanations down the decades of 'Milner's War' or a 'Capitalists' War', and sometimes even of 'Chamberlain's War' had resolved the knotty question of why war came in 1899. Instead, the debate over its origins is still not yet quite finished. Historians continue to ponder a basic question: why did Britain resort to a confrontation which its colonial secretary had earlier predicted could turn out to be 'a long war, a bitter war, and a costly war'?[25]

Probably the first point to emerge from scholars who have laboured on the subject is that the war was not all down to hustling imperial figures. Its cause or causes cannot be ascribed simply to the individual motivations or peevish personalities of Salisbury's colonial secretary or his South African high commissioner, however influential their position in the British political spectrum. While their urgings were assuredly part of the immediate slide into war, they are not 'guilty men' upon whom the war can be blamed. This would be to substitute effects for causes, for a pushy man like Milner 'may have helped to stir the pot, but he did not supply the ingredients'.[26] Clearly, the source of those needs to be identified.

There is common agreement on one factor – the war for South Africa serves as a textbook illustration of the argument that it is hard to find any war which could be termed 'accidental or unintentional'.[27] This was a war deliberately initiated in the conviction that the objectives of victory or staving off of defeat could not be attained effectively other than through fighting. Another given is that, in its origins, this was emphatically a British rather than a Boer war.

Naturally, both during the war itself and in its immediate aftermath, imperialist commentators claimed that the Boer republican leadership and their Transvaal oligarchy bore responsibility. An obdurate President Paul Kruger lacked the moderate good sense to yield to the essential internal reform of his state necessary to ensure harmony and security in the Southern African region. Hard-faced in its diplomatic dealings, it was the belligerence of the South African Republic which forced the pace, by getting the Orange Free State into line behind the blunt Boer war ultimatum of 9 October 1899.

The fact that it was the Boers who issued that ultimatum rather than the British (who had already drafted one under wraps, a month earlier, just in case the Boers dawdled) made the republicans the aggressor. They were outfoxed diplomatically and, perhaps no less importantly, initially surrendered some moral ground to their adversaries and critics. For an appreciative Salisbury, this relieved his government of the need to explain 'to the people of England why we are at war'.[28] By then, influential imperial pressure groups and much of the metropolitan press required little further explanation. For some time, they had already been working up the notion of a combined South African Republic and Orange Free State conspiracy to dismantle British supremacy in the region, the prelude to the imposition of a unified Boer or Afrikaner republican dominion over the rest of South Africa.

Perceptions of a wolfish Transvaal also coloured settler reaction in British South Africa. Even for leading conciliatory and pacific Cape liberals, such as John X. Merriman and James Rose Innes, the 'hostility' and 'impracticable attitude' of the Transvaal leadership, and of Kruger in particular, were making it impossible for a reasonable Anglo-Boer settlement to be given a chance. The president's bloody-minded exercise in warnings and ultimatums, and failure to grasp the need for progressive reforms 'as necessary for his own future as for that of the whole of South Africa', meant that he risked 'forfeiting all claim to sympathy and consideration'. In the language of current world politics, he was inviting 'regime change'. As the war crisis deepened, some prominent members of the Cape Afrikaner Bond party who had little stomach for war were similarly alarmed by the Transvaal. J.M. Hoffman (who would go on to work in a Boer ambulance unit during hostilities) was one, whose view of the 'attitude' of 'Krugerism' turned to 'contempt'.[29]

In fact, within the Transvaal political establishment itself there were voices which sounded not so very different. Kruger's Progressive Party political opponents, including generals like Piet Joubert, insisted that war was by no means inevitable, and that what was preventing a peaceful accommodation was their president's 'blind obstinacy', a trait which was playing straight into enemy hands. For the prominent attorney, Ludwig Krause, Kruger was dealing an exceptionally dangerous card. Fearful that any reform of the Transvaal would mean 'the weakening of the Kruger Party', he concentrated on demonising Progressive critics as 'traitors' and Anglophile fanatics or *Engels-gezind,* who indulged in calculating brinkmanship, and 'played the fool all over the country with a matter of life and death'. Krause was adamant that the war was 'engineered' as an ill-judged trial of armed strength 'in order that the Kruger party might remain in power'.

This has plenty of comparative historical resonance. It is, for instance, reminiscent of what some critics were saying of Britain's prime minister, Margaret Thatcher, when she first found herself in domestic difficulty in the early 1980s. In the 1982 Falklands crisis, she pushed for war with Argentina in an effort to save her position by leading her country into a regenerative baptism of blood patriotism.

In Krause's despairing judgement, an autocratic Kruger regime was risking war so as to escape domestic reform. In chancing his hand, the South African Republic's leader simply lacked the proper statesmanship of 'a sincere patriot'.[30] Such rumblings suggest that the Transvaal did not move to war as a 'united people', nor did its leading social classes necessarily endorse some pre-war national compact.

In any case, did Kruger actually want war? Or was he just fatalistically resigned to it? Of course, the Boer leadership was convinced, with good reason, that a hard line in any crisis would reinforce its position and raise its legitimacy. Yet this was not the same as wanting to plunge the Transvaal into a major war. On the Boer side, the war which came was entirely defensive, and it was on this basis that Kruger and President Marthinus Steyn of the Orange Free State had little difficulty in convincing their populations that the taking up of arms was for the survival of their independence. Indeed, on that basic score, not even bilious anti-Kruger Progressives like Ludwig Krause had any doubts about turning out for war.

The Transvaal president was certainly convinced that if they did not go to war at that moment their position would deteriorate and Boer power and control would pass into British hands. His famous mid-1899 charge against Milner, 'It's our country that you want', remains a crisp expression of what was ultimately at stake. While military calculations were to play their part in the crucial decision-making a few months later, a declaration of war against Britain had become a desperate gamble by a cornered opponent, and one which simply had to be taken. Milner's relentless quest for Boer capitulation, and his willingness to resort to force to achieve this, had ruled out any practicable policy of further deliberate delays or of appeasement. Eventually, it became time to act. Why wait for Britain to pick the moment for battle?

Another contemporary view saw the origins of the war not as an 'accidental' conflict with mainly short-term and contingent causes, but as the inevitable outcome of an evolutionary human struggle through which progressive civilisations shouldered aside conservative, stagnant and outmoded societies. Interpreted in this way, the war was a progressive colonial landmark in the 'perennial evolution of human society towards a higher state, one of many similar struggles in that unstoppable process of development'.[31] Grounded in those later Victorian biological and evolutionary arguments which accepted war as indispensable to progress, the Anglo-Boer clash was both natural and necessary. For individuals ranging from Alfred Milner in South Africa to metropolitan figures like the eugenicist Karl Pearson and Fabians like Sidney Webb, to the editorials of *The Economist*, the Boers were seventeenth-century frontiersmen, a medieval racial oligarchy, primitive stock-breeders, or sluggish nomads whose parasitic lifestyle was retarding free economic expansion. Their maintenance of feudal barriers to progress was wilfully blocking progressive development associated with a Great Power imperial civilisation, sanctioned 'by God's will'.[32] In some more menacing anti-English associations, the Boers resembled the ancient Scottish Picts and the Irish. The underlying issue was not whether the war had a particular cause, or whether that cause was moral or just: it was its acceptance as a conflict between antique and modern centuries, made inescapable by the imperatives of a Darwinist militarism.[33]

Marxist-influenced interpretations of the conflict took more than one form in Britain. For some writers in *Clarion* and *Justice*, the war was a structural or functional necessity of capitalist advance. It became in some sense a 'bourgeois revolution', an enforced stage in completing South Africa's transition from a traditional non-capitalist civilisation to a fully modern society. Through the handmaiden of war, a restive industrial and financial capitalist class was seeking to secure a political and economic system that would further its interests, tearing through the stifling protectionism of landed proprietors. Thus, the war for South Africa became a British colonial version of the English Civil War.[34]

Other radical opinion focused on the perceived relationship between the war and imperialism: here was ample illustration that militarism had become an essential cog of newly expansionist capitalism. The deployment of armaments, and the 'egging on' of conflict revealed the manner in which war had become a weapon in the competitive struggle between capitalist nations for colonial areas as vital markets for surplus production and as investment opportunities for surplus capital. Accordingly, the increasingly frenzied drive of European imperialism had, by the last two decades of the nineteenth century, made the Boer War inevitable.[35]

While the rapacity of capitalism and its relationship with imperialism was part of such contemporary explanation, other, more precise factors were also identified. For some Labour critics as well as Radical Liberals, war was being fomented by shady special or 'sectional' interests intent on provoking a situation which would lead to colonial annexation. Such meddling by meretricious colonial capitalists had already been detected in places like Egypt and China; now it seemed to be South Africa's turn. Thus, Fabian dissidents like Ramsay MacDonald and Bertrand Russell blamed 'the imperialism of capitalism' for manipulating 'vainglorious nationalism' as a cover for greedy individual capitalists to grab all they wanted. The Radical Liberal intellectual J.A. Hobson, in various articles and in his major 1900 book, *The War in South Africa,* charged that sordid interests in the shape of Transvaal mining magnates had pulled the levers of war and conquest as a contemptible alternative to the 'natural' growth of commerce. Much of such British criticism was directed towards 'militaristic' and 'speculative' means, not at expansionist ends. It was anti-war, not anti-imperialist.[36] Meanwhile, within the Transvaal, too, leaders such as the state attorney, Jan Smuts, and the state secretary, F.W. Reitz, along with Witwatersrand papers like *The Standard* and *Diggers News,* proclaimed that behind the intensifying war crisis lurked intriguing mine-owners and capitalist speculators.

Smuts concluded confidently that the war was not being unleashed as a fight for British 'national' interests. 'As the Boers read the situation,' he declared, 'the one issue was whether the mine owners had to govern the Transvaal in their own interest; the British flag was a minor phase of that fundamental issue.'[37] In this, he was much of the same mind as Hobson, who in his 1901 *The Psychology of Jingoism,* lambasted the manipulation of patriotism as a 'screen' by cosmopolitan capitalist forces. In the case of the British cause in South Africa, when 'businessmen . . . require a screen, they find it in the interests of the country, patriotism. Behind this screen they work, seeking private gain'.[38]

For radical British interpretations the issue was invariably capitalist imperial aggression and not empire itself, for by the late nineteenth century the dominant feeling was that Britain needed continuing worldwide expansion to stay alive, just as a fish required water. Thus, for Ramsay MacDonald, while the war was a blatant instance of naked capitalist greed, the desired evolutionary outcome in

South Africa was *still* British supremacy. Similarly, the Liberal, Lloyd George, assumed 'that the peace and prosperity of South Africa depend upon British rule being supreme in that part of the world', something which would have been attained naturally and legitimately 'by pacific methods'. There was thus no need to work up an expensive war on the basis of bogus motives, especially one which would consume funds urgently needed for domestic social reform.[39]

Whatever their varied understandings, these contemporary perceptions engage with the question which has preoccupied historians up to the present. The coming of war should not be taken as the outcome of a single event, and clarifying its cause still boils down to explaining why Britain harried the South African Republic to a point where the Boers opted to attack in order to try to preserve their independence. Clearly, at the most basic level it is about the balance of causality: how far was the 1899 eruption determined by more gravitational or underlying forces, and how crucial were the immediate preoccupations of politicians and officials?

To make basic sense of how the war crisis developed, a short and simple narrative context is useful.

By the second half of the nineteenth century, the patchwork region that had become known as South Africa was held together not by any remotely common culture or political coherence, but by an encrusted British imperial presence which either enjoyed acceptance or commanded pragmatic accommodation. Roughly one million white inhabitants populated four settler states, consisting of the Cape Colony, Natal, and the distinctly backwoods interior Boer states of the Orange Free State and South African Republic (the Transvaal). While these cast a jaundiced eye upon the intrusive influence of the British and their juiciest colonial berth, the Cape, whatever 'the ambitions of their creators, the Afrikaner states were inexorably part of the informal British Empire'.[40] Under the 1852 Sand River Convention and 1854 Bloemfontein Convention, that cost-conscious 'reluctant empire' was content to leave emigrant Boers alone to manage their ramshackle establishments.

British interests puttered along through the 1850s and 1860s in a fairly sedate imperial situation. There was no rival European challenge to Britain's domination of external South African trade, and its strategic position appeared impregnable. Transvaal attempts to establish an outlet to the sea through Delagoa Bay in the

Portuguese territory of Mozambique had failed, sealing Boer commercial dependence on the British ports of Natal and the Cape. And Simon's Town naval base, the symbol of Britain's control of the sea route via the Cape of Good Hope, was more than safe. At some stage, Britain could try to cajole all the settler states into some collaborative white federation under imperial auspices, not least to stitch together a common policy towards governing conquered Africans and organising the efficient supply of their labour. If this looked potentially awkward given independent Boer republican instincts, it was also a fairly distant policy interest.

EASTERN, CENTRAL AND WESTERN FRONT TOWNS AND PORTS

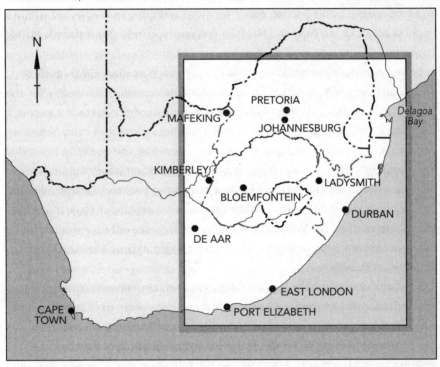

Affairs remained like this until the beginning of the 1870s, when the rapid development of the Kimberley diamond fields began to galvanise and transform what had previously been a mercantile agricultural economy. South Africa suddenly became more valuable as a field for large-scale capital investment in mine-based industry and in railways, driving the British stake deeper. For those with an eye on future share prospectuses there were also reports of possible gold deposits in the eastern Transvaal. The unresolved issue of extending imperial control now moved sharply up the agenda. Firstly, speculative capitalists were keen on seeing growing investment and trade backed by the British flag. Secondly, settler federation appeared a more urgent and also more affordable enterprise. Thirdly, for strategic interests concerned with the security of the Cape sea route to the east, it was now preferable to have South Africa's hinterland and its mineral deposits under Britain's thumb. To these considerations were added disputes involving competing Boer and black claims to diamond diggings, chronic armed skirmishing between Boers and Africans driven by the rising market for land and labour assets, and friction over Transvaal meddling in the flow of African migrant labour to the Cape and Natal. It was now apparent that 'informal British hegemony' would no longer suffice.[41]

Following Britain's annexation of the Griqualand West diamond fields in 1871, its colonial secretary, Lord Carnarvon, initiated a confederation policy for the South African territories. His 1870s initiative for a sturdy centralised state put a premium on economic imperatives. By phasing out rickety and inefficient non-British states, an integrated governing entity would be able not only to service mounting industrial demand for transport provision and labour supplies. Even more, it would provide the teeth to close remaining pockets of African landed independence, incorporating inhabitants as the mass labour force of a stable imperial dominion. For Whitehall, national settler responsibility would also be likely to reduce future demand on imperial military expenditure and other colonial financial aid.

Yet, far from opening the sluices, federation won few converts. Absorption did not excite the self-governing Cape, and the northern Boers were less than lukewarm about negotiating away their independent identities. But Carnarvon was the dog with the bone. With the Transvaal bankrupt and menaced by powerful Zulu armies, he levered the republic into the British empire, annexing it in 1877 in the quaint belief that this would achieve his aims. Instead, it scuppered the federation initiative completely. Annexation inflamed anti-imperial feeling within Boer communities throughout South Africa, and was also condemned as a blunder by moderate English-speaking Natal opinion. Undeterred, Sir Garnet Wolseley, Britain's Transvaal overlord, announced that 'so long as the sun shines, the Transvaal will be British territory'.[42] It did not shine long. By the end of 1880, the republican Boers had had enough, and rose in armed rebellion. Flagged on by militant women, commandos with customary logistical support from African combat auxiliaries overwhelmed slim and poorly prepared British garrisons, and in February the following year heavily defeated their redcoat enemy at Majuba Hill, a loss which included the life of the British general, Sir George Pomeroy Colley. A 'humiliation and a critical blow to Britain's position in Southern Africa', the outcome of the Majuba battle was that 'confederation was dead'.[43]

Although not quite Khartoum on the scale of late-Victorian imperial trauma, Majuba provoked mockery everywhere, even in the Caribbean, where it became parodied in a popular calypso melody. Like the preceding 1879 Isandlwana defeat by the Zulu, the disaster rankled especially because it represented humiliating national loss to an inferior colonial adversary. In the political culture of Tory imperial patriotism, this reverse was not something to be easily brushed over. There was lost glory to be restored. For the republican Boers, meanwhile, Majuba signalled not merely an ignominious British retreat, but the potential to push their power into the Southern African region more generally, probing the empire's soft spots and making other kinds of trouble.[44]

With Irish troubles already on its plate, Gladstone's Liberal government opted for a negotiated peace rather than renewed battle, something which greatly irritated a crusty Queen Victoria, who grumbled, 'I do not like peace before we have retrieved our honour.'[45] Under the 1881 Pretoria Convention, the Transvaal reverted to full internal independence, while Britain retained a token 'suzerainty' in respect of its relations with foreign powers, frontier zones, and the distinctly petty issue of African rights. Through a diplomatic Resident in Pretoria, British interests were to be upheld, if in a somewhat antechamber style.

Still, while a forward federation policy had been derailed by what it regarded as its 'War of Independence', Boer or Afrikaner nationalism did not yet present any immediate threat to Britain, even though a good many Conservatives and Liberal Imperialists warned that it did. So did some English opinion in Natal, which worried that the wider nationalist stirrings sparked by the war of 1880–81 presented 'a threat to British supremacy and the future of Natal as a British colony'.[46] In reality, with its earlier annexations of Basutoland in 1868 and Griqualand West in 1871, the margin of security for Britain's essential interests continued to be substantial, even massive.

That margin of trade and influence was also watched both in the west and to the east. The imperial gaze grew especially vigilant in 1883, as strategic power rivalry reared its head with Germany taking possession of Angra Pequena Bay on the west coast, north of the Cape Colony border. Two years later, Britain annexed the Tswana territories of Bechuanaland to block oozing Transvaal expansion which looked as if it might eventually lap up against the recently declared German protectorate of South West Africa, even if Germany's acquisition was in itself 'relatively worthless or utterly insignificant'.[47] Eastwards, the remaining free parts of coastal Zululand between Natal and Portuguese East Africa (Mozambique) were annexed between 1884 and 1887 to block off Transvaal access to the sea which might have freed it from commercial dependence on colonial British ports. Then, at the end of the 1880s, the perpetually hungry mining baron, Cecil Rhodes, pushed through an occupation of Matabeleland and Mashonaland to the north. This British-imperial company enterprise not only provided a base for expansion beyond the Zambezi, up Rhodes's favoured 'Suez Canal to the interior'.[48] It also completed the convenient triangular cordoning of the South African Republic.

In all this, the British were still careful not to tread too heavily upon Transvaal corns; they observed a loose balance of needs and rights. Thus, one annexation was accompanied by a relinquishing of residual controls over republican 'native policy'; similarly, in return for Boer restraint upon westward movement, Britain dropped the term 'suzerainty' from the provisions of the 1884 Anglo-Boer London Convention. This intriguing period of empire and republican interplay, based on nervous stability, served to establish Transvaal independence or 'sovereignty' as something continuously debatable, its meaning and limits inherently re-negotiable or re-definable. While a restored post-Majuba Republic was keen to assert its control over its own affairs, and not to yield to such impudent British claims as the right to move imperial troops through Boer territory at will, another 1877-like breakdown was avoided by contractual treaty or convention-based dealings.

Equally, so long as it slumbered within an imperial Southern African economy, the South African Republic could only dream of real independence. Its new post-1883 president, Paul Kruger (a flinty figure who had risen to power during the detested British occupation), continued to seek that elusive Portuguese East Africa railways artery to Delagoa Bay (now Maputo), a direct line to Kimberley, and a customs union with the Cape to beef up its revenue. By the mid-1880s, these initiatives were either barely making headway, or were more or less dead. Given some new forward movement, it seemed that London might yet be able to nudge along a settler state association, a bloodless sub-Limpopo version of the 1867 Dominion of Canada. With federation under a measure of British control there would also be less need for the War Office to fret over the potential political difficulties of having to turn the Cape peninsula anchorage into 'a Gibraltar' to patrol the India sea route.[49]

But seemingly fluid conditions were not destined to solidify in quite the way anticipated by Britain. In 1886 the discovery of Transvaal gold dramatically transformed the position and prospects not just of the Republic but of South Africa as a whole. The emergence of a mineral revolution in a marginal state long saddled with virtual insolvency rapidly renovated Kruger's country. More than this, it turned the Transvaal's Witwatersrand into the economic hub of the entire subcontinent, the power of its industrial revolution producing 'a pronounced northward shift in the balance of economic power in Southern Africa'.[50] Gold rapidly overtook diamonds in export importance, and in not much over a decade the fabled Rand mines had become the world's largest single source of gold, their rising production accounting for more than a quarter of total international output. Everything that had gone before, whether Cape wool and diamonds or Natal coal and sugar, was eclipsed by a gold industry which began to hammer the economic, social and political structures of South Africa into the grid of an industrial civilisation.

The tremendous impact of this mineral-based industrial revolution forms one of the most powerful themes in the history of modern South Africa, and has generated a body of writing longer even than Paul Kruger's imposing beard.[51]

As Transvaal gold set the pace in sustaining the complex late-nineteenth-century international monetary, financial and trading system, presided over by the Gold Standard and centred on London, capital investment flooded in. It came overwhelmingly from *rentiers* abroad, the lion's share from British investors but also from French and German capitalists. Most estimates suggest that the British stake comprised three-quarters or more of the £75m foreign investment on the Rand at the outbreak of war. While countries such as Australia, Canada and Argentina were also key markets for British investment and trade in this period, they were certainly not collared as an investment enterprise with anything like the fervour of the South African mineral boom. One significant consequence was that South African ore reserves became an increasingly crucial commodity for the protection of Britain's commercial advantage in the world economy and for its supply and servicing position in the international trading system. It was due to the Rand, for example, that the Bank of England was able to double its volume of gold reserves in the first half of the 1890s.

For an impoverished agrarian Boer state, the swarming mineral revolution had its own decisive outcomes. First, in becoming the wealthiest region in Southern Africa, revenue mushroomed: by the mid-1890s, income had already multiplied more than twenty-five times over the immediate pre-1886 years. Previously, 'the Dutch in South Africa had had the numbers but not the money; now they had the money too'.[52] Second, the effects of gold radically reshaped the social framework of the Transvaal. Production demands required a new mass inflow of cheap, unskilled African migrant labour from elsewhere in the region, including the British South African colonies. Within Boer society itself, inflated land prices due to vaulting agricultural opportunity, and speculative enclosure for prospecting, intensified pressures on available land. This accelerated growing class stratification, worsening the malaise of *bywoners* or landless, labouring tenants yoked to the farms of wealthier Boers, and increasing the difficulties of many other displaced 'poor white' squatters.

Within this white underclass, cultivated populist resentment perceived foreign capitalists and prosperous black peasants as a principal threat to wellbeing. At the same time, a patriarchal ruling class of Boer notables on the make, including such leading Calvinist squires as Kruger, Louis Botha and Piet Joubert, freely milked major or minor government office and backstairs influence to amass land for large commercial farming.[53] The seismic pressures exerted by growing industrial and agricultural transformation naturally affected both republics, making settler society increasingly restive. To some extent, fractured social forces could be knitted together by populist perceptions of 'alien' domestic or foreign perils which endangered a traditionalist burgher order of *het volk* or 'the people', threaded by large families and buttressed by customary female involvement in social and civic spheres and in rural homestead life.

A no less interesting side of this picture is the singular failure of Boer capitalist enterprise to break into the mining industry itself. No indigenous mine magnates, or Randlords, homed in, and skilled white mine work was not for uneducated and inexperienced Boer labourers. Accordingly, with no defining social shift into the new industrial sector, the political structure and sense of identity of Transvaal Boer society remained pinned to a conservative agrarian order. At the same time, that population occupied a country which had now become home to fragmented and divergent white societies. Into a Calvinist religious state traditionally riven by localised rivalries and factionalism, yet stitched together by kinship, communal social solidarities, and an independent identity hardened by recent anti-imperial conflict, came an enormous influx of overseas immigrants or Uitlanders. Mostly European, and overwhelmingly British, a wave of skilled industrial workers, professionals, merchants, managers, and fortune hunters became concentrated in the mining mecca of Johannesburg.

This mostly parvenu imported society of over 100 000 people, some 75 000 of them British, and over two-thirds consisting of single men, entrenched itself as an alien, English-speaking frontier vanguard. Held in low regard by many republican burghers as transients of dubious morals, and tolerated by the Kruger government as economic mercenaries who had no legitimate claim to citizenship or a political stake in the republican order, the intrusive Uitlander presence could not be anything other than a growing predicament for the Boer authorities. And this was not solely because of the British habit of using Transvaal Sundays for pigeon-racing rather than prayer.

By the later 1890s, republican male burghers may already have been outnumbered by Uitlander men. On one hand, this fanned anger over continuing disenfranchisement of a white Johannesburg community which provided the Republic with a very large proportion of its public money. On the other, it also tightened the resolve of the ruling Boer oligarchy to resist any democratising encroachments upon its closed governing system. Stern from the start, the Boer constitution barred Jews, Catholics, and any other male non-Protestants from *Volksraad* or parliamentary membership, and from holding any civil or military office.[54] A flood of foreigners could not be assimilated into republican politics, for conceding meaningful rights would fatally undermine the Boer monopoly of power. Enfranchised immigrants could tilt the balance of power towards mining interests, deliver political control of the state to English profiteers, and finally square the circle by easing the Republic back into British hands. Of course, for opposition Boer Progressives, the outcome of a more liberal white constitution looked nothing like as apocalyptic. A nicely balanced clientele of reformist Boers and moderate English Uitlanders would not necessarily mortgage Transvaal national interests. Instead, it could increase legislative pressure from the Volksraad upon the Kruger regime over government corruption, largesse, and the cosy fixing of profitable economic arrangements to enrich the state's cronies.

Within the ruling establishment and its small political community, there was no question of transforming the political character of the state, and a series of stringent laws were enacted to make the acquisition of citizenship hard going. Through the later 1880s and 1890s, this was a leadership which conceived of itself as both rightfully predominant and increasingly threatened. Security lay in absolute mastery of the political apparatus, fiscal levies upon the gold mines, and manipulation of the economic arena through tariffs and preferential monopolies, or concessions, over dynamite, railways, and alcohol. These costs yielded increased state revenue and fattened German, Dutch and other capitalists who buttoned Kruger's ear. But they also burdened the balance sheets of the mining industry.

General anti-Boer Uitlander antagonisms (over everything from education to policing) and sectional mine grievances (over the industry costs imposed by state policies) intensified through the post-1886 decade, culminating in the emergence of a patchy and ineptly-led political reform movement on the Rand. This pressed for liberalisation of a state 'in which those who felt that they contributed most to the wealth and revenue of the country were effectively discriminated against and excluded from citizenship and political power'.[55] In Britain, the imperialist press and other forces swung noisily behind an ill-treated Uitlander interest. Enfranchisement, it was claimed, would turn a corrupt Boer fiefdom into a modern and purposeful industrial state, efficiently serving the needs of its wealth creators rather than those of an arrogant, obstructive and anti-modern rural dynasty. For Whitehall's high commissioner, Sir Henry Loch, a potential revolt over Uitlander rights promised to clear the ground for renewed imperial intervention. In 1894, with a nod from influential mining interests, he began to tinker with the notion of staging an imperial annexation in support of rebelling immigrants, in order to make the Transvaal a British colony. But the Colonial Office would not give a nod and a wink at this, fearful of condoning a deluded insurrection which could well provoke another Anglo-Boer war.

At the same time, by no means all Uitlanders were anti-Republic malcontents. To be sure, there were influential business and professional coteries quite intent on putting down permanent roots, and psychologically incapable of playing second fiddle to the Boers, whom they considered not to be up to the job of managing a modern urban industrial society. But outside this boardroom of pro-imperial interest, attitudes were more mixed. Content to make their pile as temporary migrants, many Uitlanders had scant interest in the franchise. Others had no relish for the more onerous obligations of republican citizenship, such as compulsory commando service. Artisan radicals wavered between an anti-Johannesburg capitalist rapprochement with the government and visions of a cosmopolitan smallholder republic. They had as little love for British imperialism as for the existing Boer system. Then there were those more established British settlers who had lived in the South African Republic long enough to have become disgruntled with Britain's ineffectual meddling in Pretoria's affairs. Although keen 'to reform the Republic's existing institutions', they strongly opposed 'proposals to bring the state under imperial control'.[56] Lastly, German, Scandinavian and other continental Europeans, to say nothing of nationalist Irishmen, had some difficulty in identifying with an Uitlander campaign run as a unified British imperial cause.[57]

With the mining community issue simmering away, events lurched deeper into crisis around the mid-1890s. In 1894, the Transvaal completed an eastern rail link from Delagoa Bay to the Witwatersrand, not only giving it coastal access beyond Britain's exclusive sphere of influence, but also threatening the important goods revenue of the two British colonies. As if this were an insufficient demonstration of its independent new wealth and greater assertiveness, the Transvaal also established diplomatic relations with Germany. While Berlin's extension of patronage did not necessarily imply an immediate challenge to British regional supremacy, it was not there simply because Kruger was proud of a personal family lineage east of the Elbe. German approval of the Boer refusal to enter a Cape-based customs union looked to be an ominous encouragement of greater republican independence from British commercial arrangements. So, too, did the deposit of German capital to assist the 1894 formation of a South African Republic National Bank.

For Whitehall, such moves did not bode well for protection abroad. Then, in 1895, an emboldened republican government sought to rub in its improved railways position by imposing steep haulage tariffs on Cape goods trains and then blocking colonial efforts to circumvent this through the use of road transport across Transvaal territory. This 'Drifts' crisis (so-called after Pretoria's closure of transport fords or 'drifts' over the Vaal river) produced a standoff with the Salisbury government, which swung firmly behind Cape insistence on the rights of free commercial access under the London Convention. With a terse ultimatum which took things suddenly to the brink of war, Britain threatened intervention unless the traffic blockade was lifted.

Kruger grudgingly capitulated and re-opened the drifts, thereafter accepting a tariff agreement. Yet this appeasement could not rescue a deteriorating British situation to the south and east. With increasing trade diversion, the economic grip of the Cape (and, to a lesser extent, Natal) had been growing more slippery. Now, there was a further unsettling possibility: might the Transvaal's new influence not turn to decisive leverage over the Cape Colony? Might the northern Boers not try to reel it in, in their evident aspiration to slip the leash of British supremacy?

As imperial attitudes hardened, the key men of the 1890s hustled forward. Frustrated by failure to check the Transvaal's rising wealth and power by encirclement and the raising of a countervailing Rhodesian 'Second Rand', a pathologically plotting Cecil Rhodes hatched a conspiracy in 1895 to tip the Transvaal into British hands. The ambitious Cape premier, who fancied himself as a would-be viceroy of a united white South Africa, established a secret armed enterprise to overthrow the Kruger government. It enjoyed the connivance of 'Slippery Joe' Chamberlain and his South African high commissioner, Alfred Milner, together with some mine owners who sought a more amenable business order than that currently provided by the Republic. While a harnessing of capitalist interests with imperial political objectives seems to have been perfectly evident, which was the cart and which the horse has long remained the subject of historical controversy.[58]

Rhodes's rash plan was to cook up an Uitlander rebellion as a pretext for an invading British colonial police column led by a trusted lieutenant, Dr Leander Starr Jameson, to stage a supporting invasion to safeguard imperilled nationals. Once the Rand had been seized, a solicitous imperial power would intervene to bring peace and mediate a safer British future for the troubled Boer state. What spoiled matters was the Uitlander failure to take up arms on cue, and the madness of Jameson's hopelessly undermanned and poorly primed force in pressing on with its quixotic mission regardless. Having already lost any element of surprise days before, Jameson and his raiders were easily cornered by smirking

Transvaal commandos early in January 1896. An utter fiasco, justly termed one of the 'great cock-ups of history',[59] the Jameson Raid inspired a flood of clashing imperialist and pro-Boer literature, animating such diverse figures as G.K. Chesterton, Rudyard Kipling and Olive Schreiner. It also galvanised the Boer nationalist cultural community, whose writers trumpeted the preservation of sacred freedom against underhand imperial violence. As an example of brisk and bungled British imperial adventurism, the Jameson Raid is almost without modern parallel (with the possible exception of the botched Suez Canal invasion of 1956).

For London, the results of the 1896 fiasco were predictably dismal. Rhodes was disgraced, Britain was condemned internationally for its implication in a murky conspiracy to snatch an independent Christian state, and there was heightened bickering amongst British Liberal Imperialists and Radical Liberals over imperial claims upon political morality: the Raid had raised the issue of power over principled diplomacy in a most uncomfortable way. In South Africa, far from toppling Kruger, Jameson's intervention strengthened his diplomatic, psychological and moral position. Justifying suspicion of British intentions, it enabled the Transvaal to solidify further its republican alliance with the Orange Free State, boosted Kruger's previously shaky electoral popularity, and spurred the growth of anti-British, republican and nationalist passions within Boer populations elsewhere in the region. More widely, the Boer leader enhanced his international standing. For a breathless Jan Smuts, the Jameson Raid was the greatest stimulus to a pan-Afrikaner consciousness since the 'glorious liberation in 1880', quickening the 'national heart' of the Afrikaner.[60] While this may have been stretching things a little, colonial Boer sympathies for their beleaguered Transvaal kin certainly increased substantially. Even the Cape African newspaper proprietor and journalist John Tengo Jabavu found British buccaneering against the Boers as distasteful and illegitimate as any predatory sortie against Africans, although few blacks would have shared that view.

For his part, Kruger was adroit. Despite a baying Volksraad, he dealt magnanimously with seditious Uitlander conspirators and sweating Jameson raiders, and became more accommodating of the grievances of Randlords who yearned for a less parasitic agrarian state, more favourable industrial legislation, and labour policies which would hasten the delivery of more African migrant workers to the Rand. While the mines remained discontented over such thorny matters as government-imposed monopolies and a regime burdened by tribal graft and inefficiency, the Boer landed oligarchy became far more solicitous of industrial needs after 1896 as notables moved to modernise their republic. [61]

At the same time, Kruger's ruling clique did not neglect to apply some stick. Just as British and South African public attention focused ever more intensely on the Uitlander question, Uitlander political activities were curbed, and Pretoria set its teeth against any constitutional compromise in which political control might slip out of its hands. Its defensive capability shaken by the Jameson incursion, the Transvaal also began to prepare for a war which looked as if it might well be around the corner. A new military alliance treaty was concluded with the Orange Free State in 1897, affirming mutual support against any external threat to independence. Kruger, long criticised for being too sluggish about modernisation, now began to tackle the issue, not least by providing security. The republic embarked upon an expensive programme of major defence works, stockpiling of supplies, and a rearmament of its forces with imported weaponry, largely from Germany.

Previously, the Dutch had had only the numbers and the money. Now, they had the Mauser rifle too. They also had a further token of German approval. The Kaiser dispatched a congratulatory cable to Pretoria on the defeat of the Raid. Even as a watered-down version of Wilhelm's fantasy of landing German marines to strut around Delagoa Bay, the gesture was inflammatory enough. It incensed the British government and touched off a wave of imperial patriotic sentiment, providing a powerful tide for the Conservative administration to ride its South African preoccupations.

Some in South Africa saw in the Kruger Telegram evidence of Germany as a future patron and protector of Pretoria. However, rather than a clear-cut German challenge to British assumptions of regional paramountcy, it was more of a cavalier diplomatic manoeuvre with repercussions which Berlin tried quickly to contain. Nonetheless, it seriously deepened London's unease over developing relations between Germany and the South African Republic. In a significant way, the Raid had crystallised the linkages between 'Transvaal power, the wealth and needs of the mining industry, Uitlander rights, British supremacy and the prospects of a united South Africa'.[62] It further aggravated British-Transvaal tension, but the issue is whether or not it made war inevitable. Certainly, in the immediate aftermath of the Raid, neither side wished to bring on war through risky ultimatum or threat. Nonetheless, it remains a watershed moment, for hereafter the republican regime had the internal cohesion and spiky resolve to ensure that if Britain wanted its way, it would have to be through war. Jameson's attack had confirmed just what the stakes were.

For two further years there was stalemate and restraint, although no sign of any resolution. Chamberlain's decision to turn Uitlander grievances into a high-minded infatuation with civil liberty and political freedom took off as a popular campaign for the cause of empire, mobilising press opinion and pressure groups like the pro-British South African League in both Britain and South Africa. In 1897, determined to force the pace through diplomatic pressure, the colonial secretary posted Alfred Milner as South African high commissioner. Haughty, supercilious, and a self-proclaimed 'British Race Patriot', Milner was contemptuous not only of Boer republican claims. An advocate of a more highly integrated imperial order, he also regarded Cape and other colonial Boers with considerable disdain and suspicion, viewing them as disloyals who could not be assimilated, part of a rising 'Afrikanerdom' constellation which had to be smashed.[63] This was not too promising a basis for productive Anglo-Boer diplomacy.

Although neither Salisbury nor Chamberlain were wholesale war enthusiasts, hoping rather that Kruger would succumb to bluff or threat before snapping, they were equally set on forcing imperial supremacy or paramountcy on the Boers, 'whether peacefully or not'.[64] If this meant war, there was natural concern about public opinion and diplomatic repercussions on British interests elsewhere. To the world at large, it was essential that things looked intolerable for Britain; negotiations for a reformed Transvaal had to be genuine, and the chosen *casus belli* legitimate. For his part, Milner was increasingly dismissive of what in March 1898 he termed 'the waiting game'. Acknowledging the only conceivable outcome as 'reform in the Transvaal or war', he was more impatient than his political masters to clear the decks for a conflict he not only accepted, but craved.[65] In effect, Chamberlain relinquished things to Milner, a man unlikely to go fishing or to the races when there was a crisis to worsen. Hope of acceptable reform looked lost by the end of 1898, a year of resounding electoral victory for Kruger and his championing of nationalist republicanism.

A beavering Milner, together with his subordinates and allies, prodded and cajoled English press and public opinion into talk of intervention over the franchise and other Uitlander 'wrongs' and 'injustices',and then proceeded to do what was necessary to scupper any Anglo-Boer compromise, and to nudge along a final showdown. Early in 1899, bargaining between the republicans and the Randlords over possible franchise concessions was sabotaged, as this threatened to cool a hot political temperature. Ideas from pacifist Cape and Natal elements for regional South African policy conferences on such issues as European immigration, met with indifference. Instead, a series of trumpeted Uitlander petitions to the Volksraad and to the Queen, requesting reform and protection, focused things nicely for the high commissioner, who fired a round of sulphurous dispatches, enlarging old complaints and dredging up further disputes. These included a famous May telegram, in which Milner depicted British subjects as 'helots' enslaved by Transvaal tyranny – a distressing scandal which was crying out for forceful resolution.

Milner – deaf to the conciliationist pleas of the poor old Cape colonial moderates, anxious anti-war Natalians, and of some Orange Free State and Transvaal 'progressives'– kept pushing to the limit on the franchise disagreement. He had energetically massaged British opinion on this, and believed that if the Transvaal did finally cave in, it would be delivered through its British vote. With his back to the wall, an outwardly intransigent Kruger was now ultimately prepared to concede a franchise liberalisation in return for some imperial restraint. But such bargaining was spurned. For its part, the republic rejected demands for a joint Anglo-Boer enquiry into the Uitlander political problem, on the reasonable basis that it undermined its sovereign rights to internal autonomy.

Following the failure of a mid-year Bloemfontein Conference to achieve any compromise deal, and a tearful Kruger's memorable observation that what Milner wanted was not the franchise but his country, the Boers grasped at a last straw in August. They consented to a five-year retrospective franchise right demanded by Milner, in return for guarantees of non-interference in their internal affairs, a relinquishing of the assertion of imperial 'suzerainty' or supremacy, and submission of outstanding disputes to future independent arbitration. There was by now little possibility that Britain would agree upon statutory conditions, especially not those suggested. Rejection again confirmed thinking in Pretoria and Johannesburg that the issue was not Uitlander rights. As Smuts wrote in August to the Cape Afrikaner Bondsman Jan Hofmeyr, the dispute was not over the basis of the franchise law, but 'about possession of this land of gold.'[66] Given that perception, it is not surprising that friendly German, Dutch and Belgian diplomatic advice to accommodate British obligations failed to sway Pretoria.

In response to the reassertion of claims and demands for further Uitlander concessions, the Republic withdrew its compromise settlement offer on 2 September, and fell back on its earlier 1899 proposal of a franchise based on a seven-year residence qualification, again contesting Britain's 'suzerainty'. A week earlier, Milner had declared the 'South African question' to be 'purely military', and Chamberlain had obligingly assigned troop reinforcements. Britain had also begun to use its diplomatic leverage over Portugal to curb Transvaal arms imports through Delagoa Bay. Such brinkmanship increased republican determination not to yield. For Smuts, the Transvaal would sooner 'again take up arms' than submit to a 'humiliating solution'.[67] Tortuous political exchanges continued through September, as Britain bided its time. This was spent awaiting reinforcements, preparing brusque war terms, and hoping for a prior Boer ultimatum which would provide the just cause needed to quieten lingering Liberal and Labour murmurings that Boer shortcomings did not warrant war. At its last pre-war Cabinet meeting on 29 September, the Salisbury government was confident of sufficient domestic support.

Meanwhile, Bloemfontein readied itself to fight alongside its neighbour. At the end of September, President Steyn's Volksraad pledged full treaty and other assistance. On 2 October, with both states mobilising their commando forces, the South African Republic's president advised his legislature that war was now imminent. Convinced that a snap offensive would be to Boer advantage (and mindful of being caught napping, as in 1896), Kruger and his ally presented a joint 48-hour ultimatum to the British Agent in Pretoria on 9 October – just pipping Britain's own ultimatum. Republican demands left no room for any further wrangling. Britain was to agree to arbitration on all 'points of difference', and to an immediate withdrawal of all its forces, be they those already menacing Boer borders, reinforcements stationed elsewhere, or troops already en route from any part of the empire. On the evening of the next day these terms were tersely rejected. For haughtier Whitehall minds, it was disagreeable enough for a great power to have to negotiate with a small African state managed by ruffianly Dutch farmers. This last impertinence was too much. For Salisbury it did the trick, relieving his government of responsibility for justifying the war to the British public.

The Boer republics opened hostilities against Britain with a formal declaration of war on 11 October and a cross-border advance into Natal. Publicly sure of a swift victory, a bellicose Chamberlain was optimistic, even smug. In the previous week, Milner had scoffed at the notion that simple farmers might hold out for more than a moment against regular soldiers. Such confidence was not shared by the British general, Sir George White, who had left Cape Town early in October to take over Natal command. In his view, the Cabinet could well find itself in a pickle if the country would have to be reconquered from the sea. With hostilities underway, even Milner felt a shiver, contemplating 'a bad time before us' as his empire confronted 'the greatest strain put upon it since the [Indian] Mutiny'.[68] On the other side, an ageing Kruger dug into his Calvinist Puritanism and was bitterly apocalyptic. An American journalist was assured that the price Britain would have to pay for Boer territory would beggar the most metaphysical imagination.[69]

So much, then, for the relentless pace of events. It is easy to see why figures as different as Smuts and Winston Churchill considered the Jameson Raid the real declaration of war, or why an apprehensive Merriman, with the start of the American War of Independence on his mind, feared that its 'first shot may well be a South African Lexington', with consequences far more unpredictable and dangerous than in 1881.[70]

To turn now from such immediate gambling to the war's underlying causes is to contemplate a historiographical Mount Everest. The long shadow which it casts is a larger interpretative picture that requires some concluding light. Here, in weighing up a larger interpretative picture, the bringing on of war cannot be ascribed solely to Milner and Chamberlain or Kruger, however important their individual responsibility. Nor can the cause of Uitlander rights be seen as a prime motive, whatever its obvious centrality to the 1890s crisis; at bottom, this was really a functional pretext for the larger issue of who should enjoy untrammelled authority over Southern Africa.[71] It is no easier to accept that war arose from republican intrigue or design to reclaim all of South Africa as a Dutch 'Africander' possession. While the spectre of an ascending 'alliance' or 'dominion' of Afrikanerdom had become increasingly influential in British thinking after 1896, there was little material basis for a republican-ruled Cape and Natal. On its own, the Orange Free State had no particular quarrel with British power and the

Transvaal and pre-war Natal maintained a cosy coexistence for good economic reasons. Crucially, too, there was also no common vocabulary of united purpose between colonial and republican Boers, whose sense of nationality and identity derived historically not just from membership of a constructed people, but also from territory and regional political cultures.[72]

Of long explanatory significance is the thesis, in various versions, that the war was basically a product of late-nineteenth-century economic imperialism, a push to exert control over or to entrench leading access to the vital Transvaal gold fields. As already noted, the notion of a capitalist war gripped republican leaders as well as late-Victorian British radicals, for whom a 'parasitic imperialism' was the 'civilisation of De Beers'.[73] That general conclusion has also been echoed by such eminent modern historians as Eric Hobsbawm, for whom 'whatever the ideology, the motive for the Boer War was gold'.[74] But this argument has not had an easy ride from critics. In the first place, it has been pointed out that Britain did not invade the Transvaal directly to control the mining industry; its capital investments could see to that. Similarly, British access to bullion did not require the creation of a Crown colony and British governance.[75]

Nor, in this assessment, is it tenable to claim that a knot of grumbling mining capitalists amounted to a conspiracy, exploiting Anglo-Boer antagonisms to engineer the removal of Kruger's regime and its replacement with an administration more attuned to special industrial needs. In reality, Rand capitalists were not a united pro-war front. If anything, war looked frightening and costly for mine operations, and the most that can be said is that the anti-Kruger antagonisms of the mining interest and its local press allies helped to feed an atmosphere of crisis. Indeed, for the most part, capitalists remained willing to deal with the Boers, and would assuredly have settled for more helpful labour accords, industrial commissions and accelerated modern state reform. As the only partisanship was that behind dividends, interest and profits, the Transvaal might as well have been in South America. Moreover, there is no really clinching direct evidence that in resorting to war the Salisbury government was itself driven by concern over the conditions and profitability of the gold industry.

In this view, all that can be said is that the mining interest went along with force, trusting that battlefield victory would usher in a freer kind of capitalist regime. For Britain's end was not the gold supply as such, but the imposition of its political will over the Transvaal, and affirming British supremacy for the laying down of a loyalist South Africa. It was not pushed by economic determinism but by the decisive need to affirm imperial political supremacy.[76]

Nonetheless, that Britain did not go to war *for* gold does not mean that the war was not essentially *about* gold's overarching effects. This takes us back to the old argument over whether or not war was necessary to modernise the Transvaal. Undoubtedly, the country's image as torpid and anti-modern now appears much less clear-cut, and one suggestive view is that what disturbed Britain was not so much Boer antipathy towards mine costs and other Uitlander complaints. It was much more the use of protectionist state economic policy to foster indigenous national industrial growth. For Kruger, who personally thought gold a divine provision to end hard times, greater economic autonomy through developments such as the state dynamite monopoly, republican mint, national bank, and control of the railways could now realistically be pursued. Coupling political sovereignty to economic independence would increase Boer capacity to dictate the development of a wealthy and powerful state with the muscle to draw in slack British colonies, while any protectionist moves would imperil British market preference. As both imperial politicians and local capitalists swung behind demands for a more accommodating Transvaal, so there was shared anxiety over its drift towards economic modernisation and autonomy on a tide of tariff protectionism.[77] The paradoxical assertion in much imperial propaganda, that the republic's problem was that it was somehow either 'feudal' or 'medieval', and yet also South Africa's potential 'centre' or 'capital state', is a contradiction still well worth considering.

Linked to the latter perception were renewed late-1890s concerns over the Delagoa Bay connection. Britain had long wanted to block the Boers' eastern harbour link and to exclude any rival European power like Germany or France from commercial or political holdings in Mozambique. An 1898 Anglo-German agreement on Britain's Transvaal paramountcy was meant to stabilise the Delagoa Bay position. But it was to prove less than perfect for it conceded business development of the port to the market. When that concession went to a German-backed company, Britain faced a newly awkward situation for its Southern African position and 'vital interests'. It was no idle speculation to see the consequences of an improved port facility serving the Transvaal as well as European rivals. This deepened worries about the commercial interests of the Cape and Natal, the security of their sizeable British investments and the future flow of gold to the Berlin and Paris money markets. And it fuelled anxiety about the continuing predominance of British trade with the Transvaal should Germany or France use an expanded Delagoa Bay route to penetrate a growing Boer market.

Aside from the economic stake, by the end of the 1890s there were naval fears over the strategic implications of independent Mozambican dock development. With direct access to Transvaal coal, any European maritime rival with a Delagoa base could menace the vital Cape route as well as bolt the door on inland British trade. So, whether it was foreign commercial interests squeezing in on trade routes, or apprehension over rivals securing naval bases in the territory of weaker powers (as had recently already happened in China), security also moved up the imperial scale. Disquiet was not eased by speculation in 1897 that Berlin would boost German business development of a Delagoa Bay concession to service a planned new Transvaal steamer line, entrenching advanced German marine expertise in the area. Against this, talk of Simon's Town being put at risk on account of the Transvaal was a sideshow.[78]

Deep down, and intersecting with British economic and strategic interests, was the critical question of who Southern Africa *was for*. The answer, Britain, had long seemed obvious enough to the British. But, by the late 1890s, establishing supremacy looked easier said than done. If there were no declared German ambitions in the Transvaal, Berlin's nibbling on the seaboard to its southeast still threatened to dilute that exclusive predominance which so preoccupied Downing Street. And that supremacy looked to be no less unsettled by both Germany and France entering the auction for Transvaal favour, thereby inflating its influence and independence. All this appeared discouraging for the future of the Cape and, especially, a financially rocky Natal.[79]

In imperial defensive scenarios, there were two maturing and corrosive insecurities by 1899. One was that a straining and protectionist Transvaal, aided by railways spoils and port advantages, might simply cast off on its own. What would happen then? Shrugging off remaining dependence on British territories, it was conceivable that the Republic might get a larger share of South Africa after all. But the worry was not merely that of the Transvaal's potential ability to suck adjacent territory into some anti-British, republican *Mittelboer* zone. It was the prospect, clear to the British prime minister's son-in-law, Selborne, and to other officials, of the damage a restive, demographically expansionist and increasingly cosmopolitan Republic could do to British interests if left to develop unchecked.

What guarantee was there that a rich and defensive nationalist Transvaal, thick with Americans, Germans, Scandinavians or other dubious Europeans, would not ally itself with a foreign power?

After all, influential 'Continental' republicans were already embedded in the Transvaal state, recruited by Kruger to make good technical and managerial deficiencies in its infrastructure. For those British officials who believed that all this pointed to Germany, bodies like the Pan-German League provided brooding confirmation of their worst fears. They harboured notions of German–Boer affinity and asserted that the Boers were the outriders of German expansion.[80] Even as things stood, the challenge of fixed Boer republicanism to Britishness jeopardised the attainment of a South African federation as a segment of that 'unified white empire' which Chamberlain felt could help to rebuild Britain's competitive advantage over newer world powers like Germany and the USA.[81]

Any erosion of British power was considered disastrous, and not merely because of its consequences for the control of South Africa. Resolution of this problem had also become essential to maintaining confidence in Britain's ability to defend its vital imperial interests. For what was at issue was more than British prestige in Southern Africa or in Europe: it was the standing of its governance throughout the empire. For the Colonial Office, the case for upholding British 'prestige' was virtually as compelling here as on the Indian frontier. Therefore, for Chamberlain, if the British position in South Africa was 'at stake', so was 'the estimate of our power and influence in our colonies and throughout the world'.[82] If Paul Kruger provided a peephole into an imagined imperial abyss, the only way to block it was a convincing demonstration that defiance of British paramountcy would not pay. That made a showdown imperative.

Such were the elements which culminated in deadlock diplomacy and mutually misguided military conceit. By then, hostilities were being egged on by the belligerent and militarist surges of late-Victorian public opinion, and across class and party lines. Having implanted an aggressive imperial campaign to jack up British prestige and to secure the sovereign rights of freeborn Britons in the colonial world, it would have been difficult for any British government to back away from so great and public a cause.[83] At this level, it was never a matter of Britain making war *only* to protect its trade and investment or to make certain it retained its supremacy in a juicy part of Africa.

What, then, emerges from all this? It is now probably generally accepted that the precise balance between economic, strategic and political factors remains difficult to strike. But in any equation, the critical importance of gold reserves and supply to Britain's financial position in the international economy cannot be discounted. Had the Witwatersrand become famous for asparagus, there would surely have been no war crisis. At a time of intensifying competition from rival powers, London's traditional world money-market role needed the tacit assurance of uncomplicated political arrangements in the Transvaal. With a friendly regime in place, the mining industry would then be free to concentrate on improving its efficiency and performance in a more economically liberal environment. Then, the British government could have slept easier in the knowledge that the Bank of England would retain control over the disposal of South African gold, and remain impregnable in its leadership of the international gold standard.[84]

The other major consideration is the connection between confidence in Britain as the world's financial and commercial centre, and the peace and security of its empire. As the power of that empire gradually declined through the later nineteenth century, relations with economic competitors and peripheral colonial societies became more 'marked by increasing demands and diminishing tolerance'.[85] Less and less could be left to chance when possession of a formal empire was essential to international predominance. Chamberlain made much of this, a politician who 'sought to convince the public as never before of the cardinal importance of the Empire and of the need to cultivate and consolidate it'. And that public was as much Melbourne and Durban as Glasgow and Birmingham.[86] The colonial secretary stood for an authentic imperialist collectivism, fed by policies which would combine integrated development abroad with domestic economic and welfare reforms. In time, this organic unity would become a largely self-generating affair, befitting a national revitalisation of the British imperial race. Its commercial basis lay in the idea of a preferential imperial customs union, within which free trade would prevail, removing any protective colonial tariffs against goods from the mother country. For a Chamberlainite advocate of empire preference and imperial federation, it was only through a more efficient empire that Britain would stop losing ground in the world economy.

The highveld had become one of the more vulnerable places, a spot where that empire could start bleeding. Perhaps as pivotal as Egypt to the British position in Africa, South Africa also appeared to be a case of nudging at back-door independence. This would not do, especially as British 'vital interests' in Southern

Africa were not solely strategic, a matter of safe naval stations and ocean lanes to India. The future of capital and commodity trading markets had become no less an issue, as had the need to resolve Cape, Orange Free State and Natal–Transvaal railway disputes in order to establish a viable rail communications network. In the face of some waning of influence, there was something to be gained by ramming home imperial supremacy, and much to be lost by not doing so. For, in a fundamental sense, South Africa had become an exemplary case of national interest for the British governing élite. After all, for much of the nineteenth century it was axiomatic that 'the security and vitality of Britain's economy and society depended upon the retention, defence and whenever necessary, the extension of the empire'.[87] South Africa fused all these necessities, and added the upholding of Great Power prestige. If Britain was willing to threaten war with France over its West African interests in 1898, there could be no question of its readiness to use force for South Africa. Without that intervention, there could be no knowing whether, in the longer term, South Africa would end up as a new Canada or another United States.[88]

When war did come, it brought a familiar lesson, namely, that forcing a war was not the same as determining its course. Milner committed a mistake in manoeuvring the enemy into war for which his generals were not completely ready.[89] In this, even Chamberlain was not an entirely ignorant politician. Just a week before hostilities he was a little worried that 'our troops, unlike the Boers, cannot mobilise with a piece of biltong and a belt of ammunition, but require such enormous quantities of transport and impedimenta'.[90]

There was nothing new in that. For some years Chamberlain had been urging the Cabinet to strengthen Britain's South African military presence, something which had usually been resisted by the Treasury and by colleagues wary of overdoing things. Yet, for much of this time, the colonial secretary himself had been thinking of armed force more as a means of keeping matters astir, as an intimidating factor in negotiation, rather than for its employment in actual warfare. On the other hand, others in the Cabinet, not least Salisbury and the war secretary, Lord Lansdowne, grasped the eventuality of war more firmly, and took its requirements rather more seriously. At the same time, they also shared Chamberlain's grasp of the consequences of an operational commitment with a limp ending. Without a war, how could the value of any expenditure wrung from a reluctant Treasury be reasonably recovered?

From August 1899 onwards, the stage was set for Britain to handle its war preparations very gingerly, with a War Office full of misgivings about Cabinet equivocation over military measures, and with the government deliberately ambiguous over whether it would be peace or war. The classic calculation, for Lansdowne, was to avoid any action which could prod the Boers into starting a war which, just conceivably, might still be avoided. It was precisely this risk, of a pre-emptive enemy strike, which Chamberlain continued to dismiss.[91]

This sort of political balancing was all very well, but did not do much to advance the state of British military preparedness for an impending war which was likely to come sooner rather than later. If threatening words could not be backed up convincingly with military deeds, there would be a price to pay.

3
SADDLING UP

BOER WAR AIMS WERE SIMPLE AND STRAIGHTFORWARD — THE RE-
tention of the internal political independence of the Transvaal, respect
for its post-1881 independent status, and a repudiation of imperial
'suzerainty'. Above all, command of the South African Republic would have
to remain unequivocally in Boer hands.

It was by no means Paul Kruger alone who was profoundly influenced by the
belief that through years of struggle and sacrifice the Boers had come to own
the Transvaal. Members of its Calvinist clergy and intelligentsia, its professional classes and its leading urban commercial and financial strata shared this
view. The mineral wealth of the Witwatersrand was a final vindication of their
nineteenth-century Israelite quest for the promised land, a providential reward
to make up for beleaguered and impoverished migrant beginnings. Endowed
by history and sanctified by Calvinist Protestantism, the republican nation
state required resolute defence against predators, be they Zulu warriors, anti-
republican Uitlanders, or Britons wearing red or khaki.

Among the white rural landless and other poor people there was a dusting of
Old Testament prophets, millennial visionaries and passionate fundamentalists
for whom a defensive war was something to be met with more than a religious
sense of fatalistic acceptance. It was also an emotional opportunity to bring
about a purification of the Transvaal. Successful resistance would see off both
foreign invaders and the corrupting modernisation represented by their mines,
ideologies and debased value systems. What could then be reclaimed was some
lost Boer Arcadia, in which pre- or non-capitalist needs and practices could once
more prevail in a gentler and more communal society. Thus, if peace could no

longer be preserved, so be it. An anti-alien war could renew the Republic, with victory providing the basis for a protective social order which expressed the 'true character' or 'real spirit' of its people.[92] Still, judging from the work of historians of the pre-1886 Boer republics, the good old days were somewhat less rosy for the poorer whites who lived through them than for those tramping demagogues who now nostalgically imagined them.[93]

For most ordinary Boer men and women, a war against Britain was a matter of survival. Even if the chosen method of defence would be the invasion of British colonial territory, it was widely understood to be a defensive enterprise. At the same time, the extent to which support for war represented some universal nationalist ardour must surely remain an open question. There is no doubt that modernising, urban-aligned and educated middle classes identified deeply with a republican state patriotism exemplified by such national figures as Jan Smuts and Marthinus Steyn, ironically the respective bearers of a Cambridge and London education.[94] But Dutch/Afrikaans 'continental' republicanism is unlikely to have encompassed the entire Boer population, most of whom inhabited an agrarian world thick with localisms, resilient kin loyalties, and devoted ties to farmsteads. A glorious republicanism had as little resonance for many rural Boers as did nationalist euphoria among rank-and-file Italian peasant conscripts in war against Libya in 1911 or later during 1914–1918.[95]

Yet little or lukewarm identification with a republican statism did not mean lack of popular support for taking up arms. Instead, the basis of support for a national war effort rested upon some quite discrete understandings of the meaning and objectives of a defensive mobilisation. To put it another way, for the anti-imperialist Pretoria press this was a war to ensure the continued existence of the Boer state and the future of a free republicanism. For the large rural patriarchs of the Transvaal and Orange Free State it may have been more an effort to defend defined territorial influence and community. For ordinary farmers, the stakes probably narrowed down to responding to a perceived threat to their homes and agricultural livelihoods. And for agitated women it amounted to a fight in defence of a traditionalist home community against threatening alien intrusion.[96]

There was no uniform Boer republicanism. At the outbreak of war these essentially conserving elements simply came together in defence of the homeland. This, as many writers on war have noted, has long been one of the most powerful motivations in the will to fight. On that score, there was assuredly something to defend. Part of the legitimacy of the Boer state lay in the fact that it was not completely neglectful of the welfare needs of its poorer rural burgher electorate, hard hit by severe drought in 1893 and a crippling rinderpest cattle epidemic in 1897, to say nothing of locusts and malaria. By the late 1890s the Kruger government was spending almost one third of its annual budget on relief to distressed whites. Britain was just another pestilence.

In the meantime, while the standpoint of justified defence was obviously vital to the persuasiveness of the Boer case in Europe and North America, the republicans themselves were not wanting in pugnacity. Responding to bullying British diplomacy with a strong threat of their own, Reitz and Smuts declared it the task of all Boers to unite militarily to bring about a 'Free, United South Africa', an ambitious national Afrikaner republic stretching from the Zambezi to Table Bay.[97] This confirmed the most apprehensive imperial speculation about the Transvaal and its sub-imperial intentions. But the Reitz-Smuts grand design remained more offensive bluster than an achievable objective. The first republican columns assembling on the Natal front may have been itching to get at the enemy, but few in their ranks could seriously have believed that this would be a fight to knock the British out of South Africa altogether. Many more, egged on through September by a pro-war republican press and a seething Volksraad war faction, simply fancied their prospects of achieving a headlong military victory and thereby swiftly repelling Britain. Newspapers on the tables of Pretoria's generals, such as *Ons Volk* and *Land en Volk,* pointed out repeatedly that Boer arms had been effective on a previous occasion. Why not again? The Transvaal wished for nothing more than another Majuba Hill.

On the other hand, the Boers wished for nothing less than the involvement of surrounding Africans. Their war aims turned on the simple need of a limited political community; its fight for independence required black compliance rather than alliance. Not only was there was no basis for Africans in the Boer republics to be convinced of the necessity for war. On the other hand, there was every basis for assuming that discontented peasants and labourers would be more likely to favour the imperial side. For them, the disruption of invasion might well be a blessing by diverting the Boers and loosening their grip. In this sense, the immediate reality of war confirmed the narrow territorial legitimacy of the republican state. It was not least for this reason that Boer war policy excluded any arming and enlistment of African groups as contractual allies. Here, the issue was not simply one of weighing up the risk or reliability of black collaboration. For 'the prime condition for Afrikaner survival', more crucial even 'than independence from the Empire', was 'the constant subordination of the African communities'. For Smuts, this meant that on no account could 'the coloured races' be allowed to become 'the arbiters in disputes between the whites' for fear that they would become 'in the long run the predominating political factor or "casting vote" in South Africa'. This was 'the cardinal principle in South African politics'.[98]

Because of source limitations, it remains exceptionally difficult to obtain a full picture of the range of African sentiment and responses to republican war preparation. Very broadly, what can be assumed is that in parts of the countryside there would have been indifference and antipathy, or perhaps some level of anticipation or even conviction that an imperial invasion of the republics could overturn Boer authority and lead to more favourable terms of existence for workers and agricultural tenants. On the other hand, for those male servants traditionally socialised and acculturated as loyal commando *agterryers* or after-riders, here was another war in which their functions of skilled military aid and dependent solidarity would be utilised by Boer masters. If there was a recognisable black loyalty to the republican cause it was here, in the individualistic and personalised form of the experienced and trusted servant auxiliary.

Other positions were fairly clearly defined. Some pre-war British propaganda had focused on the discriminatory treatment meted out to British Coloured citizens in the Transvaal, with a straight-faced Chamberlain even announcing that one of the causes for which Britain was going to war would be to ensure that victory over the Boers brought 'kindly and improving treatment' of 'countless indigenous races of whose destiny' a self-reproachful imperial power had been all 'too forgetful'.[99] Steeling themselves for war, the small Coloured community on the Rand looked to British success. So did many African mineworkers, fondly believing that an imperial order would in some way relieve them of an oppressively regimented labour regime.

Many more did not await the outcome of a Transvaal war. Between May and October 1899 economic slump on the Rand, and growing fears of what looked to be an unavoidable conflict, triggered a 'mass exodus' of around 100 000 African, Coloured and Indian people, who scrambled for the Cape and Natal to escape being stranded in the Republic. In flight they joined a corresponding mass of white foreigners. Nearly 100 000 miners, artisans and other able-bodied Uit-landers 'not interested in fighting for Kruger's franchise' or fearful of 'impress-ment by the Boers' headed for the sanctuary of coastal colonies.[100]

If republican war aims were plain, those of the British were only a little less so. They hoped for a transfer of power in the Transvaal. The installation of a pro-imperial government would keep it unambiguously within the British orbit, uphold London's regional paramountcy, and bring the territory into line with unification or federation objectives, thereby ensuring that a dense web of impe-rial economic interests would be secure against a potentially damaging nation-alist Transvaal economic bloc. As Chamberlain put it in September 1899, what had to be terminated was the existence of a 'pure Dutch Republic' flouting, and flouting successfully, British control and interference.[101]

Initially, this did not necessarily mean the practical imposition of sovereignty over the Boers. In that sense, this was not conceived of as a classic war of colo-nial conquest to annex the Transvaal and make it a directly ruled colony. Most historians now accept that that decision was only taken after the war had started. First prize for the Colonial Office was a client regime in Pretoria which would create a pro-British state based on more modern and efficient institutional struc-tures. The Transvaal could then be safely left to make itself. On the face of it, it is at this level that the wants of vested capitalist interests, like mining and its in-dustrially based social groups, coincided fairly neatly with those of Whitehall.

Naturally, both sides had an eye on the international repercussions of war. Given the strains of Great Power rivalry and Britain's growing diplomatic isola-tion by the end of the 1890s, the Colonial Office sought to keep the crisis con-fined to an Anglo-Boer domain to ensure that it would not become a factor in established imperialist rivalries. In the weeks leading up to war there were cer-tainly some recurring worries about potential German, French or even Russian meddling, which could seriously heat up the conflict. A notable concern, already well represented in public debate because of anxiety over economic competi-tion, was Germany. The Transvaal was depicted as a garden of this alien growth, with the *Pall Mall Gazette* even classifying its Boers as 'honorary Germans'.[102]

Such spleen was predictable given the mood of the later 1890s, a climate ani-mated by periodic international crises, naval challenges, patriotic vigilance, and a shrill distrust of foreigners and their intentions. The same anxieties gripped some British colonial politicians in Natal and the Cape. Prominent amongst them was the Cape colonial premier John X. Merriman, convinced that military entanglement would render Britain so dangerously exposed that unfriendly states could hardly be expected to remain aloof or neutral. When he termed the commencement of war a South African Lexington, he had in mind France and the discomfiting eighteenth-century colonial precedent of the Franco-American alliance against George III's British empire.[103] Yet apprehension over European rivals or opponents being drawn into hostilities was misguided. Governments and the public in Germany and France may have greatly relished Britain's Transvaal difficulties, but in the imperial partition of Africa, South Africa was acknowledged to be British turf. Pretoria would receive no pledges of official military assistance. At the same time, Britain had no need to secure allies: it had, if need be, the resources of an empire.

Just as it was in Britain's interest to keep the struggle at the level of a backyard colonial war, so it was highly desirable for the Boers to encourage European interference. W.J. Leyds, the Transvaal foreign secretary and Kruger's envoy in Brussels, did what he could to try to bring this about, by cultivating the more ferociously anti-British press in France, Germany and the Low Countries, and by opening urgent lines of diplomatic communication with Britain's principal Continental rivals.[104] On their part, these rivals never seriously contemplated involvement, although in the opening phase of the war Germany, France and Russia would briefly mull over the idea of diplomatic intervention to try to put pressure on London to come to terms with the republicans. But, as a military proposition, any move by other powers to help the Boers in countering the British was never practical. Intervention would be nothing more than a lingering dream, as remote as the notion that the war in South Africa might become a world war.[105]

Nevertheless, the mirage of Cossacks to Klerksdorp or Prussians to Potchefstroom loomed over what constituted the Boer war plan. This notion, by all accounts solely devised and presented by Smuts, was some years in the making and was both bold in conception and fairly detailed in its grasp of the essential requirements for a successful offensive. It was evidently the only plan for war the Boers had, and it was certainly the closest the republics came to formulating a strategic vision. Although ambitious and imaginative, the plan was longer on the importance of timing than on sound and intelligent generalship.

Crafted as an intricate memorandum, tabled on 4 September for submission to the Transvaal Volksraad, Smuts's perceptions came to form the basis of a common strategic scheme for both republics, as much of its effectiveness lay in close coordination between a Transvaal and Orange Free State war effort. For the young state attorney, vigorous political and economic mobilisation was as important as decisive military action. The first thing was sedition, or at least an attempt at encouraging it. In an assessment of enemy weak points, one assumption was that Britain had now grown vulnerable under the sheer weight of its empire. With an imperial structure increasingly 'strategically over-extended', Whitehall was at the mercy of a worldwide Malthusian army of impoverished and discontented subjects, countless rebels and innumerable plotters.[106] By encouraging Irish Fenianist inclinations within the empire, Boer republicans could hamper any enemy war effort by helping to ignite difficulties on other fronts, and not only on the Irish Sea.

The more hopeful of the Pretoria observers foresaw the possibility of Britain's Transvaal troubles being eclipsed by ever greater difficulties elsewhere. Pressure on Britain in South Africa could open India to pressure from Russia. More widely, it could pose a temptation for the Franco-Russian alliance to become aggressive, a recurring concern for both the War Office and the Admiralty.[107] Such Boer calculations were by no means implausible. Smuts was right about the low level of British self-confidence in Central Asia, and about rising anxieties over imperial defence capacity and costly military burdens. But he also failed to appreciate two critical considerations. One was the nature of British national interest in South Africa. Its Transvaal problem, unlike India, was bound to be temporary and one which was likely to be resolved. The other was the British foreign-policy imperative of conducting negotiations with rival powers over the protection of interests. Last, the idea of a contagious Boer republicanism corroding the worldwide imperial fabric implied a formidable propaganda campaign far beyond the slender means of the republican camp.

Local horizons were more realistic. Acutely aware that the republics would not necessarily command the total loyalty of their populations in a testing struggle, Smuts put a high priority on domestic propaganda efforts. These were directed not only towards Boer citizens of the British colonies but also at neutral or irresolute republican inhabitants, such as those in the Orange Free State who had not come to view Britain as a natural foe. Trade and commercial affinities between Free Staters and the British Cape were deep, and neutrality seemed reasonable enough. Against this, northern republican appeals promoted a heightened sense of 'Afrikaner' nationhood and national patriotic duty in the event of war. Leading republicans sought to fashion a war culture rooted in moral mobilisation by depicting a Manichean conflict between the rapacity of mercenary Rand financiers and mine magnates, and the 'freedom', 'independence', and 'righteousness' of a small and plucky 'Africander people'.[108] Smuts' own influential contribution, produced with the assistance of the no-nonsense lawyer Jacobus de Villiers Roos, was an impassioned 1899 republican tract, *A Century of Wrong*, which denounced the enemy as 'the lion, the jackal, and the vulture', driven by 'the lust of robbery and the spirit of plunder' to fall upon a 'wounded antelope'. Concluding that what approached was 'no War' but rather an 'attempt at Infanticide', Smuts fashioned a compelling polemical vocabulary which reverberated with familiar Boer religious, national and carnivorous imagery.[109] It was also carried to Britain and published in English by the Radical W.T. Stead's *Review of Reviews*.

What connected *A Century of Wrong* to the September war memorandum was a sense of righteous Boer power, and a feeling that its time had come, provided the republicans could get the upper hand. Smuts therefore envisaged an economic policy to boost military effectiveness. For a start, there was ample agricultural capacity which could be readily diverted to creating a food supply for fighting forces without squeezing domestic consumption in the countryside. In the absence of farmers mobilised for commando service, continued agricultural production could be sustained by controlled African tenant labour or commandeered work parties. In a farming community, one of the benefits of the mobile commando system was its flexibility, through which all men in the field need not be removed completely from critical stages of the agricultural cycle. Food crops would become a servant of strategy.

To enhance the production of war material, the plan called for accelerated development of new light industries, aided in urban areas by the requisitioning or commandeering of raw materials and the brisk procurement of plant by a powerful commissariat commission. This would ease the supply of clothing and basic nutritional requirements (such as bread, jam and biscuits) to Boer forces. To build up stores, commissariat organisation would also be able to siphon off supplies held by wealthy capitalists or to lean on fat individuals for patriotic donations. Some leading Transvaal industrialists, like Sammy Marks, knew all about smart moves and responded positively to Kruger's call. At the same time, great importance was accorded to the need quickly to set about controlling and boosting armaments production by coordinating the conversion of Rand mine foundries and machinery firms into munitions factories to hammer shrapnel and turn out shells. Provision had also to be made for import-substitutionist technical services for such things as artillery maintenance. Self-sufficiency was a priority: with war under way, the British Fleet would be able to mount an arms blockade close in to Delagoa Bay, the Boers' only free provisioning point.

Ironically, the commodity which had helped to bring war upon the republicans was also the means of bankrolling their own war effort. Smuts's planning assumed continuing gold production and a 20 per cent war levy on output. In return, there would be the provision of a 'protective' regulatory environment to maintain the supply of materials and labour, and measures to encourage skilled mine staff, even if British, to remain on the Rand. It also envisaged increased output, if need be through the administration exerting direct control over the most profitable mines, or through actually taking over some operations and working them as government mines.[110]

As long as the Transvaal state had the ability under its 1898 Gold Law to mine gold, and confiscatory powers under martial law, to scoop up raw gold supplies and coin, it would be able to pay for the war without any panic over its fiscal capacity to sustain large increases in expenditure. The solution to another Treasury concern was straightforward. To stop money leaving the Republic in the form of wages, all the earnings of departing Cape and other African mineworkers were seized at frontier crossings. Sullen and despairing black labourers were among the first to sacrifice for the Boer war effort. Given a policy of radical government economic intervention and controls over reasonably good resources, no major war borrowing was envisaged. Nor was there any need to worry about the political consequences of heavy taxation, even if the republics had possessed the administrative capability to impose new cash levies on their farm populations to fund defence.

Best characterised as an executive discussion document, Smuts's September strategy is a singular but significant indication of the ways in which the governing republican élite, or at least those elements which believed that everything had to be subordinated to supply needs, fixed on the methods necessary to organise a major war effort. This was to be based on intensely ideological popular mobilisation, and the first resolute steps towards the development of a command war economy. Yet to what extent the Smuts Plan came to structure the Boer war effort is not so clear. While the Kruger government and Transvaal Volksraad appear to have backed it strongly, the level of support within military command remained uncertain, with some writers even suggesting that far from there being any strategic consensus, the Smuts vision had little serious impact on actual Boer strategy.[111] Indeed, at this strategic level, what evolved was not necessarily a coordinated operational agenda so much as contending perspectives of the republican campaign. These were embodied in leading personalities, not all of whom were famous for tactical flexibility or for consulting with others about what to do.

Naturally, there was general acceptance that the Boers had to wage an offensive war. Here, again, it was Smuts who articulated a clear strategy of deep penetration. Given the military situation, everything lay in timing. Schooled in a crucial breeding ground for master strategists (the largely student Stellenbosch militia), Smuts urged Boer command to prepare for a rapid opening offensive. By concentrating their armed weight for a pre-emptive knockout blow before the arrival of British reinforcements, the republicans could immediately gain the advantage. Eastwards, a shaky Natal could be taken at minimal cost. A sharp westerly thrust would cut the vital single-track rail artery connecting the Cape Colony with Rhodesia and the intermediate supply links between Cape Town, Kimberley and Mafeking.

The scales were finely tuned. An attack could not be launched until seasonal rains had provided adequate grass to relieve mounted commandos of the lumbering encumbrance of forage carts and the need to establish and maintain a run of fodder depots. Delay, however, inevitably provided Britain's garrison with further time to ship in reinforcing contingents. Running against the clock, and gambling on good grass, the Boers had to launch a war before an expeditionary force seriously threatened.[112]

In the first instance, therefore, the key was a rapid, heavy advance on British colonies while conditions remained easy. Once they had broken through light British forces already mustered on their borders, the republicans anticipated that not much else would stand in their way. Having punched through Natal and the Cape, taking all of the former and much of the latter with the aid of Cape Boer allies, movement would be replaced by position. With northward supply lines secure, the Boer armies would establish sturdy, first-line defensive positions deep inside occupied colonies. Holding down enemy territory would enable them to frustrate any forward movement of the main British reinforcements, due before the end of November. In this scenario, victory was considered perfectly attainable, provided war could be carried to the neighbouring colonies and kept there, even if it turned into Smuts's nightmare of a lengthy and draining struggle.

It was essential to block any move on the republics. With over 2 000 miles of frontier, their borders were exposed on too many flanks, and they were far too short of soldiers for adequate defensive fortification. Their only bastions were designed to overawe the enemy within. Four costly rear fortresses for Johannesburg and Pretoria served little purpose other than to give any uppity Uitlanders a fright.[113] So a deep Natal–Cape attack looked a fair gamble. If it did not bring a quick victory, it could still produce a stalemate or deadlock to compel London to make a compromise peace. Equally, launching a prompt offensive was justified by more than the prevailing military doctrine that in war attack was essential, even for defence. It had also come to form a core ingredient of Boer military culture. African fighting, whether with Zulu, Pedi, Sotho or Swazi, had invariably been a test of movement and charging down. Recently, headlong and headstrong rebelling burghers had also overwhelmed their British enemy in short order at Laing's Nek and Majuba. The natural fighting heritage embodied in nationalist discourse was not so much staying power as supreme will for the unstoppable offensive of 'wild' Boers.[114] That culture of dash was what determined military effectiveness.

Beyond this, there were more inflated hopes of what could be achieved thereby. Again, in Smuts's conception, a spearhead which tore right through to the coast could prompt otherwise hesitant European powers to intervene, particularly if the Boers had provided the necessary tokens of diplomatic goodwill (or mining rights) to Continental capitals beforehand. Astonishing as it may seem, this assumption lay behind the idea and planning of a singular 'march' or 'ride' to encircle and capture Durban. Among some mobilised burghers there was excitement about a conquest of the British colonies, including a ripple of millennial relish that the republics would gain the bounty of the sea. In this view, Natal was a great prize, a lost natural cornerstone of republican power which years ago had been rolled away by avaricious British 'usurpers'. Invasion was to be nothing less than a just restitution of the lost 'heritage' of a mythical Boer land, originally validated by civilising trekker occupation[115]

Even an otherwise level-headed Deneys Reitz, the capable son of the Transvaal state secretary, recorded that as Boer 'salvation' lay in 'rapid advance', there was 'not a man' amongst invading commandos 'who did not believe that we were heading straight for the coast'.[116] This was a case of chewing at more than one could swallow: lunch in Ladysmith, dinner in Durban. Once accomplished, Britain would face humiliation. Its soldiers would be steaming for a hostile port, and could well find themselves on ships which commanded the sea, yet were unable to make land. If armed hostilities turned out to be a swift affair, resolved 'perhaps within one year', Smuts envisaged the subsequent creation of his 'United South Africa', a non-imperial state in the form of an Afrikaner Republic, 'stretching from Table Bay to the Zambesi'.[117] Otherwise, the price of failure was chilling: a war which might bleed the Boers into submission through attrition. Smuts's sober reflection would come to prove bleakly prophetic.

But, at the outset, the Boers had the initiative; all that mattered was ensuring that they retained it. For a start, the republics appeared to have the means to launch a climactic assault on British positions. Their armoury was extremely well stocked, Kruger having lost no time in getting things going after partial mobilisation in response to the 1896 Raid had revealed inadequate equipment, obsolete firearms and ammunition shortages. The amateurish legal tradition of the Boer citizen army, which prescribed that each burgher provide his own personal gun and ammunition, was superseded by government issue at a cost which exceeded £1m. Between 1896 and 1899 Transvaal annual budgets allocated over one third to defence expenditure. Commandant-General Piet Joubert, the dapper Transvaal commander-in-chief and a fairly consummate operator, was able to order virtually everything he thought was necessary. Adding to around 42 000 older-model British and Austrian rifles, he procured over 37 000 of the latest .276 Mausers, 'the finest infantry arm in existence',[118] the same effective Krupp weapon which had mown down many of Theodore Roosevelt's Rough Riders in the 1898 Spanish–American War. To this store, Orange Free State command added around 13 000 further Mausers – virtually sufficient to meet Kruger's desire for each burgher to have a reserve rifle.

In all, the Boer armies had over 102 500 good-quality rifles, a supply augmented by a large rural stockpile of personally owned arms, some in the hands of farming women.[119] Effectively over-provisioned with guns and ammunition reserves, it was envisaged that the surplus could be utilised by Boer rebels in the Cape. The 1899 attachment of black auxiliaries to republican forces was part of fighting tradition but, apart from that, reserve weapons transportation on a large scale would require the use of sizeable numbers of *agterryers* as gun-bearers and in gun maintenance. Having these extra men and even more guns undoubtedly helped to lift republican morale and, while of course not every mounted infantryman was cocky, it is easy to see why many felt strong and confident of their chances.

The Boer commando's close relationship with the rifle, its mythic measure set by the early nineteenth-century tradition and the history of the Voortrekker and his lethal *Voorlaier,* was now modernised by precision and reliability. Through natural aptitude, marksmen could carry the older romantic inheritance of prowess with the trusty family musket into the handling of new, regulation-issue firepower. Not for nothing did Boer general staff lay such store by possession of the Mauser, with its clip-loading, rapid-fire capability. So did their men, with many burghers personalising weapons by engraving their names on the butt.

Moreover, the Boers had more than just the pick of modern rifles. Their *Staadtsartillerie* or artillery corps (the republics' sole, and minuscule, standing army) had guns which were newer and considerably more modern than those of the British Army. As limited training and financial capacity would obviously never have sustained a gun-for-gun arms race with Britain after 1896, the Transvaal concentrated on acquiring the most modern available weaponry and high-quality expertise in tactics and other gunnery procedure. To this end, whopping commissions fattened Kruger's various contract agents in continental Europe, who increased in number, and in price, after the Jameson Raid. Their orders amounted to an emergency rearmament programme. One of the more ingenious post-1896 Transvaal rumours was that of a conspiracy by a couple of powerful Randlords to spirit Kruger away and replace him with a more pliable Piet Joubert. This was supposedly tumbled by European arms dealers, who alerted the president's *Geheime Dienst* or Secret Service. Continental merchants had no wish to see a profitable Anglo-Boer war averted.

In addition to French Creusot heavy guns and field guns, and Krupp howitzers and field guns, Joubert plumped for a batch of advanced Maxim-Nordenfeld quick-firing field guns, British but not yet in British Army service. The

Orange Free State, whose heavy arsenal was leaner than that of her wealthier republican ally, still had an established *Artillerie Korps* equipped with new Krupp models, as well as older Armstrong and Whitworth ordnance. Serviced by the new state foundries and ordnance workshops, the republics could deploy over a hundred highly mobile guns. Some two dozen of them had rates of fire faster than anything currently in the hands of the Royal Artillery. With these went a shell stock of about 108 000 rounds laid in from continental European manufacturers. Along with ample powder and metal for some local shell assembly, these pieces were considered generally sufficient for a short offensive war.

A few of these pieces were kept warm in the later 1890s with African sideshows, bombarding recalcitrant chiefdoms into submission with minimal wastage of shell. These grand exhibitions of Boer military prowess, it has to be said, were mainly a way for old Majuba fire-eaters, like Commandant-General Joubert himself, to put on imposing new airs. In the event of a longer war, shell supply was bound to become a complication, as it was simpler for the republics to buy stock than to invest in large-scale armaments production. This would indeed turn out to be the case in the coming war. Quite apart from the effect of its naval blockade, Britain paid off several French and Belgian firms to ensure that they would not supply war material to the republics for the duration of any conflict. After March 1899 not much more could be brought in anyway, after a £25 000 order for Creusot quick-firing guns and another for field-gun rounds failed to arrive. Inevitably, artillery replacement was also destined to be a problem as anything captured could not be replaced by foreign suppliers. In the long run, the Boers would be hampered by a limited import-substitution capacity in this sector.

Scholars have suggested that the Boers paid little attention to gunnery in tactical planning.[120] But this was plainly not the case after the Jameson jolt. Younger officers from leading Boer families were dispatched to Germany and the Low Countries for artillery training, and the *Staadtsartillerie* barracks in Pretoria contracted former German gunners and engineers to provide technical training for recruits, and their drill books were quickly translated into Dutch. The 500-man Orange Free State *Artillerie Korps* also engaged several German officers. Some, like Major Erich Albrechts, were veterans of the 1870–71 Franco-Prussian War, in which artillery had been of crucial importance. Expansion of the Transvaal artillery corps from 100 to 400 gunners, with a well-trained and disciplined reserve of 550 men, was conducted under close German supervision. Field artillery preparation concentrated on rapid mobility in the field, the use of long-range, heavy guns using shell with time-delay fuses, accurate range-finding across large, open terrain, and the stealthy deployment of equipment. It was fitting that Boer heavy gunnery tactics, like so much of their weaponry, should be adapted in one form or another from an obliging German army.[121] In their imported Prussian hats, trained personnel regarded themselves as distinctive heirs of the Prussian fighting tradition, even though they might have been a little short of siege experience against European capital cities.

Drawn from landed or other wealthier and more educated backgrounds, and more self-disciplined than the average irregular, Europeanised artillerymen formed a small standing-army élite, a cadre of army careerists set apart from those whose routine commando obligations did not run to knowledge of trigonometry and ballistics. As with those Boer professionals and students in Holland, Germany and England who returned home at the outbreak of hostilities to take up arms, here was a cluster of altruistic men acutely aware of the national cause, and with a consuming soldiering will. As one of them declared, if it took war to secure 'the future destiny of our nation on earth', that would be welcome. Unsurprisingly, a big war could also provide opportunities for national fame and personal promotion through battle experience more challenging than the occasional bombardment of peasant enemies.[122] These men carried little trace of the entrenched civilian mentality which common burghers brought into commando service as part of the tissue of their fighting sentiment.

Confidence and optimism in the potential of artillery tactical mobility was shared by republican commanders. General Ben Viljoen, for instance, immersed himself in the study of technical conditions, penning a series of articles on the lessons of Franco-Prussian War strategy and tactics in the prominent Transvaal papers, *Land en Volk* and *Ons Volk*.[123] Indeed, Boer generals were fond of the didactic study of foreign wars, with professional knowledge of the conduct of not only the 1870–71 conflict but also the Napoleonic Wars, the American Civil War and, by no means least, because of its inspirational legacy as a struggle for national independence, the American War of Independence. It is thus wrong to assume that all that Boer military leadership knew of were African colonial clashes. It is equally misleading to suggest that only a single Boer soldier (General Piet Cronjé) 'ever made a serious study of modern war';[124] and it is at best whimsical for one scholar to conclude of this prominent 1880–81 veteran that 'his military studies were almost certainly restricted to the campaigns of Joshua and the prophetess Deborah'.[125] The spiritual inspiration of the Old Testament may well have been deeply instilled in Boer generals, but they were not without some knowledge of Napoleon and Clausewitz. Although professional military leaders were few, the Boers were able amateurs and were not unmodern in their knowledge of how to go about waging war.

One element of this was the skilled use of heliograph apparatus in commando training, during which mirror messages could be flashed over distances of up to a hundred miles by operators specially coached by the artillery corps. Another was intelligence. Between 1896 and 1898 the Transvaal intelligence department spent over £286 000 on information-gathering, expanding its roll of agents and rewarding snoops lavishly. Monthly monies for men in Natal and the Cape Colony reached £1 500. On the Rand, £850 went to trusted foreigners keeping a watch on any British Uitlander intrigue, and over £900 was remitted abroad to agents in Britain. Some of these, it was reported, had been briefed to keep tabs on and to evaluate the loyalty of Irish troops or other 'alien elements' in the British army.[126] As far as can be determined, republican intelligence was directed not so much at clarifying enemy intentions and strategy, as Boer leadership considered these to be fairly self-evident. Instead, effort was concentrated on obtaining an intelligence picture of the state of imperial preparations and British morale, and of what Britain might deploy to South Africa when mobilised, the speed with which it could be shipped there, and the strength of local British garrison forces. On the last score, the information gleaned was accurate enough. The British had barely 20 000 troops in South Africa, while the Boer states could quickly field at least 50 000 men. The republicans knew well that their military advantage was sufficient for the immediate move, with Smuts, for example, calculating that the enemy would require an army corps of at least 150 000 troops to hold off the republican forces.

British intelligence in the later 1890s emphasised that mounting Boer military spending had not worked to much advantage in administrative coordination and in establishing more cohesive supply systems. Staff work remained weak, and fragmentation of command over support activities made for an organisational machinery which was at best inefficient, and at worst simply incapable of focused operational planning. Entrenched discretionary powers at lower levels in the chain of command also bred corruption in the handling of stocks, with requisitions favouring those merchants most willing to nod through backhanded commissions to commissariat stores officers. It seems that only Bibles for commandos were entirely exempt from requisitioning deals, probably due to God's design. Given the feeding frenzy of widespread graft under the Kruger administration, it is not surprising to find that the *krijgscommissaris* or war commissariat was similarly contaminated by shady practices. With inefficiency and corruption hampering the preparedness of their bureaucratic machinery, there is undoubtedly a good deal to the view that the Boer armies were 'administratively weak and not really capable of a major offensive'.[127]

Operational organisation was certainly short on inventory control and centralised systems of materials procurement and handling. Still, leadership generally did not conceive of the war lasting any extended length of time, and the campaign envisaged was considered sustainable by the republics' logistical capacity. Secondly, for the majority of Boers this was neither a war cooked up by government, nor a burdensome minor expedition imposed by their ruling élite; it was 'a war for their national independence, which concerned every single burgher'.[128] Individual motivation, ingenuity at cutting corners, and the Boers' famed independence of mind would compensate for any systems deficiency – or that, at least, was the anticipation.

Third, while the conflict may well have been 'the last *laissez-faire* war'[129] for Britain, it was far less so for the Boers. The Transvaal government took over the Netherlands South African Railway Company and assumed direct control of major wagon convoys and their routes. By September 1899 it was requisitioning draught animals, carts, horses, grain, fodder, tinned food and clothing from merchants, shopkeepers and ordinary burghers. As *The Times History of the War in South Africa* recognised, the Boers relied very heavily 'on the power of commandeering'.[130] Fourth, and no less significant, was the degree to which the provisioning work of Transvaal and Orange Free State commissariat commissions, council, and committees was augmented and eased by the private supply of essential commodities. Its basis lay in a coil of social relations thickly oiled by custom, prerogative, usage, and prerequisite. Wealthier burghers entered the field not merely with their obligatory mount and initial ration reserve, but with an accumulation of carts, wagons, horses, reserve stores and dependent or coerced African servants to attend to organisation and maintenance. Supplemented by commandeered horses and transport, this helped to ensure that poorer burghers who had no war goods of their own would be provisioned. At the base of the Boer war-supply system was an acceptance that defensive need might require some social distribution of surplus property. There were also strong voluntarist impulses. Newspapers and well-heeled residents funded commando supplies of tobacco and spirits. From abroad, France provided army hospital stores, while Scandinavian, Russian and Dutch sympathisers opened subscription lists to fund equipment and even weaponry.

The final logistical cog was the household, especially in helping to service nutritional and clothing requirements. While formal fighting mobilisation was obviously a male affair, directed through a stoutly patriarchal Boer political system, output and distribution needs incorporated substantial numbers of women. As producers of food, as seamstresses or boot repairers, or as overseers of African servants and herdsmen, industrious wives or sometimes mothers ran supplies of meat, biscuits, clothing and footwear to individual burghers in commandos. The image of the hardy *vrouw* or woman, or of dutiful servants dispatched by her, trekking from the farm to a commando camp with a cartload of protein, fat, wool, and leather, is perhaps one of the more telling images of the scale and commitment of the Boer national war effort. In reality, it reflected the closeness and intimacy of ties between commandos gathering for the front and their fortifying domestic domain, and the significance of powerful familial exchange between Boer soldiers and their home front. There, the customary responsibility of women was substantial, and with it came corresponding authority in crisis.

If committed women were accustomed to getting commandos off the mark, what kind of citizenship soldiering did they represent? A creation of eighteenth-century Dutch-colonial frontier society, the armed *kommando* or civilian militia initially had no standard roll, but instead relied on the turnout of a rough assortment of Dutch East India Company soldiers, white farmers, and Khoikhoi and Coloured men who were either collaborators or forced conscripts. Service at this early stage lacked both structure and any developed notion of racial preference. There were too few Boers, many ducked call-ups, and shirking Cape farmers would frequently elbow Coloured labourers into military duties as substitutes. In the later eighteenth century, settlers often comprised only a minority of men fulfilling commando obligations in white frontier communities.[131]

As the classic military formation of the Boer republics, the commando system experienced continual institutional development through the latter half of the nineteenth century. In a significant recomposition, it became more white under Transvaal and Orange Free State gun laws which forbade Africans from possessing firearms. It also became more centrally planned. By the 1850s there had been a transition from improvised arrangements, in which dispersed civilians were subject to service on a territorial basis, to commando law in the Orange Free State, in which all white males between sixteen and sixty were obliged to register for armed duty. By 1890 Free State men had to participate in annual *wapenschouwingen* or military camps. It became a statutory requirement for men in both republics to own and maintain weaponry and basic military equipment, to have equipment inspected regularly, and to participate routinely in designated field exercises and camps.

What this amounted to in the Transvaal by the later 1870s was an obligation that able-bodied men complete at least three months' full-time military service. Mobilised through a spread of some forty Transvaal and Orange Free State electoral or magisterial districts, the timing of deployment was swift. In the event of threatening hostilities, individual commandos, each providing his own rifle with thirty rounds and a horse (mostly rugged, unbending and swift Basuto ponies), could be ready in a week, mustered in four rising age-bands starting from 18 to 34, and ending with an under-16 reserve. For the Boer states, the advantage of commando-based defence was that their combat power could be delivered through the small savings and assets of a community. It was an economical option for governments which lacked the fiscal base and tax-extraction capacity to maintain anything other than a negligible standing force and small police corps. The absence of any formal regimental system, and the practice of appointing only establishment staff for actual war, also meant large economies in services, professional officers and administrative staff. In sum, the commando net institutionalised a cheap form of reservist conscription which trawled virtually the whole of the able-bodied male population. Peacetime in the republics meant regularly replenishing the appetite and fitness for war. In war, not only republican citizens but all official 'inhabitants' (such as Orange Free State British male residents) were liable to be commandeered for service.

How many of a combined burgher force could be counted as really effective or competent soldiers seems not to have greatly worried Boer onlookers and commentators in the 1890s, nor sympathetic Dutch, German, French and other foreign observers. If rather short on drill, dress and taut discipline, the 'spirit', 'dash', 'reliability' and inherited 'frontier talents' of commandos were considered more than compensating virtues.[132] No longer were Boer riflemen simply seen as capable of dispatching any 'uncivilised' enemy, like aggrieved Pedi or Swazi, still spoiling for a fight. Having already bloodied Britain's nose once, they were judged sufficiently tough, resourceful and tactically adept for a major offensive war. There was no shortage of romance about Africa's outdoor Boers being born to soldiering by instinct and by the blood tax of bodily service. Unlike slack metropolitan Europeans, they did not have to be made into soldiers by parade-ground generals.

These forces had a fairly well-articulated chain of command, with 'democratic' or elective structures which were completely alien to regular armies. Based on commando territorialisation, every locality had a peppering of *veldkornets* or district field officers who served under another elected *kommandant* or principal military officer. Higher command of militiamen and all professional forces was assigned to a *Kommandant-Generaal* or commandant-general, also elected and invariably a landed Boer notable. A final feature was the direct insertion of the elected state president into military matters. In both republics, war declarations and martial law authorisations were not simply imposed by the state president and his consultative executive council. Each Transvaal and Orange Free State commando had a powerful elected *Krijgsraad* or council of war, its legitimacy resting in the elected status of veldkornets and commandants in association with the president. This war collective voted on operational movements and battle planning after consultation, in a kind of shotgun caucus.

At the end of the chain, going into battle was an elective business. Rhetorically, this participatory military democracy was underpinned by a good deal of flannel about equalising citizenship. But muddiness was its virtue. Contentedly democratic propertied men used their office, clientage networks, political toadying, and dodgy cattle or land transactions to secure the rewards of nominations or the attachment of high political patronage. The result, in the Transvaal, was a system of popular military participation checked by the purchasing power of numbers of favoured elite 'Krugerite' officers, as in the case of General F.A. Grobler. His 'chief qualification seemed to be the power to utter silly jokes and to laugh at them himself . . . probably he was chosen for the purpose of keeping the burghers in a good humour. But, then, he was a staunch supporter of Kruger'.[133] In command, the enduring deference and oligarchic balance of forces within Boer political culture assuredly left their mark.

Even so, the egalitarian plumage of the commando remained an article of faith, and one which increased in standing as war approached. Thus, *Land en Volk* and *De Republikein* reminded literate Boers of their proud eighteenth-century republican inheritance. They were straddling the Jacobin tradition of the 'nation in arms' and the heady manhood suffrage democracy of the American Revolution, with its citizen army fighting successfully for popular rights and independence against a degenerate and old aristocratic foe. In assessments of their army's effectiveness, the more bookish of Boer generals, like Ben Viljoen, celebrated as unique the imagined lack of social divisions in which, within commandos, officers and men were indistinguishable, and where an ordinary soldier of poor social origin could be promoted on ability through the ranks to the very top of the officer corps.[134] In this fanciful notion, such camaraderie produced a fighting unit far more cohesive and dedicated than a British army hampered by the rigidities of class hierarchy and by mutual incomprehension between strong rural men and weak urban recruits.

By the late nineteenth century, to be a male citizen of the South African Republic's *volksdemokrasie* or people's democracy, or to be of military age in the Orange Free State (sixteen years), was more or less by definition to be a member of a commando. This was the key to citizenship and the franchise, to masculine status and identity, and to any sense of both military and civic duty to defend land, freedom, and the state. Bearing arms was also pivotal to the socialisation of young Boer men, with competitive traditions of individual marksmanship and horsemanship providing a distinctive 'rite of passage'.[135]

As a compound of individual ability and virtuous communal endeavour, the commando was a regimental expression of Boer ethnicity, in spirit at any rate. It embraced acting as the redcoats or kilts of frontier republicanism. This ethos was reinforced by the status of blacks on commando as auxiliary retainers, and by the mating ritual of substitution, whereby conscripted wealthier burghers could meet military obligations by stumping up for a poorer stand-in. With the fee running at up to £90, rich sleeping-partners were providing capital for lean fellow citizens.

Around this apparent unity under arms, however, Boer society continued to carry its old troubles of fierce factionalism, regional and district animosities, and class and sectarian religious rifts. Furthermore, not all ordinary citizen-soldiers were happy to make good their legal obligations to attend annual field camps and to perform unpaid commando duty. The main source of discontent over militia demands were poor whites who lacked the means to equip themselves with weaponry and equipment, and whose families faced increased privation through the loss of productive male labour to periods of military requisitioning. In the Orange Free State in the 1890s, there were growing concerns over the reliability of the *bywoner* class, which was centred upon its preparedness 'to take up arms in defence of republican independence'.[136] Still, by 1899 only about ten per cent of burghers were not effectively armed.

No less interesting, if perhaps more obvious, were some other commando characteristics. Membership was by no means confined to individuals who owned barns and stables. Some were banded in distinctive *dorpskommando's* or town commandos, drawn from the urban possessing classes. Although lawyers, merchants and teachers were sometimes said not to put up too easily with slumming down alongside common farmers, they were not short of an ideological sense of national obligation and were organisationally adept. Republican forces had no formal training establishment; nor did they develop any regular disciplinary regime for soldiers, leaving it to individual commanders to devise their own instruments of control. Although wearing no regular (or recognised) uniform, their soldiers' garb and bearing announced their business. Generally neatly jacketed, frequently wearing a collar and tie or even a cravat or bow-tie, commando dress peaked with a customary felt hat, the Boer answer to the French army's sacrosanct red trousers, *le pantalon rouge*. For added flair, these were often worn tipped up on the right, a fashion to be later mimicked by nationalist Irish Volunteers in the 1916 Easter Rising, who would dub their slouch hats 'De Wets' after the admired republican general. The primacy of experience and seniority, as well as patriarchal authority, was marked by heavy beards, displayed by most men over thirty and the object of considerable grooming and preening.

Wholly at ease as a mounted infantry, commandos had their rifles slung across their backs and leather bandoliers strapped over their chests. As befitting a force which believed it had God on its side, all men carried Bibles: even in their doctrinal Calvinist diversity, they shared a common understanding about religious devotion. They also shared a liking for military ceremonial, fashioning glorifying battle insignia, flying flags, pennants and banners, and commemorating significant past victories by putting up stone cairns or scoring rock faces.

Boer militia also gained through the continuing use of black auxiliaries as a labour and technical-skills subsidy to keep them in the field. While Africans were excluded from the republics' gun-bearing culture, their *krijgswette* or martial law provisions made allowance for *kleurlingen* or Coloured men to be called up. Of course, what it meant to be Coloured was by no means all that obvious. In places, the colour line in white-supremacist Boer society was just a trifle porous, and not all enlisted commandos would have changed complexion when scrubbed. Far more than this, though, it was the incorporation of *agterryers* which counted. Able mounted servants and gun-bearers, these men serviced a range of vital needs: gun-loading and maintenance, transport of reserve ammunition, tending of horses and repair of saddle equipment, carrying of bulk rations, treatment and bearing of the wounded, dispatch riding, and scouting. As one leading military historian has suggested, a lot of hard work is required to keep a fighting force together in the field, so that, ultimately, 'war is a form of work'.[137] Bidden to make war their work, commando dependants embodied that in the truest sense.[138]

The scope of that work was also wide. To *agterryers* fell responsibility for the finer conveniences of life on the hoof – cooking, and brewing morning coffee. When pressed, Boer command could swallow hard and sometimes deploy auxiliaries in direct combat roles. A leading modern historian of the commando has ventured an average operational ratio, in a normal commando complement of 1 200 men, of one *agterryer* per every four to five burghers, At the outbreak of this war, that meant that well over 10 000 auxiliaries were pulled into campaigning.[139]

Estimates of the total strength of republican forces at this juncture still vary. By October there were some 55 000 to 60 000 men available for deployment, of whom between 35 000 and 42 000 were mobilised and in the field on the southern borders of the Boer states. Depending again on differing calculations of the level of mobilisation, the effective field force represented no more than about fifty-six to sixty-five per cent of fighting capacity.[140] The balance did not comprise idle stay-at-homes. Men had to be assigned to other sectors, such as policing and the guarding of farms against African interlopers, and to stamp Boer garrison authority on the frontiers of such potential African enemy territory as Basutoland and Swaziland. There could be no question of flinging the entire force at the British.

The republics could also count on some loyalist pro-Boer combat reinforcements. Internally, upwards of 2 000 pro-Boer Uitlanders either joined standing commandos or formed national fighting brigades and corps, which also attracted a swarm of late-adolescent adventurers (such as bull-necked American ex-Indian fighters) from countries partial to the Boer cause. This volunteer list was long. It mustered Germans, Dutch (including the military attaché to the Transvaal), Scandinavians, French, Italians, Irish, Americans, Greeks, even a Jewish Ambulance Unit, and Russians, some of whom threw in their lot with the Boer cause in the belief that it would provide handy experience for that inevitable future war with Britain.[141]

Externally, the republics banked on the armed collaboration of improvised bands of colonial Boer rebels who were expected to oppose the British wherever they chose to strike. Even though prominent Cape Afrikaner Bond politicians like J.H. Hofmeyr made it clear to Kruger that a mass Cape rebellion looked improbable, northern leadership remained convinced that at least 5 000 to 6 000 sympathetic rebels would be ready for war. This calculation made some sense. Indeed, in the war itself, more like 10 000 such men would turn out, and prospective rebel numbers might have been far greater had invading Boer forces charged harder through the Cape and Natal.[142] But even without these colonial collaborators, the republics assembled easily the largest modern army yet seen in South Africa. Its backbone was the cream of the mounted militia. Physically tough, crack shots with advanced smokeless Mausers, formidable in the saddle and proud of their veldcraft, these were good irregular soldiers, quick to the colours, and high in confidence in 1899. Springing from a settler society attuned to warfare, their commanders knew how to manoeuvre riflemen to maximise the impact of their fire, and how to minimise exposure to anything returned by opponents.

Even if the coming war turned out to be lengthy, leading figures like Smuts envisaged that when things turned towards irregular warfare the independent Boers would shine in a guerrilla struggle sustained here, there, and everywhere. What 'everywhere' meant was probably not quite decided. At this stage most ordinary burghers were not conditioned by any pan-republican nationalism. Unlike the Boer élite, they were bounded by their borders, which confirmed them as Free Staters and Transvalers.

None of this did much to frighten the more bellicose pro-imperial voices, either in Britain or in its South African colonies. For *The Economist* and *The Spectator*, Boer fighters were no more than 'stock-breeders of the lowest type', at best 'a rough mob of good marksmen' who would be unlikely seriously to test a

British army ready to flatten them at negligible cost to the Treasury. 'Preposterous', concluded the *Cape Argus,* for whom Boer claims reportedly 'evoked contemptuous amusement, mingled with satisfaction at the tension being at last ended . . . the ultimatum was received in military circles with the greatest enthusiasm'.[143] Such equanimity was bolstered by common press perceptions that the War Office had things well in hand. Even if there were any delay in the arrival of an expeditionary army corps, it would not hamper the British mission. The Boer army had no men of talent, its organisation was too much of a muddle for any sustained campaign, and many commandos, once short of food and stores, were likely to return to their farms before any action. This was the view not merely of the *Liverpool Echo* or the *Huddersfield Examiner:* it was also Chamberlain's assurance to the Queen on receiving the Transvaal ultimatum. Perhaps this was the only opinion his obstinate and crusty sovereign wished to hear.

As already noted, there had been some initial uncertainty over how best to handle the issue of beefing up Britain's South African position. Although the realistic possibility of a military contest had been on the cards for several years, up to the very eve of declaration the roll of the diplomatic dice had still assumed that Kruger's nerve might finally fail. The Transvaal would yield on the franchise demands, given a clear British undertaking not to challenge 'the independence of the South African Republic'. For a Cabinet insistent on dragging out the matter, it was obvious that any premature strengthening of the imperial garrison would expose Britain's aggressive calculations, accelerate the Orange Free State's gravitation towards the Transvaal, and risk a row with the Cape and Natal, neither of whose governments was keen to see a diplomatic confrontation turn military through impetuous warmongering.

Granted, a negotiated settlement tolerable to both sides would have calmed the Salisbury government's worries over domestic opinion and partisan parliamentary division. Even so, the logic of any tactic of intimidatory pressure upon the enemy while continuing to negotiate with it would have justified significant mobilisation well before an impasse looked likely. Crucially, this did not escape the notice of the army commander-in-chief, Lord Wolseley, who grasped the facts of the situation: Britain's negotiating posture had to be fortified. In memoranda through June and July 1899, an apprehensive Wolseley pressed Lansdowne for authorisation to amass essential stores and food reserves in South Africa, and to quickly strengthen the British garrison establishment through the dispatch of

10 000 troops to Natal and the Cape. The estimated cost of these measures was £500 000. After Majuba he no longer held the view that the Boers were 'poor silly creatures' who were 'playing at soldiers' and were 'far inferior to the Zulu'.[144]

In terse warnings to the Cabinet, Wolseley stressed that not to stiffen the military position would be a dangerously false economy, for Britain's whole situation would be thereby imperilled. The only hope of getting the Transvaal to cave in, and thus to avert war, would be an overwhelming show of force. His recommendations were turned down twice by Lansdowne on the grounds that circumstances did not yet justify heavy reinforcements, and that it was too tricky to do anything until all negotiating options had been exhausted. All that could be risked by August was the dispatch to Natal of a small contingent of 2 000 men. To Lansdowne and Salisbury this may have seemed diplomatically prudent. But in military terms it was folly.

Wolseley was incensed by what he saw as misjudgement by Lansdowne and other politicians and their alarming inability to grasp the true nature of British military strength. His retort to Lansdowne's rejection of his proposals was that, if war came and not enough had been done to bolster the position of British forces, the initiative would be surrendered to the enemy with serious repercussions for British national prestige. For the commander-in-chief the problem was not British inferiority: it was a lack of political will to utilise its superiority. Baldly summarised, such ill-feeling between War Office soldiers and the politicians over activity – or inactivity – clearly made proper war preparations difficult. It was not until September, late in the day, that the British Cabinet turned seriously to the fundamental problem that its South African garrison was far too weak to do much. It was obvious that its established force would not only have to be brought up to strength, but also increased in size through the shipping in of a strong expeditionary contingent. Now, a worried Salisbury wanted Chamberlain to ease up on Kruger so that Britain could get things into place.[145]

Yet in these early days, aside from worries over the delay in sailing time, the British army did not take long to get going. A mobilisation scheme operated smoothly, and the raising and dispatch of the first regular army expeditionary corps of 30 000 men to Natal ran like clockwork, prompting a satisfied undersecretary for war to declare the army 'more efficient than at any time since Waterloo'.[146] Indeed, so effortless was mobilisation that between early October and the end of January 1900, over 112 000 regular troops were equipped and transported to South Africa. Victorian merchant enterprise, embodied in Britain's mercantile marine, possessed significant capacity.

If the early position in Natal and the Cape was looking a little precarious, the arrival of reinforcing troops from India would be sure to extricate Britain from any difficulties. That, at any rate, was how a good few saw it at the beginning. At the same time, not everyone in London was sure that this was a war which would be quickly decided. Just as Smuts had pondered the terrible possibility of a lengthy and wasting struggle, so Chamberlain weighed up the prospect of 'one of the most serious wars that could possibly be waged', to follow his earlier, sobering Commons remark on the chances of a long, bitter, and costly engagement.[147] On the Left, meanwhile, some socialists predicted that financing a major war effort would spell trouble for the Treasury and lead to possible social unrest, as a lingering colonial conflict would take an inevitable inflationary toll of workers' living standards.[148]

Most calculations, though, were sanguine. For months, war with the Boers had hardly been thought to require heavy preparation. Initially, the Salisbury government estimated that the task would need no more than 75 000 troops, would incur a negligible casualty rate, would last between three and four months, and would cost perhaps £10m or £11m. This Cabinet estimate, in effect the equivalent of about ten Majestic-class warships, was not the kind of figure to give the chancellor, Sir Michael Hicks Beach, too many sleepless nights. Accordingly, war would now get under way with no long-term approach to cost and only the most minimal short-term provision, with the Treasury estimating £5m for the mobilising and transporting of 50 000 troops. Victory would be secured for no more than £600 000 per month.[149]

Away from South Africa, Britain's generals also believed that they had the measure of the Boer republics. Possibly the most famous illustration of this was an exchange between Lansdowne and General Sir Redvers Buller prior to the latter's departure as commander-in-chief to assume command in Natal. By this account, all was now set for Buller to commence his planned advance around two days before Christmas, requiring no more than a month to knock out the Orange Free State and then plunge beyond into the Transvaal, needing only a further fortnight to reach and take Pretoria.[150] It was all as if there would be virtually nothing in his way.

Back in South Africa, however, informed military staff spotted one or two impediments. For this, we need to go back a few months, to a moment when Milner had thought that a tough show of force might bring the Transvaal to heel. With tension mounting in May 1899, the high commissioner and his military secretary, Hanbury Williams, had had a tart exchange with Sir William Butler, commander-in-chief of the British garrison in South Africa since late 1898. As ever, Milner wanted a sabre-rattling initiative. In this case, it was to see whether Kruger could be intimidated by a feint, involving an advance of Natal British troops to the northern frontier shoulder of Laing's Nek, just inside the colony. This was an unhappy spot for Britain as in January 1881 Colley's infantry had been all but routed there. It seems that Butler had scoffed at the idea, insisting that a minimum of 40 000 men would be required even to begin to face down the republicans.[151] He did not share Milner's belief that the Transvaal's social crises of the 1890s had so damaged its economy and weakened its defences as to make it ripe for the taking.

Butler's natural inclinations were to go more carefully, hence his reluctance to antagonise the republicans by also reinforcing Kimberley, and a determination to concentrate on guarding the interior approaches in expectation of a moving Boer encirclement. Acutely aware of its vulnerability, he was panicky about the defence of Natal, for which he claimed to have secret strategic proposals which were kept firmly under wraps. An officer with South African experience dating back to the 1870s, Butler was also of pronounced conciliationist instincts. In his view, rogue mercenary elements for which he cared little (Rhodes, the Uitlanders, the South African League) were criminally intent on causing a needless war which would place Britain under dangerous pressure. 'Let us', he suggested to the War Office in June 1899, 'leave the Jews and their gold alone'.[152]

Recognising that he was unlikely to get an energetic offensive commitment from Butler, Milner successfully intrigued against him, carping on his Irish Catholic origins to paint him as a suspiciously lukewarm imperialist and an Irish Home Rule milksop. The general had to go; he was too much in the rear, too prone to worry, too prejudicial towards, and contemptuous of, the Randlords of 'Jewburg',[153] and rather too respectful of the rural virtues of the yeomen Boers. Milner engineered this early in August, a tricky month for dealings with Kruger, and a time when British South African forces still consisted of just two cavalry regiments, six full-strength regular infantry battalions, and three light field batteries, their howitzers easily outranged and outmanoeuvred by the Boer Krupps.

Troops brought in from India, with a further small infusion of New Zealand and Australian contingents, raised regular-force strength for colonial defences, but British forces were still outnumbered by virtually two to one. Nevertheless, for most observers national superiority against a 'mob' or 'tribe' of marksmen was still expected to take care of any deficit.[154] It was almost as if the efficiency of mobilisation and smooth dispatch of a regular army corps to Natal had brushed aside other troubling questions of military preparedness. For this was a war which would require different tactics, a different administrative establishment, and different methods of command from the routines that characterised imperial Britain's small-war expeditions for most of the nineteenth century.

For decades, beginning with the 1904 Royal Commissions on the War in South Africa, writers have addressed the question of the inability of the British government and its War Office to perceive properly and prepare for a difficult war of which there had been at least three to four years' warning. It would be tedious to catalogue in detail once again the pre-war deficiencies in preparation and infrastructural machinery, and the strains to which the military establishment would now become subject. The problem was that no one listened to the few who rang alarm bells over inadequate preparation for the task ahead. For, in its distance from the home base and the extent of its operational area, even for a short campaign South Africa was likely to be a tough undertaking. While comprehension of what would be needed to maintain, service, and supply a large force in a distant field would improve significantly in time, its absence at the beginning was striking. For Lansdowne and Buller, too much was seen through a glass darkly, if it was seen at all. That applied quite widely, for 'staff, troops, and service corps were scarcely better prepared than their commander to face the task ahead'.[155]

Ammunition of all kinds was in short supply, as were modern quick-firing guns, with ordnance factories poorly placed to change stride quickly. Field artillery could deploy more guns than the Boers, but it was disadvantaged by traditional theory and rigid drills which were dear to it. Deployment in far-forward positions and in bunched batteries may have been potent against vulnerable spear-carrying warriors and in drills at Woolwich and on Salisbury Plain. It was, however, not ideal practice for a campaign in which exposed gun teams and horse lines would be within reach of coordinated, long-range rifle fire from entrenched positions.

The standard British infantry weapon, the .303 Lee-Metford rifle, was accurate and reliable, save for an occasional tendency for its wood to shrink in very hot weather, loosening rivets and causing the butt to slide off.[156] If infantry tactics and fire training had been stepped up in recent years, accuracy was not their most obvious strong point. While close formations and steady volleys had been lethally effective thus far against a charging peasantry on foot, this was not necessarily the best kind of instruction for coping with a more modern kind of colonial 'small war'. Moreover, most of the newer infantry recruits were urban men from large industrial cities, with little experience of movement across wide open spaces, and unused to operating in the dark or in extremely variable weather. For these, there was little realistic prior training for South African conditions.

Then there were other limitations in both strength and ability. The ordnance department was short of hands, stores and servicing capacity, with no planned systems for field-depot ammunition supply to the front. Warehouses lacked replacement reserves of basic equipment such as saddlery, and hospital reserve stores were negligible. The decisive element in all of this was the severe logistical demand to be made on Britain's supply services for South Africa, ranging from the provision of transport and the international procurement of items like mules, to the moving of arms, stores, animals and food and other equipment. Supply-service need was likely to be immeasurably greater than in any conflict since the Napoleonic wars.

To these problems could be added a further difficulty. If British statesmanship had been insufficient to prevent war, the craftiness of the Colonial Section of the Intelligence Division had been enough to aid contingency planning, but to little effect. When war was declared, ministers complained that the government had had as much anticipation of war with the Orange Free State as with Switzerland, with Buller declaring his surprise that 'the enemy who declared war against us is much more powerful than we expected'.[157] Enemy strength and armaments greatly exceeded expectations, nothing on the theatre of operations had been furnished to assist tactical training, and the pitiful inadequacy of mapping had left imperial forces in a precarious position.

In reality, under Sir John Ardagh, director of Military Intelligence, the gathering of information on the enemy had been systematic and remarkably accurate.

That it was still limited was due to pinched resources. As Ardagh was later to point out to the Elgin Royal Commission, when the Division discovered that the Boers had been spending £340 000 on intelligence in the two years leading up to war he requested £10 000 per year for counter-activity. After some quibbling, he was grudgingly granted £100. Typically, the devising of a comprehensive military map of the theatre of war came to nothing, as it would have needed a large grant and several years of 'secret service' work by fake civilian travellers to chart topography, and to document the location of roads, rail connections, bridges, rivers and other features essential to the requirements of military cartography. Such an enterprise was considered politically impossible in the sensitive circumstances of the late 1890s.

Where Ardagh was able to do something, intelligence was impressive. In 1897 and 1899 the Division issued a series of early reports on the likelihood of war, warned that it would be costly and difficult, and accurately determined enemy intentions, military expenditure and arms levels. Memoranda in June and August 1899 stressed the probability of full Orange Free State–Transvaal military collaboration, and a handbook on South Africa provided a fairly precise tabulation of what the enemy had. All of this revealed an alarming disparity in the capabilities of opposing forces in October 1899, an intelligence assessment flawed only in the sense that the problems were possibly even worse than those portrayed.[158] Ardagh's warnings did not go entirely unheeded. Senior military figures (including Buller) foresaw danger in moving too rapidly towards a war ultimatum while they did not have a full army corps on hand. But his warnings were not effectively absorbed by a War Office which lacked a proper General Staff for advanced contingency planning and for seeing to appropriate levels of preparedness. Communication between those who were posting key intelligence information, regular staff administration, and decisive government figures like Lansdowne, remained laconic, incomplete, or otherwise poor.

Taking into account reservists, the size of the British army in October 1899 was about 320 000 men, drawn from a society in which military values had been spreading, so that by the end of the 1890s over 22 per cent of the male population of Britain and Ireland aged between seventeen and forty had had some kind of army or semi-military experience. As yet, 'there was little expectation that such a potential reserve of military experience would need to be tapped in any way'.[159] The Victorian army had undergone a long period of organisational reform under

Edward Cardwell in the 1860s and 1870s, and economy-based policy adaptation in the late 1880s under the secretary of state for war, Edward Stanhope. To assist government estimates, provision allowed for the army's dispatch of no more than two corps for any overseas service, after calling up its reserve. The Stanhope policy was now about to fail its South African test.

The garrison battalions stationed in South Africa were experienced and proficient, as were units dispatched from India, Mauritius, and the Mediterranean. But the army, in general, was rather less so. Previous campaigns had invariably been short and limited, with little need for large-scale manoeuvres and complex communications. Most generals had little experience of handling very large bodies of troops, and instead of a standard system for the transmission of information between commanders and their subordinates there was a woolly space. Meanwhile, at the bottom, the general calibre of ordinary soldiers was not high. Suffering from wastage of trained soldiers through short-service enlistment, the army found itself 'unable to compete with urban rates of pay, and handicapped by the contraction of its traditional sources of supply – the rural population and the Irish in particular – it depended heavily upon the urban unemployed'.[160] A few months of regular food and barrack-square exercise achieved something towards making the men fit, but South Africa was a fairly tall order when it came to endurance. A campaign here represented weeks on packed troopships, hours in poorly ventilated trains, days alongside unsanitary rivers and streams, and fatiguing marching and fighting across difficult terrain.

From their inception, other general studies of this war have, from one angle or another, stressed that all was not well with Britain in coping with the coming challenges. Levels of 'preparedness' or 'readiness', particularly in minor tactics and logistical planning, were to prove woefully low. While that much is obvious, it would be equally wide of the mark to suggest that the British army had by now somehow grown short of war experience, or had no idea of what to expect in a colonial clash. By the end of the nineteenth century, a series of colonial campaigns had provided it with very considerable 'small war' experience. Even if South Africa would turn out to be more than expected, it was 'the 226th colonial campaign' fought since the accession of Queen Victoria.[161] This pedigree should have eased the transition to the running of a more weighty and complex exercise, but the British would begin by making a mess of things.

Why had preceding war experience not served well in the preparation? When it came to calculations, perhaps these wars of empire were not much of a guide. Small wars were highly varied in nature, and did not easily provide a standard model for operational planning. Too much was unpredictable for firm lessons or lasting principles, whatever the efforts of Colonel C.E. Calwell's influential *Small Wars, Their Principles and Practice* (1896), to provide generalised strategic assumptions.

Arguably, what counted no less were the basics of Victorian small wars. In these, Britain had superior rifles and guns, better-trained, better-disciplined and better-nourished troops. Under the inspired generalship of a Christian commander, victories against weaker adversaries came about through early decisive blows, followed by the complete dispersion and suppression of opponents. London was thus spared the challenges and costs of prolonged campaigning, and the need to absorb new tactics to meet the firepower of modern weapons already seen in the Franco-Prussian War and American Civil War. Cut down to essentials, the country's only lengthier expeditionary involvement earlier in the 1800s had been the Crimean War of 1854–1856. Even there, it had been limited in scale, with fewer than 100 000 troops put into the field.

Small wars with small armies were not about expansion, duration, technical adaptation, or administrative capacity. They were about achieving success based on personalised qualities such as courage and moral character, negligible casualties and minimal cost. When the odd thing did go wrong, this was easier to brush aside than to absorb fully into military thought. Thus, for Wolseley and those in his 'African' army faction, much of the blame for Majuba lay in the use of an Indian army contingent, by nature undisciplined, full of drink, and ridden with venereal disease.

As this implies, the British were not without some lessons in what proficient irregulars could do against its regular troops — yet they profited curiously little from their preceding Transvaal experience. And Britain would now learn, far more resoundingly, that the Boer republics were not 'backward' in the sense of Burma, Egypt or the Sudan. Sweeping advances with machine guns which had shredded the Sudanese along the Nile would not do the same against a camouflaged and entrenched enemy able to make best use of broken terrain. Nor would steam gunboats be able to take the Orange River. Even more importantly, inadequate longer-term logistical planning would not do against a mobilised 'national patriotic' population able to keep up prolonged warfare. And professional British troops with Maxims would not soon be able to overcome twice their number of Boer commandos, despite Wolseley asserting just this towards the end of 1899. To be sure, the British army in 1899 was not entirely without an idea of the need for adjustment to changing tactical conditions, and of the training requirements of 'a new and flexible discipline of the battlefield'.[162] But this was still some way short of practical application. The prevailing assumptions of the next war were that it would again be small, and that nothing very fancy would be required.

4

EMPIRE UNDER SIEGE

OSTILITIES BEGAN NOT WITH ANY GREAT ENGAGEMENT, BUT WITH a skirmish. On 12 October, at Kraaipan railway siding some thirty miles south of Mafeking, a Boer patrol from forces commanded by General Piet Cronjé sabotaged a railway line, checking the advance of a British armoured train conveying munitions and other urgent stores to the town garrison.

Led by Koos de la Rey, soon to become a rising star, an 800-strong commando called up field artillery which briefly bombarded the stationary train from a distance of about 2 000 feet. This onslaught produced a swift surrender; the Boers took away the wounded and prisoners, among them African and white railway workers.

The mechanised passage of arms and troops between Mafeking and the south had now been cut, and the Boers commanded its southern approaches, ready to open a line of advance.[163] Yet to sustain a casualty, they had inserted the first wedge of the overall republican move to sweep into Natal and the Cape Colony, and to seal off the railways as a strategic avenue of British advance northwards by throttling the line at the key points – Kimberley, Vryburg, Mafeking in the Cape, and the Ladysmith junction, the principal northern Natal town and railhead up from Durban.

Logically enough, the whole Boer strategic conception turned on control of the rail system, its trunk routes a pivotal element in transport and communication over the great distances between the colonial coastal fringe and the republican heartland. Invasion routes were all aimed at denying the enemy use of lines of advance. The Boer purpose was to sever rail routes to the coast to prevent the British from moving reinforcements from the ports to an interior theatre of operations. At the far end of a successful offensive lay the blockading of Durban and Cape

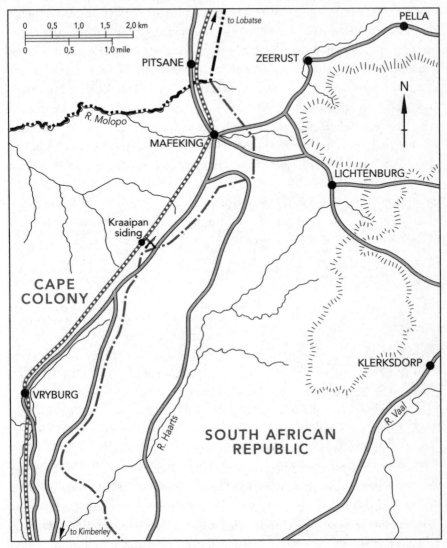

Town, and the promising augury of a negotiated peace before it all turned too bloody and destructive. This meant menacing several areas at the same time. Commandos moved westwards into Bechuanaland and Griqualand, southwards across the Orange river to threaten the internal territory of the Cape, and eastwards into Natal.

These opening moves favoured the Natal front, for reasons involving a fine mix of military hubris and judicious political calculation. First, Transvaal leadership was understandably partial to the known campaigning advantages of the territory around Majuba and Laing's Nek, the towering but manoeuvrable ridges straddling the main eastern corridor of advance through the Drakensberg mountain range. First Boer War (Transvaal War) veterans like Piet Joubert, Piet Cronjé and Christiaan de Wet had a good nose for the inspirational significance of a site where Britain's red line had previously been too thin and too short. Second, there had been a forward deployment of some British cavalry and infantry to the northern junction and colliery areas of Dundee and Glencoe. This had been ordered by Major General Sir William Penn Symons in response to urgings from the colony's governor, Sir Walter Hely-Hutchinson, that Natal be reinforced well inland of Ladysmith, headquarters of the main British force. A further consideration was the political need for some show to remind Boer stock farmers in northern Natal to stay put, and also to keep surrounding Zulu communities calm. Inquisitive Africans were to remain neutral, at least until nodded into controlled collaboration on British terms.[164]

With reinforcements on their way, Penn Symons in Dundee appeared confident. But Glencoe and Dundee were weak spots, and the siting of an inferior British force of 4 000 troops during September and early October provided the Natal-front Boers with an inviting opportunity to punch a hole right through the first enemy lines. Preparation was simplicity itself. Joubert concentrated a mass of 14 000 Transvaal commandos, reinforced by 6 000 Orange Free Staters led by General Marthinus Prinsloo, along the upper northern reaches threatening the apex of Natal. The chances of failure were small.

Third, Natal was fancied because the Transvaal did not have an entirely free hand to dictate republican strategy. The Steyn administration was lukewarm about mounting a major invasion of the Cape from the Orange Free State, due in part to the honourable tenacity with which the Cape prime minister, W.P. Schreiner, and its chief justice, Sir Henry de Villiers, had pursued Anglo-Boer mediation through the last few months of the crisis. Even if virtually everyone in Bloemfontein understood that a big rush at the colony could well deliver rebel recruits to the republicans, a prevaricating Marthinus Steyn remained concerned with proper presentation of a 'just-cause' defensive alliance with Kruger. As correspondence with Joubert made clear, it was Pretoria's war, and the role of Bloemfontein was to keep up as its ally.[165]

Given that understanding, the Transvaal could not count on the Orange Free State taking the initiative to open accounts with a heavy push southwards into the northern Cape. So, again, a major Natal effort proved irresistible. Not only was it a topographically difficult region over which to establish coordinated defence. Not only had the British made their position more assailable by helpfully dividing and exposing their available forces beyond the Tugela River. Not only did the Boers find the route through the Drakensberg barrier fairly soft going, with no bridges blown, no passes mined, and the Transvaal-Natal railway route nicely in repair to enable the movement of supplies. A further advantage was that the two Boer armies could be combined with relative ease, on almost equal terms, for a breakthrough.

Already on the verge of retirement in 1899, Major General Sir George White, the dithering Natal commander-in-chief when war erupted, had grudgingly agreed to urgent pleas from Penn Symons and Hely-Hutchinson for an advanced detachment to be posted in the far north. This dispersal, which left only 8 000 men at Ladysmith, increasingly alarmed White as a bisecting Boer push could break communication lines between Dundee and Ladysmith and isolate them from the rest of the colony.

Buller, the incoming expeditionary commander, foresaw an even more calamitous opening outcome. In a perceptive judgement, he concluded that as the entire northern Natal salient was so vulnerable to frontal attack as to be indefensible, any position there would be overwhelmed. To make matters worse, the net could also close in another direction, through additional flanking offensives from the eastern Transvaal and western Orange Free State, across the Drakensberg. Just as Dundee and Glencoe were being lopped off, so a converging pincer movement could menace Ladysmith. Concluding that there was too much dangerous ground to contest, Buller favoured pulling the British defensive line right back, if need be even well south of the Tugela.[166] He did not get his way with Penn Symons, White or the War Office, and was in any event not in an effective command position before 9 October. Thereafter, he was to have other problems on his plate, which would soon culminate in the unravelling of a previously accomplished soldiering reputation.

It did not take long for Natal to become seriously disputed territory. On 19 October an advance Boer unit pushed through to Elandslaagte on the rail line just south of Dundee and Glencoe, pounced on a British supply train, and easily occupied the settlement. Under British noses, connection between Lady-smith and Dundee was swiftly severed. For triumphant commandos, the mounted photographic pose in front of a captured train was to become an early celebration of bravado and optimism, and one destined to be repeated. Meanwhile, in Dundee, Penn Symons did not feel that he could do much. Writing off the capture of Elandslaagte, this headstrong and opinionated commander did not expect the republicans to have the bottle to take on a full and fresh British brigade. Although alert to the moving presence of Joubert's forces, a peculiar insouciance seemed to settle upon him. Despite being 'aware of the poor training of his own infantry battalions'[167] he made no effort to entrench his troops nor to devise other effective cover. He had a cynical view of the Boer armies, believing that their mounted riflemen were semi-trained levies, and no match for the superior technical preparedness and disciplined aptitude of his regulars.

But his enemy was full of fight, and was to choose its ground well. The Boer forces were large enough to divide into two attack formations. One, under General Daniel 'Maroela' Erasmus, placed itself on the flat Impati highland overlooking the plain occupied by the small colliery settlement. The dominating Talana Hill, with heights reaching 500 feet above the depression in which Penn Symons' troops were encamped, was occupied by a force led by General Lukas Meyer. At the same time, Erasmus, a man normally known for wilfulness and for being out of touch with events, was one of those considered by the patrician Ludwig Krause as 'hardly fit to be employed, even as a common soldier'.[168]

From these crowning vantage points, the Boers unleashed a thumping bombardment of Dundee. Before firing began, a British patrol had stumbled on Meyer's assembled force of 4 000 commandos in the dark, with one sergeant managing to slip off to warn his garrison commander of the strength of the enemy approach. His alarm was brushed aside by Penn Symons, but at dawn on 20 October, the Boers' intentions became clear. Thousands of their soldiers could be seen lining the hills, from which the artillery bombardment was directed. With their customary talent for preparation and contriving surprise, the Boers had quietly run guns up by hand in the darkness, digging small pits along hillcrests to keep muzzles at low level and to provide alternating dugouts for the routine shifting of artillery pieces. Gunners also took particular care to water the ground heavily, or to lay the skins of freshly slaughtered cattle under their concealed Krupp howitzers, to minimise the dust thrown up on discharge.[169]

The surprise was total. The British field force soon found that Boer weapons had been positioned beyond the range of their own garrison artillery. But Penn Symons' troops managed to rally, to limber artillery into a more effective position, and to direct a screen of returning defensive fire against the Boers. This was sufficiently ferocious not merely to keep their guns quiet, but to spread panic through their firing line; over 1 000 battered and shaken commandos melted away. An emboldened Penn Symons then ordered a frontal attack on Talana, sending his cavalry between the two hills. With Erasmus's troops bedded down on Impati, this was risky, but his opponent was not one for wait-and-see observation. Meyer, meanwhile, sited part of his force on Lennox Hill, adjoining Talana to the south. Luckily for the British and maddeningly for the Boers, a lethargic Erasmus was in no mood to harry enemy troops. The commando culture that regarded a military force as a group of independent equals always had a price, as leadership now discovered. Within republican ranks, there were to be murmurs about replacing senior officers like Erasmus with men of stouter character, and even a sardonic belief that the republican position would have been better advanced if 'independent' commanders, who had decided 'to carry on the war' according to their 'own bright ideas', had 'been shot as early as Dundee'.[170]

In the event, it was Penn Symons who died, fatally wounded in the Talana assault and carried away by his soldiers as they held off the Boers and retreated to Ladysmith. The high ground of Talana was taken by the British, and Dundee was saved, in a fairly sombre victory. Great damage had been done to British confidence, and even though they had prevailed the cost had been quite considerable. Boer casualties were 140; field force losses 546, or more than ten per cent of the total complement deployed. Some British infantry were the victims of shrapnel fire from their own guns, as battery rounds fell short of the crucial margin between friend and enemy.

During this engagement, the British decided to confront the Boers at Elandslaagte, northeast of Ladysmith and a position which presented a further threat to White's base. Scouting information reported that it was lightly defended, although General Johannes Kock and 1 000 soldiers were in the vicinity to raise numbers and to secure things for a move on Ladysmith. But here the initiative had already passed to the British, who on 21 October pressed forward from Ladysmith to re-establish the head link between Elandslaagte and Dundee. The

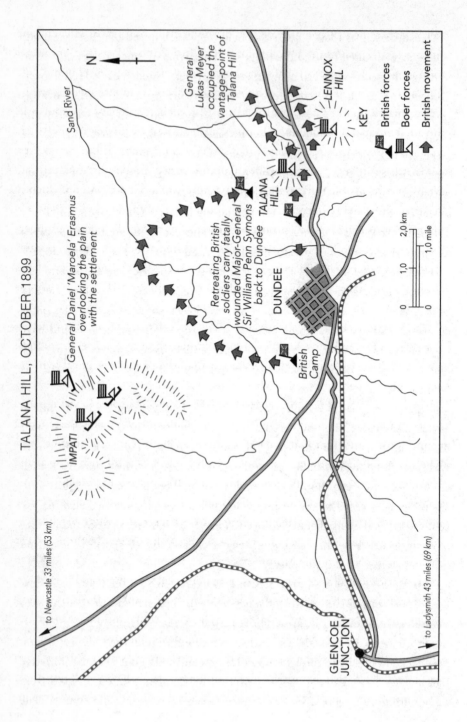

TALANA HILL, OCTOBER 1899

General Lukas Meyer occupied the vantage-point of Talana Hill

General Daniel 'Maroela' Erasmus overlooking the plain with the settlement

Retreating British soldiers carry fatally wounded Major-General Sir William Penn Symons back to Dundee

LENNOX HILL

TALANA HILL

DUNDEE

British Camp

IMPATI

Sand River

KEY

British forces
Boer forces
British movement

2,0 km
1,0 mile

to Newcastle 33 miles (53 km)

to Ladysmith 43 miles (69 km)

GLENCOE JUNCTION

men who planned the blow were two of the British army's most efficient and austere tacticians, infantry Colonel Ian Hamilton and Lieutenant General Sir John French, an expert cavalry force commander and 'prototypical blimp'.[171]

The occupying Boers were fated to be outnumbered and outmanoeuvred by a coordinated infantry and cavalry attack. Entrenched and behind earthworks threaded around the ridges and koppies just south of Elandslaagte, they were squeezed by a pincer movement which brought continuous and thick rifle fire, while British infantry drawn up in a flanking thrust closed in. Attempting to establish a defensible retreat, the Boers withdrew to a hill position on which to make a stand. Their two commando guns could do nothing to counter the shell-fire of 18-gun British field batteries. In intense fighting, the embattled Boers resolutely defended their position against repeated attack, and then counter-attacked. After a final climactic British assault, Kock's defending Transvaal and Orange Free State commandos crumbled as French and Hamilton's troops stormed through.

The surviving Boer force was routed. But the collapse was to bring further slaughter. As commandos fled their trenches and took to their horses, traditional hard-riding British cavalry charged in with lance and sabre to cut down cornered and terrified Boers, whose famed fleetness had deserted them. Observing the gruesome effect of men being slashed to death, one infantryman was repelled by his vision of 'a stinking knacker's yard'. For exultant cavalrymen, the outcome confirmed a conviction that even an obdurately 'hard' enemy would be overwhelmed solely by 'dash' and steel. If anything, Elandslaagte, with its aged and broken General Kock himself mortally wounded, diminished that enemy, turning him into inferior prey. For Lancers, 'it was not even . . . as though their army were fighting real soldiers. The enemy were a mob of farmers, dressed in black frock-coats, riding ridiculous little ponies and carrying Bibles under their arms'.[172] The virtual annihilation of the escaping Boers left the republicans with a legacy of virulent hatred of British cavalry. Commentators in Bloemfontein and Pretoria reacted with revulsion at what was considered an atrocity, akin to the earlier spearing of Christian trekkers by 'savage' or 'barbarous' Zulu or Sotho adversaries.

Yet, despite the Boers having broken and run, the outcome of the Elandslaagte affray, for the British, was mixed. Even though their enemy suffered fifty per cent casualties, the British themselves were hardly unscathed, having lost just under one-tenth of their strength. And this sacrifice had still not tipped the strategic balance in northern Natal towards them. They lacked the power to continue holding a salient which remained vulnerable, and lacked the means to engineer a decisive battle to extinguish the republican offensive. So White now abandoned Dundee and Elandslaagte, and drew back to Ladysmith, leaving behind a well-provisioned camp and a dying Penn Symons.

With the Boers closing in on retreating and increasingly fatigued British troops, whose progress was being hindered by flooding rivers and enveloping mud, White resolved on carrying the fight to his opponents before they bore down and attacked him. In a last move before Ladysmith became encircled, he launched a concerted flanking assault, with strong infantry brigade and cavalry detachments, aimed at surprising the Boer position and doing sufficient damage to reverse the entire course of their eastern offensive. His plan was ambitious, addressing the need for a northwards thrust to cut off retreating Boers who were expected to make a run towards Newcastle before skulking back to Majuba and Laing's Nek, this time to lick their wounds. The élan bequeathed by a century of victorious colonial campaigns and punitive expeditions was still keeping buoyant 'the "over by Xmas" mentality'.[173]

But, on 30 October, it was to turn out badly for the British. Poor reconnaissance, misjudgement of Boer positioning, and a blur of confusing and hesitant orders left White's dispersed forces in disarray and at great risk. For the Boers had been anything but idle.

With his luck running out, White deepened the confusion by ordering a wholesale retreat in response to an unverified alarm that Orange Free State forces were massing to attack Ladysmith from the west. By now, the republicans had become too informed and too strong, and were tenaciously led by Lukas Meyer. At Lombard's Nek, they outflanked their enemy and maintained devastating fire until resistance petered out. Simultaneously, at Nicholson's Nek, the British played into their hands by basing themselves on the more precarious half of the pass, allowing their adversaries to occupy the more secure half from which to mount an attack. Orange Free State commandos under De Wet overwhelmed them. When his troops began to give up of their own accord, their commander, Colonel F.R.C. Carleton, resigned himself to the inevitable, declaring a ceasefire and surrendering around 1 200 men. Some of them were tugged across Boer lines by African servants 'dressed in kilts', evidently stripped from the corpses of Gordon Highlanders at Elandslaagte.[174] The republicans sustained some 200 casualties. These essentially diversionary battles had involved something like evenly matched forces: their outcome for the British was galling.

White's hand was spent. His troops, demoralised by having been shot to pieces for no gain, fell back towards Ladysmith as the encircling Boers closed in. By the end of October, the largest British force in the country was trapped inside a town which some felt was the last remaining obstacle to the invaders heading for Durban. In itself no great prize to be gained, Ladysmith waited to be swallowed by an enemy whose communications and supply were rapidly improving. But, then, instead of capitalising on its success, the Boer command proceeded to squander its precious advantage at a pressing moment. And reinforcing imperial troops were now seaborne.

As local British forces headed for Ladysmith under hastily improvised artillery

LADYSMITH, OCTOBER 1899

KEY

British forces
British movement
Boer forces
Boer movement

NICHOLSON'S NEK

Orange Free State commandos under De Wet

to Newcastle 31 miles (50 km)

PEPWORTH HILL

LONG HILL

SURPRISE HILL

Modder Spruit

N

LADYSMITH

LOMBARD'S NEK

0   1,0   2,0 km

0   1,0 mile

Lieutenant-General Sir John French's troops

to Colenso 16.5 miles (26.5 km)

cover, Joubert eased the pressure. Instead of sending his mounted forces in rapid pursuit, as some of his chafing commandants and many of his veldkornets expected, he reined in his army. With the town still poorly barricaded, the chance of forcing through a British capitulation was lost. Then, having declined to drive home its advantage before the defenders could dig themselves in, Boer leadership decided to sit out the confrontation. Joubert encircled Ladysmith and laid siege from 29 October onwards, an investment which was to last a full four months, ending only on 28 February 1900, when British reinforcements finally relieved the garrison. The republicans had locked their forces into a fixed position, thereby effectively immobilising their Natal offensive.

Petrus Jacobus Joubert's hour was over. Before the war, the assignment of the ageing sixty-eight-year old veteran to preside over the eastern invasion had met with scepticism and even scorn from his younger, more fiery and more imaginative rivals. The 'old General' or 'Kruger's dog' was judged at best irresolute and procrastinating, and at worst feeble and timid.[175] There was particular contempt for his attachment to an afternoon nap and household comforts. He evidently believed in marching on his stomach, and on campaigns he routinely took along his spouse, Hendrina, accompanied by her servants and household cattle, partly to ensure that that stomach would not go empty. But, as Ladysmith revealed, he was no Napoleon, displaying a reach which constantly threatened to exceed the grasp of his armies. Despite holding almost all the trump cards, and despite full knowledge of where and when Ladysmith defences were fairly thinly held, Joubert risked little in attempting to find a back door through which to overrun the town. One has no need to be too hard on him, as he has been well enough derided already for bull-headed tactical inflexibility and a failure of strategic imagination. But it must be said that he was a mediocre commander who had probably got too far on political cronyism.

Smuts may have had his strategy, but clearly its implementation could not be left to generals in the field. In order to report to the Pretoria government on campaign conditions, he personally visited the Natal front on a number of occasions during the opening phase of hostilities. What he saw around Ladysmith was a costly bind, at a stage when the strategic need was to leave the siege lines just near enough and strong enough to deter any major British garrison counterattack and to invest the bulk of the commando forces in maintaining the offensive towards Durban. If the republicans were to settle for a war of place and position, they would have to be in a commanding spot on the coast, either menacing Durban or, ideally, entering it. Then, and later, Smuts and other younger leaders were to fume over a stubborn subversion of grand strategy by generals too old, too cautious, and too cranky to perform.

With the backing of his personal council of war, Piet Joubert saw the siege of Ladysmith as an achievement. After all, the priority was not to capture it, but to keep it ringed in depth with commando *laagers* or encampments. Maintaining the investment was the means of impeding a British offensive against the Transvaal from Natal. It was, however, a misconceived calculation, which has rightly been termed 'one of the most serious Boer tactical errors of the war'.[176] The siege diverted thousands of troops from offensive campaigning, and kept them largely idle. At the same time, the republicans lacked the numbers to do much during an extended siege. For their war effort, this represented a woeful confusion of strategic intentions. Furthermore, the state of affairs created by Joubert played right into British hands, even if he failed properly to comprehend it. White found himself able to tie up much of the invasion force in a tactical concentration for which it was especially unsuited, and for which it was ill-equipped with heavy guns. Boer military culture and disciplinary capacity did not raise commandos to conduct interminable fixed siege operations.

The siege of Ladysmith, like the other celebrated republican sieges of colonial towns in the opening phase of the war, was to remain a desultory business throughout. The besiegers rarely looked as if they had the will actually to take the town. On the other side, despite dwindling reserves and increasingly grim conditions which were to see ten deaths per day from disease, white and black rarely looked as if they were about to be bled into surrender. Both sides seemed to conform to tit-for-tat shelling and tit-for-tat forays against each other's lines. It was scarcely serious fighting, and all it really did was to underline the extent to which the antagonists were not merely becalmed, but marooned. If this set-piece illustrated anything, it was the degree to which both republican and British command were becoming reliant upon the labour or other services of black workers, much of it commandeered, some of it collaborative, to maintain siege operations. The British exploited the presence of the large number of African and Asian labourers who, after fleeing the Natal coalfields, had sought refuge in Ladysmith before the siege commenced. For their part, the Boers conscripted Africans into work parties to destroy railway track and to dam up the local river. They also armed a small number of retainers to stand relief in outposts at night.

Whatever this wearing down of the British garrison accomplished, those outside were hardly elated. Some Africans who deserted the Boer camp actually slipped *into* Ladysmith, in the belief that conditions there might be better than being constantly ill-used.[177] More telling was the ebbing of the spirit, morale and discipline of ordinary burghers, who were simply ground down by the lack of any sense of gain or purpose. Joubert's troops whiled away their days boozing on brandy, pilfering, slipping away on leave to check on home harvests or market conditions, and pining for the beaches and bananas that lay beyond their grasp. Their loss of faith in Joubert in particular seems to have been all but complete. In December, there was already growing frustration with his brusque dismissal of rank-and-file ideas, one of which was to construct shallow 'zig-zag trenches so as to get nearer and nearer the town every day' in order to 'have the enemy under rifle fire from all sides'.[178] Similarly, commandants were irritated that their general was not moving swiftly to adopt what seemed to them the inviting tactic of damming up the town's Klip River in order to flood the trapped British into surrender. Such was the glum Ladysmith record after several months of mutually dispiriting endurance, and of random deaths from shrapnel and typhoid.

Equally, the republicans were not in any sense contemplating a reversal of their occupying position in this eastern theatre. In December 1898, Butler had been advised that while the 'northern strip of Natal may be occupied by the Boers', it could be considered 'unlikely that any further serious advance . . . would be undertaken'. At most, 'raids' involving '2 000 to 3 000 men' were 'to be expected' and to be adequately guarded against.[179] But the advice had missed something. By now, Boer gains in Natal were also causing trouble for still vague British campaign planning. This planning involved the 'interior strategy', in which a strong expeditionary force would roll directly through the Orange Free State and assume control of Bloemfontein. In the immediate present, White's job had been to hold off any Natal offensive until his position could be strengthened by a weighty western expedition against the republicans. In this, however, he failed. Indeed, the British inability properly to secure the colony against its predator, and the apprehension this produced, completely changed the picture. At the outset, Britain would first have to restore its tottery Natal position.

The other leg of the Boer offensive aimed to make a hole in the Cape Colony. Here, General Piet Cronjé and a well-provisioned force of between 8 000 and 9 000 men, which had at its disposal almost a dozen guns, including a heavy Creusot siege cannon, fixed on Mafeking as a first target. Dozing close to the western internal border of the Transvaal, this typically small colonial African town presented an opportunity for action. It was a place barely known to outsiders − if it was known at all, it was doubtless only in its role as the largest railway depot between Kimberley on the Orange Free State border and Bulawayo in Rhodesia.

In some ways, Mafeking offered itself to the republicans. Its siting on the rail link to the north had some strategic significance. As a commercial and trading enclave in the Bechuanaland Protectorate within the Cape Colony, it held useful stores and provisions. Lying less than ten miles from the Transvaal border, there was barely any need to bother about supply lines. And, lastly, there was a powerful emotional and patriotic reflex about the Mafeking area. It was from here that Jameson and his raiders had set out to terminate the South African Republic's independence; and the man who had run them to ground then had been Pieter Cronje. For all that, though, Mafeking was not necessarily, from a detached viewpoint, an obvious military focal point for hard Boer campaigning.

Appointed as general for the Western Front by Joubert in September 1899, the sixty-three year-old Cronjé had a reputation as a dour and headstrong leader. A religious fundamentalist prone to prophetic visions, he occasionally expressed his ideas through symbolism and allegory rather than by clearly formed Dutch sentences. In anticipating the war, Cronjé was confident that Britain would not be able to crush the Boers. His assigned military adviser, the younger Jacobus Hercules ('Koos') de la Rey, had nothing like the same confidence. But this did not mean that Cronjé did not count: a pottering siege was precisely the kind of eventuality with which his temperament could cope. Indeed, as with Joubert, holding position enabled him to retain a close connection with femininity and family. His wife, Hester, habitually accompanied him to war, one of a small number of Boer women in laagers and trenches in the early stages of hostilities who ignored directives barring them from the field and from entering the front other than as nurses. For Hendrina Joubert and Hester Cronjé, infiltration of a masculine world of fighting was more than merely an adjustment to the dislocation of war; it was equally an active identification with the republican war effort and the adoption of a nurturing role. For an American press correspondent with the Boer forces, the most potent expression of that support was the ritual oiling and loading of Cronje's rifle by his spouse. It is worth noting that, in a limited way, the Boers were replicating common African practice in areas like West and Equatorial Africa, where the sustaining of military campaigns by followers had long been something of a family business.

At the time, what ensued at Mafeking left unclear exactly what had been gained by either side. It was by no means certain that a fight should have been carried on here at all, let alone a confrontation which would last a whole seven months. The defences of the administrative capital of Bechuanaland had been roundly neglected by the Cape government for, as war approached, it was reluctant to provoke the Transvaal by carrying a military position to its very border. Far from requiring force and firepower to protect it against invasion, Mafeking was considered sufficiently remote, and sufficiently small (1 500 white and 5 000 black inhabitants, mostly in the adjoining African settlement of Mafikeng), to be spared. Denied military protection by Cape authorities, who had shrugged off pleas and warnings, the white town fathers eventually acted for themselves and roped in Colonel Robert Baden-Powell and his Bechuanaland Protectorate Regiment.

By the latter half of September, Baden-Powell, although at first reluctant to consign any of his men to Mafeking, was persuaded of the need to garrison his force in defence of the town rather than have it quartered in one or other part of the nearby countryside. Given the position of the Cape government, which was to keep out of the way of trouble, his defensive preparations were effectively undertaken in secret, although the significance of large supplies being run into Mafeking was not lost on nearby Boers. He then moved in his entire regiment to deny the town to the republicans. Even fully assembled, this contingent was not large, amounting to 750 trained troops and mounted police and a scratch rifle guard force of around 450 semi-trained volunteers raised from the local white citizenry. His artillery provision was also seriously inadequate, consisting of a few outmoded, slow-firing muzzle-loaders and a clutch of light guns. In all, it did not look to have the makings of a strong defensive position.

Mafeking hostilities began with a few skirmishes and light sniping. As Cronjé's forces closed in, Baden-Powell launched several flanking sorties to try to break up the front of the advance while the Boers were still at a distance. The sorties were easily beaten off, and the republican general urged 'BP' to surrender to avoid loss of life and damage to the town. Baden-Powell rejected the offer and, his troops still firing to harass the enemy, fell back into the settlement. Having failed to force the issue in the field, the Boers then surrounded the town, consolidated their lines and, on 14 October, began a long investment. Curiously, aside from this initial belligerence, thereafter 'relatively little real fighting took place for the remainder of the siege', to quote the most informed historian of late-Victorian Mafeking.[180]

However much the siege of Mafeking (and of Ladysmith and, to a lesser extent, Kimberley) would go on to grip the popular imagination of the British public, there was just not much to it. For here, the war ground to a virtual standstill. Inside, Baden-Powell established a defensive ring of trenches linked to a cluster of small forts, all looping around Mafeking and the segregated African *stadt* or location of Mafikeng. Outside, the republicans threw up an encircling chain, its largest links provided by several commando laagers. Behind this cordon, the Boers also held several fortified elevated positions. Some bemused journalists pondered a military situation which at first glance looked somewhat ambiguous. Was Mafeking actually being besieged? Or were the Boers simply laggard in not surging forward and carrying the town's defences? For his part, Cronjé seemed content to behave as if he had plenty of time. Indeed, it was only when British relief forces began to break through, in May 1900, that he launched an extended attack to try to take the position.

For most of the time, Cronjé's operational aim was to keep the siege alive. Reluctant to risk real losses, Boer command resorted to shelling and 'Mausering' the town from a secure distance to increase the burden of defence. Cronjé's heavy Creusot 'Long Tom', capable of engaging a target from a distance of over 6 000 metres, looked a fearsome weapon, with the mechanical capacity to flatten and terrorise the beleaguered population into submission. In fact, while it combined heavy military power and the myth of a war monster, it was not that much more lethal or destructive than the Krupp field guns which the commandos also ranged against Mafeking to no very great effect. Ammunition was of uneven quality; fuse malfunctions were common, and shells produced limited explosive power.

Mafeking was closed up by the Boers in the sense that normal communications between the town and the outside world were severed, but never in the sense that it was sealed. The relative ease with which both white and black inhabitants could on occasion weave their way through the sentry lines was doubtless because the lines were thinning. Operations had started with the deployment of around 6 000 Boers around the town, but after just a few weeks this had been whittled down to little more than 2 000. Burghers either decamped to do a turn on their farms, were diverted to other fronts, or were hauled away into diversionary raiding elsewhere. As the strength of the siege force was allowed to fluctuate, so the power to mount anything much more than intermittent assaults drained away. Cramped around Mafeking, some of Cronjé's more obvious problems mirrored those of Joubert at Ladysmith. These boiled down to maintaining the spirit and commitment of immobilised soldiers, holding the loyalties of grumbling commandants and veldkornets, ensuring that burghers did not lurk in laagers to avoid line duties, and coordinating artillery, light sortie and picket operations to avoid a daily muddle.

The confrontation became little more than a matter of finding ways to sustain momentum beyond campfires and breakfasts. Inside the town, Baden-Powell had to take special pains to organise a reasonable muster of able-bodied defenders, obviously a vital requirement for the holding of its defensive circuit. Mafeking's white citizenry, for the most part wanting nothing to do with the war, resigned themselves to having to provide 300 men for the Town Guard, and even this was grudgingly given. Traders with Transvaal commercial connections had a greater interest in buying peace than in fighting for victory; they felt no pro-British attachment and considered service obligations unfair. Others resented having to turn out as substitutes for troops who, in their view, should have been dispatched by either the Cape colonial or the imperial governments. Even the more loyal and conscientious recruits in the Town Guard and Bechuanaland Rifles became glum, their distrust and disgust rising in response to the haughty treatment and mean rewards doled out by Baden-Powell's military authorities. As citizen soldiers, well-off Cape English colonists resented the rather unequal sharing of discomfort and deprivation. Their world of exposed and wet trenches, and the airy neglect of the commanders, was in sharp contrast with that of Baden-Powell and his staff officers, who enjoyed solid shelters, medals, and brandy with soda.[181]

Tactics mattered more than politics during the siege, and the presence of blacks around and within the sphere of Mafeking operations was a factor. It partly assisted the needs of both sides, and partly complicated them. Reclaiming local loyalties, Cronjé's force secured the willing cooperation of old Boer allies, the Rapulana-Barolong, whose leadership furnished scouts, messengers and labourers. About 300 men were also armed and posted to trenches and fortified points, while others not dug in were deployed to raid enemy livestock and as cattle guards. But not everything could be taken for granted. Working at cross purposes with Boer designs, the wilful Rapulana seized chances thrown up by the siege to pay off personal scores with the Mafeking Tshidi-Barolong. These acts of random aggression added to Boer uncertainties.

Mafeking command was also manoeuvring, operating and pulling. It was able to unleash the Tshidi-Barolong, who had long experience of collaboration with the British against the Boers. Baden-Powell knew better than to leave Mafikeng exposed beyond his lines of defence, which would create a fatal gap through which Mafeking's defensive foundations might slip. About 500 armed Barolong were stationed to defend the African quarter and to provide cover for the southwestern cordon of the town's defence. In addition, small armed companies were organised from other inhabitants, drawn mostly from the Mfengu and Coloured communities. These intermediaries, far larger in number than the white defenders, both stocked defensive lines and beavered away at intermittent and risky raids on Boer lines to scoop up cattle. The rudimentary labour required for fixing defensive works like shelters and dugouts was provided by Africans, while the crafty retrieval and delivery actions of black scouts, spies, and runners made up the kernel of Baden-Powell's local military intelligence. At great personal risk, especially in the early months of the siege, these runners also kept wire agencies and newspapers in the world outside in touch with the Mafeking crisis, or at least a jaunty version of its truth pushed through by Baden-Powell and his vigilant military censors.

Described wryly by *The Times'* siege correspondent, Angus Hamilton, as 'young, as men go in the Army, with a keen appreciation of the possibilities of his career',[182] Baden-Powell proved a dab hand at releasing outnumbered, poorly briefed, and ill-prepared forces to attack well-fortified Boer positions to negligible gain. Yet this did little to damage his growing external reputation as commander, and still less were there serious questions about what had possessed him to station his force in a spot where it would be holed up uselessly for months. He was left to flourish, and by the end of 1899 'The Defender of Mafeking' was projecting its siege for all the world as if it were some sort of Troy of the Bechuanaland Protectorate, with the town's commander 'an icon in the pantheon of imperial heroes' – a role he was happy to play'.[183]

The celebration of Baden-Powell overseas was not shared by too many white and black townspeople, who were fast growing sceptical of the benefits of making imperial history under the command of a man of enormous determination and rather less humanity. Even though food for whites would never be in seriously short supply, the authorities improved the odds in the early months by denying provisions to trapped African refugees. Baden-Powell's ultimate intention was to drive those Africans who were surplus to essential defence needs out of Mafeking so as to conserve stores. For people who were liable either to be cut down or hounded by the Boers, the choice was between intense privation and virtual starvation inside, and the mortal danger of the republican lines. The Mafeking commander probably did more to worsen African mortality rates than to inflict damage on the Boer invaders. Granted, he did set up soup kitchens serving horsemeat, but there were 'not many horses available to be eaten by the besieged Africans'. [184]

The day after the dreary Mafeking sideshow got under way, the republicans began their third large investment operation, putting Kimberley to siege on 15 October in an action which would last for four months. While not an obvious strategic cornerstone of British defence like Ladysmith, it had enough as an upcountry communications site to draw in the Boers. Unlike Mafeking, both military and political opinion had a sense that here was a weighty prize, the loss of which would both damage and humiliate the imperial camp. Kimberley housed the De Beers diamond industry, making it a plum repository of money, coal, foodstuffs and other stores, railway equipment, engineering workshops, scrap iron (potential shrapnel) and dynamite.

General Christiaan Wessels, commandant-in-chief of the Orange Free State forces, and his war council had little hesitation in committing resources to a move on Kimberley in the hope of spooning its captured materials onto the republican war plate. Kimberley and its diamonds were also synonymous with the cavalier imperialist, Rhodes, a tempting nose waiting to be bloodied. A number of republican journalists and politicians wanted Kimberley solely because it would mean the capture of the famous financier. As an exquisitely telling political blow, it would raise morale in the field and inspire the Boers to ever greater efforts. Even in a phase of the war especially short on common sense, to have made this British figure the justification of an assault on Kimberley was odd. Still, as an Irishman conscripted for commando duty observed wryly of his fellow Kimberley attackers, 'they believe that if Rhodes and Chamberlain were out of the way it would be all over with England'.[185]

Kimberley ended up as the culmination of a minor offensive south of Mafeking, running along the line of the rail system. Koos de la Rey and other more decisive commandants who were determined to hurry on the war, coordinated a rapid movement through small Griqualand West villages like Taung and Kuruman, riding virtually at will, picking up rebel recruits, forcing white police and Coloured guards into frontal engagements where they could be outnumbered and outgunned, and scaring unfriendly black civilians into passivity. There was nothing to halt their advance until Kimberley, a town of 13 000 whites, 7 000 Coloured people and 30 000 Africans, 11 000 of them mine workers. Although inviting encirclement, its surrounding terrain was not particularly to the Boers' liking. Unlike Ladysmith and Mafeking, it had little by way of koppies or other elevated ground to serve as strong points from which to direct firepower.

Under the command of Colonel Robert Kekewich, an able and clear-thinking North Lancashire Regiment officer, Kimberley had a small but effective garrison, its professional complement consisting of 400 troops of his own regiment, a Royal Artillery company, and one from the Royal Engineers. These regulars were augmented by a mixed force of trained and experienced colonial mounted infantry and police, and a town militia. With De Beers itself raising and arming about 3 000 irregulars, the town rapidly mustered over 4 000 men under arms. As the Cape government again dawdled over a defence commitment here, Kekewich knew very well that time was running out. In the days immediately preceding the arrival of besieging Boers he had pegged out a line of field fortifications around the town, arranged artillery to cover vital spots (for instance, the water reservoir) and worked out where reserves were most likely to be needed to seal gaps sliced by any republican breakthrough. Largely due to Kekewich's initiatives, the Kimberley force did not stand around to await the arrival of the enemy. Morale was fairly high, and early on cavalry and infantry raiding parties made intrepid efforts to topple enemy bridge-heads that were being planted ahead of a concerted strike. The raiders were able to create some obstruction, but after losses they had to fall back from ground controlled by the converging enemy.

The key enticements of Kimberley were also what increased its defensibility. Aside from levies of armed men and the capacity to draft supplies of non-combatant labour, De Beers' jutting mine dumps (up to seventy feet high) became fortified vantage points. Meanwhile, the mining industry provided barbed wire for fencing (hard on horses, to say nothing of their unseated riders), ample telephone connections for perimeter look-outs, engineering floorspace, machinery and skilled labour for diverting to the production of armaments and armour, searchlights to keep any creeping Boers blinking, and deep mine tunnels as shelter from bombardment for resident white women and children.

Nor was that all. 'It is hardly an exaggeration,' concluded *The Times*, 'to say that Kimberley is De Beers and De Beers Mr. Rhodes, so huge is the property and wealth of the company and so great the power exercised over it by Mr. Rhodes.'[186] Inevitably, then, the mines also supplied their omnipresent master. A man who had made his pile by waging war in the sphere of capitalist monopolies, he now switched his vaulting ambition to influence and command in military dealings. As the embodiment of De Beers, Rhodes laid out his claim to a big say in the conduct of Kimberley's defence in a way he knew best. By provisioning and providing a large company of irregulars, supplying rifles, and extracting ammunition from mine workshops, he was effectively financing siege defences from his own pocket.

Contemptuous of the garrison commander, Rhodes constantly rowed with Kekewich over needs and tactics, second-guessing his orders, making independent preparations, and otherwise meddling shamelessly to try to influence the running of defence operations. If garrison commanders or, for that matter, the British Cabinet, could not be bought or dragooned, they could at least be shouted into listening to the Rhodes line on the Kimberley siege. For Kekewich, the problems of the Boers outside were probably little worse than the annoyance of an interfering Rhodes inside. As one authority has suggested, 'If one of the main objectives of the Boers was the capture of Rhodes, there must have been numerous occasions during the four-month siege when the garrison commander would have been glad to hand him over to their tender mercies.'[187]

The Rhodes line emerged in the first few weeks of the Kimberley investment, and was to do the rounds for the rest of the siege. It held that there were 'hordes' or 'legions' or 'swarms' of Orange Free Staters massing to storm the town, that pressure was rising rapidly, that things were perilously close to breaking point, and that the fall of Kimberley was imminent. On 16 October, he commenced what would become a bombardment of urgent requests to highly placed contacts like Milner and Lord Rothschild, pleading for the immediate dispatch of relief forces to avert 'a terrible disaster', even a 'catastrophe'. A shrill demand was that no British offensive against the republics could even be contemplated before Kimberley was saved. The entire future of the British expedition against the Boers, it seemed, turned on the danger of the town's capitulation.

This ran counter to Kekewich's perception, which was that the position was *not* absolutely critical. Rhodes, therefore, did not disclose the dispatch of these telegraphic alarms, and it was only when an African runner brought a query from British general staff that the Kimberley commander discovered that he was close to surrender. Kekewich was stunned. Thereafter, relations with Rhodes turned ever more tense, and were only to worsen through the coming months. Unfortunately for Kekewich, Rhodes could not be hushed. After Kimberley's southwards telegraph line was cut on 14 October, and the garrison had to resort to heliograph transmission to a watchdog station further down the line, Rhodes simply had his own heliograph equipment constructed in De Beers' workshops. He had no intention of complying with censorship provisions, of double-checking with military authorities, and least of all of having to await a turn on the official signalling mirror.

Observers began to report that the frequency of Rhodes' communications soon exceeded those of the garrison. Many of them were targeted at an already cultivated British press which was taken with the mining magnate's imperial allure and was eager to create another heroic Victorian siege persona. Kimberley had thrown up a bold and independent figure, once again identifying the need of empire as his need, and acting with singular energy and resolve to tackle its military crisis. While recognising the degree to which Rhodes was using his personal influence and power to ensure that Kimberley would not be lost, some of his more astringent critics hinted that the De Beers heliograph was also being used for the more usual cost-benefit analysis. There was something to this. Rhodes did not sacrifice share dealing and capital commitments when Christiaan Wessels arrived, and even managed to pocket a small independent diamond mine during the siege.

As Rhodes maintained his personal grip, the 4 800 Orange Free State commandos around Kimberley maintained their strategic grip. Steyn had judged a force of this size sufficient to overrun it, or at least to mount a siege of such concentration as to make its position untenable. To strengthen the assault further, with the support of Kruger he urged Cronjé's war council to dispatch Transvaal troops to swell his ranks. De la Rey and his commandos were then sent southwards from the Vryburg district on 17 October to provide Wessels with additional weight. Stationed not far away himself, the Orange Free State president set out for Kimberley on 23 October, believing that personal showings at the front would boost morale. A canny and imaginative politician with the right patter, Steyn knew well how to exploit further his already good rating on the lines. Aside from inspecting field positions and meeting ordinary burghers for expressions of personal solicitude and encouragement, he attended intelligence briefings and discussed attack preparations and other war planning with officers.

The president was not the kind of political leader who had little to do with war other than to authorise the mobilisation of men and approve expenditure. Prepared to travel as far as would be needed, Steyn took the opening Kimberley action very seriously, and assiduously outlined his understanding of what should follow its success. With the town secured, enlarged Orange Free State and Transvaal forces would maintain their combined strength in the area. One part would stand on the defensive, protecting the southern border of the republic, while another would clip across the Orange River near Hope Town and push hard into the northern Cape. Here, Steyn confidently anticipated, large numbers of republican loyalists would rise in rebellion and throw in their lot with the invaders.

The offensive might possibly have taken this shape had republican command in Griqualand West opted for attacks sufficiently heavy to breach Kimberley's defences. Instead, the siege was allowed to grind on dismally to no very obvious territorial purpose. Early in November, Wessels decided that he could destroy the target, without risking his troops, by resorting to sustained bombardment. Still he hesitated, signalling his intention of delivering this fatal stroke. A general not lacking in a strong personal sense of moral decency and honour, his surrender ultimatum to Kekewich allowed a period of grace in the event of its rejection for the evacuation of all women and children before the start of shelling. It was a bit more than 'civilised' war and its restraining rules of engagement. From Wessels it was also a shrewd psychological tactic to fray the enemy's nerves.

Boer command also produced an astute deal providing relief for 'any Africanders' who wished to leave Kimberley for safety beyond *their* lines. In this political game, Kekewich and Rhodes were willing accomplices in duplicity. So as not to undermine morale, they buried Wessels' offer of general security for those traditionally most at risk under fire, and only posted the offer to receive anxious Boer families. In any event few of these budged. They were nervous about what could be seen as a declaration of republican allegiance, or were worried about dispossession of property in reprisal under martial law conditions, or feared the likelihood of social ostracism when they returned to resume life in Kimberley.

When heavy Creusot shells did begin to rain down there was considerable panic, as brief but intense bombardments threatened not only key sites such as the mines and water reservoir works, but several other parts of the town, killing or wounding a trickle of white and black civilians. But relatively little fell apart under concentrated or stray shelling, much of which just spent itself. Kimberley was not short of men with respectable military engineering talent, nor of ample conscriptable African labour. Thus, fortified tunnels, sandbagged bunkers and thick earth cushioning provided by shelters dug into mine dumps were proof against even heavy 100-lb shells. This helped to minimise white casualties, but even exposed black inhabitants were largely untouched by random artillery strikes. Heavy gunfire was meant to suppress Kimberley's defences and to soften things up so that it could be seized at low cost to the Boers. But it was a conspicuous failure.

As with the other misguided and drifting investments of garrison towns, what the Kimberley attackers lacked as much as anything were the banks of heavy artillery and reserve shell supply necessary to resolve stubborn sieges successfully. So the Kimberley action turned into another familiar story of stalemate, a low-intensity affair with republican forces seemingly unable to do much more than trade artillery fire with the defenders, give as good as they got in running mounted sorties against enemy redoubts, and load their food supply system through sporadic cattle raiding and the seizure of agricultural produce from surrounding areas. As a point of assault, all Kimberley really did was to hobble a planned republican war of movement in the west.

At the same time, the impact of Boer investment was considerably diminished by the ability of the garrison authority to shield the dominant political community from some of its most injurious effects. Here, as elsewhere, there was no acceptance of any 'equality of sacrifice', nor any attempt to enforce 'fair shares' to sustain and protect whole populations. In Kimberley, supply and distributive problems were resolved essentially by displacing much of the routine deprivation and danger of siege life onto African residents. This meant, for example, that when control of De Beers' fresh food reserves was taken over by military command, the focus of official provisioning became white inhabitants. While scurvy was deflected here, it soon engulfed the compounds of African mine labourers, adding to the death toll from typhoid and dysentery. Of the some 1 500 Kimberley deaths during the course of the siege almost all were black, and a good number of these were children. Africans were supposedly mellow about all this, their behaviour 'throughout the siege was very good; they were quiet and orderly and there was little grumbling'.[188]

The insistence of the Boers on keeping men and materials committed to clearly unproductive siege offensives has prompted a number of historians to account for their failure in terms of a customary tactical mentality or of 'natural' mobile combat instincts. Not only was the immobility remarkable. It was an unnatural and ineffective departure from the known and preferred way of war. Traditionalist military culture and shallow discipline did not raise commandos to conduct fixed siege operations; to the contrary, a loss of flexible mobility in the field stifled innovation, spontaneity and fighting conviction. Typically, therefore, one authority on this war has stressed 'the first principle of Boer tactics' to have been 'mobility above all'.[189] In the main, the conduct of all of these fixed-position engagements did seem counter to the Boer mode of warfare, one fashioned by a heritage of roaming pastoralism and flurried land or frontier wars.

Still, the practice of besieging the enemy until its resistance broke was hardly novel to Boer command. In the mid-nineteenth-century Transvaal, resisting Ndebele had been readily put to siege by commandos. In the 1870s, some of the Mafeking Barolong had defied encircling Boer forces for a stupefying two years; the 1899 siege of the area amounted to the Barolong's sixth such experience. Indeed, in the previous year, Joubert had used heavy artillery against African foes who had gone to ground, blasting away the only obstacles − rocks provided by nature − in order to tighten the noose.

The real problem for the republicans was more that the present sieges were a different story. Town garrisons with reserves, firepower, coordination, and more modern defensive technologies proved a far harder nut to crack. While the Boers had artillery, there was not sufficient at hand for continuous massive bombardment. On the other hand, any attempt to overwhelm the enemy by running at them in preponderant force involved an acceptance of casualties far in excess of those to which Boer forces were accustomed. Therefore, if the attack approach of Joubert, Cronjé and Wessels was exceptionally careful and cautious, this was probably due at least in part to a sense that they had to go carefully with their men.

While they obviously enjoyed a numerical advantage in the opening offensive, Boer reserves were not abundant, and little thought seems to have been given to the contingency that at some point a British relieving army might arrive. Then, the want of numbers to repel the advancing forces would be bound to tell. Furthermore, this time, unlike colonial siege operations of the 1840s and 1850s, there was no straightforward battering-ram tactic to wrap things up. Previously, breaking the back of resisting Africans who had bunkered themselves into defensive mountain strongholds had been brutally straightforward. Commandos, sometimes with the assistance of African allies, would either blast in the roofs of caves, block off water supply, or touch off engulfing wood fires across cave fronts to suffocate those besieged.[190]

Nonetheless, the republicans' strategic siege problems did not mean that elsewhere they were unable to advance fairly easily where British defensive lines were appreciably thin and seriously stretched.

At the end of October, Steyn abandoned tact in his dealings with the quivering Cape Colony, bringing to an end the moderate and conciliatory hopes of its W.P. Schreiner administration that it might be able to duck a colonial combat involvement. On 1 November, Orange Free State commandos crossed the Orange River and, confident in the knowledge that they had farms and stockpiles on which to draw and local rebels to recruit, advancing forces overran rural frontier districts, driving both eastwards and westwards. They achieved immediate success. Able to count on only a small minority of white colonial loyalists, the magistrates turned to the willing help of anxious African and Coloured citizen volunteers to try to defend their villages and tiny towns, and held their breath. Confronting superior combined invasion forces, well-armed and amply provisioned, novice local militia and scratch guards with little training and less depth could barely do anything more than exchange a few blows before giving up the unequal exchanges.

During November, Steyn's army, with eager collaboration from insurrectionary Cape Boers, took places like Aliwal North, Dordrecht, Albert, Colesberg and Barkly East as it cut a swathe through the east. To the west, the Boers ran through Vryburg, and later Kenhardt, Prieska, and Gordonia, virtually at leisure. This wedge, driven in from the Orange Free State and with a rear reserve line, established a threatening strategic perimeter for the Boers, extending gains across a pocket of eastern and central or midlands localities. The occupation of Colesberg by the combined Transvaal and Orange Free State commandos of Schoeman and Grobler actually took them to within striking distance of the important Naauwpoort railway junction, as they assembled just thirty-five miles to the north. In Burghersdorp, a force under Du Plooy and Swanepoel had the potential to do something other than to rest and routinely plunder local black inhabitants. Positioned only forty miles southwest of an Aliwal North rearguard, they were set for a joint disruption of British communications by attacking the main coastal rail line to East London.

The speed of such breakthroughs surprised and alarmed British observers. In these areas, invading Boers now had a fairly solid base, not stiff enough to give them meaningful control over the edges of their boundaries of occupation, but enough to lay further claims and to look increasingly scary. In the euphoric view of some commandants, what lay ahead was almost open season. As imperial and colonial forces might have to be reduced or pulled out altogether to reinforce relief actions in siege crises, they could continue to take villages and other minor settlements with decreasing potential resistance from Cape Mounted Riflemen and Cape Police contingents. While Buller was compelling queasy Cape authorities to mobilise 4 000 African field force levies to hold the borders of eastern Mfengu and Thembu districts, all this meant was that Boer forces would have to think twice before raiding the Transkeian Territories to run off livestock, grain and forage.[191] With control of key rail points in the central Cape midlands, and an accumulating rebel colonial reserve, commandos could form an offensive line running west from Barkly East to Gordonia, secure from any British flanking attack or counter-offensive from the rear. The route to Cape Town, Port Elizabeth and East London then lay open. That, at least, was how some of the more optimistic spirits in the field saw the prospects.

Consolidating captured ground was obviously crucial to all of this. In that respect, while the Boers were not usually famous for being like-minded, like-willed, and obediently disciplined, they moved with speed and purpose to co-ordinate their linked occupational authority into a form of rough and rolling conquest regime. Geopolitically, as in Natal, occupied districts were formally annexed as republican territory. Northern Boer command created a new administrative structure which rewarded southern rebels for their military, political, protein, horse and grazing subsidy of the invasion by lifting them into positions of official authority as upstart district veldkornets and *landdrosts,* or magistrates.

In effect, the invaders and their local collaborators suspended Cape Colony sovereignty in an ambitious sweep to 'republicanise' British territory. Naturally, many Cape Boer rebels welcomed an instant, fictive, Orange Free State territorial legitimacy. But white loyalists and black citizens who bonded themselves to a sense of being imperial British subjects, were affronted by misrule. In annexed districts, established colonial domination through wage dependence, clientage, other social bonds and the rhetoric of British civilisation and protection, gave way to fierce sanctions as occupying Boers indulged in exhibitions of oppressive new power. As studies of wartime black experience have emphasised, new republican pass controls were rigorously enforced, labour was forcibly commandeered to service commandos and to work on friendly supplying farms, existing labour disputes were resolved through the dispensing of rough justice, tribute was exacted, and better-off blacks were dispossessed of rights, both propertied and petty.[192] As a fearful band of Coloured teachers and artisans declared in September 1901, 'Free State Dutchmen' were 'Boer hyenas' who would enslave them.[193]

To be sure, the Boers did not exercise much discretion over the conduct and terms of local occupation. Thus, there were few if any friendly gestures towards Cape black society calculated to extract goodwill or deference. This left an immediate need to make the meaning of conquest tell, through tough and showy exhibitions of authority and power which invariably made inhabitants intensely resentful of the abrupt and unwanted change of masters. What might have remained sullen acquiescence or neutrality in these frontier areas became simmering hostility which would soon begin to gnaw away at the republican camp. At the same time, while rising black resistance to commando incursions was the outcome of the intransigence of the Cape campaign, it was equally also the product of the imported doctrine of Boer white supremacy and the repeated desire to assert what commandants habitually termed Republic Native Law across the Orange River.

In other respects, even though the frontier districts invasion had failed to trigger a large-scale Boer colonial rising, the republicans had exploited the political ecology of small urban enclaves, creating distracting problems for the British through the isolation and capture of pockets of rural territory and endangering sectors of their communication system. For all this, there were still some oddly neglectful things. Amidst the excitement at the symbolic stroke of Boer armies crossing the Orange River, no move was aimed at seizing the strategically important railway bridge on the Orange. And, more generally, while the chances of reeling in active Boer support were reasonable in the Cape while comparatively negligible in Natal, the southern campaign commitment remained fairly limited.

By the last week of November, the pattern of the opening offensive was set. Imperial command had misjudged the level of reinforcements required to ward off an early republican strike. Moreover, the British took time to get things under way locally. This ensured that Boer leadership could exploit their edge of temporary superiority without having to test the issue in major battle. In Natal, British garrison power had been knocked back and immobilised. To the west, attack against border garrisons had sealed them off, obliging them to dig in. Meanwhile, other swift incursions chipped away at the British position, opening a menacing frontier gap between ground ceded and a British colonial rump which still had fairly little by way of defensive depth.

But then the republican impetus started to run down. Seemingly left hanging in the air, Boer forces turned towards a defensive stance as their forward thrusts began to ebb. With a British counter-offensive already beginning to darken the picture, it seemed to some French observers that there would be no easy resolution to the conflict.[194] This apprehension would indeed prove to be true, and not only for the Boers.

Whatever had been accomplished by Pretoria and Bloemfontein, the advance was obviously not enough to create conditions for a speedy end to the war, and on realistic bargaining terms. W.J. Leyds and other Transvaal diplomats lacked a crushing blow to emulate Majuba Hill, and upon which they could have tried to exploit their military successes politically. Then, that might have enabled them to recall Milner to open peace negotiations. For many republicans and their sympathisers in the Cape and abroad, this could have settled the war fairly, and could also have finally cleared South Africa of future Anglo-Boer quarrels.

Intriguing as they may be, these speculations are probably less important than the associated question of where the republicans went, and where they might have gone. One view is that the Boer war plan 'was achieved. With three main towns invested, the British would now have to try to relieve them.' That meant having to tackle the Boers 'where they had all the advantages, in prepared positions, held in strength but which they could abandon when they wanted and operate as guerrillas against the more stereotyped British'.[195] Unlike the Zulu, the Boers were less compelled by the economic strains of mobilisation to seek out decisive early frontal battles. Or, taking another perspective, despite letting opportunities slip, 'the Boers had achieved their first strategic aim: that of sealing off all the garrisons'. With that accomplished 'on all three fronts, it was time for the second strategic aim: to dig in and block the advance of Buller's forces. If they could hold them off, it should be possible to starve the three beleaguered towns into submission'.[196] These actions represented easy gains, for which a low price would be paid.

Against this, there is what is perhaps best termed a might-have-been argument or proposition. Here, several factors are of particular relevance. While the war crisis pushed the Boer states together, it took Steyn too long to get proper mobilisation going. With both republics having to mark time to synchronise their joint operations, the mobilisation timetable only came into effect in the Transvaal on 28 September, and in the Orange Free State on 2 October. Had the last throw of the dice been accepted to mean the commencement of fighting, the Boer time advantage would have been that much greater, and the first British reinforcements would not have been disembarking in Durban before that October ultimatum. It was more a case of not knowing when to start than not knowing when to stop.

A second inference, already touched on, is that by grounding so much of their campaign in 'coalescing around Mafeking, Kimberley and Ladysmith, the Boers lost their best opportunity of avoiding ultimate defeat'.[197] By immobilising their forces, a desultory siege movement proved to be a trap for the besiegers. Poorly led and lethargically conducted, the wrong engagements sapped offensive spirit and doomed the hope of a successful short war. If anything, the grizzly, ageing generals in charge of these essentially futile operations behaved as if the republics wanted a long one.

This deepened division and acrimony within the Boer officer corps. From the outset, questions had been asked about the ability and vision of high command to run the offensive. Its stalled pace did much to strengthen ongoing doubts about the competence of a supreme command consisting of elderly and dilatory men like Cronjé and Joubert. Criticism was partly generational. Able, ambitious and impatient younger commanders such as Koos de la Rey, Christiaan de Wet and Louis Botha were contemptuous of those they considered to be arthritic amateurs. In part, it was also social and political. Those with the drive and faith to renew momentum lacked the authority to pull things off because older military notables had the prerogatives of patriarchal seniority to block them from power in the field. High command rested in the hands of those who owed their position less to ability than to favouritism, factional twists, or fawning personal services to the Transvaal president and his clique. Lastly, among the small but restive urban 'educated Africander' soldiery, lawyers, teachers, ordinary state officials, beneficiaries of European travel and the like, there was a bemoaning of the failings of a band of 'country' or 'bush' Boer generals who were too pre-modern to ensure success. Inflexible, obstinate and ignorant of anything other than hugging the ground and holding defensive positions, they were incapable of addressing fundamental campaign problems.[198]

One of these, leaving aside the bottleneck of delayed mobilisation, was the imposing level of order demanded by the strategic plan of a two-front war. This assumed that the republics would not gain enough if they fought at full campaigning strength on a single front. Smuts was not wrong about this. But a combined two-front attack required that more time be spent on detail, precision planning of a pattern of aggressive operations, and the machinery for centralised command to ensure effective coordination between generals. Those in charge, however, were not brilliant at Napoleon's dictum of unity of command. By most accounts rather slow to tell one another what was going on, Cronjé and Joubert were isolated, indecisive, and unable to organise their strength in such a way as to take decisive advantage of opportunities. For example, they ignored the ease with which their forces were being provisioned on the Natal southern front.[199] Thus, if Boer forces were increasingly under-extended in their Mafeking and Kimberley operations, commandos were not being transferred quickly to maximise force against Natal. For that matter, given the promise of the Cape as a theatre of operations because of its republican loyalist support base, the effort there was too small-scale and sporadic to make a really deep hole. Commandos ended up staying, rather than pressing forward to positions from which it would be more difficult for them to be knocked back.

Finally, it goes more or less without saying that want of numbers was an obvious hindrance. While thousands were sent to ring Mafeking and Kimberley, only about 2 000 men were available on the western border of the Orange Free State for forward deployment. On this last point, one suggestive comment on the misdirection of republican strategy is forceful. The inevitable conclusion is that the Boers allowed themselves to become too hypnotised by sieges, beguiled by the reclamation of the spiritual lower plateau of Natal, by the harvesting of Durban, and by the lure of an artery to the sea. Had more weight been added to the western front, the unleashing of between 30 000 and 40 000 well-prepared riflemen into the Cape Colony might conceivably 'have radically altered the course of the war'.[200] As things stood now, that course was set for a British counter-offensive. It would be launched in Natal.

5

THE EMPIRE STRIKES BACK

D URING THE FIRST WEEKS OF FIGHTING, CORRESPONDENTS OF PRO-
imperial newspapers in Natal and the Cape gradually tempered their
boasting. The republican advance implied that things were less than
'perfect' for the British position, declared a writer to the *Umtata Herald*. Another
concluded that insufficient heed had been taken earlier in the 1890s of the alarming increase in the power of 'Boer militarism'. Instead of wasting time on who
was to be given the benefit of the doubt over the Jameson Raid mess, Britain
should have moved decisively, there and then, to put the 'emboldened' Boers
out of business. From Durban, a *Natal Witness* correspondent queried the reliability of journalists who had been scornful of republican capabilities, and were
now having to report the 'dangerous' and 'injurious' gains of the Boer forces.

Alongside this, anti-imperial reaction is well illustrated by an awareness in
Ons Land and *Het Zuid-Oosten* of the immediate vindication of a 'just' war by the
victims of calculated British aggression. One reader reminded others of Reitz's
rousing 1899 manifesto to the Orange Free State burghers, calling for exertions
to make 'a great day', its success affirmed by the knowledge that 'the God of our
Fathers will be with us in our struggles'. Not all resorted to a religious vocabulary to link war achievement to fundamentalist Protestant doctrine. Milder colonial Boers merely expressed a quiet optimism that British 'difficulties' would help
along a compromise peace, without victors or vanquished, on 'honourable' terms.
After all, with Britain now facing calamity in Ladysmith and Mafeking, hostilities were surely unlikely to be prolonged.[201]

Within British territory, this combination of loyalist settler unease and republican satisfaction did not represent any crisis of civilian morale, in the sense

that we would understand the significance of that factor (and its influence upon army morale) in a context of 'total war'. In all, it was too spasmodic and too diffuse. Moreover, if General Sir George White was short of victory, colonists in Cape Town and Durban were not short of food. There, the real effect of the republican strike was an unsettling of more confident opinion. While there was continuing anticipation of a short war and decisive British victory, it had become clear that if matters were not to become too prolonged, far more would have to be undertaken. The British would have to dislodge the occupying enemy from colonial territory and then carry the republics.

Given the balance at the outset, it was not altogether surprising that the war should have gone badly for the British. The Boers had the troops, the equipment, the field intelligence, the mobility and the armaments to shake the enemy. Britain now moved to recover its position against the background of a still pervasive fighting mentality whose simplicity has been sketched by many writers on this war. In essence, to quote one historian, its basis was an indefatigable sense of unreality, of illusory beliefs, 'the Boers with their memories of Majuba, the British because they refused to admit that a handful of farmers could withstand large numbers of regular troops accustomed to victory'.[202] It was no less illusory to suppose that the British had a properly planned offensive strategy. As the 1904 Royal Commission on the War would go on to note, while Britain had an agreed 'line of advance', its expeditionary force lacked the guidance of a formulated 'plan of operations' upon which to base detailed campaign organisation or an envisaged sequence of battle. The lack of effective central coordination and planning was not helped by some fairly surreal behaviour by senior figures in London. Wolseley was in direct personal confrontation with the unsmiling and supercilious regime of Lansdowne, a Cabinet superior he damned as a 'cock sparrow of a Jewish type'.[203] What Lansdowne in turn thought of his military subordinate is not recorded as candidly. Nonetheless, as Wolseley was rumoured to have had a lowly social pedigree, he is unlikely to have been outdone in bigotry by a former Indian viceroy. The squabbling of these imperial warlords was to hamper the development and application of strategic thinking from the centre.

The cause of that difficulty was ultimately deliberate procrastination and spiteful deception. Thus, in mid-1899, Lansdowne's response to competing claims from Wolseley for 50 000 troops to defeat the Boers and the chancellor, Michael Hicks-Beach's insistence on maintaining a tight-fisted 'Gladstonian' Treasury, was to be ostentatiously busy with other matters. Then, he selected August deliberately as an unhelpful time to go off on holiday to his ample Irish estates. Having little but contempt for the bureaucratic authority exercised by despised War Office 'clerks', Wolseley's riposte was to economise on his urgent minutes to Lansdowne about the South African military situation, leaving out the increasingly detailed field information at his disposal from some accurate and sobering intelligence assessments. If these critical calculations did reach Lansdowne eventually, it was through the novel channel of Chamberlain and the Colonial Office.

The outcome of these astonishing exchanges was that the commander-in-chief's prescribed 'preparation of schemes of offensive and defensive operations failed to be enacted in any systematic fashion'.[204] All one had from the imperial core was Cabinet approval of a loose plan of a direct expeditionary force advance to Bloemfontein through the Orange Free State, the weaker, closer and more exposed of the Boer states. In the periphery, its only contribution was the local defence strategy for Natal and its strategic coal supplies, planned by the now deposed General Butler. The British had no clearly prepared or structured offensive beyond a vague grasp that their forces would have to be deployed forward for a conquest of the Boer republics. 'We would advance until there were no longer any Boers in sight, and then pass through all such openings' was the sarcastic recollection of a West Yorkshire Regiment officer.[205]

As already noted in an earlier chapter, what first took a bite out of the British 'interior strategy' was General White's defensive predicament in Natal. The idea of lancing Steyn's republic with a western offensive which would at the same time cauterise Natal was discarded. It was too late to assist White to repel an invasion by easing pressure in the east.

Arriving in Cape Town on 31 October, Buller had just over a week in which to fix upon a strategy and get a move on. His original proposal had been devised on the basis of intelligence estimates and War Office thinking during 1896 and 1897. These had envisaged a 'main line' of advance running west of the Drakensberg, based on the Cape Colony and steering well clear of any potentially dangerous entanglements in the tricky mountainous terrain up the Natal route to the Transvaal.

A veteran of the Anglo-Zulu War, Buller knew enough about South Africa to appreciate which ground would be easiest to traverse. That was to be found by ensuring that the spearhead of an offensive rolled along the rail line through Bloemfontein to Johannesburg and Pretoria. There, the open plains of the high-veld would provide a good road for marching British forces and their huge flow of supplies. But, for the Army Corps, central strategy was now superseded by a decision to salvage Natal. Much of November was spent preparing for the Buller offensive, pushing troops into position, attending to transport and provisioning needs for various fronts, recruiting Africans to service army field requirements, and awaiting the arrival of further reinforcements, not merely from Britain but also from Canada, Australia and New Zealand.

The most pressing problem had been a shortage of troops in the operational theatre: with an Army Corps now numbering 47 000 and rising, the seriousness of this difficulty was diminishing. In search of a winning stratagem, Buller divided his assembled forces. With 20 000 soldiers, Lieutenant General Lord Methuen was to retrieve things to the west, carrying an assault along the western railway to relieve Kimberley, and thereafter opening a straight line of advance into the Orange Free State, crushing the enemy's northern districts. Lieutenant Generals Gatacre and French were to stage a counter-offensive in the Cape Colony, putting an end to the Orange Free State invasion by descending on commandos in the midlands, around Colesberg, Stormberg and Naauwpoort, and by clearing the upper interior route to East London.

Buller took upon himself the crucial responsibility for getting the Natal menace out of the way, committing to this more than half of his army corps. Given that, by November, there was probably little room for second thoughts, there was no obvious flaw in Buller's strategical thinking, or nothing 'intrinsically misguided', to quote a modern military historian.[206] For all that, something appeared wayward and brittle about the Natal situation and Buller which captures the early aura surrounding military affairs, of personal calling, of destiny, of heroism that lay around the advancing imperial enterprise. White's commanders, Lieutenant General Sir Francis Clery (whose prominent side-whiskers were dyed blue) and Major General Neville Lyttelton, were unsentimental about an unlucky superior whose authority seemed to have been reduced to a plaintive heliograph from Ladysmith. With others, they implored Buller as South African commander-in-chief to move swiftly to turn the Boers out of Natal and to win the war from there.

From London, an incensed Wolseley denounced White and his 'little army' for an 'ignorance of strategy' which had proved disastrous for 'all the scheme of this war'. Put into retreat more by his own feeble tactics than by the Boers, his consequent precariousness had made it obligatory 'that we have to relieve him'.[207] As for Buller, he was rather fond of Natal, familiar and fortunate campaigning country for a soldier who had won the Victoria Cross for rescuing British wounded from the Zulu in the 1879 war. South Africa's 'garden' colony was in some ways a familiar cultural stamping ground, as inviting, bucolic and replenishing as his own Devon estate. Self-indulgent, and reputedly fond of a daily pint of champagne, the sixty-year-old general resembled the empire at its most stertorian: ponderous and puffy in appearance, he possessed 'great girth, multiple chins, flushed complexion and walrus moustache'. Attentive to the welfare of his troops, Buller was held in high regard by the rank and file, and was said to have inspired 'devotion'.[208]

Buller fended off strong political opposition from Milner, who wanted him to make the Cape his first order of business and not undertake a thousand-mile voyage to Durban. The general had a firm sense of the kind of mark that needed to be made. Although to date he had rarely commanded more than a few thousand men, his considerable experience of war against colonial peasant enemies had convinced him that a strategy of conquest directed at towns or capitals was often insufficient to bring hostilities to a successful conclusion. Ultimately, that could only be attained by eliminating or subjugating every belligerent in the field. With the major Boer forces infesting Natal, the enemy war effort could be fixed and destroyed there. The British had been handed an unmissable opportunity.

One factor in all of this was that Natal was in no imminent danger of sliding any further under the republican thumb. Once in the colony, Buller himself did not exactly behave as if this were the case either, spending time in Durban and Pietermaritzburg and only ambling up to forward positions in Frere after eleven days. Joubert's commandos, meanwhile, had done little more than work their way around Ladysmith. After much strategic hesitation and delay, the Boers had ventured the barest advance southwards of the siege sector. Merely 3 000 men had ridden on, with no more forthcoming. Natal's military outlook was, in its way, *both* simultaneously urgent *and* relatively assured.

Elsewhere, on 23 November, with Kimberley in his sights, Methuen began his advance from Orange River Station near the western border of the Orange Free State. Revelling in the glory of his first independent command, he notified

Kekewich that his 1st Division field force of 8 000 infantry would arrive to lift the siege within a week, bar any check at the Modder River. The Boers, in readiness to stall the British advance after thorough reconnaissance, had begun to disperse their disposable troop strength in small contingents at a number of raised positions with good observation and wide fields of fire. North of the Orange River near Belmont, Commandant Jacobus Prinsloo and 2 000 Orange Free State commandos topped a hill position, under orders to hold off Methuen's force until Cronjé could slip down reinforcements from Mafeking.

Closing up, and knowing that they were the stronger, the British decided to take the Boer position in order to remove any flanking threat to their line of communications.

In many respects, Paul Methuen had prepared well. His attacking troops made their way forward under cover of darkness, their officers hiding their shiny buttons and sword hilts, or discarding swords altogether, stripping the shine off rifle butts, all to make themselves less conspicuous to beady-eyed Boer marksmen.[209] There had already been ample indications in Natal of the threat to exposed officers in battle. A greater similarity of appearance between officers and men was one obvious way of countering disproportionate losses and their likely effect upon morale and effective line command.

Unfortunately, cursory scouting and sketchy mapping meant that the coming of dawn caught his force at an alarming distance from the enemy position with virtually no screening. One soldier recalled a heart-stopping moment, clawing forward through a strangely 'full stillness'[210] and expecting the Boers to open up with every passing second. This came in the form of concentrated crossfire, its costs borne mainly by the Grenadier Guards. Nevertheless, overall losses were reduced by Methuen, who had sensibly thinned out rather than massed his advancing troops. Moving across the veld in open formation deflected some of the force of blanketing, repelling rifle fire. And, however tenacious, Boer resistance could not prevent the British from getting onto the slopes of their defended koppie and swarming on until it became clear that the outnumbered commandos could not sustain their defences. Before their losses mounted further, the Boers slipped away from their fighting lines and fled northwards. For the British, a pulverising frontal infantry attack had done the trick in the small battle of Belmont, but at a disagreeable cost. The losses suffered by the republicans were only a third of those by Methuen's force, and the withdrawing commandos were able to recover.

Having pushed Boer outposts farther up the railway corridor, the British then resumed their move against enemy strongpoints.

Meanwhile, the Boer command also had to confront the cost of killing and dying. Aware that Methuen's march had only been temporarily hindered, ordinary burghers grew increasingly disenchanted with Prinsloo's leadership and tactics, a large number finding this sufficient cause to leg it home to check on their crops and the welfare of their families. Against this, the arrival of De la Rey with advance reinforcements and provisions dispatched by Cronjé did something to lift morale and introduce more cohesion. But the intrusive influence of Boer personal and private concerns continued to sap levels of service commitment and combat performance. With so many commandos having trickled away, all Cronjé's contingent did was to raise Prinsloo's strength to around 2 000, its original size at Belmont.

On 25 November, four of Methuen's infantry regiments pounced again. At Graspan, De la Rey had positioned his force along the summit of an arc of koppies, thickly fortified with earthworks and with swift and smartly secured evacuation outlets. This position was fairly easily located and targeted by Methuen's observers. Preceded by heavy artillery bombardment of frontal entrenchments, which drove the enemy firing-line back from the summit, British infantry stormed in. After a bitterly fought engagement, the Boers again yielded to superior odds and fled on horseback, harried by British shelling. The fugitives dragged away most of their dead and wounded along with rifles scooped up from abandoned corpses.[211] Once more, Methuen had prevailed. Yet, again, it had been a bloody effort with the British casualty rate of 300 more than double that of the Boers. As victories go, Belmont and Graspan were minor affairs, however fiercely fought. If beaten there, the republicans were nevertheless still able to save something. For, by tactically abandoning their posts to regroup, they continued to elude the British to fight another day.

More of that fighting, and in greater earnest, lay almost immediately ahead. If his advance was not going quite like clockwork, Methuen was still certain of reaching Kimberley almost as scheduled, his objective now only some twenty-five miles away. In his calculations, the last remaining defensive point of any consequence left to the Boers was Magersfontein, twelve miles southwest of the town. By now, it was anticipated that the republicans would be too spent to put up any further substantial resistance. But something unforeseen happened next.

With the British line of advance taking them inexorably to the Modder River, De la Rey glimpsed good fortune. There lay a chance to exploit a good position and he fixed upon shrewd tactics to do so.

De la Rey discarded the traditional use of rocky koppies in establishing defensive sites. As they were vulnerable to artillery attack and their lower slopes provided good covering space for advancing troops, he now exploited other natural positions. This involved entrenching 3 000 commandos along the banks of the Modder. Rather than use the river itself as a barrier ahead of its trench defences, he decided to front it with well-prepared and well-concealed trench lines and a dispersed cluster of well-prepared battery positions. A dense line of vegetation aided concealment and provided cover, while the ground behind the defenders sloped down steeply to the river line, hampering enemy observation and offering good protection from British fire.

Conversely, the ground southwards between the Modder and Methuen's advancing troops was both wholly exposed and rising neatly, ideal for delivering the quarry to De la Rey's guns. For that, the Boers had actually watered the ground ahead of their trench line, setting down rows of marker stones in measured distances to aid the accurate adjustment of rifle sights in immediate preparation for firing. At short range and across a flat trajectory, this camouflaged and level sweep of field marked a diversion from the customary Boer battle tactic of firing downhill from a crest.[212] De la Rey, no self-sacrificing romantic, recognised that the Modder River provided two key factors crucial to sustaining the fighting efficiency of his troops. One was the strength of concealment, the advantage of surprise, and a virtually impregnable position. The other was that the choice of terrain made it difficult for commandos to break and run willy-nilly if their defences were in some way to be breached. As any retreat or escape would involve fording the river, the Boers would first need to inflict sufficient casualties to make the British waver or to inflict disarray to achieve the necessary breathing space for a withdrawal across the water barrier.

Methuen set off at dawn on 28 November for the Modder, a man on the make who considerately scheduled a late breakfast for his force alongside the railway stop on the other side of the river. He had been advised by advance scouts of Boers milling around ahead, but took little notice of reported sightings, believing that the enemy were all falling back towards Magersfontein. Counting on nothing more than a rough-and-tumble skirmish with the retreating enemy, he ruled out the possibility that their command might have made any tactical innovations to use the Modder as a defensive line. Given previous British experience, this was probably a fairly reasonable judgement. It also meant that Methuen set out in ignorance of the precise whereabouts and intentions of the Boers.

The Modder River ambush, for that is what it was, pinned down the exposed British with raking volleys for the whole day, forcing virtually the entire, broad front to go to ground and to stay there while attempting to return fire at an unseen enemy, whose smokeless powder helped keep them hidden. With little by way of defensive fire control, conditions for the attackers in this unrelenting engagement were horrendous. With voracious ants and searing heat adding to their misery, desperate soldiers, already exhausted by lengthy marching and maddened by thirst, were cut down as they stumbled around in search of water carts. Part of Methuen's force did in fact, eventually, manage to stage an assault which broke through a section of the Boer lines, and the troops crossed the river to turn on their enemy from the rear, but they were beaten back in pitched battle. Here, the Boers were not to be panicked into flight, despite losses which included the death of De la Rey's own son.

The Boer commander's objective had been to delay and to do damage to Methuen's advance, and in this the Modder River battle had been satisfactory. A 10 000-strong British force lost 500 men, and Methuen himself was wounded. Yet, while De la Rey wanted to build on his strong show by running in further reinforcements from Cronjé, he now came up against the limits of the republican model of command by mandate. A council of war vote directed an orderly retreat towards Magersfontein for a major stand in order to retain the Kimberley position. Methuen looked to the morning of 29 November for a renewed assault, only to find that the enemy had abandoned its position during the night. The Boers can hardly be said to have been beaten in battle, and they remained uncaught.

As Methuen's bruised army now wound its way on towards Kimberley, the woes of Buller's generals elsewhere were just about to begin. In the Cape midlands, the central front, French brought up his mounted force to seal off the Colesberg area against further Boer probing. This was to be the beginning of over three months of duelling, virtually without pause, with neither side showing any inclination to give serious battle. Numerous expeditions were sent out from field bases, but the republican invaders continued to overstay their visit, inflicting

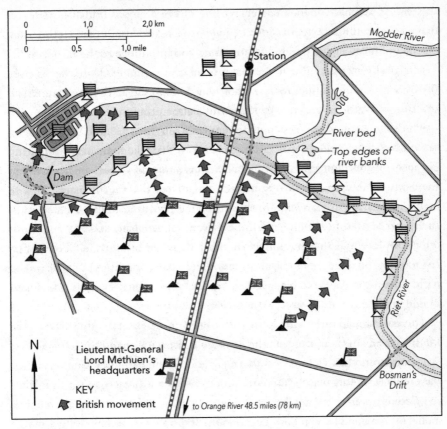

increasing frustration and fatigue on the British. Still, as yet, French was in no danger of defeat. The same however, could not be said of Major-General Sir William Gatacre, who was now about to make a calamitous move.

In the third week of November, several days after Gatacre had established his headquarters in East London, Orange Free State commandos occupied the Stormberg junction. A commander of some political intelligence, he judged that safeguarding imperial prestige in such vulnerable districts was essential if estranged Cape Boers were to be kept in line. Pressure had to be applied, and quickly.

But time and distance were against Gatacre. His own force was too distant to block the republican incursion on 22 November, and French's cavalry brigades were almost 100 miles away to the west, combing the countryside around Naauwpoort. Aware that the republican command could take immediate advantage of this gap to feed forces into the very heart of the exposed midlands, Gatacre moved. Arranging to have his force of 3 000 troops railed to Molteno, the station closest to Stormberg, the British planned for a surprise, concerted attack on the enemy position, held by 2 300 commandos under General J.H. Olivier, before the Boers could do another run. To consolidate his strength, Gatacre counted on drafting in a further 500 men from an established post in the area.

The plan required good, smooth assembly arrangements, and here problems set in immediately. No troop reinforcements were diverted to Gatacre's command because, in some tangle of confusion, his orders were never delivered. Furthermore, the trains failed to run on time, raising anxiety that the force might not all arrive soon enough to take part in the Stormberg operation. While Gatacre eventually mustered a full complement in Molteno, some of his soldiers, worn out after spending hours in the sun before being corralled into a train for a lumbering journey, only reached their destination very late at night. As he planned an eight-mile night march to his target to launch a dawn assault, mounting delays obliged him to drive his already tired troops at a punishing pace.

The envisaged line of attack for the column had been directly through the known terrain of the pass through which both the rail line and the road fed into Stormberg junction. But a report that Olivier had concentrated defenders in the pass to meet any incursion head-on, promptly caused Gatacre to turn his force in a flanking westerly direction, pushing troops through the Kissieberg heights, a natural bastion of steep koppies. This involved a considerably longer march over rough and broken countryside which had not been adequately reconnoitred. In a lapse over attention to detail, the commanding officer of the Molteno garrison was not advised of Gatacre's abrupt change of direction. This ensured that the British medical and supply column continued to roll grandly along the main road towards Stormberg and a hideous muddle.

On the evening of 9 December Gatacre began his planned descent, with a night advance by weary and cursing troops who were by now sorely in need of rest and refreshment. Unused to night operations, they were also badly short of prior training. In another bizarre piece of carelessness, no scouts were dispatched to sniff ahead, even though there was uncertainty over the exact positions of Boer forces on the approaches. By now, the offensive was inviting disaster. Next came something close to pantomime. In the dark, threading their way through a clogged terrain of rocky outcrops and confusing defiles, Gatacre's novice guides became hopelessly lost and, bafflingly, failed to tell their commander to put a foot on the brake. Perhaps they thought that suicidal pretence would allow them to live to guide another day.

When dawn broke, 3 000 British troops, exhausted and disorientated from a draining march on empty stomachs, had indeed reached the Stormberg valley. On the map, however, this actually increased their peril, for they plainly did not know where they were. Gatacre certainly had few reliable clues, and seemed to assume that his path was taking him towards the targeted railway pass. His officers and men were sure that they had ended up just ahead of the front range of the identified heights. In reality, they were about to be caught behind them, and at a nasty disadvantage.[213]

The more advanced of Boer pickets on the crest of the Kissieberg swung around almost in disbelief, and sounded the alarm. A bewildered Gatacre turned to face an enemy thought to be in full defensive position, and launched an attack, thrusting frantically to get battle under way at full strength. The British appeared to have no inkling at all of the real weight of the enemy along the Kissieberg; Gatacre's information about Boer numbers had been about as reliable as that of their location. This position was, in fact, relatively lightly held. But it was formidable high ground. Even fresh troops familiar with the terrain would have found an upward assault impossibly heavy going given its steepness, formidable rock outcrops and precipices. It was to be neither the first nor the last occasion in this war when the run of lumpy terrain played a crucial role in determining the balance of advantage between opposing forces.

Inevitably, Gatacre's fatigued infantry, trying doggedly to scale the heights, spent themselves on the unremitting roughness of the Kissieberg. Some managed to secure a precarious position near the summit, squeezing into crevices to prepare for a closing assault. But even this advance was illusory, to be destroyed at a stroke by the poor fire control of their own supporting artillery. Aiming against the blinding sun, their shells ripped away many of those who had found a foothold. The assault was a fiasco, and soon the British turned tail and began to move down in demoralised retreat.

With the operation in disarray, Gatacre now tried to march his dispirited force back to Molteno, only to run into more disaster. Commandos harried their enemy from a second direction, putting the British under flanking fire from the west.

As it was, the republicans did not press their advantage very heavily; their mounted riflemen had other fish to fry. To Gatacre's relief, the engagement inflicted only ninety casualties, and he resumed his retreat.

If ever there was a South African War general with a knack for forgetfulness, it was William Gatacre. By all accounts, in beating a retreat he seems to have forgotten the plight of 600 of his men, still stranded on the Kissieberg slopes as the triumphant Boers converged. After hours under a blistering sun, they crawled down to surrender. Conceding that its admiration for British arms was beginning to take a few knocks, the *Cape Mercury* suggested that the 'painful'

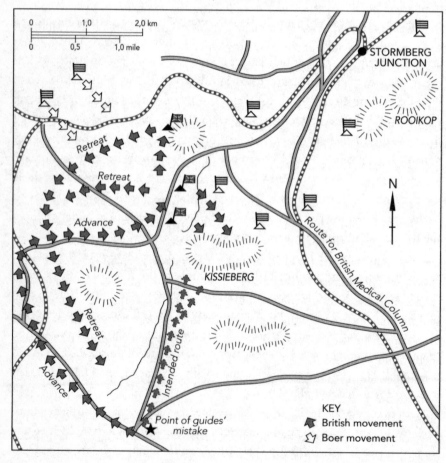

STORMBERG, DECEMBER 1899

and 'shameful ... Stormberg disaster' was indicative of a lack of proper attention to 'growing examples of proper Boer strategy'.[214] Local Mfengu transport auxiliaries were a little more blunt. At Queenstown's Army Service Corps remount depot, African workers staged a comic dance mocking the débâcle, in which General 'Backacre' (as he was increasingly dubbed by his own men) was played as a cornered beast by a 'whitened-up' mule wagoner. This impudence so incensed a Rifle Brigade transport officer that he docked his muleteers' monthly bonus.[215] Hereafter, Gatacre consolidated in the Queenstown area, protecting it until March 1900 without much fear of the enemy taking ground from him.

While Gatacre was being pursued to defeat, Methuen was enlarging his force to 13 000, confident that an offensive dominance would enable the British to take Kimberley. But Cronjé, too, was busy finding the commandos to swell his entrenchments around Magersfontein mountain. All was set for a strike. Methuen suspected that the Boer positions were reasonably strong, but he could not know exactly how strong. In planning his attack, he moved methodically. The British began with a heavy artillery pounding of the Magersfontein hills to spike republican defences before advancing (on 11 December). The standard tactic was Modder River simplicity – a brisk night march along the railway line with no flanking diversions, followed by a hard dawn strike to overwhelm the enemy.

But again, as at Modder River, the defenders were full of guile. As the battles were fought on an ever larger scale, their tactics improved. Instead of bunching their forces on high ground to hold the Magersfontein summits, the Boers had opted to form a long defensive belt along the base. This was another uncomplicated and effective De la Rey plan. His men dug a substantial line of deep trenches and rear pits (as medical and supply stations), snaking across some twelve miles in a crescent formation virtually at ground level. An imposingly long trench line reduced the risk of outflanking. In addition, their position's sculpted narrowness and thick internal earth cushioning provided maximum protection from British shrapnel. Casualties even from a direct hit by a British shell would be minimal.

Complementing these natural defences was a man-made one. Commandos ran a profusion of barbed wire across the line of approach ahead of their trenches, firmly compacted into the earth and studded with clanking tins as a trip-warning. This kind of lacerating barrier had been extremely effective against British advance at Modder River, where a Highland Light Infantry assault in poor light had been upended by a wire line, with troops in disorder trampling one another in their frantic efforts to break clear. The use of barbed wire in this war is usually associated with the British, as an iron cage around their internment camps or as a relentless weapon employed to encircle a weakening guerrilla enemy in the latter stages of the fighting. Yet, the impact of its earlier use by the Boers should not be underestimated, not least the cold proficiency with which their command turned to stock-farm fencing to repel Highlanders instead of jackals.

Although by 11 December the republicans had committed a force of 8 500 men to Magersfontein, an instinctively tentative Cronjé thought that De la Rey's frontal deployment was potential folly, too risky a way of making a stand. But the Orange Free State president, on another of his back-slapping tours of the front, gave De la Rey an overriding free hand. And luck was to be with him. The difficulties of the British, again, were created by their lack of foresight, shaky coordination and general confusion. Thinking that he had battered the enemy to pieces through an intense artillery bombardment of the slopes of the main Magersfontein hill, Methuen tried to storm the position. For this, he assigned a dawn assault to the Highland Brigade under the energetic and breezy command of Major General Andy Wauchope, descendant of a wealthy Scottish mine-owning family. On this occasion, however, Wauchope was apprehensive ahead of a night march. There had been little basic reconnaissance: poor weather had grounded a vital observation balloon, and his troops, clinging to guide ropes in the dark, were having to advance across a sector turned to mud by a pelting thunderstorm. In the early dawn hours of 11 December, 4 000 Highlanders, bunched up in close formation, negotiated their way to a forward position about 600 yards from Magersfontein hill. The exact whereabouts of the enemy were still not known.

That enemy, however, was wide awake. At almost the exact moment the British force began to disperse from thick assembly to group fighting formation, it was enveloped by concentrated Boer rifle fire. Dying, wounded and terrified, Wauchope's column halted in surprise and disarray, losing any meaningful sense of direction. Amidst stumbling confusion and panic, there was little organised return of fire, nor was there much consideration of how to recover or to effect a managed retreat. For Wauchope, the consequences of misjudgement were catastrophic. The majority of his kilted force clung to the base of the hill throughout the day, raked by commando fire, scoured by the fierce sun, scrabbling on ground teeming with ants and flies, out of cartridges, and short of water. A few small parties ripped off khaki to camouflage their kilts and crawled up to huddle on higher slopes. Yet that was only to imperil themselves further.[216] Estimating that the full Highland contingent had gone to ground at the foot of the heights, Methuen's rear gunners pulverised the upper slopes and summit areas with shrapnel. They did virtually no damage to the Boers. The barrage did, however, batter their own troops. Moreover, British battery support was doubly wasteful – the sporadic igniting of powder charges by the Boers well away from their line deceived artillery observers about their true positions.

During the course of the day there were a few desperate lunges towards De la Rey's trench line, but steady and accurate fire cut down attackers. One storming party did eventually prise open a gap in the barrier and charged through in force, with the intention of scaling Magersfontein hill to threaten the flanks of their entrenched enemy. But, as this small body of troops moved forward, it collided with none other than Cronjé himself and a detachment of his commandos, short of their bearings but alert. The confrontation quickly flared into a vicious battle in which the outnumbered and out-gunned British either died or capitulated. Then, a concealed Orange Free State commando wormed its way out in force around the edge of the Boer entrenchments and closed in to attack the right flank of the immobilised Highlanders. There was very little cover, and what remained of British cohesion dissolved.

Sensing that their line of retreat was coming under threat from this flanking assault, Wauchope's bloodied force broke into panic-stricken flight, their dark kilts a clear target for Boer marksmen, who were soon joined by gunners to press home the rout. Methuen's reluctant order of a full retreat amounted to little more than painful recognition of what had already been decided by his men. As it had become clear, by the following day, that the Boers were not planning to repeat Modder River and abandon their positions after repelling the enemy, the British had no option but to withdraw in the teeth of exceptionally stout defence. Their casualties were considerable, numbering about 1 000 against Boer losses of 250. Among the dead was Wauchope himself, no more to be the beneficiary of the hefty dividends of his family's mines.

Reined in by his own instincts as well as by Buller's command, Methuen then took no further initiatives. He fell back on the defensive, treading water until Cronjé evacuated Magersfontein three months later. The battle had been a

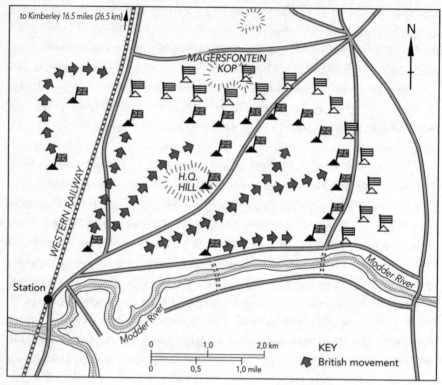

harrowing experience, and among its combatants there seems to have been some resigned understanding of its tragic costs, enough regret to curb the killing frenzy. During a natural lull in the fighting, medical officers and stretcher-bearers were by common consent permitted to move freely and to work on those wounded who were marooned on the battlefield. Wounded survivors of the British frontal assault who had been felled very close to the Boer trench line testified that commandos had yelled out promises not to fire upon any walking wounded, provided they discarded weaponry.

Finally, following the completion of Methuen's retreat to the Modder River, the two sides came to a lenient armistice arrangement. This permitted the return of some Highland infantry to retrieve their wounded and to inter their dead, a sombre and hushed assignment in which the Boers, clambering out of their trenches, offered the assistance of blankets and shovels. Some observers at the time, and some later historians, have argued from the evidence of such humane trans-actions that the nature of soldierly combat in this war was governed by ethical or chivalrous restraints. These, it has been said, upheld standards of honour and mutual empathy among adversaries, expressing the moral spirit of a final nine-teenth-century 'gentlemen's war'.[217] Leaving aside its predictable romanticism there was, perhaps, something to that elusive vision in the aftermath of Magers-fontein, if only in the sense of mutual shock that this was an African colonial war in which European life was losing its premium.

As Gatacre and Methuen slumped into the ignominy of decisive defeat in the central west, Britain's eastern campaign went ahead in Natal, with Buller trying to retrieve the situation. Around Ladysmith, little had changed by December. The siege rumbled on, with neither side displaying any flexibility. Buller en-camped at Frere on 5 December, in very low spirits about the way the war was going. In a classic lament to Lansdowne, he conceded initiative to the republi-cans, declaring that they 'have had the whip hand of us ever since the war began' in obliging the British 'to attack with inferior forces their superior forces in selected positions'.[218] How Buller saw matters is probably reflected even better in his massive overestimation of enemy strength around Ladysmith. The real figure was around 8 500 men, not the tens of thousands of his imagination.

On the day following Methuen's flight from Magersfontein, Buller left Frere with 18 000 troops and set out towards Ladysmith. His opponent, Louis Botha, commanding a comparatively modest commando force, anticipated that the Brit-ish would again follow the direct railway line to their objective, and planned to repulse an attack by building weighty trench systems in the huddle of koppies just north of Colenso, which commanded a wide view. Dimly aware of the strength of this Boer position, Buller had initially decided that he would not be drawn into an encounter, and contrived an advance which would neatly bypass the waiting enemy. If things had been going well for his generals in the Cape, that, possibly, would have been that. But news of the Magersfontein disaster, coming close upon the setback at Stormberg, impelled Buller to action. Although unsure of exact enemy numbers and positions, he opted for a direct strike against the main Boer force around Colenso. He abandoned his earlier intention to reduce the risk of over-exposure – by simply holding the Boers to their Colenso lines and then marching on to Ladysmith along a westerly outflanking route. Instead, he now chose to force a spoiling frontal battle at a fairly serious geographical disadvantage.

The north bank of the Tugela River, which ran through the direct approaches to Colenso, was backed by solid heights which dominated the more modest southern slopes. There were passable drifts, but as these fords were obvious funnels for any enemy assault, the defence grip was kept tight to spike any offensive. Behind this outer line lay a further strong reserve position, to which defenders could withdraw in the event that their frontal chain snapped. This comprised a forbidding base of mushrooming koppies and massed rocky outcrops, a sheltered back-land into which commandos could retreat, dig in, and sit tight. In Buller's command there was certainly some apprehension over the terrain advantages enjoyed by the Boers along their ten-mile front, but not of a kind that could not be ignored.

Although Buller's direct offensive may have been playing to Boer strengths, General Botha was not without a few difficulties of his own. While he needed to make the most economical and effective use of his troops, it was too risky to shorten the republican line. Dismayed by scout reports of the size of the enemy columns, hundreds of Boers lost their stomach for what promised to be a fearsome battle and turned tail for home. Experienced commandants also knew something of Buller's hard-nosed earlier pursuit of the Zulu, and his reputation made some of them jittery. A third problem was the difficulty of assembling the number of troops needed to hold a front lengthy enough to ensure that the defences could not be out-flanked. Posting men to hold key high positions which were not integrated into the defensive line posed morale and discipline problems. Botha's commandos refused flatly to occupy any detached point which ran the risk of being encircled and overrun. Deployment to the defence of Hlangwane hill only proceeded after threats and bullying, and then on the chilling basis of drawing lots, a method insisted upon by the unhappily resigned commandos.[219]

Dispensing with any attempt at secrecy in the timing of attack, the British launched, on 13 December, an intensive bombardment of the Boer position with an assortment of heavy field and naval guns, blasting enemy entrenchments and earthwork entanglements with lyddite shell. Having chanced a run at the enemy's toughest points, Buller counted on his artillery to pave the way for a breakthrough by dismembering republican defences and either flattening or demoralising occupying commandos through intense shock. Although two days of this ensured that the defenders paid a price, the weight and depth of republican placings provided good protection against both explosive and shrapnel. At the same time, just as the bombardment was all but useless as an aid to the British, so it proved a help to Boer preparation by clearly signalling the launch of a major enemy assault.

The British plan of attack was spectacularly inept, and it would turn out to be costly. Buller's forces had to push forward at a slow pace over dangerously exposed ground in full daylight, attempting to fix on an enemy whose defensive density was not properly known and whose advanced positions had still to be definitely located. The main assault committed two brigades to a dual and parallel offensive, one brigade to mount a frontal strike against the Boers' Colenso stronghold and the other to force its way around to peck at the right rump of the republican position. This was designed to carry the British forces across the Tugela River, in order then to join up and establish a commanding position. Buller easily had the troops for this, and more. In that, he was probably right had all things been equal. At the same time, a mounted brigade was sent to take the upper reaches of the Hlangwane position; two additional brigades were retained in reserve. Conscious of the power at their disposal, many of Buller's officers were bristling to get at the Boers before they could run away. Such sports bloodlust was, however, dangerously misplaced. Colenso was not some grouse moor.

Right from the start, the battle brought grim memories of the Magersfontein disaster. Colonel Charles Long, in command of the artillery brigade division, had been assigned to protect the central advance with what was expected to be the usual method of shelling the enemy front from the rear of his advancing infantry. But the impetuous gunner was no stick-in-the-mud traditionalist. Together with several of his more experienced officers, he had worked out an approach which had already been applied effectively elsewhere in Africa. This was to dash his guns straight up to a startled enemy; take up a parade-ground position, follow the firing drill, and then smash the ranks assembled before them with a steady discharge of explosive and shrapnel. Long had no authorisation to experiment with this tactic at Colenso, and had not advised Buller of his intention to try an independent initiative in close-quarter gunnery.[220] Still, as this had been devastating against the Sudanese in 1898, Buller's artillery commander was all for trying the tactic to break what he perceived as agricultural warriors on the Tugela.

However, Colenso was not the same as Omdurman. On the morning of 15 December, Long deliberately ran his batteries well ahead of the infantry brigade which he had been ordered to accompany on its march. After one or two perfunctory stoppages, supposedly to permit trudging infantry to catch up, he shrugged off repeated requests to slow down and raced well ahead, quickening in pace as enemy positions were spotted ahead. Long soon ended up half a mile in front of his infantry and roughly the same distance from the bank of the Tugela. Selecting a promising, flat, open piece of terrain on which to bring his guns into action, he dispatched a scouting officer to survey the forward ground to make sure that it was secure and free of snipers or threatening outworks. As the position received the nod, he galloped to the front of his batteries to direct firing operations. Magersfontein had, of course, shown that reliable reconnaissance was hard to come by in largely unknown Natal countryside. Failure to make allowance for this would now have fatal consequences for the British artillerymen.

As its guns rolled forward, Long's unprotected brigade ran into a dense wall of rifle fire and shrapnel from thickly concealed enemy positions 1 200 yards ahead across the Tugela. Rapidly finding their range, entrenched riflemen toppled most of the artillery officers from their horses, including Long. Their stricken gunners, unable to establish the bearings of a well-hidden enemy, fired erratically and to no avail. With hundreds dead and many more wounded, the survivors withdrew to safer covered ground, abandoning their guns and other equipment. Some suicidal sorties were attempted to try to retrieve the weaponry, but each failed. After several hours, concluding that the battle was lost, Buller called off any further rescue attempts. Discarded guns were hauled off smartly by the Boers, who crossed the Tugela and descended like vultures to grab the tempting spoils.[221]

This was not the only one-sided confrontation. The other main assaulting brigade, under Major General Arthur Hart, made progress sufficiently slowly to allow the Boers to plot its advance and to ward off any charge. As Hart's troops cautiously pushed towards a ford in the Tugela, angling through a sharp curve in the river, they were suddenly mown down by heavy fire from three sides. With Hart's brigade trapped in close formation, the ambush was bloody, with the British dead and wounded mounting to over 400 within little more than thirty minutes. Halting and then breaking into scattered and barely coordinated groups, fragments of Hart's force stubbornly formed and re-formed in their efforts to maintain the fight. It was courageous, but futile. The strident insistence on a close-order, parade ground advance over open ground against Boer entrenchments had been very costly. 'Hart had his usual slaughter,' observed a mordant Major Henry Wilson, concluding that he was 'a perfect disgrace . . . quite mad and incapable under fire'.[222]

As Buller's reserve brigades began to head out towards the offensive line, the realisation seemed to dawn that he was walking into defeat. He gave up the engagement, stopping new troop deployment and recalling ammunition and supplies being fed to gun batteries on the bank of the Tugela. He also had, finally, to relinquish the guns judged essential to blasting away the Boers around Ladysmith. Any continuation of the offensive to relieve the town appeared lost. For the British, Colenso had miscarried horrendously, with Buller's army losing some 1 130 men to republican losses of forty commandos. The *Cape Argus* was not the only paper to call it 'another Majuba' or 'a second Majuba'.[223] Faced with calamity, Buller's responses amounted to something like a declaration of bankruptcy. To a bemused Lansdowne, he confessed to being 'frightened' by the 'utter collapse' of his troops, neglecting to explain the misguided route of attack that he had inflicted upon them.[224] And, on 16 December, there was a sensational heliograph missive to the hapless White, in which a despondent Buller suggested that if Ladysmith proved unable to hold out for a further month, the garrison should expend as much of its ammunition as possible and seek 'best terms' with the enemy. The British Cabinet was dismayed by this blushing display of candour by heliograph, with a grumpy Lansdowne warning that the loss would be regarded as 'a national disaster of the greatest magnitude'.[225] A chastened Buller returned to the campaign, hoping for no further mishaps.

Stormberg, Magersfontein, and Colenso represented the high-water mark of conventional republican success in the field, in which the advancing British had been fairly easily held at bay or roundly beaten in surprise counter-attack. These 'Black Week' reversals or disasters, as they became unpopularly known in Britain, also brought low its commander-in-chief in South Africa. Militarist and patriotic sentiment was outraged by the continuation of the sieges and by the humiliation of battlefield reversals inflicted on a powerful army by a pastoralist militia. Liberals sprang to the defence of honest but ill-used British soldiers, attacking the government for taking risks with the Boers while neglecting

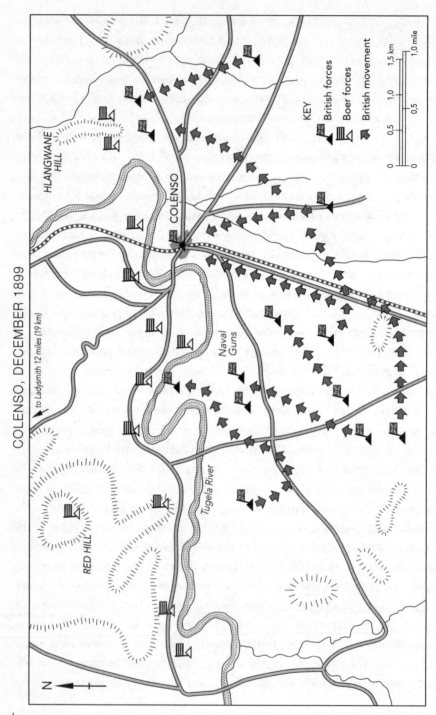

COLENSO, DECEMBER 1899

HLANGWANE HILL

COLENSO

to Ladysmith 12 miles (19 km)

Naval Guns

Tugela River

RED HILL

N

KEY

British forces

Boer forces

British movement

0   0,5   1,0   1,5 km

0   0,5   1,0 mile

adequate military preparedness.[226] Stung, the War Office moved to replace a now inglorious Buller. Natal had finished him, and his lame-duck sacking was unavoidable. Critical historical assessments of his South African leadership are legion, although Thomas Pakenham has made a case for a fairer credit rating.[227] Perhaps the truth about Buller lies somewhere between his second-rate generalship, and the fact that it was his misfortune to have been placed in command at a stage when no one could really have succeeded against the Boers. Perhaps anyone given his hand would have come up short.

His chronically intriguing successor, appointed just two days after Colenso, was Field Marshal Lord Frederick Sleigh Roberts, who had already been badgering for some time to be given the British army's South African command.[228] With the spartan Lord Horatio Herbert Kitchener as chief of staff, Roberts had much to do, and he was soon receiving the men to do it. In the days immediately following Black Week, a full field force of 47 000 troops reached South Africa, and before the end of 1899 further divisions of 20 000 regulars and 20 000 volunteers had been mobilised and put to sea. Their new command, Roberts and Kitchener, reached Cape Town on 10 January 1900. Now, if any confirmation were still needed, it could be nothing but war to the finish.

In this temporary lull, the republicans were not doing very much to settle the outcome. The British failures of Black Week had prised things open, almost inviting a capitalising counterstroke from some bold and resolute Boer leader.

Exposed to a broader offensive, the Cape Colony virtually asked for deeper penetration to throttle the strategic junction of De Aar, thereby severing Methuen's supply lines. On the eastern front, almost half of Natal remained under the enemy thumb. With the British confined or paralysed, rampant Orange Free State commandos in their most southerly groupings had pegged out a substantial swathe of land running down to within 120 miles of the Indian ocean. One purposeful Boer strategy at this stage, now that the invaders had been rocked back on their heels, might have been to launch a counter-offensive against Gatacre and Methuen's forces, which were dispiritedly binding their wounds and counting their corpses. Yet, the Boers failed to press their advantage. Aside from a few minor scraps in the Cape, there was barely any further contestation or serious fighting. Admittedly, republican command could not always assume that all of their men would have the constitution for another test. But a key factor in their restraint was the calibre of older and reticent Boer generalship which was inclined to be dilatory rather than dynamic, even when the going was good.

However galling to the imperial psyche and however injurious to the well-being of more vulnerable sections of the civilian besieged, republican siege warfare ground on in its pedestrian way. In Natal, younger Boer generals increased pressure upon Joubert to move more decisively against Ladysmith, particularly now that the Buller–White débâcle had added the advantage of good timing to an already strong position. Joubert finally ordered a heavy strike on 2 January, aimed at snatching the commanding heights of Platrand ridge from which further fire could be rained on the town. The Boers failed in their objective, but only after a lengthy, raging battle in which the beleaguered British held on at a cost of over 400 casualties, more than twice the losses of their enemy.

Meanwhile at New Year, to the west around Colesberg, French also came to a decision. Fixed on the need to prevent the republican tide in the Cape midlands from lapping deeper into the colony, a 2 000-strong force was pushed forward against Commandant Hendrik Schoeman's strong point, held by 4 000 commandos. French's initial charge was damaging, but a renewed night attack on 5 January to further turn the Boers was, unexpectedly, firmly repulsed. French had contained the enemy, reassured by Buller that his was the 'right policy. Worry them'.[229] Yet British losses were once more disproportionately heavy.

To the east, Buller himself had not yet played out his hand. Roberts allowed him continuing command of the Natal army, either through thoughtful tact or some perverse calculation that a sidelined rival might as well be given more rope. So Buller's campaign position was duly strengthened, with his forces profiting from the rising flow of reinforcements. By early January he had 30 000 troops at his disposal. At the same time, Roberts had no intention of permitting him to go about his own business without interference. While still on the way to South Africa, he repeatedly cabled his Natal commander to remain on the defensive and mark time. Any operations under subsidiary command would have to be under Roberts' overall direction. But a stung Buller declined to dance to this tune. Colenso may have got him the boot, but this setback did not mean that his punctured reputation was beyond all repair. There was still the chance of a renewed offensive to unseat the Boers around Ladysmith.

Sure enough, on 10 January, the day of Roberts' and Kitchener's arrival, Buller headed out from his Chievely camp to have a second stab at the besieged town. This time, he reverted to his original approach, which had been to hold the republicans at Colenso while his forces pushed around to bear down on Ladysmith from the west. The operation involved marching the main British forces some eighteen miles upstream to Trichardt's Drift, the chosen avenue of penetration across the Tugela, and then closing in by cutting between the hills of Spioen Kop and Twin Peaks. Buller left the implementation of this advance to Lieutenant General Sir Charles Warren, notoriously hot-tempered and on bad terms with his commander-in-chief.[230]

As estimates, for once reliable, confirmed that there were few Boers menacing Warren's chosen passage when his force set out, all he apparently needed was the confidence to keep pushing through. But Buller's army was to have a bad time even before it bumped into its first commando. The rivers were in flood, the roads were waterlogged or so washed away as to force repeated diversions, and the British were themselves so overburdened by supplies and indulgent baggage (taken on the principle of why include one mess table when two would suffice), that a journey of twenty-one miles took the best part of a week. As the Natal army panted onwards, the republicans limbered up in preparation. They scrutinised danger points and repositioned some of their front, leaving a few light lines behind outworks to keep up the deception. Dozy British reconnaissance failed to ascertain some feverish moves which had been taken by the Boers to reinforce the steep heights running to Twin Peaks. Nor did their advancing enemy latch on to the fact that the western limits of the republicans' position had actually been pushed several miles beyond where it was thought they ended. From various crests, the movement of Buller's columns lay under continuous surveillance, and British hopes of working their way round without bringing down anything on their heads were about to be horribly dashed.

On 20 January and again the following day, Warren's assault column, having found a secure foothold on the bank of the Tugela, tried to rush the enemy encampment on Twin Peaks. These attacks were beaten back. Combined with Boer pressure elsewhere, the setback soon disabused the British of any idea of easily outflanking their enemy. An apoplectic Buller urged a further sortie against the Twin Peaks position, but Warren only foresaw a third reversal against durable defences on steep ground. With withdrawal not the most ideal option at this probing stage, Warren then proposed taking Spioen Kop, an assault to which Buller consented. Rising all of 550 yards above the level of the Tugela, the Kop was seen as a commanding fire point for volleys with which to enfilade enemy trenches tucked into surrounding lower koppies. Thereby lay a way of breaking Boer lines.

In settling on Spioen Kop, Warren made a sorry misjudgement. Far from trapping the defenders, it would prove to be a hole for their attackers. This was inherently unsafe ground, a kind of no-man's land forming a salient reaching into the enemy position. Its exposed flanks and impermeable topping made it so indefensible that the Boers had themselves only committed a very light holding force there. There was no defence in depth because it was judged to be ultimately indefensible. Spioen Kop's slender picket defence, and the fact that this time surprise was achieved by the attackers, eased the opening intervention. On 23 January, a rampant British night assault, with further cover provided by thick mist, saw the Boer sentries gutted by the bayonets of Lieutenant Colonel Alec Thorneycroft's infantry, and other commandos put to flight by the British charge. Backed by an artillery bombardment to deter anyone from contemplating a return to the fight, Thorneycroft's troops deposited themselves on the summit and awaited the dawn light in which to begin exploiting their occupied hilltop stronghold.

But as the sun rose and the mist dissipated, chilling realisation set in. For a start, the British were once again not where they thought they were. Instead of occupying the summit, they had based themselves on a hazardous front ridge, an extremely shallow depression below which the ground fell away sharply to a wide plateau. Secondly, all the close approaches to their position were situated in classic 'dead' terrain that was sterilised by its angle against downwards defending fire. This was ready-made for darting commandos to snake their way to within close striking distance of the lip of ground which held their crouching enemy. Thirdly, Spioen Kop lay wholly exposed to Boer fire from Twin Peaks and other adjacent heights. Lastly, burrowing for entrenchment was an almost impossible task on the immensely hard hill rock, against which the frantically flailing picks and shovels of Warren's men could make only the barest excavation. Their moody commander, moreover, was not helping: he seemed to have calculated little beyond successfully delivering his force to its assigned location. Warren had neglected to improvise proper defensive support, had failed to lay out navigable paths for withdrawal, and would not countenance surrender. Such foolhardiness betrayed an almost criminal carelessness towards the lives of his men.

The commando picket which fell back from Spioen Kop gave Joubert and Botha plenty of time in which to react to an assault which, it was clear, would end by their pinning the enemy to a fixed point. Early in the morning of 24 January they proceeded on horseback to review their positions, distributed an encouraging wire from Kruger to officers, and told commandos to their face of the dangerous confrontation which now loomed. Urging their men to oust the British from the heights at all costs, Boer commanders threatened to flog slackers, cowards, or those who tried to dodge orders. The final and bloody phase of the Spioen Kop action now began.

Once the early-morning light was sufficiently clear for the Boers to roll their guns forward and fix their range, devastating artillery and rifle cross-fire from the adjoining heights pummelled the British position from three sides. The Spioen Kop location virtually funnelled fire into a huddled mass of unprotected troops. Warren, no longer gloating over what had first seemed to be the easy capture of the hill and dismayed by the unexpected raking of his position, now looked for a way out. Reinforcements under Major General Talbot Coke were shoved up to fortify the ridge, under the accurate barrels of Boer guns whose shells tore through the advancing force. Coming at a run across open country, they had no covering bombardment – Warren held off for fear of striking his own troops. 'It was utter madness,' recalled one infantryman, 'to have placed ourselves in that spot.'[231]

Meanwhile, in the rear, Buller was not yet blunted. Heartened by reports of Thorneycroft's night assault achievement, he ordered Warren to hand him command of Spioen Kop, which looked increasingly like a mountain-top pit which was swallowing those who had dug it. Inexplicably, Warren neglected to advise Talbot Coke, whose nimble force was feeling the weight of casualties, of this new command arrangement. Well into the evening of 24 January, with his eyes still fixed on the Spioen Kop plateau, Talbot Coke slipped down its slope for a briefing with Buller to establish exactly what was going on.

Then came a truly astonishing turn of events. As Talbot Coke's reinforcing troops more or less ground to a halt, a troubled Thorneycroft decided quite independently that his brief hour was over. Breaking off, he ordered a rapid evacuation of his over-exposed position. At that moment, it looked the sensible thing to do. This bizarre lapse in British coordination has been part of virtually every available account of the battle of Spioen Kop.[232] It bears retelling, perhaps only

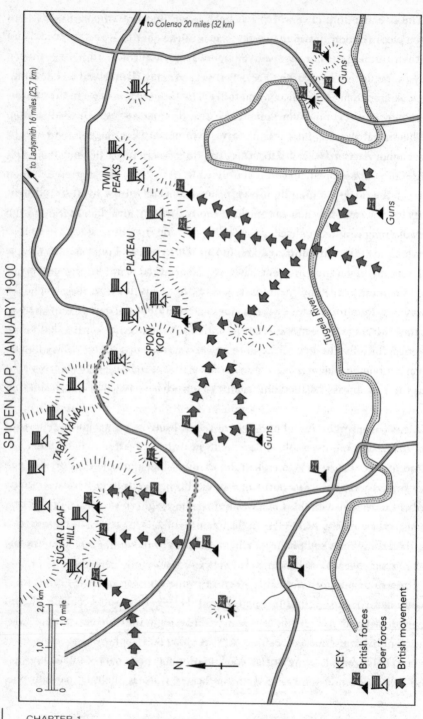

SPIOEN KOP, JANUARY 1900

to Colenso 20 miles (32 km)

to Ladysmith 16 miles (25,7 km)

TWIN PEAKS

PLATEAU

SPION KOP

TABANYAMA

SUGAR LOAF HILL

Guns

Guns

Guns

Tugela River

N

2,0 km

1,0 mile

0

KEY

British forces

Boer forces

British movement

as a text-book illustration of the poorly controlled line of command which beset British operations in the earlier stages of the conflict.

At the same time, not every advantage was flowing towards the Boers, even though the British were falling back. For, as the enemy withdrawal was developing, commando fire also began to die away. The men crammed around the flanks of Spioen Kop and on Twin Peaks were also evacuating their ground as they were gradually overcome by an infantry counter-attack in a belated forward diversionary action. It was, altogether, an odd moment of battlefield symmetry. The Boer commandos who could simply walk in to carry the shattered Spioen Kop ridge now abandoned their own positions to the King's Royal Rifle Corps. In effect, the two sides almost cancelled each other out, although in the end the republicans prevailed.

Strategically, ground lost or taken in this battle was of trivial significance: it did nothing much to alter the balance of power in the Natal theatre. It has not been judged a 'futile day', or a 'useless waste of life',[233] without reason. The action saw great efforts made by both sides and a savage confrontation of shattering intensity. Casualties from relentless shelling were heavy, with losses being borne mainly by the British, who lost over 1 100 troops killed, wounded, or taken prisoner. It is a telling fact that most of Buller's army were not even released into the battle lines. Neither Buller nor Warren was heedful of the weakening condition of their men; they merely pushed reinforcements towards the fringes of the engagement as a kind of diversionary measure to blunt the sting of main battle.

Meanwhile, although Boer casualties mounted comparatively slowly, they, too, had topped 300 by the end of the day. In scorching heat, across hard and jagged terrain, with little cover and less water, the costly tactical pattern of fighting consisted of virtually endless republican bombardment. Each side was also keeping the enemy lines under almost constant attack and counter-attack by frontal assault; there were Boer flanking attempts to carry enemy defences, and opposing British formations were either wilting, just holding firm, or falling back briefly before having their front sufficiently stiffened to surge back to regain position. On and around the British defences just about every piece of ground was frantically and bitterly contested in pitched battles. Entrenched or rutted belts of that ground, a kind of no-man's land, held the broken remains of those who had been killed, most of them British. The scene was nightmarish: wounded men crawled, others were quietly dying; everywhere there were torn corpses already darkened by their mantles of ants and flies, and, as night began to draw in, the more isolated bodies, slumped in rocky extremities, were being sniffed and dismembered by hyenas.

For the wounded, the only safe passage away from the battlefield was the Natal Indian Ambulance Corps, funded and otherwise supported by the pro-imperial merchant and professional interests collected around M.K. Gandhi. Comprising a company of some 1 100 bearers, mostly of sugar-estate indentured labourers together with a sprinkling of artisans and middle-class volunteers, it remained perilously close to the firing line, ready to stretcher Buller's casualties from Spioen Kop. While the locally raised Corps was to be used in a number of major eastern front engagements, clearing this arena was by far its bloodiest im-mersion in battle. Gandhi's volunteers 'won great admiration from British com-mand for its endurance in dangerous conditions and preparedness to tackle the messy business of seeing to the maimed and the dead'.[234]

Perhaps the single most striking photograph from this stage of the conflict was the grisly image of hundreds of dead British infantrymen stacked up in their trenches, some visibly mutilated. The scene underlined the reality of an offensive which was now taking an ominously bad turn. That said, Botha and Joubert had burdens of their own in the Tugela sector. In their lines, too, the horrific conditions around Spioen Kop had begun to tell on morale. So did the sapping exertion of repeated attacks on the cornered British, each time being beaten back. Each may have produced a few more yards' progress, but that was all; a deciding breakthrough remained elusive. One part of the republican prob-lem was lack of numbers to sustain an offensive spirit. Fatigued and drooping commandos, close to breaking point, had few reserves on hand to provide line relief. Again, a familiar index of collapsing resolve was defiant desertion, with increasing numbers of Boers ignoring the pleas and threats of their commanders to continue fighting.

As the day ground on, disenchanted and demoralised burghers flitted away homewards, sometimes taking only their rifles and ammunition while leaving behind almost all their personal belongings right down to tobacco and Bibles.[235] A number of observers have credited the moral exertions of Louis Botha with having saved the Boer forces in the Tugela basin from complete rout. His per-suasive zeal notwithstanding, it seems apparent that by nightfall the hard centre of the defence line was crumbling away inexorably. In truth, here, too, it was just about all up, although precious little advantage came of it for Buller.

Indeed, if there was a peculiarity about Spioen Kop, it was that neither side grasped quite how badly its adversary was doing. Close to the end of their tether, British officers concluded that before orderly movement around their tenuously held position became impossible, they should break off and retreat in advance of any authorisation from Warren. They seemingly had little inkling of how much Botha's own lines were buckling, how many of their enemy were quitting the battlefield as well. Far from exploiting any moment of advantage for fresh onslaughts, the faltering, combat-fatigued men relaxed their grip. When Warren heard that commandos had given up the fight altogether, he was intent on staging a renewed assault. But Buller had come to accept that his wilting troops had borne enough. In ordering a comprehensive withdrawal across the Tugela, he simply gave up. Equally, there was no republican stomach for any pursuit. In the very early hours of 25 January, probing Boer scouts found Spioen Kop deserted. An extraordinarily resilient Botha then performed one further act of endurance, scratching together a band of commandos to dart up to the summit to demonstrate that the engagement had paid off. However, with so many fighters having fled, there were relatively few left to recognise the gesture.[236] It was victory in a battle which, in a sense, almost ran down of itself.

Shrugging off the outcome of Spioen Kop, Buller returned to the focal point of his strategy, an offensive large enough to deal with Ladysmith. At this stage, a disgraced Warren could be blamed for the late-January failure. Back in London, *The Times* continued to urge 'the British nation to keep a stiff upper lip'.[237] As the hunger, dysentery and general misery of the siege situation worsened, Buller worked up another offensive to relieve White, who was wrangling with the War Office over what was now looking dismayingly possible – a surrender of the town. Like some other early British planning, Buller's renewed sortie amounted to little more than charging the enemy at its secure holding points, where the likely depth and defensive line formation had not been adequately established. While he had plenty of anxieties, unfortunately, too few of these seemed to be tactical.

Buller, resolved to simplify and to hasten the line of advance, moved to carry the Boer defences on the Vaalkranz and Doornkop hills. Once these were overrun, the British could hope for an unimpeded thrust through to White. They did not expect much resistance: many beaten commandos had fallen back to republican territory, and with Botha himself having left the fighting zone, it seemed that success might at last smile. With only very minor opposing forces holding the hills, it was assumed that a numerically strong attack would do the trick.

On 5 February, Buller forged ahead with an army of 20 000 men, some of its officers convinced that, with such resources, Boer nerve would now break completely. At first, matters did indeed seem to be going their way, as a brigade under Neville Lyttelton sliced through to the dominating Vaalkranz headland, beating down fiercely held Boer lines. Lyttelton's force then looked to a converging assault to consolidate the initial successful push, a move which would close up Doornkop. The entire advance was based on a staggered series of diversionary troop movements and feint attacks designed to bluff the defenders as to where the British really aimed to make their chief gains.

But Buller's adversaries were not taken in. Unexpectedly dense fire struck the British head on, severing planned coordination between the attacking infantry and cavalry. Buller then stopped. Feeling inclined to break off the action, he wheeled away from his Doornkop target. Now, instead of in an improved position, Lyttelton found himself in one significantly more precarious. The Boers ahead of him, anticipating further blows, moved rapidly to switch resources into the depleted defences commanded by a nervous General Ben Viljoen. Botha was recalled from Pretoria and, with the defenders' delaying capacity now strengthened by more than 2 000 men, by sunset further British action to capture Vaalkranz had been thwarted.

Neither side had anything to spare with which to clinch an advantage, so Lyttelton urged an uncertain Buller to stop hanging about and reopen the original strike against Doornkop. Buller did not like the suggestion, although he did consider it. Neither could he conceive of any other way of going forward. He hesitated, committed reinforcements to Lyttelton but then watered them down, consulted with an alternately reproachful and wearily resigned Roberts, and tinkered with various offensive preparations. Well into the following day, he was still dithering.

By then, Boer leadership had decided not to await any further attack. Towards dusk they concentrated their commandos, made sure that the wind was continuing to blow towards the enemy, and fired the grass and scrub as screening to cover a coordinated angling assault, which struck hard enough to set back the British. Late on 7 February, a wobbly Buller decided at last to withdraw, having lost over 400 killed, wounded, or missing. Four days later the entire Natal force slumped back to its Chievely starting base. They had sustained another 2 000 casualties in all in this failed effort to demolish republican defences.

The confrontation at Vaalkranz and Doornkop marked the end of the opening British operation in one important sense: it was to be the last set-piece action in the old Black Week style. Even General Buller seemed finally to realise that something was going badly wrong, and that the successful resumption of a British advance required other ways of securing and retaining the initiative. The key to that leap forward, to which we now turn, had little to do with consuming sieges or formidable battles, and rather more with logistics and improved mobility, adherence to more exacting techniques and tactics, and elaborately prepared movements of encirclement.

A major change was about to be made in the method the British would adopt to conduct their laborious offensive.

6
THE LONG ROAD TO JO'BURG

THE BATTLE FOR LADYSMITH HAD REACHED STALEMATE, BUT ITS CONclusion was close. On 17 February 1900, General Buller made another effort to relieve the town, now into its fourth month of siege and hanging on desperately for his liberating army.

After the three consecutive setbacks, his prospects looked bleak, but his luck finally began to take a turn for the better. At first, though, the British move made an inauspicious start. The familiar, crawling progress of their overweight army (its commander never one to stint on troops' provisions), further impeded by ground grown almost tidal through severe rains, gave the republicans plenty of opportunity to make a stand on their threatened Colenso front. It looked as if the old story of a Natalian road leading nowhere might well be repeated.

The Boers brought in reinforcements to strengthen their key hill positions, but could only muster some 5 000 commandos. Their command was now also facing serious distractions to the west, events which were bottling up men. And Buller had a better tactical plan.

This time, instead of drawing the enemy into a single converging battle, the British sweep towards Ladysmith took the incremental form of well-rehearsed assaults against a crop of defensive koppies to the east of Colenso. For this, Buller decided to direct the whole of his army, now swollen to 25 000 men, against enemy positions. Crucially, in carrying their renewed attack the British began to do more. As they approached, troops constructed defensive field positions as a forward screen. Tighter signals coordination between moving infantry and artillery meant that bombardments of Boer defences could be lifted at the moment that the men stormed out of their trench lines. It was still a gruelling, stumbling passage against ambushing sharp-shooters. But despite the heavy fire, Buller's forces broke through, overrunning a succession of hills and triggering Boer flight from a further hill base. With these defensive strongpoints out of action, the Tugela line was finally broken and Buller had secured an opening to Ladysmith, though still a dangerous one.

Aware that their enemy now had no defence in any depth, the British believed they faced little more than brittle rearguard resistance. Exhausted, depressed by the elephantine strength of the enemy, the Boer defensive effort was finally at an end.

As their front began to melt away into mass flight, a hard-pressed republican command began bickering over the conduct of affairs in Natal. A fatalistic Louis Botha, realistic in his perception of the odds against him, was resigned to the unstoppability of a growing commando stampede, and argued for abandoning Ladysmith altogether before all remaining order broke down. It was an early lesson in what could no longer be withstood when 'the English' were pouring in in such droves.[238] Kruger, however, was all for staying in the game, believing that the dispatch of the increasingly arthritic Piet Joubert to the Tugela would somehow persuade burghers to get on with the manly task.[239]

At the same time, the remaining republican main body was not completely at a loss over what to do about the continuing British advance. Having acquired considerable bridging proficiency in the sodden Natal countryside, Buller's force hardened its breach of the Boer defences by throwing a pontoon across the Tugela to shift men and equipment into and through the valley on the northern bank. As the head of the column pushed beyond the far shoreline, their adversaries struck back. Crammed into a cluster of flanking hills, they caught the British on the move, subjecting them to withering fire. Buller, nevertheless, continued to send his troops across the river, assembling them on the narrow bank where they simply backed up behind their disabled advance column. In four days of hard fighting, the British struggled to hack away those defences on the upper reaches which were checking their thrust, while the Boers launched a desperate assault to close off the advance. The remaining koppie positions then fell into Buller's hands, but not before his force had sustained 1 400 casualties. On 25 February the fighting came to a halt, Buller and Botha having agreed to a ceasefire in order that their men could turn away from killing, bind up their wounded and inter their dead. During this interlude the British withdrew across the Tugela, prompting some commandos to hope against hope that they might yet have prevailed. But their position was lost.

Buller was drawing back only to re-form in order to attack afresh, and the assault came on 27 February (ironically, the anniversary of Majuba Hill). The panic-stricken defenders, pulverised by artillery fire which shrouded their positions in thick clouds of dust and spinning stone splinters, took off in complete disarray, followed by British infantry with lunging bayonets. Botha had no hope of holding a firm rearguard behind which commandos could fall back along an orderly riding escape route. It was just as well for him that Buller stayed his hand and did not press pursuit.

After the best part of a fortnight's heavy fighting over the Ladysmith position, the British had built up momentum and were conserving an offensive surplus. The Boers were on their knees. Joubert, now a sick and ailing man, merely drifted, while around him the erosion of morale intensified with awareness of serious reversal on the western front.

Rarely one to keep out of the way, Kruger again urged that the Boer forces stand on the defensive. Cronjé heard him out respectfully, but had sense enough to discount presidential pleas. In no state to deter fresh onslaughts, he authorised the tired republican command to abandon the Ladysmith siege lines altogether. Few, if any, of those holding these lines were much put out by this, swiftly rolling up tents and loading wagons to wind their way back to the homesteads of the interior countryside. It was sobering confirmation of the blunder that led the Boers to maintain static positions around Ladysmith. Having failed to break in from a superior position, they now flaked away.

On 28 February, a British mounted brigade pushed through an open door to relieve the town. Buller sealed victory two days later with a more grandiose, stage-managed show in which he and White turned out for a solicitous pumping of hands. It was an unusual public display. The general had, hitherto, not exactly been a friend of the press, empowering Natal military intelligence to censor news telegrams and to intercept letter dispatches conveyed by African runners. He did not want any correspondents' reports on Ladysmith's sliding morale, its diminishing supplies, and the atrocious state of its hospital camp to be disclosed to the Boers, fearing that news of the messy state of affairs could have encouraged an attack. Having largely infiltrated the runner circuits, the Boers probably knew all this anyway.[240]

Reimposing control had cost the British Natal army around 5 500 casualties, something which took the gloss off Buller's memorably hearty special order of 3 March, in which the offensive became an enthralling enterprise, a further 'glorious page' to add to 'the History of the British Empire'. The Natal town's 'hollow-eyed' inhabitants were less ecstatic, worn out by the miserable game of 'waiting for Buller'.[241] Back in Britain, news of the relief of Ladysmith went to patriotic heads, bringing celebrating crowds onto its streets. Yet there were also sceptical observers who concluded that it was scarcely a triumph, and that Buller and White would have done well not 'to crow'.[242]

Not that any of this mattered to the dislodged republicans, who by early March were in full and disorganised retreat. Irate commanders attempted to stem the flood by issuing hollow threats to shoot their horses, confiscate their stores, or to torch their wagons. Among some younger and more resolute officers, there was still a lingering hope of keeping a bit of something going in the Natal theatre, but it was a forlorn one. Falling back at a trot up a familiar route, commandos stripped their Elandslaagte provisioning base of anything portable and incinerated the rest in a roaring bonfire. Leaving behind a fiery scar, they were out of Natal – but not out of the war.

By this time, Lord Roberts was rapidly extending his controlling share of the imperial advance. What faced so calculating a man was the obvious physical problem of South Africa, its size, and the vastness of its veld. Through all the extensive desk-bound calculations and strategy briefings that informed him ran common campaigning sense. The only way to snuff out the enemy was to penetrate through to strategic points to carry a hostile veld and deny it to the Boers. Part of his solution lay in numbers.

By early 1900, with major imperial reinforcements continuing to stream in, he had amassed a force of more than 180 000 soldiers, an army whose size was now already virtually the size of the total combined white population of the republics. Another part of the solution lay in the manner of advance. This was not a war which would be won by railways. Roberts concluded that a push all the way up the rail routes in order to keep close supply lines would play into Boer hands. It would give the enemy the advantage of knowing when and where best to strike, and where to base or shift defensive strongpoints. Having massed his forces, therefore, he decided to assemble just north of Orange River Station, and then to run hard east and west, pocketing strategic gains in a lunge right into the marrow of the Boer states.

The opening move was intended to carry the British across more than 120 miles of open countryside, in a westerly direction along the rail line to Kimberley, and then to unleash forces in an eastwards drive away from the railway to a central consolidating point just south of Bloemfontein. There, astride the railway and menacing the Orange Free State capital, Roberts envisaged that so critical a national situation for the Boers would force them into battle, which in turn would draw commandos away from the Mafeking, Kimberley and Ladysmith sieges as well as the Cape midlands. The war would be fought within the Boer states; and the increasingly disorderly Boer armies could be destroyed. The prime objectives were to force the capitulation of Bloemfontein, and then of Pretoria. Thereafter, the British could snuff out any remaining opposition by cutting off access points – taking command of the eastwards branch line to Durban, and controlling the inland coastal link from Mozambique.

Offensive preparations were made on the customary elaborate scale, their nature chronicled in quite stupefying detail by some previous histories of this war. In fact, the makings of an effective field force may be fairly easily grasped in summary terms. For the British, the running of the war now became both more composed and more exact in intention. Thus, Roberts made a basic contribution to the education of his troops through the wide dissemination of instructional 'Guidance' notes on 'South African Warfare', stressing the survival imperatives of improved shooting, rapid movement, proper systems of concealment, and a freer hand to take independent, individual initiative against their enemy. Colonel Percy Girouard, who, as director of railways, had been moving on from Sudanese labour to the recruitment and control of Ciskeian and Transkeian workers in South Africa, was entrusted with rail schedules and timetables.

The British also desperately needed more horsemen to throw against an enemy comprised of natural mounted riflemen who were well able to fight from the saddle. Their command had barely 14 000 mounted men available in October 1899. Under the severe and bristling John French, a new cavalry division was formed and, to beef up deficient reconnaissance capacity and to make British mobility tell, the complement of mounted infantry was greatly increased. Every battalion had to provide a mounted company, and these were augmented by local colonial mounted-rifle contingents. These were irregular 'bush' units, such as Rimington's Scouts or 'Tigers' (so dubbed because of the strips of leopard fur worn on their hats), mostly enlisted Uitlander riders who knew the countryside well, could speak Dutch, and had some interpreting facility in African languages.[243] Unsurprisingly, some of those enlisted irregulars also possessed other, less admirable qualities: the smouldering resentments of marginal men, or drifters with a taste for violence, or antisocial misfits with scores to pay off and an eagerness to take on any dirty work.

This mounted infantry expansion was accompanied by enhanced efforts to make the British forces less conspicuous targets. Grey horses were dyed to provide a camouflaging zebra effect which was more difficult to pick up at a distance; cavalrymen's buttons were dulled by brown leather, and mess tins and lance butts were painted over to prevent them from flashing in the sun. In addition to having to train urbanised infantrymen as riders, some of whom thought that horses were fed on beef or mutton, the animals themselves had to be obtained. Commandeering or the costly purchase of mounts from Cape farmers or African peasants produced some, but not nearly enough. In any event, local ponies met light Boer requirements, but tended mostly to buckle under the weighty paraphernalia of a fully equipped cavalryman or mounted infantryman.[244] By early 1900, Roberts had already brought in more than 12 000 horses from Argentina, Australia and Britain itself, with many hundreds of thousands more to come. The maintenance of forage and other supply systems would soon overwhelm a poorly staffed and massively overburdened remount department. By the end of the war, 66 per cent of all the horses used had been ridden to death, turning South Africa into a kind of imperial knacker's yard for what the Australian writer, 'Banjo' Patterson, called the battered old campaigners.[245]

Roberts took two other steps to increase field force efficiencies and to establish an expanded and more predictable communications environment. Colonel George Henderson, the director of Military Intelligence, began to coordinate the compiling of a comprehensively detailed map of his planned theatre of operations, hoping thereby to reduce that persistently worrying margin of territorial unfamiliarity. Secondly, Roberts and Kitchener reorganised and unified the existing dispersed regimental transport and supply system into a general transport train, splicing together column ox-wagon and mule-cart companies into a makeshift single-service department. This, though, was staffed by mostly inexperienced transport officers who found themselves floundering. Dispatching an army from Cape Town to Pretoria was equivalent in distance to moving it from Vienna to St Petersburg, and demands on British supply, from raising transport and procuring forage to lifting food and stores, was already a daunting enterprise. The wonderful plan for technical cohesion managed to make matters worse as trickling, consolidated convoys became stuck through error and misfortune. Unintelligent meddling in this sector did Roberts no credit, and after groaning under it for an alarmingly long time, the army was obliged finally to restore a version of its own traditional, decentralised, and dedicated transport system.[246] Roberts liked to be in charge, but by no means was everything under him run competently.

Other early signs, however, were more positive. In selecting renewed avenues of advance, the army sought to guard against further defeat in the field by preserving the advantage of surprise. Up to now the Boers had had plenty of warning, but now Roberts contrived a clever ruse. By the beginning of February, he had mustered around 60 000 soldiers in an assault column occupying the forward ground between the Modder and Orange rivers. Tailing south, it reinforced French's force outside Colesberg, and its coiled presence induced Cronjé, entrenched behind Magersfontein, to assume there would be a direct British move from there towards Kimberley. To cultivate this perception, military intelligence turned from mapping the sectors ahead to the assiduous peddling of casual reports, rumours and semi-confirmations. Some of this carefully crafted misinformation was dribbled out by well-paid African spies and snoops in the employ of intelligence officers.[247] Cronjé took the bait, drawing in around 8 000 soldiers to repel an anticipated frontal attack.

On 11 February the British came, but they cut eastwards in a wide circling movement from their Orange-Modder base, with the intention of outflanking Cronjé's defensive position and then readying themselves in strength to fall on the enemy headquarters. Confronting this approach, the Boers could have punctured the British supply lines at De Aar and Naauwpoort, but this opportunity was not taken. French's cavalry division was pulled up from Colesberg and given orders to grab the fords across the Modder and Riet rivers as a corridor of infantry advance, and thereafter to wheel around the republican position at Magersfontein for a run at Kimberley. Astutely leaving behind their tents as further deception, the British set out in darkness, with Cronjé only some hours later dispatching General Christiaan de Wet to keep pace with French's manoeuvre. The uncertainty created by intermittent British changes of direction soon began to wear on Boer nerves as frustrated commandos waited for a sign of resolution. When and where would their enemy try to strike a blow?

French kept his nerve in the toiling drive (11 to 15 February) through fierce heat, but lost a good many horses, with over 500 dying or broken through lack of water, adequate forage and exhaustion from pulling a train of heavy guns. As the British advanced to within a few miles of Cronjé's main camp, the Boers, still unsure of their enemy's intention, reinforced their defence of the southern approaches, throwing a shallow, crescent-shaped front south of the Modder River around Klip Drift. But French had planned well, and the Boers were too out of touch to notice the impending enclosure of their position. The fords were seized by the British, and the Kimberley advance then opened in a thundering rush. Early on 15 February, 6 000 cavalrymen moved in a wild charge across the open, flat, undefended countryside between Klip Drift and Kimberley. More than 800 Boer riflemen broke ranks and fled after a few random rifle volleys, knowing that to stand against such odds would mean not merely defeat but the near certainty of death or mutilation. French seized the opening he had been seeking, and thereafter wasted little time in pushing his fatigued troops in a closing line of advance around and above Kimberley. In the face of this commanding encroachment, backed by the replenishing weight of a large army now moving northwards, the republican siege position began to break up.

As French moved in on Kimberley, part of Roberts' following infantry columns veered off to take Jacobsdal, where Cronjé had very recently abandoned his headquarters, and to obliterate what was left of a resisting Boer presence in the area. But elsewhere not quite everything was going the way of the British. Towards the very rear of Roberts' advance, his inviting transport column of some 200 stockpiled wagons provided an opportunity for De Wet to make trouble. Leading some 1 000 horsemen, he attacked the supply train, cleverly aggravating the commotion by firing into the oxen to make them stampede (and, in due course, seeing that their African and Coloured drivers were treated with the usual leniency). Roberts, worried about exposing his lengthening communications line between the Riet and the Modder to possible attack from Cronjé, decided against any doubling back to recapture lost transport and stores, leaving his sweating and hungry men to pay the price with half rations or less.

Boer forces around Kimberley were now, more than ever, in the wrong place. With their numbers already falling off, they were too weak to make a stand, nor were they able to forge a reinforcing connection with Cronjé's distracted force at Magersfontein, which was being squeezed hard by a Methuen onslaught. There were a few half-hearted attempts at staging a fighting retreat, but these dissolved on realisation of the strength of the British cavalry bearing down on their flimsy lines. Flattening themselves as best they could, commandos crept away in a general abandonment of their position and headed for home. In some rough semblance of coordination, Cronjé retreated east while General Ignatius Ferreira led his Orange Free State force in a northerly direction, saving the republicans further injury. Meanwhile, Rhodes, never one to let an opportunity slip, muscled forward to welcome French as one John the Baptist to another, bold men of empire who had done the right thing by meeting Kimberley's need.

After this, brushing aside urgings from some subordinate officers to regroup for a counter-attack, a dispirited Cronjé decided to leave the central sector and pull back towards Bloemfontein. The Boers vacated their Magersfontein defences under cover of darkness. Around 5 000 commandos (some with their women and children in tow), 500 wagons and thousands of reserve horses, found an exit gap in the British lines through which to slip away into the Orange Free State. Heavily encumbered, they made exceedingly slow progress, giving French an opportunity for a further turn of the screw. Counting on his troops' growing combat motivation, he risked a smaller force of 1 200 to head off Cronjé's wagon convoy. On 17 February, aware that they were being pursued in turn by over 1 500 fresh commandos under Ferreira (who was committed to a diversionary operation), the British met the retreating enemy force at a drift on the Modder near Paardeberg. Keeping at a distance, French shelled the Boers, splintering wagons and pitting the ground. Cronjé became stuck.

French remained on the alert for Ferreira and another looming threat in the shape of De Wet and his 1 500 commandos. But his worries were eased on the following day with the arrival of Kitchener's substantial infantry complement. Having driven his troops hard – they had covered over thirty miles in twenty-four hours – a headstrong Kitchener moved immediately to an all-out assault on the enemy laager, evidently relishing the latitude of command granted him by Roberts. Eager to wipe out the Boers and achieve quick victory, he made no great effort to think through the offensive coordination of his 15 000 troops. Most of

his officers appear to have been left in the dark, while any who may have perceived the possibility of confusion stifled their doubts in the presence of an aloof
and intimidatingly relentless commander.[248]

Sure enough, the British ran into resolute resistance. A series of strong attacks
broke down against repelling fire from commandos dug into concealed positions
around the river bed, and Kitchener's assault waves broke into fragmented formations. Advancing or stopping in haphazard fashion, some units were yanked
forward by impetuous, fire-eating younger officers. There was plenty of fire to
eat: late in the day, the British eventually created a combined line of attack, which
was upended by a diversionary assault from De Wet. His twisting horsemen rode
up close without being detected, and then stormed in to capture a commanding
British hill position (which would later become known as 'Kitchener's Koppie').

This audacious incursion, and the arrival of Ferreira's force and other light
reinforcements from Bloemfontein, eased the pressure on the Boers, even if slightly. By nightfall on 18 February, Kitchener's remorseless offensive had slackened.
Men were withdrawn and guns wheeled back to pick off an approaching attack
from Ferreira and incoming Bloemfontein burghers, and to retake the elevated
position seized by De Wet. Gripped by some streak of cold courage, the entrenched commandos against whom Kitchener had launched his massive assault
had not given up their position on the Modder. They could do little more than
hold on, but were still able to make the enemy pay. By the time British command
decided at last to call off the fighting and dying, almost 1 300 troops were dead
or wounded, while the defending Boers had suffered 300 casualties.

But the outcome at Paardeberg was not to be decided by this particular piece
of brutal cost-benefit balancing. Cronjé's position, split between commandos dug
in on one bank of the river and a bunched wagon laager on the landward side,
was desperate. A break-in by more strong reinforcements might have opened a
fighting way out, but nothing was forthcoming. De Wet and several of Cronjé's
own subordinate commanders pleaded with him to strip down to the minimum
essentials and implement a speedy evacuation before his encampment became
entirely surrounded. The general's adversities were growing crueller as the odds
lengthened. Many of his men lacked serviceable horses or, indeed, any escape
mount, while the abandonment of trundling wagon transport put at risk the lives
of accompanying Boer women and children.

Paardeberg illustrated that the departure of Cronjé's commandos for the offen-

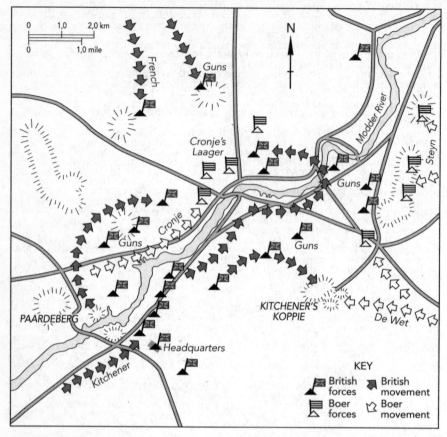

PAARDEBERG, FEBRUARY 1900

KEY

British forces
Boer forces
British movement
Boer movement

sive front did not necessarily mean leaving all families behind. In some respects, this war belonged to an earlier African age. One or two women in Natal Boer lines had already been killed or wounded; for some of those destined for this battle zone, there was no gender-related or generational sphere of safety. Tipped right into the arena of armed struggle, around sixty women and children became part of the laager's frantic battle of endurance. They included the commander's spouse, Hester Cronjé, 'sometimes referred to as the petticoat general'.[249]

What was Cronjé to do? Clinging to a faint hope that Bloemfontein would surely find something to spare to help to tide over his crumbling position, he decided, wrongly, to stay put and to soldier on. Elsewhere, nerves were cracking at the prospect: many commandos had concluded that the game was already up.

It is difficult to generalise about the sturdiness of combat mentality or fighting will, but even a passing familiarity with the character of this conflict confirms the pervasiveness of an inherited Boer soldiering sensibility that was more impulsive or wilful than well drilled. Burghers were mobilised irregulars who weighed up military prospects individually as they went along, something invariably expressed most forcefully in the customary practice of volunteering for a particular battle.

Paardeberg would be neither the first nor the last engagement of the war in which many commandos would sooner shirk duty and duck away from an unequal pitched battle than take a stand when the tables against them were stacked so high. To some degree, it may have been that these were too domesticated or civilianised, cautious soldiers who were 'only too glad to exchange war for home'.[250] Learning through the trauma of war how to subordinate family and intimate local ties to national need required a long-suffering stoicism. Equally, burghers who were unprepared to hazard their lives for officers who were trying as best they could to get their commands obeyed were not necessarily displaying 'unmanly' behaviour. They were maintaining an operational ethos. For commandos, taking up battle was an elective business, and they were unaccustomed to service as sacrificial shock troops. In all, this also reflected an unobtrusive Boer way of war, built up from earlier tactical experience against large forces of Zulu foot soldiers, when commandos were unyielding in their defence of strong positions but were always ready to ride away when it looked as if they might be overrun.[251] At Paardeberg, although by now increasingly unable to run, combatants grasped that what counted would not be courage but the probable loss of life or limb.

Determined to see to that, Roberts hastened up, arriving on the morning of 19 February to take direct command of the action. His opening play confirmed all Boer fears of a ferocious encounter. Roberts' response to an envoy sent out to propose an armistice in order to attend to the dead and wounded was brusquely dismissive. Surrender alone would halt the battle. Cronjé rejected this ultimatum and deepened his resolve to fight it out rather than submit. But Roberts was by no means fully confident; he recalled the sudden setbacks near Colesberg and Arundel, when Boer attacks unlocked an opening towards his creaky and exposed supply lines. As he now needed to resolve matters without any further delay, he intensified the pressure by turning his entire force on Cronjé's enclave.

The only real opposition came from some brief diversionary skirmishing following a mishap within the Boer lines. After Ferreira had been shot dead by a vigilant but short-sighted Boer sentry, his commandos were roped in by the agile De Wet, who for some days harried the British with mounted charges, inflicting losses. Forcing the enemy to commit a superior force of combined cavalry and infantry against his elusive commando, the Free Stater succeeded in squeezing his way to Poplar Grove, a spot much further along the road to Bloemfontein.

Meanwhile, Roberts bludgeoned his trapped target. On 21 February, the fourth day of the onslaught, he slackened, formally recognising the presence of women and children in the Boer position. For once, humanity took over; he made Cronjé an offer of safe conduct, promising to see the civilians through the British firing line and away from Paardeberg. The civilians failed to appear. Cronjé then made his own safe-conduct overtures, but his offer was spurned, and a fight to the finish reaffirmed. If the unprotected women and children with Cronjé's force did not leave their sinking ship, it was only because they refused to leave, or because those on the bridge refused to release them. For the moral compass of both warring sides, this must have been a sobering moment. But it was one which soon passed.

Justly known for efficiency rather than squeamishness, Roberts returned to battle, keeping up an artillery bombardment with lyddite shell before the infantry were sent in to pick up the pieces. For an enemy cordoned into an enclosed area, the power of the British bombardment was a nightmare, as were the rapidly deteriorating conditions within the encampment. Roasted by the heat, without sanitation, and assailed by the reek of decomposing animal carcasses which increasingly polluted the waters of the Modder, the trapped Boers faced the prospects of succumbing not only to fire but to disease, starvation and total exhaustion. The lives of some cornered commandos bearing festering injuries from earlier engagements were preserved with stubborn dedication by their nursing kin, or by fellow burghers and *agterryers* with traditional healing skills.

Meanwhile, in the republics, the agonies of Paardeberg provoked national dismay and a clamour for the dispatch of all available troops.[252] Little came of this. De Wet, although never timid, was still in a kind of secondary relieving position, or thought that he was. He believed that a sharp diversionary strike could loosen the British grip sufficiently to enable Cronjé to find ground across which to try to break free. But this required bringing him into prearranged planning and timing, which proved impossible: poor weather persistently frustrated heliograph transmissions to the laager. It was not just the British who were finding terrain and climate a problem. But, on 24 February, De Wet finally managed to slip one of his best available men through enemy lines to bring Cronjé into the picture: pack up and await the signalled break.

Again, the elements intruded. The swampy Modder rose rapidly under sudden heavy rain, necessitating a Boer bridging effort before any move could get under way. A frantic start was made, but on 26 February the British hauled up additional howitzer batteries and the Boers' last hope was taken from them. The next day Roberts launched an attack in full fighting strength, aggressively advancing his men to within fifty yards or so of the commando entrenchments. He was as eager as any British officer to get Cronjé by now, determined to turn to ash triumphal Boer memory of the taste of Majuba. At the end of their tether, and with nowhere to bolt, the defending Boers could not hold out and surrendered with a spontaneous ripple of white flags. A reluctant and dejected Cronjé fell into line, formalising capitulation on 27 February, just a day before Ladysmith would be retaken by his enemy.

Owing to the protective depth and thickness of their entrenchments, most of Cronje's laagered commandos had escaped the worst of the bombardment, taking a modest 150 casualties. But the overall Paardeberg loss was heavy: over 4 000 casualties, and close to 4 000 combatants taken captive. Neither, with 1 300 men, were British losses light. They also failed to salvage enemy armaments and equipment, shrewdly tossed into the Modder by Cronjé's force.

The collapse at Paardeberg and the surrender of virtually ten per cent of the small Boer army was a devastating blow to the republics' war effort. Indeed, in some respects, it even looked as if it might bring the conflict to a sudden conclusion. Engulfed by the sombre prospect of outright defeat, home-front morale in both republics plummeted. Out in the field, many combatants simply gave up the fight, saddling up of their own accord and racing homewards. There, they ran into widespread female anxiety and even animosity for having abandoned their patriotic duty to defend republican territory from invasion. From March it was, according to a Dutch volunteer, 'almost impossible to hear a patriotic word' among disconsolate fighting burghers.[253]

In their occupied southern pockets, alarmed leaders had more pressing demands than that of debating, collectively in war councils, precisely what to do next. Facing a near total breakdown of command structures, their greatest difficulty lay in keeping their troops in place. But the retreat was now in full flood, if not completely in disorganised panic. Thus, with impressive speed, Koos de la Rey and Hendrik Schoeman galloped most of their men back to Bloemfontein, effectively abandoning the central front.

The western front was to become a similar story. Here, with the exception of the siege line at Mafeking, the Boer line of advance more or less collapsed. Some of the republican 'progressives' who had had misgivings about the whole armed enterprise now had their qualms confirmed by crushing defeat in the field. Following the turnaround from the Tugela and the Modder, it seemed to have become nothing but 'everlastingly retreat, retreat', in the words of Smuts, 'wearying, dispiriting retreat'.[254]

Predictably, such pessimism bred recrimination. The most disenchanted critics blamed Cronjé for the whole Boer offensive having come to nothing. Within republican command, he was roundly censured for his obstinacy in disregarding repeated warnings in the field from De Wet, De la Rey and other senior officers. He had, they said, clearly risked being caught at the Modder in a trap of his own pedestrian making. At least there was no need now to engineer his dismissal from the sinecure of an ageing generalship. That was attended to by the British, who conveyed him to Cape Town with other prisoners. Accompanied by his wife and his Tswana personal attendants, Cronjé was then shipped off to live out the war on the island of St Helena, exiled behind an Atlantic curtain of indifference. For the republicans, Cronjé was the figure most responsible for a great failure. His real sin, though, was to have promised more, and lost all.

At the same time, Cronje's removal, and the fact that Joubert was fast dying, provided an unanswerable argument for restocking high command with a younger military leadership which would be more able and enterprising, and also less likely to throw things away by fighting the wrong battles. Louis Botha was made commandant general of the Transvaal, while Christiaan de Wet took over the Orange Free State. Enhanced authority was also conferred on Koos de la Rey, while Jan Smuts was given the chance of showing more of himself at operational level. These men were quintessential partisans, nationalist military entrepreneurs who looked to bring to high command a greater stringency and capacity to prepare for and to face the next round of the war.[255] De la Rey and De Wet had the biblical inspiration of a fundamentalist Christian warriorhood, zealous in belief 'that by opposing British imperialism they were on a crusade for the Lord'.[256] Both veterans of the 1880s conflict with Britain, they had already demonstrated a flair for running swift movements in the field.

Now in the throes of a critical struggle simply to hold the republican position together and to prevent their campaign from falling apart, the next step for this new generation of Boer generalship was to come back in force – a tall order. What they faced were dejected and dishevelled troops and commando desertions galore, with some throwing away their equipment as if the war were finished, others knifing away the flanks of dead horses for food.[257] If not yet ready to quit, many men were aching for rest and respite. Many were set on a slippery run homewards to save their personal holdings rather than the republican cause.

Meanwhile, Roberts' large advancing army wound on with every hope and intelligence indication that it would soon capture the Orange Free State capital. Unlike most African or Asian peasant adversaries, the colonial Boers looked to have the basic political trappings of European opponents, with a defined capital as their centre. Buller for one, however, had always been sceptical of a 'capital' strategy, believing enemy territory too large and its chequerboard of rural communities too fragmented to be intimidated into surrender in this way. Yet Roberts always assumed that the conventional toppling of their capitals would finally finish off the Boers.

Given the lukewarm attachment or even indifference felt by remote rural commandos towards the national pulse of an 'Afrikaner' state capital, Bloemfontein was not a precious town that too many felt would be worth fighting for. Orange Free Staters generally had not invested emotionally in its most important streets. But, for commanders like De Wet, something was at stake. Determined to disrupt the British advance, he mustered 6 000 commandos and entrenched them at a fancied Poplar Grove position. Along the route to Roberts' objective, burghers occupied a lengthy line along knotted ground on both sides of the Modder. Here, they awaited the British. Although strung out impossibly thinly, there was still the hope that disciplined and accurate fire would halt a hugely superior advancing force.

On 7 March, Roberts moved to the attack, committing a large enough number of men for a looping encirclement of De Wet's resisting line in order to strangle its occupants by cutting into their flanks. Instead, the impending confrontation turned into a flop. Kruger had arrived that very morning for consultations with

De Wet, and the British envelopment caught the enemy camp on the hop. With French's cavalry ahead and bearing down on the bonus of a highly exposed political target, Boer forces drew up their transport and pulled back rapidly towards Bloemfontein. With his way open, Roberts and his force of 40 000 men surged on towards the capital, moving at will, with some units on the fringes looting provisions, gutting livestock and incinerating property.[258] By the early months of 1900, the British, by burning the homes and crops of burghers on commando service and leaving farm inhabitants without shelter or sustenance, were already beginning to lay waste.

As the invaders moved to secure control of the administrative centre of the Orange Free State, their adversaries continued to reel back in growing numbers. Those who had caved in had shrugged off dire threats from their command, including bluster from Kruger that police reserves would be used to propel men back, if need be shooting any fleeing deserters. However, alongside a ragged, bitter and disconsolate collapse of republican formations, the Boers still had reliable troops. These included ideologically ardent foreign irregulars in the Orange Free State whose fierce republican attachment was especially relished by Steyn and his immediate circle. The president, incidentally, was pinning hopes in March on a Russian move on India that would frighten Britain. Provided the Boers could hold out for a further couple of months, the distracted British might yet be obliged to negotiate a peace.[259]

Although in no state of strength or preparedness to do much fighting, Steyn and De Wet hustled about in an attempt to improvise last-ditch defences of Bloemfontein and continued to display defiance. Formal confrontation around Kimberley and Bloemfontein was now close to being over but, outside the capital, De la Rey still had claws. Although only able to cluster a small force of 1 500 commandos, he lay in wait near Driefontein (Abraham's Kraal), tracking enemy movement. The British had to be lured on. Little remained other than to force some sort of spoiling encounter. In due course, De la Rey collided with French and his 10 000-strong cavalry force, obstructing their advance for a full day before being forced to withdraw.

Bloemfontein fell on 13 March 1900. Marthinus Steyn's belief in running things to the wire with some improbable national blood sacrifice came to nothing. It was superseded by the more prosaic spectacle of a handover managed deftly by the town's leading landowning and commercial élite. The attorney John

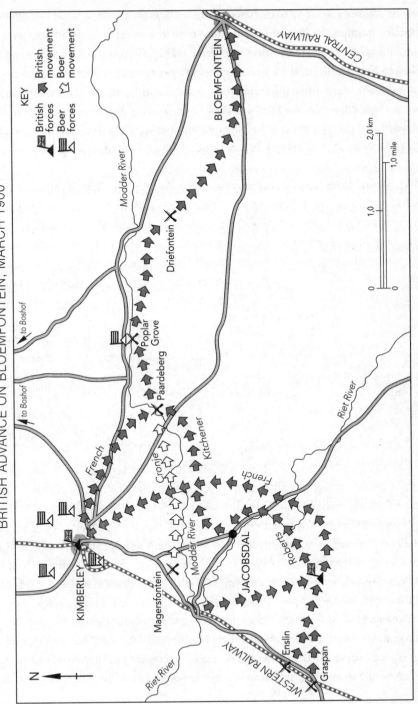

BRITISH ADVANCE ON BLOEMFONTEIN, MARCH 1900

KEY

British forces
Boer forces
British movement
Boer movement

BLOEMFONTEIN

CENTRAL RAILWAY

Modder River

Driefontein

to Boshof

Poplar Grove

Paardeberg

to Boshof

Cronje

Kitchener

French

Riet River

French

French

KIMBERLEY

JACOBSDAL

Roberts

Magersfontein

Modder River

WESTERN RAILWAY

Enslin

Riet River

Graspan

N

2,0 km
1,0 mile
1,0
0
0

Fraser, a former Speaker of the Volksraad, and B.O. Kellner, the mayor of Bloemfontein, embodied a leading Afrikaner-Scottish and Afrikaner-German urban coterie which liked to make speeches. Provided his position was flattered, Roberts liked to hear them. Driven by consuming self-promotion, he was an experienced manipulator of a captive imperialist war press, ensuring that in the taking of the town, the sunny side of affairs was fully covered. Working always to 'ensure favourable reporting', Roberts had excluded a young Winston Churchill from his Bloemfontein retinue, having had enough of his acerbic reporting.[260]

With Steyn having scurried off northwards on 12 March, on one of the last trains to roll out before the British cut the line, Roberts and his spouse found an open door to the presidential residence. Another such opening was to Bloemfontein's mostly wealthy and welcoming British Uitlander citizenry, the men with a good grip on the decanter and the women a deft hand at the running up of silk Union Jacks. The capital's Sotho labourers were also welcoming, with some demonstrating their gratitude by ransacking the Orange Free State artillery corps barracks and looting other Boer property.

For the British, the seizure of Bloemfontein was an interim controlling objective: it would do as a base for the critical strike at Pretoria. In the meantime, however, the military occupation itself was not without its troubles. Although an important theatre for republican nationalist politics, the Orange Free State capital was a little town, with just over 4 000 white and black inhabitants. Its garrisoning capacity was now to be tried severely by the 50 000 soldiers marched in by Roberts. The trying conditions in and around the capital proved debilitating for already tired, poorly nourished and seriously overstretched troops. More than just lengthening sick parades, the Bloemfontein camp concentration stretched sanitation facilities and hygiene maintenance to fatal limits. A severe outbreak of enteric fever, or typhoid, turned a packed capital into a vast and growing military hospital. A hunt for beds and accommodation by the occupation force was soon leading to the widespread commandeering of buildings and usable trappings, including schools, clubhouses and the parliament house itself. By early April, almost a thousand troops had died in what was to become merely the first of a series of flaring outbreaks of disease.[261]

Another factor which retarded the rapid renewal of Roberts' active campaigning was the seriously depleted supply level. A necessary prior step was to bring in replenishing columns, which would gather some of their fresh provisions while on the hoof through the surrounding countryside. Farms which had been losing African labourers and tenants to auxiliary service with the British army now began to lose foodstuffs too. While resting and resupplying his tired army, Roberts moved to clarify a tough new political position for subject Boers. He had already declared a confiscatory intention whereby men who were absent from their farms would forfeit their property. In March, a published proclamation specified that burghers within a surrounding ten-mile jurisdiction of the capital had to surrender or risk expropriation. Although the level of compliance with such intimidatory measures would certainly have been variable, the British were signifying that their imposed new sovereignty had sharp teeth. More broadly, the Boers had to be made to feel the loss of their own statehood. In due course, Roberts extended an amnesty to all Orange Free State burghers (with the exception of their leadership) on condition they returned home, relinquished their arms, and took an oath of allegiance.

The circumstances of that Boer leadership were dire. Not only had the short war ended up in the doldrums, but the prospects of fighting a longer encounter had been critically reduced. Displaying just how blinkered it was in its understanding of international politics – the intricate business of wheeling and dealing in the global context – Boer command tried gamely but unsuccessfully to unlock European patronage and protection. Given that the imperialist will to prosecute war looked rather unlikely to falter, what might make Britain hesitate? Perhaps, the restraining factor of European assistance for the republican cause.

In pursuit of an anti-British imperialist aid alliance, three envoys were dispatched cap in hand to several overseas capitals. Two members of this mission, A.D.W. Wolmarans and C.H. Wessels, were drawn from the prominent 'Hollander clique' of the Kruger faction, with the third, Abraham Fischer, dispatched by Steyn. But, while they were received by the Netherlands government with beaming smiles and found its Hague and Amsterdam populations a nest of singing pro-Boer birds, the Dutch state had no desire to tread on British corns. For Queen Wilhelmina's cautious ministers, it was the Kaiser's voice alone which might draw together some collective anti-British initiative on behalf of the republics. But, in turn, Germany looked to the United States for support, fully aware of the potential leverage which America was acquiring through the increasing flow of its financial credits to London after the outbreak of war. There was no need to read *The Economist* or *The Wall Street Journal* for Berlin to know about

British borrowings, not only of American capital but of American gold as well.

Yet, against that, there was always something more to the Anglo-American connection. In this case, it lay principally in a reciprocal understanding between British and American leaders of the war aims of their respective colonial worlds. In contrast to other European states, Britain had adopted an indulgent attitude towards the United States in its pursuit of conquest against the Spanish in Cuba and the Philippines in the later 1890s. In turn, Washington ignored political pressure from organised Irish-American and German-American groupings at least to disavow Britain's aggressive South African war policy. Unable to bring other governments to consider any assistance, the republicans' emissaries of March 1900 had to content themselves with trawling in public funding for the Boer cause, of which there was a good deal forthcoming through lotteries and other subscription drives by prominent Dutch pro-Boer societies (such as the energetic Haagsche pro-Boer Vereeniging).

Meanwhile, Roberts prepared for the next stage of his advance. The Transvaal was beginning to steel itself for a coming onslaught, and there were growing suggestions that the Boers did not have to wait helplessly – for they had another card to play. It was, some believed, a trump card: republican control of the wealth and strategic power of the Witwatersrand. Always a lingering undercurrent in thinking after the outbreak of war, talk of how to exploit it grew louder after the completed capture of Bloemfontein. In March, newspapers with a close ear to the Kruger government carried both insinuation and outright argument that not only should the mines be destroyed, but that any Uitlander property which could not be usefully requisitioned or confiscated should also be demolished. Indeed, both within the ruling executive and among ordinary Volksraad representatives, there was heady discussion and debate over the radical option of wrecking the gold mines ahead of a British invasion. Some of its advocates did not mind too much about consequences: it was simply a fine chance to whip Britain. Others were made eager by an incoherent Boer anti-capitalism, with the gold industry reviled not so much because it was capitalist as because it was foreign or alien. A number of influential iron-rod republicans, including Reitz, favoured blowing up the mines as an incandescent retribution upon the Randlords, whose capitalist greed was still considered largely responsible for having brought on the war.[262]

On the other hand, others, including Kruger and Joubert, made a little more effort to think out the strategic issue of what to do about the golden calf. Killing it in a vengeful rush of blood was imprudent. It would not do for the reputation of the South African Republic for it to be stung by European accusations of state recklessness with property and market rights. Besides, the republicans' war chest needed gold production to continue. It came back to finding the balance necessary to energise a war of recovery, something that could be achieved by squeezing the owners of the mining industry. It was self-evident that the Rand's nervy mine bosses were vulnerable to emergency impositions or to being intimidated by the threat of wholesale confiscation or dynamiting of their properties.

For a little while, the gold industry seemed to offer some illusory prospect of a way out. By threatening the future of production, the Transvaal could remind German, French and Belgian financiers that their returns could not come cost-free. One possibility was that by taking the mines hostage, the republican government might even compel foreign states to take up its cause, if only to ensure that, in their desperation, the Boers did not jeopardise vital world financial assets. Another, even smarter variation, was to dispense with idle threats and to seize the mines from their British owners. Then, by selling them off to non-British foreign interests, the Boers could redistribute some of the burden of their war effort to a new breed of Rand financiers and speculators who would have an obligatory stake in propping up independence.

Rumours of preparations to have the mines dynamited soon saw the likes of Sammy Marks scuttling off to prevail upon Kruger and his executive council, upon Joubert, and even upon field commanders like De la Rey and Botha, not to sanction the wanton destruction of mine property. The call was to stand firm against the apocalyptic visions of an overheated Reitz, who felt that if his state was to be conquered by the demonic English, it ought to be left ruined, 'like Sodom and Gomorrah'.[263]

Sensing that the economic future of the territory was what mattered, most guardians of the republican order were temperamentally against any war strategy of this kind. Boer society was probably incapable of such choreographed state depredation in any event. Ideological constraints were powerful. State order was deeply imbued with propertied values and protectionist patterns of individual ownership. Joubert and other well-connected members of a Boer élite with a zest for land and mineral speculation were clearly unlikely to lead any assault upon key property, whatever its ownership and whatever their national cause.

These were, after all, men with a healthy appreciation of production and profit.

While Botha and other commanders agreed on relieving the mines, they had no desire to leave the military situation in the hands of Roberts and an uncontested march to victory. Brushing aside urgings from some influential Transvaal citizens, including Pretoria's chief justice, to consider laying down their arms as the cause looked lost, it was decided at a key war council on 20 March to continue the struggle. The debate was hurried and decisive. What emerged was a blunt appreciation that the nature of the war had changed radically and rapidly. With head-on conflict at an end, and with a crushing advance by a vastly stronger adversary, what was required from the republicans was a riposte. That could not amount to simply waiting in defensive positions. War would have to be carried to selected points at which the enemy could be struck successfully. As that meant hunting the British, the Boers had to become much lighter and more efficient in the field.

For a start, action was taken to deal with issues that had been thwarting the proper deployment of commandos. Leave for fighting burghers was cut, and discipline was to be enforced more rigorously, with resort to military courts. Along with this, De Wet urged the wholesale abandonment of burdensome wagon laagers, which inhibited speed, stifled flexibility, and offered too obvious a target for enemy guns.[264] Commandants who resisted trimming their wagon transport were removed. Abolishing wheeled columns for pack horses also meant tightening, or solidifying, combat units. Ending or at least reducing wagon resources removed the kind of Paardeberg entanglement caused by the continuing presence in some commandos of older women and children. In such instances, male guardianship was an operational handicap.

What command needed were better selected and domestically unencumbered troops, younger fighters who would take on the harsh rigours of campaigning in open veld and bush, and who would be far more habituated to travelling light. Smuts, in proposing that landdrosts form systematic recruitment committees to scour local districts and to dragoon every available able-bodied burgher into service, had in mind a much newer type of man. This was a sort of pastoral Boer samurai but with Protestant perseverance, and with a true sense of what it meant to be a responsible and selfless patriot. These new combatants were urgently needed to repair a campaigning position in which 'the great majority thought more of their farms, their families and their private affairs, than of the fate of the republics'. Their forces could have no reasonable hope of making headway while 'a spirit of civil self-interest as distinguished from military self-sacrifice'[265] continued to contaminate the Boer rank and file.

Such worries were certainly justified, underpinned by the alarmingly positive response to Roberts' proclamations, in which some 12 000 to 14 000 commandos were to down arms and surrender between March and July 1900. But even so resigned a situation did not dash moves to try to improve the Boer position in late March, any more than did the death of Piet Joubert around the same time. While the Boers were in no state to beat back Roberts, they could still make him bleed. To do this, De Wet conceived a renewed two-pronged offensive which would draw his forces into the wide spaces north of Bloemfontein to bring on the British. They would then be struck at from the southeast.

This was conducted with considerable efficiency. On 30 March, Christiaan de Wet in alliance with his brother Piet and General Andries Cronjé, turned the British into quarry to be hunted, with De Wet's creeping scouts monitoring, from distant patrolling margins, the movement of a British force from Thaba Nchu to Bloemfontein. The commando leadership was able to anticipate the precise march route of the enemy column, and made its plans. At Koornspruit at dawn on 30 March, 400 Kroonstad and Bloemfontein commandos, armed with Krupp field guns and other artillery pieces, took their mounted adversary completely by surprise. Major General Robert Broadwood had neglected to send any scouts forward to scent out what might lie ahead. While his troops held on and wriggled free of the ambush, they suffered severe casualties: 150 soldiers killed or wounded and 480 captured. He also suffered serious equipment losses, including ammunition carts and provisioning wagons, several hundred rifles, hundreds of horses and pack animals, and a batch of Royal Horse Artillery guns. One of the first acts of De Wet's concealed riflemen was to fell gun-battery horses, to check their deployment and eventually to force the retreating British to leave the weaponry behind. In their withdrawal eastwards the Boers were jubilant, having taken negligible losses (five dead, eleven wounded).

Their spirits lifted by a satisfactorily one-sided clash, De Wet's forces derived an immediate tactical opportunity. The very next day, 31 March, commandos mounted a direct assault in the same area, this time against a small pocket of British infantry holding the pumping station and waterworks at Sannaspos. Situated on lower, undulating terrain just to the east of Bloemfontein, a section of approaching ground could not be tracked by its lookout point and helio-graph warning station. This provided a corridor along which De Wet's force, riding at night and quietly holed up during the day, sneaked forward. Again, the British were caught napping at dawn, and De Wet attained his objective, seizing the waterworks and cutting off fresh supply to the town. This worsened the typhoid epidemic which was eating at Roberts' army, bringing close on 2 000 deaths before the end of April. A regular counter-offensive had begun, even if based more on single military blows than on any gaining of ground or effective extension of power.

More followed. Early in April, de Wet detached 800 men from his snaking column of 1 500 commandos and struck at the British for a third time, at Red-dersburg, about thirty-five miles south of Bloemfontein. His foe, under the blight-ed command of Gatacre, had been assigned the task of bringing the southern districts of the Orange Free State firmly under the British heel. Staging a rapid approach and preparatory bombardment with quick-firing Krupp guns to press his advantage, De Wet then encircled the enemy and squeezed hard until they accepted defeat. Handing over their arms, they passed into captivity and con-finement behind barbed wire on a republican farm. British casualties exceed-ed 590 killed, wounded, or taken prisoner, while republican losses were once more slight. For the simplest of surprise moves, a considerable reward had been reaped.

The Orange Free State's forces were still haemorrhaging burghers from their combat musters, but for the moment De Wet's heartening strikes ruled out any further thought of breaking off. Commando strength was now also being aug-mented by a steady drizzle of men who, having been permitted to return to their farms on submitting to a British oath of non-belligerence, now slipped back to rejoin the fighting ranks. It seems doubtful, in any event, that all of them had meant to honour their submissive undertakings. Where the British were pass-ing, or had established a clear and undisputed hold, farmers had to act in a compliant way to restrain the invading enemy from a retributive sacking of their property. Whether to resume being a citizen-soldier or to remain demobilised could depend on personal circumstances; choosing one or other identity was a matter of need or calculation.

The Orange Free State Boers were also being joined by batches of migrating Cape rebels from the northern and northwestern districts, and by European volunteers such as the Irish Brigade, the Russian scouts attached to De Wet's commando, and the Kroonstad foreign corps under the prancing ex-French Legionnaire, George-Henri de Villebois de Mareuil, who had been promoted general on the sidelines after the fall of Bloemfontein. Although foreign volunteers were few, their bunched, clannish loyalties and fierce ideological adherence to the republican cause provided purpose and motivation. Moreover, their position as mostly single, urban men also meant that combat readiness was unlikely to be hampered by the occasional need to skip engagements in favour of some cattle auction.

Early in April, with the freedom to continue on the hoof and to stay on the attack, De Wet launched a fourth sally, this time advancing 6 000 commandos to threaten the settlement of Wepener, where he was opposed by a force of around 2 000 colonial loyalists, mostly unsentimental Cape Boers who were taking to the Crown for five shillings per day. With a determination that the enemy would pay heavily, the republicans assaulted the defences with repeated forays against the wavering line of a stretched adversary. De Wet seemed to relish lengthening the line of a new front, laying siege to the well-entrenched Wepener garrison for over two weeks. Moreover, he had troops to spare, posting them as a forward approach guard to cover his own position at some distance from the action.

But the British lines were not breached. The defenders were aided by having Basutoland directly at their rear, where the resident commissioner, Sir Godfrey Lagden, authorised a Sotho frontier guard of 3 000 men to deter De Wet from attempting any flanking movement across formally neutral terrain. From there, Sotho collaborators fed livestock and ammunition to the colonial force and transferred wounded and sick soldiers over the border under cover of darkness to be given medical aid. The stealthy movement and disregard of danger displayed by the incoming Sotho awed the Wepener garrison. One of its militiamen recorded his relief that they had not thrown in their lot with the republicans, given their infiltrating skill and night silence, barely talking in whispers and lighting no incriminating fires around the Caledon River rearguard.[266]

After more than a fortnight, a strong reinforcing column under Ian Hamilton arrived from Bloemfontein to relieve Wepener. Roberts' intention had been to maroon De Wet with a thick encircling movement and then to push him back against the garrison defence, forcing him to choose between slaughter and capitulation. But the Boers kept themselves fully apprised of Hamilton's manoeuvres through the dexterity of De Wet's élite scouting corps, and they engineered a proper rearguard barrier behind which to fall. Abandoning the Wepener position, commandos rode off before the approaching British could bring them to battle.

After a longer than anticipated pause, Roberts' Bloemfontein army of 45 000 troops got underway on 3 May, in several columns, on a march to clinch the war at Pretoria. To his east, Buller was crawling northwards through Natal, on a direct route to the Transvaal through Laing's Nek. The British could be delayed, but not blocked, as western and eastern offensive strategies converged. The confidence in victory could not have been expressed better than in the catchiness of the popular processional song, 'We are Marching to Pretoria', a jaunty imperial hymn to the rising dominion of the English in South Africa. Hopelessly outnumbered, the Boers could do little more than attempt to stem the pace of the enemy's advance by deflecting their passage through the river system. So, demolition squads blew the bridge across the Vet River, and shortly afterwards dynamited the Sand River bridge. This produced some twists to the line of advance, but did not stall the British, who merely sidestepped the obstacles.

Botha moved his base, angling away from Natal to the western front to carry the fight to the large invasion columns in the Sand River area. There, in an effort to upset the column connections of the British army, he pulled off a diversionary encounter against its cavalry spearhead under French. But, despite keeping French under fire for virtually a full day, Botha could not avoid having to pull back to avoid being outflanked. With the opposition shaken off, the British advance closed up again, and on 10 May threw its line across the Sand River without meeting any further opposition.

By now, Orange Free State political command was in tatters. Nonetheless, Steyn and his loyal associates continued trying desperately to keep their seat of government from toppling altogether, even if only a minority of their fighting burghers showed any intention of helping. Ousted from Bloemfontein, the leadership had moved its capital to Kroonstad, just over 130 miles north of the fallen town. There, Orange Free State and Transvaal war deputations had deliberated over what organisational combination and strategy might yet save them from quick defeat. On 12 May, the republicans had to find another location as Roberts picked off Kroonstad. Heilbron then became the new capital, those sitting there knowing only too well that it would probably be exchanged for Lindley before very long. Inevitably it was, and then only briefly, as the incursion of Hamilton's brigades on 8 May put Steyn and his government to flight even further north.

With Kroonstad pocketed, Roberts tied up his force for well over a week, despite nudging from some of his subordinates who wanted to stay on the trail. It was not a question of lacking the will to move. Extended campaigning over these distances was aggravating already acute problems of transport and supply. While the Boers had not succeeded in disabling the railway sufficiently to deny the British its use, there was scattered damage both ahead and behind, making it difficult to run up regular supplies. The Boers had the advantage of one of the traditional crafts of Irish republicanism. Plotting Fenians of their Irish Brigade had begun well-coordinated sabotage action on the communications route between Bloemfontein and the Vaal River, blowing up crossings and culverts and twisting rails. The British responded with repeated repair and river bridging, undertaken by a rugged, nomadic army of African railway labourers under Girouard, Kitchener's favoured Sudanese standby, with his handy background in engineering and colonial labour recruitment.

The advance had to be slowed down until the network was adequately restored for the ferrying of supplies: troops who gathered in places not fed by the railway were already grievously short of rations, largely because of the messy miscalculations of Roberts' and Kitchener's botched central transport reorganisation. Physical strain and dietary deficiencies naturally took their toll of efficiency and morale, a situation compounded by ravaging typhoid and the neglect of sanitation by field medical services. As more than one historian has pointed out, typhoid and the associated medical crisis experienced in the Orange Free State during May produced a casualty rate worse than that sustained in all the fighting of Black Week.[267] This time, it was plainly the fault of Roberts' bungling.

Meanwhile, far to the west, the question of Mafeking was also being addressed. Lieutenant Colonel Herbert Plumer, in command of the nearest British force, an irregular regiment of white Rhodesian mounted infantry, had already made several shallow attempts to force the siege. But, with fewer than 700 colonial volunteers and ineffective guns, he had managed to get no nearer than about five miles from Mafeking before being beaten off by the Boers. Even after Cronjé had lumbered southwards to respond to the Methuen move on Kimberley, a depleted siege force of 1 500 commandos under General Jan Snyman still had the superior strength to keep Plumer at bay. With Baden-Powell's fraying Mafeking defence line unable to hold out for very much longer, Roberts dispatched a 2 000-strong flying relief column from Kimberley under Colonel Bryan Mahon. This fresh and agile force, its movement closely tracked by the Boers, hurried in for a converging assault with a Plumer contingent expanded to over 1 100 colonial irregulars and braced by Royal Horse Artillery, Canadian guns, and Australian infantry. The besiegers launched a last desperate raid, virtually under the relief column's nose. It failed.

The defence was sustained largely by Baralong residents, who fought ferociously and then helped to harry the attacking force of around 300 Boers into surrender. Mafeking's largely African dead and wounded totalled twenty, with Snyman's losses much higher: sixty battle casualties, and over 100 commandos taken prisoner. With the staving off of the last republican fighting reserves, the raising of the siege came just four days later on 16 May.

The coming of relief was not accompanied by too much fuss in Mafeking, although in London there was a street orgy of patriotic rejoicing which bubbled on for more than two days. Still, it was more or less the last full-blooded domestic expression of a 'mood of intense patriotic anxiety', as by now it was becoming increasingly clear 'that Britain was not going to *lose* the war'.[268]

Pressing up from the south, Mahon combined with Plumer's column approaching from a northerly direction. With an opening of a light bombardment, this was enough to persuade the remaining Boers around Mafeking not to hang on. At the end of the action, Baden-Powell as press censor insistently barred the *Mafeking Mail* from running any account of the critical role played by Africans in repelling the final assault on the town, and brusquely disarmed indignant Barolong defenders. It was not until after the garrison commander's departure that their crucial participation made it into the published record.

It was now set for British forces to go through and conquer the Transvaal by taking its capital. Moving on from Mafeking to smaller things, Baden-Powell and his Bechuanaland corps returned to his secret July 1899 orders. At the outbreak of war, those were to threaten and even to raid the Transvaal's northern borders, a spoiling diversion to tie up a portion of Boer forces. Their strategic position was now, of course, vastly different. With his force ranged alongside Plumer's colonial column, there was preparation for a different kind of penetra-

Top left: President Marthinus Steyn urged his forces not 'to disgrace a Christian, a burgher and the Free State'.

Top middle: 'Best if Kruger hardened his heart and the smash came': Sir Alfred (later Lord) Milner, British High Commissioner.

Top right: A disconsolate President Paul Kruger told Milner: 'It is our country you want!'

Above: Kruger at the opening of the rail link to Delagoa Bay, 1894.

Top: Boers capture a British supply train at Elandslaagte, Natal, 1899. One train less for the inventors of the railway.

Above: Age and youth, coffee in hand and servant at the side: commandos at Ladysmith, Natal.

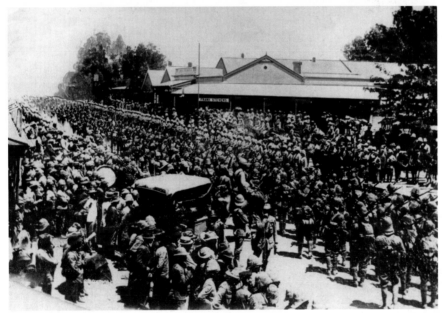

Top left: Not bearing tulips from Amsterdam: Dutch fighters join the besiegers at Ladysmith, Natal.

Top right: The troubled General Sir Redvers Buller who, according to one member of his government, 'has allowed himself to go downhill'.

Above: Made it at last – British forces relieve Ladysmith, 1900.

Top: A gunner in Mafeking keeps a cautious eye on things with his Maxim Nordenfeldt gun.

Right: Stuck in Mafeking: Lady Sarah Wilson, aunt of Winston Churchill, awaits her next carrier pigeon.

Top: Some improvement over a siege diet of stray dogs and locusts – rations queue in Mafeking's African *stadt*.

Above: Kimberley, menaced by the Boers: still mostly all quiet on the western front, with Cecil Rhodes nowhere in sight.

Top: Colonial troops and African auxiliaries at a blockhouse.

Right: At Spioenkop General Sir Charles Warren was short of what he really needed, especially luck.

Below left: Indian ambulance bearers at Spioenkop.

Below right: Civilian Boer transport conductor and African remount depot servants, King William's Town.

Top: In Cape Town Indian cavalrymen learnt that they were to groom Britain's horses, not ride them into battle.

Above: Smartly buttoned up for Transvaal commandos: in camp, loyal African *agterryers* swop horses for wheelbarrows.

Top: Field-Marshal Lord Roberts accepts the surrender of General Piet Cronjé at Paardeberg.

Above left: General Cronjé went on to make a further spectacle of himself by re-enacting Paardeberg at the 1904 St Louis World Fair in the USA.

Above right: Beware a short and poor-sighted man who is too fond of medals: Frederick Sleigh Field-Marshal Lord Roberts, five foot three inches (1.6m) tall, blind in one eye and neat as a pin.

Top: The British forces occupied Pretoria in 1900 and Lord Roberts thought that the war was just about over. But where is President Kruger?

Above: A break from either advancing or retreating, if not to unpack a picnic: troops in the occupied Orange Free State, 1900.

Above: Enjoying control of Pretoria and forgetting the countryside, infantry parade past Roberts and Kitchener in Pretoria's Church Square, 1900.

Opposite top left: Boer general Louis Botha

Opposite middle: General 'Koos' de la Rey , whose exploits included the wounding and capture of the British general, Lord Methuen (top right) in 1902.

Opposite bottom: Boer captives close to home with British captors far from home, Orange Free State, 1900.

Top: Unwilling to lose and considering the next move: Botha (seated, fourth from left) and General Jan Smuts (probably figure standing) in emergency war council near Johannesburg.

Above: They did not head up there to admire the scenery: Boer sharpshooters keeping busy.

Top: In the Cape mountains in 1902, General Smuts (sitting, centre) and officers set an example to defeatists.

Above left: 'With God and the Mauser': the redoubtable General Christiaan de Wet who always showed his enemy a clean set of hooves.

Middle: P. J. Fourie, Fritz von Maltitz and Willie van der Merwe of the Ficksburg Commando, 1900.

Right: Transvaal commando Frans Johannes Meiring is too young to grow a beard but compensates elsewhere.

Top left: For one distressed commando, 'hard is not the word for it'. Mrs T. J. Schoeman and her children, Barberton concentration camp.

Top right: For Horatio Herbert Field-Marshal Lord Kitchener what mattered most was winning the war, not counting the costs.

Above: The blockhouses were instrumental in Kitchener's victory. Here their occupants have a break from trying to bottle up the Boers.

Left: Concentration camp inmates Mrs Anna Davel and probably her daughter.

Middle: Refugees scrape an existence in an African concentration camp in Bethulie, Free State.

Bottom: Dropping their swords, Boer prisoners of war interned in Portugal pick up the pen.

Above: Smoking the war, 1900: British regular and mounted infantrymen seal the camaraderie of conquest with a smoke.

Left: Drinking the war, 2010: a red of Anglo-Boer fraternity to sip in the centenary year of Union.

tion, an invasion from the west which would strike deep into a territory held by a weakened and disintegrating army. In another part of this subsidiary pincer, the Rhodesian field force under Lieutenant General Frederick Carrington planned a way into the Transvaal from the north. And there were further major concerted movements. Buller's Natal army was inching up eastwards to hammer down the southeastern Transvaal and to unclog the second key railway artery from the coast to Pretoria. Meanwhile, French's probing cavalry headed the growing concentration of British forces under Roberts, now marching up at a brisk pace from the south. Awaiting them was no mesmerising fortress, but, rather, a wasting Boer soldier-citizenry. The war for South Africa looked all but over.

By mid-1900, British Liberal intellectuals and adherents of the country's peace movement, like the Quaker Peace Society and the International Arbitration League, were already pondering prospects of a possible conciliatory peace. Beyond this, a wider public sense of the end of the war was being reflected in pamphlets, essays, and even in a number of books which circulated amongst the more educated middle classes. One memorable example was *A Retrospect on the South African War*, conceived in 1900 and published early in 1901. It was the misfortune of its optimistic author, Sir Edward May, to have started rather ahead of time and to have finished rather behind it, too.

Equally, the Transvaal itself was not short of inclinations to surrender. In mid-May, a small deputation of influential political notables and businessmen, all cosy associates of Kruger, opened peacemaking overtures to the president on the basis that the republican cause was unmistakably lost. Evidently thinking that a peace without victors or vanquished might somehow still be retrieved, their idea was to salvage an honourable alternative to the ignominy of unconditional surrender. Announcing its action to be 'under protest', the republic should lay down its arms and then unilaterally declare the war to have ended. This would cheat Britain of the fruits of complete victory at the last minute, and also impose a moral restraint upon any continuing imperial belligerence.

This was an ingenious if odd diplomatic stratagem in these circumstances, and it remains a puzzle. It was, at any rate, an indication of the desperate state of Kruger's mind that he even toyed with the proposal as a possible means of checking further loss of life and the destruction of resources. After a brief airing, it was killed by Steyn. Kruger's ally was now far more committed than he to the independence struggle and was, if anything, all for fighting on to hold off the trauma of defeat at all costs. For Bloemfontein, too much had already been sacrificed to give up the struggle.[269]

But there was little to stop the enemy's immediate onward movement. By the last week of May, the imperial army was breasting the Vaal River on a line of march that would take it through Johannesburg and on to Pretoria. Near its crossing, a small force easily put to flight a puny Boer rearguard trying to cling to strategic command of the valuable Vereeniging colliery fields. Roberts needed to take these mines in one piece, to lighten his coaling headaches as the rail trucking line grew ever longer. In running, the Boers did not neglect defiant delaying actions, firing the railway station and blowing up the railway bridge – but sparing the coal mines from damage. No preparatory boring had been authorised for the works to be blown in and denied to the British. Oddly, the defenders seemed to have had the way but not the will.

Ahead of them, at the end of May, there was the sticky business of those other mines to be addressed. With Roberts pressing in ever more deeply, the Boers could no longer retain the gold workings to fund their war effort, and there was no reason to protect the mines. If anything, leaving them intact to be worked under British administration meant that their bullion would instead be financing the enemy's campaign. The clarion call for destruction was rekindled. In the minds of strategy-minded war radicals such as the energetic republican judge, Antonie Kock, the former state attorney, Ewald Esselen, and Reitz, the time had come to do now what could have been done justly before. Finishing off the Rand mines would be salutary for the war criminals of British imperialism. Oblivious to this, the special commandant of the Witwatersrand, F.E.T. Krause, remained watchful in absolute defence of mining property. Still, with Roberts' onward drive pushing embittered displaced Boers and pro-Boer Uitlanders back towards the Rand and its tempting touch paper, anxieties over the well-being of the mines grew once again.

By this stage, the fear was not so much a government order to destroy the mines. It had, after all, already halted some impetuous drilling of dynamiting holes in shafts in April, thereby allowing European investors to sleep more easily. The threat came more from Boer and foreign commandos who were falling back through Johannesburg, and from fighting burghers based in the city. At the end of May, these were being ordered by Krause to head out for Pretoria to buttress a republican army in the north which would continue a struggle for 'land, liberty and independence'.

Already causing maximum damage in retreat, these bands of men included no shortage of foxy saboteurs and incendiarists, and foreign anti-imperialists not at all averse to an anarcho-syndicalist line on how to bring down the capitalists' war. John Blake, commander of the First Irish Brigade, recorded how he had pleaded with a council of war on the Vaal to permit him to dynamite some mines, but in vain. He met an infuriating wall of opposition, as 'they did not believe in the destruction of property'. However, at a Meyerton war council, Arthur Lynch, another Irish Brigade firebrand, found some support from the pugnacious Boer commander, Tobias Smuts, who like him wanted to get rid of what he believed was a wicked system, 'the greed of this gold that had induced the war'.[270]

On 29 May, there actually was an abortive attempt to destroy the Robinson mine. Although winked at by Kock and Reitz, it fizzled out only at the very last minute. Botha and Krause then succeeded in scotching any further last-ditch moves on the mines. The former did not want to disown the romantic masculinity of a 'fight as men' by perpetrating 'spiteful things'. The latter was intent more on blocking any imported revolutionary radicalism from 'foreign elements, such as Socialists and the like'.[271] They were conservatives of differing ilk, but neither would countenance the destruction of strategic assets.

Louis Botha, meanwhile, still with 6 000 active commandos, tinkered with the idea of a temporary blocking defence of the heart of Johannesburg, but the strength of his approaching adversary sensibly persuaded him against anything adventurous. In any case, Boer command knew that they had lost the area, or at least that there would be nothing to gain from fighting another unequal battle. Once across the Vaal, and with only some forty miles to go, Roberts' army was already assuming tactical angling positions to carry all before it. French and Hamilton's columns were to push round to the west, closing the communications mouth provided by the main Rand road from Johannesburg to the towns beyond, such as Germiston and Krugersdorp. Meanwhile, the main force would set off in an easterly direction up the railway line to outflank the target from the opposite approach. On the way, attackers ran into the dregs of republican resistance dug into a hill at Doornkop, appropriately not far from the blackened headgear of the Krugersdorp mines.

A final Boer effort to delay and divert was launched by several hundred

Johannesburg commandos under Viljoen and a Lichtenburg commando led by De la Rey. Supremely confident by this stage, Hamilton chanced his luck by turning his infantry brigades on the Boers in an extended frontal charge without directing covering fire or bringing up artillery support. In widely separated waves, small parties of troops advanced in dispersed order up the hill in staggered stages, until Hamilton's Gordon Highlanders could close in to rip up the enemy with a raw bayonet charge. The defenders were routed, and Doornkop taken, but not without some cost to the British through well-sighted lines of Boer fire. Hamilton's infantry casualties exceeded a hundred, a loss which could have been avoided by a diversionary advance around Doornkop through a gap to the west. At the heart of this, in all probability, was a British mind mesmerised by the need to avenge Doornkop, for it was there that Leander Starr Jameson had been humiliated.

A confused period followed, with a scatter of skirmishes and sniping exchanges in and around the Elandsfontein railway junction just to the east of Johannesburg. The ominous prospect of a new phase of hostilities, that of chaotic and nightmarish urban street fighting, now threatened to superimpose itself upon what had been an essentially agrarian contest. But, after some banging away, bands of defending commandos gave up their firing lines behind covering mine heaps and brick walls, and dropped away to join the growing northwards retreat.

Instead of a chase to eliminate his withdrawing enemy, Roberts opted for a delaying armistice, so that the transfer of control could be tidily arranged.

On 30 May, the commander-in-chief's representatives, who were moving around the town on bicycles, settled on a peaceful handover of the whole Johannesburg district. Roberts was not looking for further trouble, and the Boer authorities had by then had enough of it. Looking to save what it could, the Krause administration was pleased by an agreement that protected the city and its mines. It was also more than a little jumpy about the restive effects on African labourers of continued fighting. In the end, it was wiser for the British and the Boers on the Rand to make their peace, so that black workers would keep their place, or, rather, would be obliged to do so.

Republican officials then struck a good-behaviour bargain. Boers would hold off any burning or plundering in return for a day set aside for the evacuation of the bittereinder tail of the republican army. The resisters promptly retreated towards Pretoria with their arms, including heavy artillery, other war supplies, loot and commandeered gold. On those terms, the British took Johannesburg peaceably on 31 May. There was agreement on non-belligerence from both local burghers and pro-Boers, while Roberts issued a paper assurance that women and children would not be harmed by his troops, and permitted anyone with resistance left in them to leave without interference to resume the fight elsewhere.

There was some grumbling over Krause's doings with Roberts, with thin cries for armed resistance invoking De la Rey as a trusty general who would not wish to see Johannesburg relinquished without a decent struggle. There were also rumours of daring malcontents plotting to burn the city around Roberts, alongside outbreaks of frenzied looting by blacks and poorer whites. Stiff-necked Boers, Transvaal Irish volunteers, and Roberts' Australian scouts indulged in a few final running fights at close quarters. Thereafter, the British turned to governing the city through a new Rand administration, finally realising the claim to political power of the Uitlander élite. Having either closed independent telegraph offices or placed them under military control during his advance, Roberts saw to it that the remaining press would flatter his manner of conquest.

The rigorous new occupation regime was ready to enforce the disciplinary needs of a British Johannesburg, one of which was the deportation of various foreign 'undesirables'.[272] Another was to set right a popular misconception among its African labourers, who assumed the arrival of the British had brought them a liberalising imperial freedom, so that they could continue to tear up their oppressive passes. Two months previously, Salisbury had told the Westminster parliament that Britain would be 'less forgetful' of the need for 'kindly and improving treatment' of 'indigenous races'.[273] This was not a cause for which Roberts was campaigning.

The conduct of hostilities at Johannesburg may well be seen as another of the more obvious might-have-beens of this war. The armistice agreed by the British was certainly a little strange in military terms. While it wound down the fighting, it did nothing to prevent the Boers from reassembling to renew it later in another place and on other terms. In that respect, the last straw had not broken the back of Louis Botha's army. One cosy explanation is that Roberts held off through some velvet-glove tactical strategy to bring the war to a 'speedy and humane conclusion'. What mattered was the saving of the gold mines and the taking of the Boer capitals, along the way setting shrewdly discriminating terms of conquest for ordinary Boers, lenient for some, stern for others. With the enemy flattened and the war virtually over, it seemed 'sensible and humane'[274] not to squander any more British lives by attempting a final successful showdown.

Much about this is speculative, and perhaps something can be made of it. By now, Roberts obviously judged the war to be virtually at an end, and it would have been sensible to avoid more costs in a campaign already won. Also, storming the city could have jeopardised the mines – an indication that this was a war not entirely without some practical sense.

At the same time, though, there may have been other, more cogent reasons for Britain's commander-in-chief playing the accommodating old charmer. Having experienced something of its deadly and sprawling intensity in the Indian northwest frontier's Kabul in 1880, Roberts wanted to avoid a major tussle for Johannesburg based on loose street fighting. By its nature it would be indecisive, and its unstable environment would be ripe for frustrated soldiers to vent their rage or to commit vengeful atrocities against the inhabitants. Afghan memories were instructively restraining. Another factor was the acute hunger and thirst of the British troops, who could be run short no longer. When they reached Germiston on 30 May, strained soldiers had barely a day's provisions left. Being penned into an exhaustive battle over Johannesburg was an obvious and serious worry for British forces, waiting who knew how long for the Boers to come across to parley, and inevitably running out of stores because supply lines could not easily be maintained across a clogged and unpredictable urban spread. Nevertheless, spitting on the enemy rather than swallowing it in May 1900 has been judged 'probably the most serious strategic mistake'[275] of Roberts' South African career, both by some of his contemporaries and in hindsight. In the tart view of Buller's chief of staff, he had 'annexed a country without conquering it'.[276] The implications of that form the next stage of the conflict.

7

THE HIDE-AND-SEEK WAR

ROBERTS NOW MOVED ON TO CONCLUDE HIS OFFENSIVE BY TAKING Pretoria. Johannesburg was in Britain's grasp, and there were measures in place to weed out its Boer agitators and those suspect Europeans identified by Milner as 'disagreeable foreign riff-raff'. The final and most destructive phase of the war now began.

Continuing the flanking tactic of closing and enveloping republican defence lines, which by now amounted to punching through gossamer, the British reached the hills overlooking Pretoria on 4 June. 'That holy of holies of the Republic in South Africa,' observed a flushed Smuts, 'was generally expected to mark a decisive stage . . . to the British commanders the expected final Boer stand at Pretoria and its capture' would deliver 'the *coup de grâce* to the Republics'.

This was assuredly how Lansdowne, Milner and Roberts and his generals saw things. For once, colonial opponents had a fixed 'European' capital which they prized, making its capture a decisive strategic gain. 'To the republican rank and file,' continued Smuts, the conception of Pretoria was that of 'the great Armageddon where the Boer forces, concentrated from all points of the compass in defence . . . would deliver that final united blow from which perhaps the British forces might be sent reeling back to the coast. Perhaps – and perhaps not.' For all the weakened condition of forces retreating from Johannesburg and the crippling rate of desertion, Smuts was not without faith. The fact that thousands of men still 'stuck to their commandos'[277] was animated by an expectation that the war's most crucial action would be fought at Pretoria. This was not Bloemfontein. The city contained all the republican currency reserves and reserve ammunition stores. It also had surplus food in the hands of its wealthier classes, who had been drawing heavily from surrounding farms and organised stockpiles. Within the city, petitions, meetings and the press called upon commandos to show some staying power.

Scrabbling to find men after the defection of 20 000 burghers who had been struggling to halt the British drive northwards, Boer command was able to muster about 7 000 men to meet the British attack. Pretoria also had internal fortifications. These included several formidable gun bastions, thickly proofed against artillery and with integrated electric power, and a German Siemens field telephone system, a pioneering use of modern communications in war.[278] While this may have been something to get the pigeons fluttering, field demands on the artillery corps had kept the forts short of heavy Creusot cannon and gunners. With the British advance too rapid for timely rearmament, Pretoria's forts could barely put up any blocking fire.

But this had already ceased to matter.

At the beginning of June, several Boer commanders, including Viljoen and Botha, proposed to Kruger that the war be brought to an end at Pretoria. Their case was that the Boer armies had disintegrated, and that what fighting portions had been left behind were spent. To continue would be to invite only death or captivity. Given the weight of losses since the start of Roberts' campaign, the Boers lacked the means even for tit-for-tat warfare. Paralysis was too great even to contemplate the planning of a counter-effort. Destruction of republican territory was already advanced. If hostilities continued, the ruinous trampling of occupied zones could only spread until it consumed all that was left.

The president was, by all accounts, dismayed by so defeatist an assessment, and especially by Botha's unanswerable argument that several thousand men could not hope to contest the seizure of Pretoria. Among the senior military leadership it was only De la Rey who strongly dissented, promising that if the Republic was surrendered meekly, he would run his best commandos westwards to regroup and resume hostilities from there. Ahead of a major war council on 2 June to consider what to do about the Pretoria position, Kruger conferred with Steyn, still on his toes in the far northeast of the Orange Free State. After this exchange of cables, no ruling Transvaler would ever again risk Orange Free State sensitivities in asserting their own Republic's plight.

Steyn's answer to the capitulation proposal was blunt, releasing some pent-up resentments. The South African Republic had harried his state into war solidarity, even though Britain had not at first been endangering Bloemfontein's independence. Furthermore, Orange Free State authorities had even gone on to induce neighbouring colonial rebels to risk all. Now that their Republic had lost its independence and had been flattened in parts, its ally was prepared to conclude a 'selfish and disgraceful' peace the moment warfare lapped over its borders.[279] Kruger's concern for peacemaking in order to prevent continuing devastation seemed to Steyn a wretched capitulation: too much was already carcasses and cinders for the Boers not to do the honourable thing and fight on. If it ended as defeat for the Transvaal, so be it. Even if the Orange Free State was left on its own, Steyn said, it would remain defiantly in combat.

When this blunt statement had been digested by the war council, the chance of peace was lost. If Pretoria *was* defeated, few now seemed willing to admit it. Curiously, remarkably little needed to be done at this political level to repudiate any separate Anglo-Transvaal peace. Talk of ending resistance was condemned as traitorous by the self-sacrificing, younger nationalist hot-heads for whom 'the reverses of the earlier period had been a purging and chastening process'.[280] The government, in packing its bags, was denounced for its desertion. And there were calls for all of Pretoria to be turned into an armed enclave, regulated by a military regime under a commandant-general. So that this spot would not necessarily become a final stand, the war council planned a staged defence and fighting retreat. But the conditions for that were poor.

Those disgruntled commandos who were not already surrendering or sliding back to their homes in the surrounding districts were limping into Pretoria to get drunk and to feast on the proceeds of widespread looting. As circumstances grew more chaotic, the appetites of some burghers made them more to be feared than entrusted with fighting responsibility. Abrasive contact between retreating soldiers and urban civilians was not particularly helpful to national morale. Nor was the show put up by a *rust en orde* (peace and tranquility) committee, disparaged by pro-war leadership as men scared of war and, most especially, of artillery bombardment. Quickly dubbed an *oorgee* (surrender) committee of fairweather patriots, their attempts to grasp at peace were derided as 'an exhibition of treachery and double-dealing, sickening to behold'.[281]

As the enemy closed in, Kruger's executive council sensibly put aside thoughts of serious resistance. The increasingly inert commandant, Lukas Meyer, was relieved of the impossible task of defending his capital, and the council withdrew before the president himself ended up in Roberts' hands. Together with senior members of the government, Kruger rattled away by train to Machadodorp on the Delagoa Bay line, with the sanctuary of the Portuguese East African coast ahead. Until he was forced finally to flee the country in September 1900, this rolling stock served as a sort of puffing capital, spewing out desperate telegrams to more stationary centres like Paris and Berlin. The government left behind a little window-dressing in the shape of Vice-President Schalk Burger, Smuts, Botha and De la Rey.

This was an urgent time for those left behind. Money and gold to the value of around half a million pounds was prised from the Republic's National Bank and its Mint, and a special war fund of £25 000 was also hunted down by Smuts. The Republic's paltry reserve wealth was then transported eastwards on a police train in the direction of Mozambique. Having two kinds of capital on the same line was perhaps one of the more novel moments in the history of the railway and colonialism in Africa.

As fighting commandos evacuated their lines and rode east towards the Magaliesberg, Roberts did not even have to mop up. On 5 June, with his usual exceptional sensitivity to press requirements, he put up a triumphal show by marching into Pretoria to run up the flag. The publicity was immense. To maintain the right tone in the aftermath of Pretoria's capture, the *Pretoria Friend – The Authorised Medium for Official News,* was established.

Ever ready to give Buller the benefit of any doubt, several Boer observers, Smuts included, wondered drily whether his advance through the Drakensberg had been deliberately slowed down politically to ensure that Roberts had the chance of first bite at the Transvaal. Even by his usual standard, Buller's pace looked suspiciously arthritic, not that it mattered any longer. The idea of a free republican state order had become a fiction. Now, a new imperial political formation, the recently proclaimed Orange River Colony, would soon be joined by a new Transvaal Colony to solve the question of who South Africa was for.

While the government and its generals had not stayed in Pretoria to surrender, thousands of their broken burghers were doing just that. Surrendering *hensoppers,* or 'handsuppers' were flocking to accept Roberts' neutrality-oath proclamation that had been extended from the Orange Free State. In the eyes of more speculative British commanders, any continuing Boer hostilities had to be a hollow bluff, for between March and June their military power had been wasting away. Before the end of June, almost 8 000 Transvaal commandos had voluntarily surrendered their arms. To this could be added around 6 000 Orange Free Staters. This was a grim yardstick: a combined wastage of 14 000 men represented over a quarter of all those liable for military service in both states, amounting to around forty per cent of the level of initial mobilisation.[282]

On 5 June, Roberts had almost every advantage with which to conclude the war, most of all a huge superiority in fighting numbers and equipment. His advance against a virtually unprotected Pretoria had been exceptionally easy. The remaining Natal commandos on the Drakensberg stayed clear, having nothing to spare from the thin lines of defence thrown up to try to block Buller's advance. Commandos from the western border were falling back towards Pretoria, but too slowly and too few in number to be a disruption. Directly ahead, what Botha and De la Rey had left as a command would have fallen apart at the prospect of any more hard battles.

Meanwhile, Roberts, conscious of the implications of a Boer retreat, had done his calculations. He was not too perturbed. French, sent off in a northerly direction from Krugersdorp, was to cut through the Magaliesberg and to turn east to seal off any gap behind the republican lines. Once there, it would give Roberts the opportunities to mount a rear assault on Pretoria and to cut off what he guessed would be the probable line of any Boer withdrawal northwards.

As so often in warfare, it was a seriously wrong guess by a commander. The more logical line of retreat was east. That was where the republic's government and reserves were going, and if supply and communication were to continue filtering in it could only be through Delagoa Bay. To the north lay strategically barren terrain, lightly populated with Boers, notoriously unhealthy, and poorly provided for foraging. It would have been folly for Boer forces to go into such unprotected country.

Roberts failed badly in dispatching French to close the wrong back door. His enemy spotted this blunder and, for once, were able to rejoice at the space they were being given. Had French covered the right, seaward flank rather than the left, the Boers would probably have been well and truly caught. This, as Smuts, among others, recognised, might have dealt a terminal blow to any further republican resistance.

Doggedly reorganising, the Boers soon started to show that if down, they were not yet out. On 7 June, De Wet staged a lightning raid on railway garrison posts north of Kroonstad, inflicting 700 casualties, cutting communications to the south, wrecking supplies, dynamiting a bridge, and destroying several miles of line. He knew how to play the railways game, not merely blasting track but even heating rails on bonfires until they were hot enough to twist, making it difficult for the British to straighten bent line through hammering. In such destructive proficiency, the Boer leader was a carbon copy of General Sherman on the march in the last phase of the American Civil War. Moving rapidly, De Wet's Orange Free State force continued to strike out, blowing up more bridges, bottling up tunnels, and laying risky but skilful traps in which to wound their adversaries. This involved allowing British parties to pass along routes unmolested, to build up an illusion of safety, before suddenly ambushing an isolated convoy when its guard was down. For the British, it left an increasing number of wounds to lick.

The effect of these audacious and well-prepared forays was to draw Kitchener in with 12 000 mounted men. But by then the damage had been done. By fits and starts, the Boers were getting something going, with their governments settling on a new defensive plan in which their armies would separate. By now, Orange Free State forces were down to just 8 000 commandos at the most. Still, with the great mass of the British army across the Vaal, De Wet's own small unit of experienced and accomplished veterans could be untethered to position themselves behind the enemy and cause continuing trouble with their guerrilla operations. Their commander was using surprise as his most lethal weapon, and showing what could be done with small infiltrationist forces.

Action in these shifting new front positions included a heavy engagement on 11 and 12 June, fought in a serried clump of hills east of Pretoria, which became the battle of Donkershoek or Diamond Hill. Using an imaginative assortment of emissaries, Roberts had been devoting almost a week to persuade Botha to come out from behind his mountain screen of the Magaliesberg and accept surrender. If continued, the war could not possibly last more than a further fortnight, and what could be gained by prolonging its bloodshed and agony? But Botha seemed deaf to British common sense. After a brief pause, Roberts sent out his army (on 10 June) to apply stronger pressure. Although British frontal strength had by now been depleted, he was confident that Botha's force would not pose a serious threat, and 16 000 troops were considered more than adequate for the purpose. But Botha and his commanders still had some cards to play, namely 5 000 hardened commandos, assembled from various districts and stationed to plug the tops of a triangular hill position.

Realising the holding strength of the Boers in the front apex, Roberts side-stepped and ran his attack at the enemy's flanks, menacing their usual line of retreat. This finally succeeded in collapsing Botha's defences on the left, but the right flank was reinforced, stabilised in a cut of ground which provided a natural firing trench, and which proved fairly resilient. A recoiling Roberts lost 180 men, while Boer casualties were a negligible dozen. Having frustrated the advance, Botha abandoned his Diamond Hill wing, leaving Roberts an empty space to capture. The flying Boers then withdrew their guns and transport further east, towards Kruger's headquarters at Machadodorp. This was to be one of the last real battlefield actions of the war.

With Buller at last approaching the northern Natal borders, Botha pulling back east, and De la Rey occupying the deep western Transvaal, Roberts still had at least one eye on the wriggling Marthinus Steyn. To break Orange Free State resistance in its northeastern corner, the British now applied pressure to drive their prey ever farther eastward. This forced Steyn into a series of retreats, with the Boers having to transport their administration from Heilbron to Frankfort, and then to Bethlehem. Inevitably, Bethlehem proved another narrow squeak, and in July Steyn and his commanders sped southwards.

Just a jump ahead of their enemy, they had increasingly little latitude for manoeuvre. Lieutenant General Sir Archibald Hunter was driving down from the north, and Lieutenant General Sir Leslie Rundle from the east, which gave the Free Staters no recourse other than to retreat into a wedge of land hemmed in by hills, known as the Brandwater Basin. This virtually locked in Steyn, De Wet, and Marthinus Prinsloo, chief commandant of Orange Free State forces, with around 9 000 troops. With the approaching Hunter commanding 16 000 men, the trapped Boers faced encirclement.

But before every exit could be sealed, the Boers divided and some managed to break out through a handful of navigable mountain outlets. A large column led by De Wet and accompanied by Steyn filed through successfully on 15 July and got clear away. Part of Prinsloo's command was assigned to hold open the passes until two further groups squeezed out, and then to form a retreating rear-guard for any remaining dribs and drabs. But the cover scheme came badly unstuck as the British poured into the Basin quickly, turning the Boers back. Completely boxed in, drained, fearful and demoralised commandos lost all sense of order and discipline, with Prinsloo himself involved in bitter leadership squabbles with subordinates who were trying to edge him out. It was proving virtually impossible to keep men together for any kind of cohesive defensive alignment. 'The Boer Army', as de Wet put it well, 'was in a very tight place'.[283]

The Boers thus sued for a ceasefire of several days in which to negotiate some resolution of their predicament by conferring with Steyn's headquarters. This thoroughly bemused Hunter, who anticipated that what the Boers wanted was a slackening of pressure in order to race away. As the assured winner, he refused, demanding unconditional surrender. Hardly surprisingly, Prinsloo submitted, surrendering 4 500 troops (or half the Orange Free State forces), along with 6 000 horses, 4 000 sheep, and baggage containing everything from surplus weapons to family heirlooms. Forlorn burghers without blankets asked for permission to dispatch African servants to collect them from their farms.[284]

Psychologically, this was another Paardeberg. Prinsloo and his officers instantly earned themselves the withering contempt of crusading patriots from the more impetuous, and more staunchly nationalist, younger Boer officer caste. Smuts and De Wet became the architects of a sour republican myth that Brandwater Basin had been a treasonous stab in the back. De Wet was beside himself, finding 'Prinsloo and the other chief officers there' guilty of 'nothing short of an act of murder, committed on the Government, the country and the Nation'.[285] The discredited commandant's image was not helped by his mellow fate in British hands. Rather than being shipped out to a remote Ceylonese prison camp with the rest of his men, Prinsloo was consigned to live out a miserable captivity in the soothing Cape hell of Simon's Town.

Aside from the frustration of pursuing Steyn, De Wet and the rest of the Orange Free State army in the north, Roberts had still to attend to business in the southeastern Transvaal. Here, his strategic objective was the cutting of the eastern railway link to block the passage inland of Boer supplies from Delagoa Bay and to try to reel in Kruger from his railway-base exile. The plan was for Roberts to push east, while Buller's northern advance from Natal would become the right flank of the offensive line to carry the war towards Portuguese territory. By early August, 9 000 of Buller's troops at last swung away from the Natal railway just north of Laing's Nek and moved up northeast to coordinate with

Roberts. Any remaining pockets of resistance were sewn up, and the British advance upon Komatipoort effectively severed the Boers from any remaining communications link with the outside world.

As his enemy was striking east, De la Rey saddled up west of Pretoria, demonstrating that its position was not as yet secure. He had around 7 000 loyal commandos with which to gamble. Moving fast, and aided by good scouting, this skirmishing force crashed into British posts within a hundred-mile radius west of the town, capturing some, destroying others, and brazenly taking the railhead site of Klerksdorp to the southwest of Johannesburg. On 5 August, a confident De la Rey even laid siege to a British garrison of 500 at Brakfontein, near Rustenburg west of Pretoria. The Boers were rushed by Rhodesian field force reinforcements, but held them at bay.

Republican forces which were continuing to hang on were by now split roughly into three fighting groups which, despite intermittent lapses in their command system, maintained reasonably unbroken lines of consultation. With De la Rey mounting a campaign in the western Transvaal, Botha concentrated his forces in the east, leaving De Wet to move out and cause aggravation in the Orange Free State. By now fighting virtually as soldiers on the run, the Boers attacked trains, cut telegraph wires, fired stores, bombarded outlying British military posts, and even fleetingly occupied small towns. Granted, they could not secure their trivial victories during these weeks. But neither could the British settle the contest definitively, for their occupying hold on areas such as the Transvaal's western districts was tenuous. The realisation that their commanders were already fighting a guerrilla war seemed as yet to be in few British minds.[286]

On this sustaining basis, the fighting began to fan out. In August, De Wet and his reliable Brandwater Basin veterans broke away north into the Transvaal to swell De la Rey's western concentration. Confident, clear-headed and aggressive, he wasted no time in throwing his forces against the British in battering raids from a number of directions, baffling his opponent by constant pressure across a wide front which criss-crossed the Vaal. One of these strikes was sufficiently fierce to break the security of Potchefstroom, on the western rail line from Klerksdorp to Johannesburg, forcing its evacuation and leaving the Boers 'in undisturbed possession of the town for a month'.[287] From here, burghers under General Petrus Liebenberg disrupted the railway link to the British supply depot at Krugersdorp. At the same time, though, focusing their attack on supply and communications lines quickly simplified matters for the British. With his fat cushion of reserves, Roberts was soon moving to reinforce key garrison posts on the railway south of Pretoria.

Roberts was also making a major effort to chase down De Wet and his mobile raiders. As a starting-point, the hills west of Pretoria were not a good hunting ground, and the Boers were able to manoeuvre and slip their way past their attackers and back to their operational base south of the Vaal. To end a discomfiting southern crisis, Methuen and other commanders were allocated 30 000 troops to flush the republicans out of their lair in the northwestern Orange Free State. For six edgy and exhausting weeks, Methuen's columns kept up a determined pursuit to 'corral' De Wet,[288] utilising their enormous numerical superiority and the speed of their fastest-moving cavalry to outflank snaking Boer lines of retreat. Harried hard, De Wet's commandos were compelled to stay on the hoof throughout this chase, covering over 500 miles of wild and jagged terrain. Although the British had the numbers, the large distances over which troops were having to perform and the exceptionally rough terrain sapped energies and diluted striking power. Already building up popular prestige as some republican military wizard, De Wet's ability to slip the British net only increased his stock. 'Too much and too quick on his heels to make it possible for us to finish this',[289] was the grudging compliment of one British officer.

Roberts' army encountered less trouble elsewhere. Sent to clear the countryside between the Natal and Delagoa Bay rail lines, Buller's force, which outnumbered its opponents by twenty to one, advanced on Botha's flank and broke through, swatting aside minor resistance in its path. Augmented by men released from the unproductive pursuit of De Wet, Buller's troops finally had a frontal encounter – with Botha, later in August, when the Boer general decided to stop giving ground. In the last major republican defensive positioning, Botha lined up and entrenched about 5 000 commandos and disciplined Transvaal police *Zarps* along a lengthy forty-mile front (to block any flanking penetration) near Lydenburg as a spoiling action.

With a vastly superior command of 20 000 soldiers, Buller launched a heavy assault upon the defenders on 21 August. Performing prodigies of endurance, Botha's force held up for an astonishing five days, but his front was too threadbare to maintain a coherent firing line against attackers. Perilously wide gaps between Boer trench positions widened, enabling the British to dart through and to fire upon them with slanting volleys. Staggering back as their enemy charged in to fight at close quarters, the commandos turned and fled.

East of Pretoria, the door was now permanently open. Roberts rapidly occupied Lydenburg, Barberton and Carolina, and soon moved up on Nelspruit, where Kruger and Steyn were both running out of what remaining steam they had. In the eastern Transvaal, forces still committed to the fight were also running out of secure base camps and natural shelter from which to run pin-prick attacks to slow the British.

Before remaining exit points were blocked, many worn-out commando formations broke camp and fled in various stages of disorder. Some of the most war-weary sought out the advancing enemy. Turncoat ex-combatants slid into docile new roles as imperial army guides, transport conductors, and veterinary assistants.[290] Others simply migrated away from the whole war business, reverting to a civilian identity and collecting their families, servants and livestock to trek to the safety of neighbouring territories like Rhodesia, Mozambique and Basutoland. There, they were mostly received with tolerance, and some tribute-bearing burghers even sought to put themselves under the patronage of Tswana or other African chiefs as protection against any possible cross-border Boer re-commandeering of renegade men. Yet others fell back in a straight retreat to the Komatipoort border position, staking their safety on the Portuguese.

But not everybody dodged service. Botha's most committed commandos also dropped away, but only to regroup behind the mountain barriers of the northern Transvaal.

Republican leaders could procrastinate no longer; they were now in immediate jeopardy. In response to urgings from Steyn and others, Kruger travelled to Delagoa Bay on 11 September to board a cruiser provided by the sympathetic Dutch monarchy to convey him into neutral European exile and a lavish welcome from anti-British continental factions. It was a curiously immigrant fate for an essentially anti-immigrant politician. Leaving behind Burger to discharge residual state obligations, he was never to see South Africa again, dying in Switzerland in 1904.

It is hard to resist the conclusion that the element which the ageing and frail Transvaal president lacked most was luck. He had become an increasingly marginal figure, and some within the rising new progressive and more professional military élite were not sorry to see his back. They believed that with him would go the soft-blooded, inner-circle culture of toadyism and greedy living which had so damaged the Boer war effort through lacklustre leadership, indiscipline and plain error. For the ever severe Smuts, reflecting six months later, 'as soon as we sent Pres. Kruger out of the country, and his money-grabbing, traitorous hangers-on were out of the way, the whole tone and aspect of things were altered for the better'.[291]Rid of the likes of Kruger, Cronjé and Prinsloo, martial blood would only course all the stronger.

For all Marthinus Steyn's mettle, flight for him was also the logical course, but he opted to stay and take his chances. His republic had made enormous sacrifices, and he was not about personally to give up the cause. So, with an escort of 300 first-rate commandos, his party loaded up gold and currency reserves and departed northwards on a planned route which would swing him around and back into his annexed and increasingly ravaged state.

By now, Roberts no longer saw the need for any further big blows. After a faltering start, the British had regained the initiative under his command, and in just under a year had defeated the enemy forces and had destroyed the general fighting will. Or so it certainly seemed. On 13 September, he issued a triumphal proclamation announcing Kruger's flight and giving the assurance that now the war was effectively over. By the end of that month, the British push towards Komatipoort was completed and the Mozambique communications line was gone. As their enemy approached, the Boers wrecked their wagons and destroyed surplus stores and artillery to deny their use to the enemy. Botha then halved what was left of his force to increase the British burden of pursuit, leaving the like-minded Viljoen to command the other section.

Many combatants had by now lost all heart, as morale in the eastern Transvaal continued to drain away. A British intelligence officer concluded that dispirited enemy combatants were welcoming the arrival of troops, because 'they know our growing presence means the end of this calamitous war'.[292] They had also encountered few stories of gratuitous British mistreatment of captured Boer soldiers.

Saddled with almost 3 000 unwarlike commandos and foreign volunteers who were desperate for a way out of continuing hostilities, Botha decently pushed them off towards Komatipoort and a choice between being interned by the Portuguese colonial administration or being taken prisoner by the British.

Irish and other foreign nationals were combed out and repatriated to Europe and America (to a chorus of republican reproach from Dublin, Paris and Boston).

In the last week of October 1900, Roberts proclaimed the annexation of the South African Republic. He had no second thoughts on winding down the war, assuring London that troop withdrawals could commence shortly, as all that was still required were a few policing sweeps to round up rebellious stragglers. Also in October, the Natal army was disbanded. Buller returned to Britain and still to considerable popular acclaim as the common soldier's general, the bluff if faintly ostentatious South African embodiment of Victorian military achievement. But the critical knives were out at the War Office, and he would soon be facing awkward questions about his management of the Natal campaign. On 28 November, with the war publicly declared to be as good as over, Roberts appointed the cerebral and unlikeable Kitchener his successor in command and left for Britain as yet another imperial army totem, to be rarely seen out of full dress.

While the Boers were plainly losing force in the concluding months of Roberts' command, some problems were not only persisting but growing in this transitional period. Estimating that De Wet had at most 3 000 fighting men to hand in the Orange Free State, Roberts almost ended up under-prepared.

In the tense and battered northeastern region, the impact of the attrition already being waged against farmsteads and the harrying of both women and men was ambiguous. For some, the steeply rising costs of the conflict deepened war weariness. But others faced a dilemma. For armed burghers, the choice was either to fall back to rural immiseration and an uncertain hold on the means of life, or to throw in one's lot with resumed commando activity. This could mean more than joining improvised units to hit back at the enemy, for in banding together as a fighting group there would be Crown loyalist stores to plunder, and foodstuffs to be carried off from luckless African peasants.

Zealots such as Smuts and De Wet were inclined to see in this renewed resolve a patriotic closing of ranks to fight on despite mounting hardships. Yet it is difficult to be certain of the depth or scale of such convictions in unlettered or lesser-educated burghers. Perhaps what can be ventured is the possibility that worsening conditions in parts of the countryside aided the task of some of De Wet's propagandising veterans. Dispersed into farming districts, they turned to strong oratory and the public reading of war bulletins (of varying veracity) to whip into life a localised kind of popular national resistance. To be worth anything, its rallying cries had to galvanise disconsolate men to return to fighting duties.

In these circumstances, what was beginning to show, as it was virtually bound to, was something of a paradox. It was easier getting beaten, vagrant, war-weathered men back to arms than those holed up in calmer districts which had escaped the more harrowing experiences of the Roberts firestorm. The farm-stripping and burning already well in hand under his command was by no means always aiding the objective of conquest. Far from it: some affected burghers were sticking to commandos because they no longer had homesteads and a fixed family to which to return.[293]

Commandants were already becoming aware of this unpleasant irony by mid-1900. So were the more far-sighted British officers, who worried that 'excessive' or 'unsparing' destructiveness would only end up benefiting the enemy cause by keeping combatants in the field. 'The Burgher out on Commando is bound always to his farm,' wrote one, 'by burning it and sending his family packing, we are only making him a roving desperado, consumed with hatred.' Captain Francis Fletcher-Vane was one of a good few who concluded at the war's end 'that if farms had not been burnt the war would have been sooner over'.[294] It is certainly arguable that Roberts made one of the crucial British mistakes of the war by getting scorched-earth measures underway so early in his campaign across republican soil. Not only was its terror disproportionate for an enemy which was already buckling. Worse, instead of bringing on an end to the war, its impact was far more likely to prolong its duration. As a strategic error, it would make Buller's bungling in Natal look like small beer.

By October 1900, there were between 8 000 and 9 000 burghers back in the field. The British had not anticipated having to face an opposition force of this size, and certainly not one out to create systematic havoc. Sure enough, Orange Free State commandos tried to start up a minor counter-offensive to hinder British movements, interrupt the flow of supplies, and sever telegraph communications. Abandoning their own use of wireless telegraph, the Boers split into small sabotaging parties which flitted about at night to disable telegraph loops, forcing much greater use of the heliograph upon their adversary. While the bright, clear air of the South African interior permitted mirror signals to be sent across impressive distances of up to 100 miles, they had the disadvantage of being easily monitored and deciphered by the enemy.

De Wet also closed in more boldly. On 20 October, his force attacked a column on the banks of the rail line at Frederikstad, bringing the British to a fierce pitched encounter for all of five days before reinforcements arrived from Krugersdorp to push the commandos back. For Roberts, the day was saved, but only just. At the same time, his enemy was becoming ever more confident. Believing that the British had come close to being routed, De Wet blamed his men for not occupying the entire frontal position. But some of his more wary combatants felt that at Frederikstad he was taking unnecessary chances with their lives. There was always a limit to what Boer leaders could expect from their troops.

Later in October, the Boers began to take a string of small towns in a series of surprise attacks on their British encampments, perhaps most notably in a daring assault, in bad light, on the enemy camp in the Jacobsdal market-place, a spot which had been a former Orange Free State field headquarters.

Inevitably, these remained denting incursions rather than a strategy to accumulate solid gains. For, by now, the spread and constantly improving mobility of the British meant that reinforcements could mostly be run in at short notice. Nonetheless, for De Wet, De la Rey and Botha, not everything was lost from a strategic point of view. Leaders still clung to the hope that by prolonging hostilities they might sap Britain sufficiently to bring about an end to the war by negotiation.

At the end of October, Steyn joined Botha, De la Rey and Smuts in a prolonged planning session at a hideaway west of Pretoria. This took stock of emerging republican possibilities and problems, as the picture was now looking clear enough. Britain's hope of detaching one or other republic, so as to have a greater chance of finishing off its ally, had receded. The fight could therefore be continued as a fully pan-nationalist guerrilla struggle.

At the start of the war, there had been some prickliness in respective Boer territorial ranks about being commanded by men who were not from their native republic. As the guerrilla struggle got underway, rooted regionalism may have been accentuated further by actions in which 'OFS burghers tended to fight more tenaciously than some of their Transvaal counterparts'.[295] Yet, for the republican leadership, worsening military prospects were now turning the commando into the school of the nation, a valued agent of 'nationalisation'. For, as their fortunes had contracted in tandem, so commandos north and south of the Vaal were growing more willing to mix things up and to defer to each other's officer authority. Boer field forces were not as yet down to the halt and the lame, and in hit-and-run operations casualties would be relatively light and bearable. While the ranks of good riflemen had been denuded, the remaining core was skilled, committed and nimble.

The problem was the burning and sacking. Although it was not breaking the Boers, and was actually helping to keep burghers in the war, its cost to civilians was growing greater by the day. In the northeastern Orange Free State and eastern and western Transvaal, women and children were being hammered hard. Beyond their plight lay a further consequence of rural destruction. Not only was it destroying the means of livelihood, but it was also threatening the elimination of commandos' remaining campaigning grounds. For evasive riding and counter-riding, resisting burghers needed avenues of retreat to replenishing bases, and they needed protective enclosures like the lost Brandwater basin.[296] They could not fall back to stubble. In this, something of what Roberts was doing was effective.

The only way to ease the pressure would be a strategic initiative to distract the British. Here, Botha and Steyn were not without foresight, however short they may have been on means. The Boers hit on a fresh campaigning solution, almost a grand design: it was to carry the war on a guerrilla basis back into British territory. In Natal and the Cape, it would be politically tricky for the British to teach the more disloyal rural settlers the hardships and terrors of war through farm incendiarism and wholesale evictions. And if good routes of advance were properly worked out, and surprise was sustained, then a breakthrough was possible. British second-line colonial garrisons could be disrupted as they would not know where to move until it was too late to check their opponents from securing new positions. This move was to be preceded by a strategic return to the old lure of the Rand and its gold.

Drawing up Steyn and De Wet behind a combined Transvaal-Orange Free State strike and prodding others who were more timid, Smuts laid out a far-fetched campaign to try to settle accounts through agility and intrigue. Early in 1901, the enemy in Johannesburg would be drawn away in a diversionary action, while a republican force of some 12 000 to 15 000 would be held back in preparedness to strike in a straight line through the Witwatersrand. After seeing 'all mines and mining property blown up and completely destroyed', in the ensuing confusion Botha would slip down into Natal, and De Wet and De la Rey would open a wedge into the Cape.

There seemed to be some practical and even moral justification for an action of this kind. For one thing, Smuts had decided that as the gold mines were now a British political possession, economic sabotage would be a defensible expedient. For another, a big gesture of reprisal would be grand as war bulletin news to boost the morale of the commandos. And, in a further sense, action against the industrial resources of the Witwatersrand would also show that the doctrine of levelling destruction was no longer the monopoly of the British. Indeed, it would not come even close to emulating Britain's South African war crimes. Although 'an extreme measure', Smuts stressed that the blow inflicted by mine wrecking would 'not be one-tenth of what the policy of farm-burning and women-driving was inflicting on the Boer people'. The ruining of gold production combined with a new offensive thrust could 'have had a very different influence on the future of the war'.[297]

Perhaps, but it was not to be. After the western Transvaal talks, Steyn slipped off to join De Wet's commandos, and was in their midst during one of De Wet's flying visits on the morning of 6 November. It was an unhappy visit. Lounging on a farm northwest of Kroonstad, the Boers were unexpectedly caught in broad daylight with their guard down, either snoozing or plainly idling. As the British closed in, their startled enemy scampered in leaderless flight, ignoring De Wet's frantic efforts to *sjambok* (whip) them into making a stand. The Boers lost 150 men, artillery, wagons, and stampeding horses. While Steyn wasted no time in getting away, a small rearguard took a grip and held off their attackers until De Wet was able to compose his commandos and range them against the British in a flanking counter-attack.

This seesaw phase took another dip with the arrival of British reinforcements in much superior strength. After a short-lived but ugly exchange involving snipers, the Boers' desperate employment of women and children as improvised cover, their use of mutilating dum-dum or fragmenting bullets, and some brusque post-battle reprisals, they were forced to give up. Astonishingly, however, De Wet squirmed away to fight another day. This abrupt retreat, and the simultane- ous frustration of De la Rey and Smuts, destroyed any serious prospects of a co- ordinated joint Boer strategy. The aims were now different: the Boers would continue to play for time, and make it as difficult as possible for the British to defeat them.

The last month of Roberts' command turned out to be bumpy. Fresh pockets of resistance flared up in the northeastern Orange Free State, with convoys captured and plundered, supply-train stoppages in which drivers were targeted by marksmen (this involved less effort than blocking the line), and the blasting of communications points. There were numerous such incursions, although few worthy of individual record.

By mid-November, De Wet, not one to hang about, had mapped out a penetrating route south for a republican invasion of the Cape. Alert to this, Roberts quickly sent a column in pursuit in what would become known in war folklore as the second of the 'Great De Wet Hunts'. Moving rapidly to the attack when an opportunity opened, the Boers struck at Dewetsdorp (De Wet's home town) on 23 November, duelling fiercely with its British garrison for three days until it was forced to surrender. Exulted by this strike, De Wet charged on.

Although headed off eventually by their more numerous and better provisioned pursuers, his commandos kept a wide margin of ground across which to wheel. So, even if obliged to turn around and run back to less risky northern positions, De Wet's force tied up the British sufficiently to give Generals J.B.M. Hertzog and Piet Kritzinger enough slack to take around 2 000 commandos across the Orange River and into the northern Cape on 17 December.

Exactly one week earlier, Roberts had been seen off finally by Milner, who made a big effort to show warmth to his departing commander-in-chief, despite his feeling that there was something 'almost repulsive' about the fawning over 'Bobs' [Roberts] when they were inescapably still 'in the middle of war'.[298]

By now, the Boers were doing their best to underline that reality in other areas which served as their bolt-holes. Their drowsiness was broken in part by cheering news of De Wet's fleet-footed accomplishments. His forces in the northeastern Transvaal and on the high plateau south of the lost Delagoa Bay rail corridor now began to raise their game. Botha and Viljoen had recruited encouraging numbers into their respective commands, and there was a greater will to move. Hungry for the credit of some striking victory, Transvaal leadership consolidated their units for a coordinated offensive manoeuvre to regain some forward initiative.

Early in December, De la Rey and Smuts tracked down a heavily provisioned but lightly guarded British convoy outside Rustenburg. Led on by their advance scouts, they swooped, killing, wounding, or capturing 120 British soldiers, flogging or executing over twenty African drivers, torching 115 wagons, and making off with the remainder. These contained much that, as guerrillas, they needed – medical supplies, clothing, and boots. The fact that they tossed aside the Bollinger champagne, *Grand Cru,* and vintage port can only have confirmed some British officers' prejudices about the Boers' grasp on civilisation.

Thereafter, Transvaal forces looked for bigger fish, and hooked it in Nooitgedacht gorge in the Magaliesberg on 13 December.

There, Major General Richard Clements foolishly discounted danger with his choice of camp site, placing his men at the foot of steep cliff faces. He had neglected basic intelligence, skimped on pickets for his crucial outer line, and then paid the price. Smuts and De la Rey extended the striking power of generals Christiaan Beyers and Jacobus Kemp, so that when the Boers attacked they outnumbered the British by more than two to one. Sustaining negligible losses through their tight command of the imposing terrain running downwards from koppie firing positions, commandos, mainly from the Krugersdorp, Waterberg and Zoutpansberg, drew plenty of blood. They inflicted some 640 casualties, amounting to half the strength of Clements' force, ran off hundreds of draught animals, seized over 120 mule carts and ox wagons, and fired other transport and combustible equipment. If this could be kept up in the Magaliesberg, mused one hardened and hopeful veteran, the enemy could become so depleted of supplies and impaired in fighting capacity that it might be forced to give up the countryside and withdraw to hold only the towns.[299] In the end, there would be nothing left to requisition and the British would have to bargain for peace.

This optimism, though, could only have come from reading one republican war bulletin too many.

What Nooitgedacht also revealed was a degree of Boer uncertainty of purpose and vacillation on the battlefield. Despite a rare position in which they could have finished what they had started, the Boers stopped short of a knock-out blow. They had outnumbered, outmanoeuvred and pinned down a faltering force which had little effective cover. Here, too, reliable scouting had picked up that enemy reinforcements were certain to be late in coming. Yet the Boers did not press home their advantage. Without trenches, British troops would have been slaughtered or forced to capitulate by accurate artillery bombardment. As it was, the Boer generals held off, allowing the surviving enemy troops to retreat to Pretoria.

In other respects, though, their combatants were being true to form and their command could not but be reminded of what that form was. Given the choice between foraging through the vacated British camp or straightening up to finish off the fight, the tired and hungry burghers followed their stomachs. With the essential job done, there was no need for them to chance their lives in continued hostilities, however much Beyers or Kemp might admonish them with a customary fatherly whipping. Furthermore, British prisoners were now a drag, not a gain, as there was little food to sustain them and no easy holding places to which they could be consigned. There also remained divisive differences in command objectives within republican leadership. This produced a clash of styles between a clinical and disciplined Smuts, who wanted to stay on the attack in any and every way possible, and a coarser and lower-minded Beyers, who rather relished the distractions offered to his force by plundering opportunities. The real problem was an old one: the civilian-soldier's resistance to a common elementary discipline, and disagreement within command structure over direction.

While the new year did not bring any unified republican direction of the war, at local levels it continued to flicker. Early in 1901, Botha and Viljoen linked up their columns and sought out a new operational base in the east, near Machadodorp. There, on 7 January, they chanced their hand in a daring, well-timed assault on seven thinly screened garrisons along the Delagoa Bay line, thereby bisecting British control of the eastern corridor zone. The thinking behind a stalking attack to open up a disruptive gap was enterprising. But this time, the terrain and weather worked against the Boers: heavy night fog and twisted terrain sent the commandos fumbling rather than stealing forward in attack.

Surprise was swiftly lost, and the British held firm. Meanwhile, knots of mounted commandos elsewhere continued to start running fights on ground where they felt most at home tactically, and where they judged that lighter, detached enemy forces could be beaten. While these forays produced little more than glancing blows, some could still be costly for the invaders. Thus, one shock attack in the far northeastern corner of the Orange Free State brought down a British company, with close-range rifle volleys killing more than 150 men. Although these were blistering engagements, they amounted to playing a hand. What the Boers required for 1901 was someone to conjure up a renewed offensive initiative, with a sense of purpose and a realistic end in view. The alternative was to carry on with a grinding, piecemeal approach, and merely delaying inevitable defeat.

An attempt of sorts to do just this came from an Orange Free State leadership pulled along by De Wet. It involved a return to the aborted October 1900 scheme to mount a wide, deep offensive to relieve the attritional pressure on the lower belly of republican society. On 27 January, in a four-pronged advance to enter the Cape, De Wet began to track south to cross the Orange into British territory.

De Wet's aim was to find and join up commandos and Cape colonial rebels and to impose some positioning discipline and direction over the roaming bands. Then Hertzog, now second-in-command of Orange Free State forces, was dispatched in a westerly direction. This grouping was to proceed across the trackless landscape of the northwestern Cape to the Namaqualand coast, and to open up Lambert's Bay for a rumoured shipment of European munitions and volunteer infantry. This bounty was an illusory objective, and probably the closest the warring Boers ever came to behaving like some later Pacific islanders who, before and during World War II, evolved 'cargo cult' obsessions centred on the arrival of Allied and Japanese war materials. But then, this was not always a war about common sense.

Planning to raise additional recruits from the large number of Cape republicans believed still to be willing to take up arms, De Wet intended to rendezvous with Hertzog and then to march southwest to threaten Cape Town. In a third bold entry, the hard-riding and hard-talking Kritzinger was given a 1 000-strong force of commandos and set loose in the interior lands of the Cape midlands, to accumulate more rebels, to harry loyalist white and black inhabitants, and to cause a commotion which could serve to encourage local resistance to British control.[300]

Finally, there were Louis Botha's plans for Natal. His brief called for him to move down into the Colony with around 1 000 men from the eastern border of the Transvaal. Eyes were on the British encampment at Dundee, to be followed by a stab at the railway at Glencoe to deprive the Transvaal occupation force of its principal trunk route. Kitchener, though, was not taken by surprise, and sent French and his large eastern Transvaal mounted force of 21 000 troops after Botha.

Yet, to ensure success required knocking out more than mounted burghers. The British had to ensure that their harried enemy could not creep back into territory which contained food and shelter, as well as scatterings of spies, farm-house snipers, and arms caches. Not famous for being 'soft when it came to the enemy',[301] French intensified Roberts' scorched-earth strategy behind Botha, scouring areas clean, destroying crops, live-stock, and wagons, and firing farm-houses. A punitive scouring to chill the spines of those in the field, it included the drama of a single artful blow: the dynamiting of Louis Botha's own house. Having served in the Sudan with Kitchener and Buller, French knew all about going beyond strict military necessity in irregular warfare.

Ahead of the Transvaal Boers were the key entry points into British Natal, too well-guarded or patrolled to be broken, and now backed by effective intelligence and communications systems. Break-ins by the familiar routes were blocked, and while intermittent raiding scooped up British arms and ammunition, it did not bring in good horses with feed nor replenish vanishing food stocks. There were sufficient British troops not to become over-extended in standing on defence, and by September 1901 Botha's force had been driven in on the southeastern border of Zululand.

To have continued across would have exposed the Boers to new danger. Earlier in the war, the British had relied on the mobilising of relatively 'sedate and dis-ciplined defensive bodies',[302] like the several hundred-strong Zululand Native Police, to give the Boers second thoughts about meddling in Zululand. Now, the administration looked to the far more formidable prospect of 10 000 to 12 000 warriors, bristling with assegais and some with firearms, to chase away any in-vaders. After a couple of expensive reverses against British positions in the vicinity in late September, Botha's heart appeared to be in it no longer, and his beaten commandos broke off and raced back to the Transvaal.[303] At least 15 000 British troops followed to ensure no slackening of their pace.

Elsewhere, the fluttering wings of combined Boer operations had been clipped. During February, Hertzog and Kritzinger's forces were slimmed down and pushed in a westerly direction, back towards the Orange Free State, by flying columns. While on a forward campaign the Boers were, in effect, having to act defen-sively. Their large, combined column made it easier for the British to fix their location. The Boers responded by dissolving into small commando units, which enabled them to survive parasitically, but, at the same time, it reduced their striking capability, soon restricted mainly to sporadic attacks upon African and Coloured labourers and smallholders.

But De Wet could still not be chased into ground where the British could get at him. With his quarry over the Orange and into the Cape by the second week of February, Kitchener put in thousands of troops to blanket the Karoo region, using the Colesberg locality as a logistical base. He also placed a thick line of mounted columns running south from Kroonstad to Naauwpoort in the Cape. Using the trusted bush war method of picking good troops who could travel light and handle the challenge of troublesome terrain and extended distances, fifteen British columns were set off in a third De Wet Hunt. Although the Free Stater's planned northwards retreat was cut off for a time by flooding of the Orange River, he did not lose his edge when on the run. Abandoning his remaining guns and any other cumbersome equipment, he outran his pursuers for a full six weeks, eluding every trap, until finally he was able to make his way back, to be swallowed by the expanses of the Orange Free State highveld.

Many of the British officers involved in this pursuit found the experience – of being persistently misled by an inferior force – profoundly grating. Although the threat had been removed from the Cape, it was blood that they wanted. A 'humiliating state of affairs', wrote a Namaqualand Field Force intelligence officer, 'the cheeky Boers have again been able to move away . . . . it is all as vexing as a mysterious robbery'.[304] Yet, the fact that De Wet prevailed was no mystery. On the British side, it was down to signalling difficulties between branching columns, some uncertain mapping, and key shortcomings in staff training for tactical field intelligence, with the Boers easily intercepting sensitive communications passed across without encipherment.

On the Boer side, the formula was a better mix. Its elements included better horses and horsemanship, retention of the best mounts for long-range scouting, intimate knowledge of the terrain in the southern Orange Free State and northern Cape, and an intelligence grasp resting upon a pro-republican Boer civilian population.

To these was added the ability of Boer command to deny their men the use of those cumbersome ox wagons which dragged along such vital essentials as stoves and mattresses. At this level, military matters had grown much trimmer since the first 1900 De Wet chase. Then, the general had been wary of compelling his burghers to ditch their wagons, fearing mutiny.[305] Despite facing an approaching enemy force of over 50 000 troops, the 2 000 commandos had clung to a baggage train of 460 wagons and carts. That was probably with good personal reason: wagons and animals were prized personal capital assets, without which their futures would be jeopardised even further. Now, whatever his fears, De Wet would not contemplate being hamstrung by his own laager. A guerrilla war could not be fought with bulky creature comforts which slowed movement.

Within this continuing Boer prosecution of the war there was evolving — as Kitchener, for one, rightly saw — a spreading conviction among burghers who had surrendered that there was no point in looking to the battlefield for salvation. It had also become futile for many commandos still in the field to continue the struggle in the expectation of some mirage of foreign diplomatic intervention, European aid, or an imperial loss of will. As defeat could not be avoided, a feeling was emerging that arms should be laid down voluntarily. That was essential to ending the war in a way that could provide for the making of a negotiated, soldierly peace in which the Boers might be allowed to surrender with honour. For this, an initiative was needed before the two sides were driven even further apart and more of the countryside ruined.

Those burghers whose war was over debated what to do. Towards the end of 1900, a couple of urban middle-class ex-commandos employed their riches and political pull to leave the Transvaal for London, where their persistence landed them an audience with Chamberlain. The colonial secretary was quite taken with the idea of dispatching 'peace emissaries' to the republican fighting forces to present the case for good sense, and authorised Milner and Kitchener to explore possibilities.[306]

Kitchener, who had been closely monitoring the general state of Boer morale through personal contact with surrendered Transvaal combatants and interceptions of strategic information by his improving field intelligence department, saw this as a timely intervention. Given the nod, several burgher peace committees were set up in the Transvaal, moves which then crossed over into the Orange Free State. Their Boer representatives stressed the odds against them, emphasised that no one could be blamed for yielding to defeat, and urged the commandos to create peace by disarmament. By demonstrating their pacific intentions, they 'would be assured of better treatment in future'.

In the opening months of 1901, a serious attempt to convert fighters was undertaken by the emerging peace interest, aided and abetted by the British high command. Given the increasingly scattered distribution of commandos, communication was a rather hit-or-miss affair. Still, almost 30 000 handbills and leaflets were sent fluttering into the countryside, and a small body of reliable apostates was saddled up to make contact with individual commandos to 'add reason' or to 'bring sane views' to the nightly campfire politics in the Boer laagers. The Boer peace movement also tried to make use of potential conciliationist elements which lay beyond the republics. This was helped by a memorable contribution from a fighting family bloodline. General Piet de Wet, younger brother of Christiaan de Wet, had surrendered to Methuen in July 1900, and he now led a burgher peace delegation to the Cape to foster the cause among prisoners of war held being held there. He also sought the moral support of Cape Boer clergymen and influential Afrikaner Bond personalities.[307]

But Piet de Wet and the others had a hard time of it. Most prisoners spurned those they regarded as renegades. A handful risked breaking ranks, but the moral constraints and solidarities of camp life ensured that the majority of captives stayed true to the cause. At the same time, prominent Cape Boers professed themselves reluctant to become embroiled in the increasingly bitter divisions of an internally warring republican society. There was some sympathy for the De Wet peace deputation, but any tears in response to its message were of the crocodile kind. Out in the field, it was even harder going. Peace-committee burghers found it difficult to persuade toughened commandos who, unsurprisingly, viewed them as deserters and traitors. A number were taken captive, fined, or had their property destroyed, while a few unfortunates were flogged or even executed.

Perhaps the most striking of these failed attempts at massaging an enemy surrender was that arranged personally by Kitchener himself, once firmly in charge as successor to Roberts. He had no desire for fighting on if parleying with Boer generals would resolve matters on his terms. Accordingly, feelers were put out for a Transvaal conference with Louis Botha at Middelburg along the Delagoa Bay line. Botha consented to crossing the enemy lines under safe escort, and entered the town on 28 February 1901. At this stage, Kitchener's political outlook was not especially vindictive. Provided that the Boer leadership accepted imperial annexation of the republics as final and not to be haggled over, the proposed peace terms would not be without sweeteners. This could include war-damage compensation in the form of a levy upon the gold mines, and an assurance to the Boer political élite that they would have command of their own interests and would not be subject to the will of Rand capitalists. Furthermore, there could be a general amnesty, not merely for republican combatants, but for Cape and Natal colonial rebels, too. Lastly, an improved legal position for the African majority would not be pushed down the Boers' throats in any peace settlement. Kitchener was, if anything, rather taken by the big stick of republican 'native laws', and wanted to see them embedded, not watered down by any metropolitan liberal sentiment about wider civil rights.[308]

Rarely inclined to be lenient, Milner was at best lukewarm about talks, and he and Kitchener squabbled over this and that point of concessionary peace terms. In London, Chamberlain and the Cabinet raised difficulties over a rebel amnesty and the absence of any regard for the statutory rights of Africans in any peace agreement. But Milner was interested only in obstruction, pruning back Kitchener's ideas on reparations for damage to the rural economy to limited compensation to farmers for wartime losses in horses. The armistice negotiations had as good as failed. In the event, Botha shrank from the final British ten-point peace plan, advising Kitchener that it would be difficult to persuade his fellow generals to call off fighting on the basis of such niggardly terms.

Thus, Kitchener's chances of making a negotiated peace drained away, leaving him exasperated. He was being given no political latitude by Milner and the British government, which maintained an unwavering adherence to unconditional surrender. Equally, Botha could not act alone, and those around him were not enthusiastic peacemakers. Kitchener's objective was to end the war, and quickly, but its resolution would continue to lie in the balance between what was militarily possible and politically practicable. Middelburg demonstrated the dilemma of getting one factor to tilt the other. Had the British already cornered De Wet and the obdurate Steyn, Kitchener might have strengthened Botha's restraining hand in persuading other commanders to come in on the Middelburg deliberations. As Lionel James, chief war correspondent of *The Times* concluded towards the end of March 1901, 'military pacification was now the only problem in South Africa and had not yet succeeded sufficiently well'.[309]

In an aftermath of renewed Boer pessimism over what lay above any dotted line, peace talks of this kind (or, indeed, of any kind) were ever more fiercely opposed by groups of Orange Free State officers. This applied most especially to the key figure, Christiaan de Wet. He was growing increasingly suspicious of

Botha, whose reputedly amiable correspondence with Kitchener was looking to him, ominously, as bad faith. The burgher peace movement, too, signally failed in its purpose during this phase of the war, although one scholarly authority has suggested that its propaganda effects on rank-and-file combatants should be seen as a factor behind the distinct increase in the number of surrendering burghers in February and March 1901.[310] That notwithstanding, the ultimate difficulty for peace collaborators was their inability to act as neutral mediators between belligerents. Their position could not be anything other than shameful. As men who had limply surrendered their arms, and thereby their rightful claim upon the totems of republican manhood and citizenship, they had no credit in the eyes of their ex-commanders. In operating tamely under British direction, they were Kitchener's partisan ally. In a sense, the reviled burgher peace emissaries were sawing off the very branch upon which they had decided to sit.

On the other hand, the emergence of collaborationist peace energies clearly reflected the untidy factional fissures which the war had by now opened up within the body of Boer society. One rupture was, as we have noted, the relations between surrendered burghers and uncompromising patriots who were set on continuing the independence fight, come what may. Another was disagreement among those of a more moderate nationalist stripe, who had concluded that the struggle was now hopeless and immensely damaging, and radical 'rejectionists', including women who had been maltreated by British soldiers, who wanted the fight to go on to its bitter end. Such Boer females were like the French women whose areas had been occupied by the German army by 1917. Male countrymen who had deserted or given up, found that 'their womenfolk told them to go back'.[311]

As a doctrine, actual pacifism never took hold. It is a truism that religious feeling among fighting burghers was extremely deep, but the stiff certainties of a united Calvinist Protestantism probably smothered any humanist or 'secularising' dissent from the notion of fighting a just 'English War'. It was more the case that 'the Christian faith and the war effort were closely linked'.[312] Religious faith 'kept the courage and the moral sense of the burghers up to the mark' for this was a sacrificial patriotic struggle for survival.[313]

Rather more interesting was the manner in which the war crisis unlocked less conventional expressions of fundamental religious faith — a mixture of super-

stitions, prophecies and millenarianism on the fighting front. The weirdest embodiment of this was undoubtedly an increasingly influential republican vision-
ary or prophet, *Siener* (Seer) Niklaas van Rensburg. Although regarded with
coolness or derided as crazy by the educated, more 'European' commanders
like the sophisticated Deneys Reitz and the worldly Ernst Marais, Siener van
Rensburg was able to lodge himself under the credulous wing of De la Rey in
the western Transvaal. Under this patronage, his richly elaborate prophecies and
ranting predictions were listened to avidly by ordinary burghers and the more
rustic of commanders, not least of them De la Rey himself.

Visions infused with homespun rural symbolism served as a kind of supernatural subsidy to continuing commando exertions. They included warning
predictions of precise British attacks on laagers, psychic confirmation of the
outcome of impending Anglo-Boer clashes (such as that between De la Rey and
Methuen late in the war), and various other occult observances of danger. Both
De la Rey and Steyn swore that their survival in a number of close-run encounters was due to Van Rensburg's timely premonitions of a sudden closing enemy
movement. A good scoring rate also boosted his reputation among *bittereinders*.
It is by no means easy to get a reliable sense of the influence of the supernatural
over the minds of fighting burghers. But there can be little doubt of the workings of superstitious practices among hard-pressed men in the field, desperate
for helpful omens and consoling signs.[314]

While random prophets concentrated on psychic tactical intelligence, the
Boers continued to fight on a tried earthly basis. If surprise could be achieved,
a lightly held British line could always be penetrated, and frontal forces and
convoys could still be knocked down if they were caught napping. To increase
their ability to ride faster and more freely, commandos jettisoned most of their
remaining field artillery during the latter half of 1901, sticking to minor engagements. A fair portion of this activity consisted of increased attacks on enemy
convoys which, with the approach of winter, were bringing in urgently needed
food, clothing and other supplies. The results were a mixed bag, with attackers
sometimes being beaten off by superior British firepower.

Then there were impetuous dawn assaults on troop concentrations, with riflemen riding down hard to open fire before wheeling away to avoid being gunned
down by superior fire. There were also a great many night attacks on British
camps in the eastern and western Transvaal, with the Boers sometimes preparing

hidden positions in advance to provide Maxim and Vickers guns with good flat trajectories of fire. And there were opportunities to move when the enemy strayed too near, moves which were usually too tempting to ignore.

In these tussles, the Boers tried to make up for want of numbers by employing innovative attack techniques. For instance, at the end of May 1901, De la Rey chanced upon a mounted British column camped near Vlakfontein in the Magaliesberg. General Jan Kemp brought his force of 1 500 riflemen to bear, advancing in a flanking movement along a rising incline to within 600 yards of the enemy, downing British pickets and their outlying African scouts. Cutting into a favourable wind, commandos scattered gunpowder on the ground to fire up a thick protective smokescreen, which bemused the British about the size of the enemy force. Firing from the saddle in a storming attack, the republicans inflicted 180 casualties before breaking off. They lost about forty of their own men.

Yet, the outcome of such positive strikes simply posed the problem: stealing a march on the enemy was something, but nothing like enough. In other words, the Boers faced a strategic blockage. If the British could still be damaged, they could not be repulsed. Kemp's force was cunning and courageous, but tried to do too much with too few men. Granted, time could always be gained, but for what? After the Vlakfontein battle, the British columns simply shook themselves off and resumed what they had been doing: burrowing away for hidden caches of weapons on farmland.

The republican territorial heartlands, still obstinate war theatres, became a confusing maze of attacks and retreats from place to place, the actions governed by pure chance and opportunity rather than any commanding Boer strategic aim. With few if any periods of inactivity, it was a tense and exhausting time. In June 1901, De Wet and Steyn had another narrow squeak near Reitz, in the Orange Free State, when their convoy was trapped by a British drive. A month later, in Reitz itself, Steyn was nearly swept up again when a stealthy encircling British attack netted Kitchener almost the entire Orange Free State government and its war cabinet. Although the president was able to use up another life to run another day, it was a serious psychological loss.

In September and October, with 'Boer operations on all fronts heated up',[315] matters took a slightly different turn. Having got wind of the extent to which British strength in the western Transvaal was being diluted by the need to run troops down to deal with Botha's second Natal invasion, De la Rey and his 3 000-

strong force attacked a column commanded by Robert Kekewich in the Zeerust area. The ferocity of this sudden onslaught panicked some of Kekewich's untried soldiers, set horses and mules off in a dozen directions, and inflicted a loss of 200 men. To retrieve the situation, Kekewich and Methuen combined their forces to catch De la Rey while he was still roaming around Zeerust. Instead, the biters were bitten as the Boers struck again, the weight of casualties and supply losses being borne by the British rearguard.

Just as earlier conventional campaigning included the ruthless destruction of the Orange Free State countryside to bring home to civilians the horrors of military conquest, so the guerrilla confrontation threw up one or two last-ditch battles in the old style. Towards the end of December 1901, at Tweefontein, east of Bethlehem in the Orange Free State, De Wet seized a chance to turn his 700 or so men on a scratch force of drowsing British units. Commandos reconnoitred the enemy hill-top camp for several days, selecting a prudent approach and preparing well. A slope judged too steep to assail had been left unguarded by the British. It was a fatal mistake, for a probing De la Rey had picked out a gulley through which his troops could get to the summit undetected. In the dark, early on Christmas Day, filing Boers, many in stockings or with feet bound in rags or smeared in dung to muffle noise, overran the sleeping encampment. The use of dum-dum bullets at close range inflicted gruesome casualties, with British losses eventually topping 300 men in addition to 500 horses and scores of laden wagons. This upset caused Kitchener to roll his eyes. Yet, he remained optimistic, confident that the tide could not be turned by what he perceived to be the desperate thrashing of a dying enemy. As if to confirm this, at the end of February 1902, pounding columns under General Henry Rawlinson enveloped a complete commando on its last legs and falling over to surrender, handing the British almost 800 prisoners, 25 000 cattle and 2 000 horses.

Nevertheless, several months later De la Rey was still displaying the art of surprise and behaving like a general who could not possibly return with anything less than victory. In March 1902, in the last major engagement of the war on Transvaal soil, he turned and sank his teeth into his pursuers. Once again, these were the forces Methuen was using to run him to ground in the unsparing immensity of the countryside between the Mafeking railway spur and the Magaliesberg. It was terrain which De la Rey and his men knew intimately, and upon which they had been able to lay their hands, as British command had been concentrating mostly on efforts to round up Botha and De Wet. After weeks of sharp and evasive moves to hold his enemy at bay, De la Rey sallied out in a surprise attack on three British columns at Tweebosch near Lichtenburg.

His appetite had been whetted by an action a little earlier, when his force had cracked open a convoy and removed 380 troops for a loss of fifty of his own men. Now, De la Rey pounced on Methuen himself. A combination of Boer heroics, tactical awareness of the enemy's weakest points, the rawness of British troops and damaging lapses in coordination proved both disastrous and humiliating for Methuen. Wounded, and pinned down by his horse, which had been shot from under him, he fell into De la Rey's hands, while his force sustained almost 200 casualties for a republican loss of thirty-five men. On 7 March, the British force raised the white flag. The Boers had captured their first enemy general.

Having contributed his fair share towards the destruction of crops, livestock and homesteads, that general could not have anticipated kid-gloved treatment from his captor. But De la Rey had a streak of the old-fashioned, chivalrous Christian warrior in him. And, in any event, a humbled Methuen was probably not much with which to barter.[316] He was received courteously, taken to Klerksdorp for his wounds to be treated, and convalesced on roast chicken cooked by Koos de la Rey's wife, Nonnie, a woman whose Lichtenburg house he had once almost burned. A fine balance between being fed or being choked, this was, surely, the war's greatest individual irony. Methuen's position could not have been anything other than mortifying. He was then generously released, fully clothed, escaping the fate of other captured troops who were often run off stark naked after being stripped to ease an acute commando clothing shortage.

By now, the chronic Boer supply problem was producing another surreal sight, remarked upon by a number of British soldiers who would normally have expected it in Victorian music hall or pantomime but not during armed pursuit. This was the appearance of some of the commandos in the distinctive bonnet and black dress apparel of rural Boer women, the only serviceable clothing available to the most ragged of men, now short even of adaptable grain sacks or of captured British army garments.

As a wartime tailoring phenomenon, this may be ripe for more inventive kinds of post-modern historical interpretation, in which skirts were supplanting beards as signifiers of the Boer struggle, or in which men were becoming feminised. But what it showed more than anything, of course, was the wretched condition of the Boers in the field. It was becoming an impossibly tall order to maintain operations. Since early 1900, youths, some as young as twelve years of age, had been accompanying their fathers to the front. On 2 November 1901, President Steyn issued a proclamation rendering *penkoppe* or adolescent boys liable to be commandeered from the age of fourteen.[317]

Ahead of them, their enemy's steady pushes, huge reserves, and improved logistics and army management were bringing victory ever nearer – through round-about pressure rather than any decisive stroke.

8

AGONY BEFORE PEACE

A S THE WHOLE CHARACTER OF THE CONFLICT SWUNG TO ANTI-GUERRILLA warfare, Kitchener showed his anger and frustration. He had tried his best for peaceful resolution at the abortive June 1901 Middelburg talks. Now, he turned to political extremism.

He had already caused a stir by proposing that the whole population of irreconcilable Boers should be swept up and deported to somewhere like Madagascar or, preferably, Fiji, where they could be left to rot. That 'little bluff'[318] to finish things off was one outlandish suggestion. Through July and August he and Milner for once saw eye to eye over a milder fantasy – the banishment from South Africa of the resisting republican leadership. Early in August, the British government, enthused by this stiff threat, endorsed the issue of an aggressive proclamation warning Boer officers and anyone in command of 'armed bands' that they would face permanent exile if they failed to surrender by mid-September. This fitted well with Milner's uncompromising purpose: unconditional surrender. Predictably, though, this political gambit had little effect out in the wide spaces of the veld: very few commandos buckled under the intimidatory pressure.

But Kitchener's job was the forcible defeat of the enemy and, in this respect military action was more telling than political threat. Although it thrashed about at times, mostly in the western Transvaal, the army advanced gradually and more methodically under his stern command. As in the Sudan, war here gave Kitchener the opportunity to run things in the way he liked to run them. Core staff work became more exacting and systematic, with a vast increase in the size and scope of the field intelligence department. By 1902, it had almost 140 officers, over 2 300 civilian subordinates, several thousand African and Coloured scouts and spies, and a number of surrendered Boer *hensoppers* winkled from their farms to serve as agents. Overall coordination of command and its sifting of reports also improved.[319] As this fell into place, around it Kitchener assembled part of his striking force of some 220 000 troops into bustling flying columns. The objective was to establish an almost continuous north-south front, bisecting the interior of the country from the Transvaal down to the southwestern Cape Colony. By robbing the enemy of ground and closing off exits, the British moved to squeeze the rural war into an ever more restricted space.

Before the middle of 1901, Kitchener had also grasped the necessity of throwing an impregnable bridgehead right under the noses of his enemy and to use it as a field base artery of communications, supply, and intelligence. This comprised the rapid and efficient construction of thousands of small forts or blockhouses as a fixed grid across which British columns could conduct sweeping drives against the commandos. At first built sturdily of thick stone, cost and speed requirements soon obliged Kitchener to base his protective lines upon galvanised, corrugated iron and timber block. Less squat than stone structures, these lighter bastions could be raised easily on top of thick cushions of earth and stone, providing commanding elevation and well-protected firing positions. Proofing blockhouses against assault also became easier. Boer fighting formations were diminishing both in size and in firepower as they gradually discarded their remaining artillery.

The mere presence of these little forts became an important stamp of imperial military authority. Looped together with barbed wire, and thickly compacted at vulnerable spots, the cheap blockhouse line embraced a dense system of outlying alarms and traps in defence, together with telegraph, telephone, carrier-pigeon and other signal connections to maintain communications over lengthening field fortification lines. It was a stark and simple scheme, and a great feat of military engineering. The mechanical backbone it provided Kitchener's army was increased further in strength by the enrolment of hundeds of loyal colonist guards and many thousands more of armed African and Coloured 'watchers', 'guards', 'scouts', 'sentries' and 'police' to augment local garrison strength. The British were strung out, but systematically so. Gaps for their enemy were few, and decreasing steadily as the telegraph wire controls spooling out behind columns, and power and light provision from Royal Engineers' sappers, tautened surveillance capacity.

Thus strengthened, Kitchener deployed close to one hundred columns across large belts of mapped and defined territory. Mostly brigade-sized, these became tactical areas of independent responsibility in which commanders were given their head and a large purse to engage local black field hands and herders for scouting, snooping, and other kinds of useful service. Columns of between 1 200 and 2 000 soldiers and accompanying African auxiliaries then undertook a series of drives or sweeps into the countryside between fortified British lines, to box in and pick off their prey. By early 1902, Kitchener's flying columns had come to resemble vultures swooping on the bones of the Boer armies.

The course of these gnawing operations, in which the British overhauled and then increasingly ran down their flagging enemy, involved numerous expeditions of varying effectiveness. Some were huge combined actions, such as French's 1901 sweep between the Natal and Delagoa Bay rail lines, which netted some 273 000 head of stock, 'a devastating blow to the Boer economy',[320] and a converging drive between the Modder and the Vaal some months later, to squeeze commandos against the westerly blockhouse line between Jacobsdal and Bloemfontein. It is not easy to plot a meaningful narrative pattern to these rolling actions. In general, they killed or wounded small numbers of commandos, but took thousands more captive, and carried off wagons, weapons, horses, cattle, grain, and forage supplies. Still, the outcome of individual drives was often mixed. British hunters could not always set good snares or bridge the intelligence gap between them and their prey. Cumulatively, however, this tidal erosion of Boer capacity made a crucial contribution towards the final settling of hostilities, as a cordoning of the countryside with blockhouses and wire cut the range and effectiveness of Boer raiding parties.

Blockade and enclosure also began to break the military morale of even some of the more determined resisters, such as Meyer's 800-strong commando, which just ran out of ground and crumpled into submission in February 1902. Meanwhile, British scouring movements struck out ever further, forming barriers made up of a mesh of soldiers, blockhouses, wire and even prowling, train-mounted searchlights, tightening the screw by laying in large numbers of armed African mounted scouts. Of course, it took time for this pattern to harden, and there were also regions, like the western Transvaal, where tricky terrain, troublesome water shortages, and communication obstacles made it difficult to spread the blockhouse net. Having to restore repeatedly attacked outposts and to repair rail and telegraph lines kept the British on the hop. But by constricting available territory and penning in the enemy, Kitchener was gradually countering the Boers' evasive warfare.

It was not so much that the guerrilla war was ending; it was more that the guerrillas could dictate less and less where to hit, where to run, and where to hide. For De Wet's veteran bittereinders in the northeastern Orange Free State and those of De la Rey in the western Transvaal, warfare became less elastic and more habituated to the synchronisation of Kitchener's territorial adjustments. Commando operations then became increasingly regulated by the rhythms of great British combing strokes, with the experience of repeated flight leaving many burghers exhausted, demoralised and out of fight. There was also another territorial factor that tipped the balance against the Boers. They were denied the possibility of finding fresh bases in flanking country by hostile Africans who were 'growing increasingly sharp teeth'.[321] Defensive menace from the Swazi and the Zulu checked them in the southeast; they were blocked by Pedi groups to the northeast; and, to the west, were tucked in by the belligerent Tswana. Commandos needed space in which to regain their breath, but any movement in these directions was risky.

Meanwhile, Kitchener's formula was also being extended to other fronts. The enforcement of martial law over the annexed republican states grew more widespread. Increasingly, too, British command turned imprisonment into far isolation, withdrawing most prisoners of war altogether from the theatre of war. It was cheaper, made them less conspicuous, lowered the morale of those still under arms, and would perhaps teach the Boers just how large the empire was. Following Roberts' dispatch to Ceylon of Cronjé's troops after Paardeberg, tens of thousands of prisoners were removed to camps in Ceylon, India, Bermuda and St Helena. A couple of these tiny island economies were revived by a novel new import industry: the good fortune of hosting a mass of reluctant newcomers, over 5 000 in the case of Bermuda, which consequently increased its population by more than a quarter.[322]

The outpost prison camps were rough and ready affairs with bare provisions and inadequate services. Conditions for some prisoners were worsened by stressful tropical conditions, leading to a considerable number of deaths. Given the remoteness of their locations, Boer captives, some of them young boys, were left mostly to fend for themselves, their hearts lifted by religious assembly, sports, music, carving, and other rural cultural practices carried to these distant frontiers. While nutrition levels were uneven, there were at least tobacco and chocolate perks from French, Dutch and Belgian pro-Boer sympathisers. In Ceylon, some Boers who had been pre-war addicts of that most English of games, cricket, found themselves back on the pitch. Prisoners of war turned out the form players in their camp club against the Ceylonese champions. A fraternal encounter, the Boers cared not a whit that they were 'playing against the Colombo colts, a team of colour'.[323] Only at home would that have been a problem, insuperably so for their successors in later decades. Meanwhile, for most prisoners, transportation brought a crushing kind of enforced war tourism on the imperial fringe, although a few found enough there to begin life anew, staying on in Ceylon and India after 1902 as imperial service veterinary officers, or returning from Asia to the post-war Transvaal as lecture-hall advocates of Oriental philosophy, religion and vegetarianism.

On home soil, the fighting fortunes of men who were not famously vegetarian were also being blighted seriously by growing collaboration with the British. If Kitchener did not create this, he did more than any other commander to mould it into a fairly effective imperial asset.

Since mid-1900, some *hensoppers* had been swaying from supine neutrality towards providing crafty assistance in the field for casual payment or reward. Towards the end of the war, their numbers were increasing significantly, reaching almost 4 000 by April 1902 and close to 5 500 when hostilities ceased. With no more than around 17 000 bittereinders still out at the end, the reviled spectacle of Boer traitors had become a real thorn in the side of resisting forces who were mostly in little doubt about the Anglo-Boer position.

As British annexations had not ended the war, it continued to be contested. Crown authority remained illegitimate. The independent states which burghers had been charged to defend continued to live, not only in the imagination but also in physically contested tracts of western Transvaal territory. It was to these and these only that recalcitrant Boers could owe any political allegiance. For surrendered burghers to keep their peace and their neutral place was one thing. The renegade act of becoming a collaborating British *joiner* (as it was termed contemptuously) was quite another. Technically, such treachery amounted to treason, and anyone captured ran the risk of summary execution. So, the quandary of a hard-pressed Boer society deepened as a flank of its anti-imperial war began to mutate into a festering and bitter civil war.

Kitchener grasped both the military advantage and the political value in making the most of this. The patchy and largely informal system of irregular scouting and guiding with untried local burgher corps and Farmers' Guards which had been operating since late 1900 was greatly extended, put on a more organised basis, and made subject to a more unified direction. Variously, slender lines of Burgher Police and Farmers' Guard joiners in the Orange Free State were deployed in a 'protected area' around its capital as a safe blanket for surrendered men who were trying to resume farming, and as a force to help in affirming British authority. This deployment was also evidence of intelligent thinking: propertied members would have a personal stake in trying to defend what was theirs against commando seizures. Yet, the execution of this British strategy was never entirely easy. Aside from scratchy training and unreliable individual motivation, there was also a lack of defensive depth to cover all key points, a particular difficulty when the enemy tactic was to wait, then to raid opportunistically, then to wait again, in a minor epic of unpredictability.

More backbone came from burgher guiding and scouting which, along with black expertise, formed part of the intelligence operational capability of every British column by early 1902. Across the Orange Free State, and especially in the Transvaal during later 1901 and 1902, renegade burghers improved the effectiveness of column commanders. Reconnaissance estimates of enemy movement and disposition became more accurate, confusion over place and the nature of terrain decreased, and spying and other clandestine operations (such as sneaking reliable joiner agents into commandos) picked up. So, too, did the vital predictive side of the tactical intelligence field. Many ex-commandos had a good nose for where their former bands were likely to lie up in laager, thereby assisting British night assaults on resting Boers. 'Big coarse fellows,' wrote one intelligence officer, 'but in slyness and quiet they would surprise my sister's cat'.[324] Equally, the edge that this provided always had its parallel in the enemy ranks: such skills provided the Boers with a continuous intelligence advantage right to the end. Aside from excursions into British colonial territory, the annexed republics remained the rib-cage of irregular fighting, and occupation forces found it virtually impossible to saddle up without the closest commando being alerted.

In all of this, Kitchener's calculations were rarely without a shrewd political core. In 1901, and again in 1902, he was thinking hard about rifts within the enemy camp, concluding that if by now there were 'already two parties amongst them ready to fly at each other's throat', then the way forward was to hurry this along. Thus, 'if the Boers could be induced to hate each other more than they hate the British', the outcome would be obvious, he assured Lansdowne. It would be to cultivate and to deliver 'a party among the Boers themselves, depending entirely on British continuity of rule out here'.[325]

Accordingly, he had no intention of neglecting calls from a number of more conspicuous *hensoppers*, like Piet de Wet, that more should be done to enable lapsed commandos to aid the British, so that sense and compromise could win the day. Responding to such nudging, and to his tactical sense that the use of armed Boer collaborators would ease some of the pressure on his stretched columns, in the closing months of 1901 Kitchener sanctioned a scheme to amalgamate the burgher corps. Some of them were ill-armed and were performing little more than clearing livestock from the countryside in return for scraps of loot. Now, they were to be combined with less mediocre units, properly attested, and placed under uniform conditions of service and standard British army disciplinary codes. Commencing in October 1901, local corps and scout bodies in the Boer territories were pulled into the (Transvaal) National Scouts and the Orange River Colony Volunteers. Their very names established their British militia membership of Kitchener's professional army establishment, yet with a certain ironic imperial detachment. These were, after all, the kind of volunteers for parading in Kroonstad, not Canterbury.

Enlarging the complement of enlisted 'Judas Boers'[326] required recruiting, and Kitchener got this under way with impressive dispatch, becoming personally involved in campaigning, which mostly took the form of plucking surrendered burghers from concentration camps. In addresses to assemblies, his message was sober. The guerrilla war was hopeless, and would only bring on more bloodshed and destruction. By responding to imperial need, 'joiners' would both improve their own lowly circumstances and assist in bringing needlessly prolonged hostilities to a close. Although Scout and Volunteer pickings were modest, the availability of good daily wages, regular rations, clothing and equipment, along with intimations of post-war land or farm rewards, put over 1 800 Transvaal burghers and around 500 Orange Free State collaborators under arms by the end of the war. Mindful of likely retaliation from hostile camp bittereinders towards the families of enlisted men, some of whom were receiving perks for their loyalty, the British tried to insulate them in separate camps or house accommodation in Pretoria and other towns.

National Scouts continued to be the skirmishing outriders of British columns, their various units never combining as an independent Boer-British fighting force against their countrymen and women. But they were more wounding in another way. Accepting the empire's oaths of neutrality and oaths of allegiance was already spoiling the moral order of a common republican virtue. Now, through armed collaboration, the spluttering divisions within Boer society became another part of the daily duel with the British army.

There may be something to the argument that Kitchener's burgher corps was misconceived, and that it actually made matters more aggravating for the British by hardening the determination of those still holding out. On balance, though, it is more likely to have been otherwise, demoralising in spirit and eroding of morale. Figures like Louis Botha, Lukas Meyer, and Schalk Burger were all painfully sensitive to the depressing tactical and moral climate engendered by the Scouts' formation. 'Faithless', 'unfaithful', 'abandoning' or 'failed' people had begun to aid the British to get the better of patriots in the most wrenching way imaginable. They were teaching the enemy the Boer way of 'how to wage war', how to muffle hooves and equipment to trek silently through the night, or where there were mountain channels through which to squeeze unobserved. While commandos were counting their losses, their opponents were so growing in strength through the infusion of traitorous blood that the dread time might come when fighting partisans might even be outnumbered by 'their own people' who had turned on them.[327] If by no means a principal factor in bringing about Boer defeat, the plague of collaboration was there in the final losing equation between actual hardship and loss of faith.

The leading historian of 'joiners' and their treason as a social phenomenon has provided cogent argument that it can mostly be understood as a symptom of the deep agrarian inequalities of Boer society.[328] At the start, the war provided social cement, but once things began to go badly, it flaked off as economic and social divisions worsened. Naturally, ordinary burghers would have had a range of motives influencing their actions, whether it was staying on the run as a diehard, turning in as a 'handsupper' or becoming a 'joiner'. Rank-and-file bittereinders included poor landless burghers as well as ruined individuals whose possessions had been eaten away by the scourge of war. Displaced, and with no anticipation of ever being able to rebuild a lost material existence, there was nothing left but the fight, and pride in not yielding. Equally, not every joiner was a poor *bywoner*, willing to do anything for a crust, even slipping into khaki. After all, Piet de Wet, landed leader of the Orange River Colony Volunteers, was not short of an acre, and may even have had an eye on gaining more through collaboration. Even so, in the closing phase of the war, the broad profile confirms an unmistakeable class differentiation in the social base of National Scouts and bittereinders.

Overwhelmingly poor and underprivileged 'joiners' were drawn from that discontented stratum which had long resented having to bear the costs of unpaid commando duties. Now, they were not always charmed by having to look after the assets of the wealthier while they, themselves, had none. In some cases coerced into armed service by landlords, they had never been that much of a sacrificial repository for national causes.

The post-1900 bittereinders, and especially their leadership, were mostly individuals of a different type. These were a younger, landed, urban and semi-urban Afrikaner professional grouping, in short, the 'well-to-do'. By 1902, unable to be rejuvenated by much in the way of increased fighting numbers, they were sustained precisely because they had contracted. Having become a bony core of the tried, the able and the trusted, they nurtured more stringent commando discipline, and saw themselves as the moral kernel of their cause, with 'a magnificent sense of righteousness'.[329]

The war had cost virtually all of them money, and some their relatives, and the sense of being a distinctive war generation marked them out. Like General Ben Bouwer, they had outlived scoundrels like Kruger and Cronjé, and had become a fabled kind of Afrikaner Spartan, a 'select', free-warrior 'company' who would endure 'to the end without hope of reward'; for what hung over them was 'the threat of banishment from their country'.[330] Theirs was a confinement more bitter than that of Britain's hateful camps, from which slack, surrendered burghers were now liberating themselves as Kitchener's National Scouts.

Once wartime camps moved beyond being conventional male prisoner-of-war compounds, they were to have immense consequences for the prospects of continuing Boer resistance. Right from the outset of his command, Roberts had had no doubt as to where and how to crush the resistance of his agrarian enemy. A scorched-earth policy had been implemented from March 1900 as a punitive measure against continuing Orange Free State reactions to British occupation and, undoubtedly, to bring home the hard hand of war. 'The problem of the Boers lies not only in their armies,' wrote a Sussex Regiment lieutenant, 'they are in the main a rather hostile people, who have also to be subdued in order for our present business to be brought to an end'.[331] He was by no means alone in this early view.

Neither republican government had the administrative, transport or food-supply capacity to evacuate families from districts which were being overrun, and farm inhabitants had to face the harsh consequences of a commandeering army moving through their territory, stripping homesteads of food supplies and livestock. But British forces did not stop at 'the requisitioning of food for immediate use, which all armies engage in when their supply columns cannot keep up'.[332] They did more. Families in their path faced complete displacement as crops were burnt and houses were fired or dynamited. Official targets for demolition were properties occupied by the families of burghers who were away on commando duty, fighting on against British columns, or raiding communication and supply lines, thereby compounding the long-range transport problems already worsened by Roberts' and Kitchener's ham-fisted restructuring.

Such destruction grew increasingly indiscriminate. In some instances, incendiarism razed targeted property, condemned to ash through the absence of men who were continuing acts of war instead of taking and observing Crown oaths to stay out of it. Yet, both proportionately and in total number, rural destruction bore most heavily on non-combatant homesteads which did not necessarily have any direct link to operational commandos in particular districts. A few of Roberts' officers grasped the problems posed by setting too much ablaze. Among them, there were worries that 'gross burning and gutting' was 'needlessly spiteful', and could only increase 'the offence and hatred felt by these people'.[333] Roberts, however, was for the widest application of a mailed fist. Right up to the end of his command, he continued to insist that unless the Boers generally were made to suffer for the actions of those in arms against Britain, the war would never end.

Under that command, nothing systematic was done to deal with the position of evicted families left destitute as a consequence of mass burning and culling. While a few senior officers had families assembled and dispatched to British-controlled towns, for the most part Boer women and children were left to drift through the countryside, having to fend for themselves by foraging and taking what shelter they could get, sometimes being invited into commando laagers, sometimes even straying into the odd African homestead, which could turn out to be hospitable. Africans in Boer territory, too, were themselves also having stock confiscated by the British as a means of denying fighters the opportunity to commandeer food.

In the midst of the general neglect of uprooted civilians, there were one or two displays of improvisational virtuosity during the course of 1900. In May, Major General Edward Brabant had proposed establishing protected camps for surrendered burghers, many of whom had families drifting in their wake. A few months later, some army officers north of Pretoria suggested that the only thing to do was somehow to round up wandering civilians and then to send them stumbling towards areas most infested by commandos. That would give their bobbing enemy an unwanted anchor which they would then be obliged to drag along. Roberts obligingly conducted a sample test from July, when he evicted around 2 500 women and children from Johannesburg and Pretoria and railed them to Boer forces which were retreating along the Delagoa Bay line. This was followed by a decree that all families of active commandos residing in occupied districts were liable to be dispatched to be accommodated by the enemy. This was wholesale in intent, and applied as much to the better-off spouses of government officials and office bearers as to pauperised farm women.

For Roberts, the Boers were the architects of their own deportations. Instead of behaving as neutrals, sympathetic families were aiding commando strength in the field by providing food and intelligence. At the same time, the British themselves were short of food supplies because of repeated enemy strikes against Cape and Natal rail supply lines. Naturally, Botha and others in the Transvaal leadership saw the removal of civilians as an act of retribution, cruelly heaping the costs of their struggle upon their wives and children in order to intimidate combatants into submission.

In the event, two curious twists followed those expulsions which did proceed. Firstly, families who had been bundled off to be accommodated by the enemy mostly slid back into British hands as commandos retreated without them. Secondly, the effect of driving women out to commandos seems to have been ambiguous. At one level, it cracked morale. This can be seen among distressed burghers as they realised just how marooned they had become, with even their families 'run away', 'left to the veld' or 'chased from this place to that'.[334] Yet, on the other hand, the entry into fighting laagers of embittered women, still moving defiantly under republican colours, may have encouraged or shamed some wilting commandos into straightening up.

By September 1900, the month in which refugee camps for surrendered burghers and their families (to protect men from being re-commandeered by Boer forces) were established at Bloemfontein and Pretoria, it had become obvious that the larger problem of displaced 'undesirables' could not be solved by depositing them with enemy forces. Encumbered by wagons, furniture, grain, and even stoves, women, children and aged men who had not placed themselves voluntarily under British protection were being left behind by commandos who were having difficulty enough in providing for themselves. As scorched-earth and population-clearance measures became more systematic under Kitchener, affecting both Boer lands and African peasant holdings, something had to be done about the chaos in the countryside.

Towards the end of December, Kitchener instituted a policy of what was termed 'refugee-camp' provision for the whole of South Africa. By then, there were already over forty camps, a number holding larger populations than most middling republican towns. Indeed, some of those towns, like Bethal, Ermelo and Lindley, had already been burned down.

Usually bonded to the railway supply spine, and placed close to the circuit of military administration in small towns, these concentration camps for Boer 'undesirables' held thousands of civilian inmates who had been swept from farms by burnings and the great drives mounted by Kitchener. Most camp inhabitants were children accompanied by women, together with some older men. By September 1901, there were 110 000 inmates housed in white concentration camps. Alongside them swept another flood of homeless Africans, for whom the military authorities established separate refugee camps. The size of the incarcerated populations grew during the course of 1901 as Kitchener widened the net, ordering the removal of all people from designated hostile districts which were persistently sustaining commandos.

The British government rejected criticism; the camp scheme, it said, had been imposed on it. With unprotected women and children at risk on the open veld, the only humane thing to do was to extend aid by accommodating and feeding the refugees as best it could. Just as in rebellious India in 1857, when the Victorian army had protected the sanctity of British families against an unimaginably awful fate, so it was in South Africa. Indeed, here it was even looking after innocents who were not so innocent, thereby going beyond the basic 'moral decency' and 'lawful obligations' of civilised war.[335]

There was, undoubtedly, some basis to this. Rampant burnings and confiscations were leaving displaced and unprotected families in the most straitened circumstances. At the same time, the cultivated image of British forces acting on moral compunction to moderate the consequences of the war provided another handy form of propaganda. In that message, a caring army was seeing to Boer women and children who had been deserted by callous male breadwinners, selfishly putting war above the crying needs of home and family. Outside the protective confines of the British bell-tents lay a nature black in tooth and claw, as *The Times* advised in June 1901, for to abandon defenceless civilians to the open veld would be 'to send them to starve and to expose them to outrages from the natives which would set all South Africa in a flame'.[336] In that respect, the combination of a sentimental humanitarian protectionism and anxiety over what unchecked Africans might do 'brought together two central ideologies of Victorian Britain – that of the weakness of woman and that of the sexual savagery of the black man towards the white woman'.[337]

British pro-Boer anti-war activism from the middle of 1901 onwards focused squarely on the incarceration of Boer women and children, and demanded a great deal of defensive humanitarian rhetoric about the function of the camps from government spokesmen and the pro-war press. Yet the underlying factor is that the camps were serving a paradoxical military purpose. Families, and women in particular, were not classified as combatants. Yet, 'only for the minority who actively supported Britain' were they truly refugee camps. 'For most, they were internment camps, and the people in them were in effect prisoners of war'.[338]

At one level, the camp system had to expand because of Kitchener's tactical need. 'Every farm,' he told Brodrick in December 1900, 'is an intelligence agency and a supply depot so that it is almost impossible to surround or catch' the enemy. Again in March 1901, he stressed that the position of 'women left in farms' was proving intolerable, 'as they give complete intelligence to the Boers of all our movements and feed the commandos in their neighbourhood'.[339] Occupation forces could only be effective if 'undesirable' populations were in controlled enclaves, with combatants thereby denied their supporting eyes, ears, and food.

One thing stands out at another level. For Kitchener and Milner (and, for that matter, Roberts), internment was a strategy to pressurise the enemy into giving up. In essence, the camps were to serve as hostage sites. Only by laying down their arms would burghers ever again be reconnected with their families. For Kitchener, fear of perpetual separation and loss could 'work on the feelings of the men to get back to their farms'. Moreover, through confining concentration, the insidious influence of the most bittereinder women who were 'keeping up the war' could also be negated. Here lay the only 'solution' for women who were 'more bitter than the men'. To 'bring them to their senses' the task was to 're-move the worst class'.[340] Kitchener was, again, a ruthlessly exact organiser of what needed to be done. It was not enough to unleash force and firepower against last-ditch combatants. Their surrounding families had to be scared into orderly behaviour, and kept away from fuelling the fight.

So brisk a summary as this can scarcely begin to convey the grim significance of the concentration camp trauma, reflected partially in contemporary letters and recorded oral testimony from some of the more than 116 000 inmates who fought a caged battle to keep body and soul together in what was all too often a matter of life and death. 'As far as one can see, the veldt looks quite beautiful,' wrote Gezina Pretorius from her Bloemfontein camp in November 1901, yet 'terrible numbers of people are dying around us'.[341] Nor can this volume pro-vide a full picture of the 1901–1902 political controversy and humanitarian scandal in Britain over the conduct and the prosecution of the war. The 1901 first-hand, high-profile investigative account of social conditions by the Liberal humanitarian, Emily Hobhouse, is still credited as being largely responsible for awakening sections of the British public to the plight of Boer internees. Her sobering depiction 'underpinned the publicity and campaigning activities she engaged in, which ensured that the plight of Boer women and children remained on the political agenda, in Britain especially'.[342]

It certainly helped to push onto that agenda the Liberal Henry Campbell-Bannerman's famous denunciatory Commons speech on British 'methods of bar-barism' in South Africa. There were other Liberal anti-war critiques. Aside from those aired by his party leader, many of the most acerbic came from David Lloyd George who, early in 1901, warned that 'brutal policies' might he exploited as a pretext by scheming European powers to justify their intervention on the side of the Boers. This had happened before, in 'America's colonial revolution', and the price had been the loss of those colonies. It could do so again. If that were to come about, Britain would 'have to pay the penalty, not merely of the shame of transactions in these colonies, but the more substantial penalty of facing the world in arms against us'. Salisbury, however, shrugged it off, instructing his humanitarian critics that, as war was a terrible thing, the Boers 'should have thought of its horrible significance when they invaded the Queen's dominions'.[343]

Liberal moral revulsion over the camp policy and condemnation of Britain's perceived perversion of the rules of civilised warfare came to form the most single-minded political issue of the war. On the other hand, the establishment of almost seventy African concentration camps in the Transvaal and Orange River colonies, with exploitative labour regimes and scandalously poor medical and housing provision for their tens of thousands of inmates, created no contemporary fuss. In taking stock now, there is certainly a far wider range of white and black refugee and internment experience to take into account, with recognised 'knowledge of black suffering as a result of the British scorched earth policy and the deaths of blacks in the concentration camps'.[344]

Almost needless to say, depending on the perspective taken on concentration camp administration – as inhumane, clumsy or woefully incompetent – analysis of this squalid war saga goes on and on. In recent times, it has come to encompass assessment of the extent to which 'anglicising' children's camp schools may have been educative and modernising, instilling in Boer parents and children an awareness of 'the value of formal learning in the new era'. Or, to take another case, there has even been solemn contemplation of the meaning of death-rate counts, in which 'numbers' may be seen to have acquired non-factual significance for the formulation of war memories and the combustion of later Afrikaner nationalism.[345]

For all this, when weighing up what counted in prosecuting the war, and why, the key question is, however, somewhat different. It is not that of how horrendous the camps were, but, rather, of whether they were effective in bringing on Boer surrender. Self-evidently, civilian resettlement was a key thread in the Kitchener net, part of the blockhouse lines and their interconnecting patchwork of barbed-wire squares across which flying columns cleared the countryside. Against an enemy conducting an undulating struggle based on rising, lying low, and rising, the veld had to be rendered sterile. Ultimately, the objective of scorched earth went well beyond the punishing of 'undesirables'. It was a resolve to alienate, to render troublesome tracts of the countryside uninhabitable by the removal of all civilians, crops, livestock, and stores. In some ways, it replicated what Confederate Southerners had experienced at the hands of Union generals like Sheridan, Grant and Sherman, destruction of 'the control of their domestic landscapes', and the return of a fearsome wilderness.[346] Thereafter, dusty burghers would experience what Spanish resettlement strategy had produced in the Cuban War of Independence: the surrender of demoralised, undernourished and gaunt rebels, leaving their captors the easy task of rounding up any stragglers who might still be resisting.

There is a strong argument that the early commencement of widespread farm burnings and the internment of homeless Boers was a 'mistake' in 'military terms', as it may have lengthened rather than shortened the war by freeing commandos 'from assuming responsibility for their families', thereby extending their capacity to resist.[347] Furthermore, there is a view that internment pressures did not of themselves force determined bittereinders to give up. Within camps, female opinion seems to have been divided. Relations between women with spouses still out on commando and those whose men had capitulated were reportedly 'very poor', with the latter snooping and informing on pro-fighting sentiment to camp authorities.[348]

Others collaborated with the occupation administration in other ways, while a number would probably have been dragged into forced prostitution or would have struck up friendships with soldiers in the hope of earning favour or perks to ease their deprivation. Yet others at times communicated their desire for an end to the war to combatants in the field, 'berating us', as a Transvaal commando noted in February 1902, 'for forcing them to keep on living in the midst of misery and the dying'.[349]

Alongside all this, many women remained unwavering in their defiance, a continuing source of disaffection to the British and an emotive cushion to the spirit of those Boers still out. By 1902, with fields razed, homes flattened and kinfolk incarcerated, there remained little left to be saved through a voluntary, compromising surrender. In probably the purest expression of the war's gendered dimensions, what remained for those men was to be men. As with implacable Confederate women in the American Civil War, or Belgian and French women in the First World War, so it was with Boer women. Faced with the violation of an invading and occupying army, those who did not stay in the fight to defend national independence were not fully men. There was something of that in the air around the concentration camps.[350]

In the longer run, though, there can be little doubt that civilian internment was a considerable contributory factor to the ending of armed resistance. For the camps added something to the destruction of shelter and supplies in devastated parts of Boer territory. They added fearfully high death rates, which peaked towards the end of 1901, reaching a mortality rate of 344 per 1 000 by October. Metropolitan and local anti-war critics of British 'death camps' accused administrators of wilfully callous neglect or even of near-genocidal maltreatment, including mass poisoning to wipe out the Boer population. For their part, pro-war British propagandists blamed the Boers for running up their own death lists due to their ignorance of modern sanitation, and for clinging to their own 'primitive' therapeutic practices, such as the use of noxious 'Dutch medicines'.[351]

The basic fact is that the British army was unable to maintain a decent hygienic environment even for its own troops in South Africa, who were far more likely to succumb to a faecal-oral disease borne by water, dust or flies than to a Mauser bullet. Thus, the poorly prepared and unsanitary camps run by officers seconded as general superintendents were an invitation to catastrophe − and it came, in the shape of winnowing epidemics of measles, dysentery, pneumonia and whooping cough, which bore particularly heavily on children and cut down black as well as white inmates.

The devastating impact of this high white civilian mortality on the morale of republican leadership cannot be overestimated. For it seemed to be threatening the very reproductive future of the Boer people. Smuts, for instance, was to estimate that, by the end of hostilities, over ten per cent of the Boer republics' inhabitants had perished in the camps. Developing a momentum of its own, demographic awareness became one of the more compelling restraints against continuing the war. And, in addition to civilian suffering, there was a rising gender anxiety among men that the upright, Calvinist character of what Hertzog called 'our female sex' was being eroded by 'immorality' or 'destructive moral influences', making it increasingly difficult to keep good order 'under the influence of a godless enemy'.[352]

By now, there was also a further damaging factor, one with a worrying chemistry all of its own. Since the start of hostilities, black people in various operational zones (and even outside them) had been aiding the British to defeat the Boers through irregular armed service, scouting, spying and intelligence, supplying crops, livestock, and other goods, and in providing remount, transport riding and other labour services. This was a tide which was always running the British way, and was rising beyond politically tolerable levels. As commandos in areas like the southeastern Transvaal topped up their provisions in the only way now available, through the pillaging of Zulu homesteads, so resistance intensified and began to grow increasingly more violent. In forced conditions of almost constant pursuit, night riding, and the creaming off of peasants' supplies, burghers had increasingly to manoeuvre through lands occupied by Africans. Harassed routinely by Boer forces, the inhabitants then either informed on them to British pursuers, or turned on them themselves to avenge losses.

One shock example of the latter, and a chilling indication of how things were breaking up, was a Zulu surprise night attack in April 1902 upon a small commando encampment at Holkrantz, near Vryheid. In retribution for Boer confiscation and labour conscription, fifty-six burghers were speared to death, with the vengeful *impi* (regiment) itself losing about a hundred warriors, dead or wounded. Matters were no easier elsewhere. Either there was no longer room in areas such as the far northern Transvaal, or what there was had become too hostile into which to run. Therefore, as Botha ruefully concluded at the end, 'in only one portion of the country, namely Zoutpansberg, is there still food, but how do we obtain our provisions there? It must be taken, and thereby we create more enemies . . . if the enemy were to pour into that district, the kaffirs will join against us.'[353] He and others could only sustain their operations through widening dispersal, drawing off the British and forcing them to campaign over the largest area possible. This could not be done in countryside that had been sterilised by clearances, nor in areas like the western Transvaal, where armed Kgatla had grown teeth sufficiently sharp to deter any efforts to get them to budge.

Riding south into the northern and northwestern Cape was also beginning to provoke encounters with armed Coloured inhabitants which were a little less one-sided than in previous incursions, as had been the case in Calvinia early in 1901, when local resistance led by an influential Anglicised artisan, Abraham Esau, was swatted aside by an invading Orange Free State commando. Esau's execution as a British collaborator had turned him into a Cape martyr of the imperial cause.[354]

Thereafter, though, matters grew less sacrificial for Cape resisters. In the northwest, commandos may still have met with little but good intentions from sympathetic Boer communities, but they were greatly outnumbered by a darker-skinned majority determined to fight what was seen as an enslaving republican rule. Increasingly, British colonial authority could not but rest upon the enlisting and arming of 'coloured corps', like the Namaqualand Scouts, Bushmanland Borderers, and Northern Border Scouts. Skilled horsemen, trackers, and accomplished hunters like their adversaries, between them they landed some commandos in a tough spot during 1901. Again, into the early months of 1902, these militia forces handed defeat to an Edwin Conroy commando in a crossfire ambush, a pounding engagement which has been retrieved for the historical record as the small battle of Naroegas.[355]

As if to add to a sense of impending doom, back in Boer territory groups of rural African tenants were taking up the habit of armed threat or violence in disturbingly large numbers. They began occupying land across many areas, particularly in the Transvaal, spurning customary master-and-servant or landlord-and-tenant relations. Boers obviously resisted moves to contest their authority and ownership but, as hostilities wore on, many began to lose all ability to act, and even faith in their strength. So extensive was this decomposition, and so intense the Boer–African belligerence to which it gave rise, that one historian has characterised it as the eruption of a ragged peasant war or a 'rebellion from below'.[356] Without exaggerating its influence as a force behind republican defeat, African resistance and collaboration with the imperial occupation certainly played its part in pushing the Boers into surrender. In their classic description, 'an unbearable condition of affairs in many districts of both Republics' was what the Boer peace delegates of 1902 eventually saw. Several British intelligence officers saw it no less clearly, if rather more approvingly, recording the 'discomfiture' and 'jumpiness'[357] of the enemy over its internal crisis of African resistance as the Transvaal buckled, hit from the outside and gnawed away from the inside.

Ultimately, what was left for the republicans was the Cape Colony. An unwelcome place, regulated by martial law and disciplined by rebel imprisonment and military court executions, there was not much to go on here, what with French using his standing court-martial machinery against captured rebels 'with the utmost vigour', and compelling 'disloyal Dutch' to observe the public execution of rebels in Middelburg and Dordrecht. Milner fretted over the long-term political damage such military harshness would cause, but stood by, concluding, 'who in practice was to decide which actions were necessary and which excessive'?[358]

Hertzog and De Wet, of course, had had a stab themselves at carrying war down into the Cape, between the end of 1900 and early 1901, but had ended up being worn down by their own offensives without creating any meaningful breach. Smuts had another try in August 1901, despite his own pained perception that victory over Britain was no longer possible and that the only option would be to try for a negotiated end to hostilities. If sufficient colonial recruits could be raised, and that crucial but maddeningly elusive general Cape rebellion be got under way, the republicans might endure on strengthened terms after all.

Barely slackening, Smuts nipped through British lines across the Orange Free State, got through the southeastern Cape, and settled into a westerly prowling movement along the lengthy Atlantic seaboard. It was another impressive Boer run by no more than a handful of selected commandos, distracting the British and forcing the diversion of large numbers of troops to take on Smuts' force of just over 300 burghers. Although ill-equipped, some men answered its call from the field, increasing numbers to around 3 000. Then the old story was repeated: the expedition covered too much, too thinly. And, although Cape Boers were 'better conditioned' than their scorched-earth northern counterparts, again, far fewer than anticipated took up arms to strengthen Smuts. They knew too well what they stood to lose.

Smuts' appeal to Transvaal forces to reinforce his rocky Cape position said all there was to say about a colonial rebellion, as did his May 1902 assessment of the military position there. With no more than about 3 300 men left in the fight, crippled by remount and forage shortages, and gasping for relieving reinforcements, he was at a loss. With no harvest to be reaped, he concluded that if the war was to be kept going, its southerly direction would have to be reversed. A 'continuance of the war,' said Smuts, 'will depend more on the Republics than upon the Cape Colony'.[359] That, in its way, clarified matters on the spot, stripping away remaining illusions.

As a member of Smuts' party, Deneys Reitz met with Botha and a group of 300 representatives from every surviving commando in the eastern Transvaal. What most brought home to him that 'the Boer cause was spent' was the sight of 'starving, ragged men, clad in skins or sacking, their bodies covered with sores, from lack of salt or food'. However steely their faith, their pitiful physical state meant that they could not fight on for much longer. If these 'haggard, emaciated men were the pick of the Transvaal Commandos,' concluded Reitz, 'then the war must be irretrievably lost'.[360]

At a pinch, despite few if any reserves, Smuts' forces and other republican units in the westernmost Cape were probably still able to keep up operations, trying to adapt to the changing social and political ecologies of various districts (more hostile pro-British colonists here, more open-handed Boer colonists there). They could remain an unvanquished nuisance. But it could never be more than one small move at a time. And, when that amounted to little other than sacking Coloured mission stations or executing suspected British spies and other collaborators, it was not much of a hand to hold. In any event, scrappy southern fighting bands were well outside the influence of the discipline imposed over northern bittereinder combatants in the closing stages of the war. Efficiency was much impaired by familiar commando friction over such matters as command, geographical and political connections, and personality squabbles. Indeed, right to the end, commandos were electing or deposing officers for reasons which often had little to do with their soldiering abilities.[361]

By now, leadership on both sides wished to end a wasting war and to conclude peace. There was little popular gain in the war for Britain, with spreading disillusionment over its conduct being fanned by even some of its own soldiers in the field, in doggerel poems 'which lambasted incompetent generals and venal contractors, and proclaimed the futility and pity of war'.[362] For Milner, the ruin of the overrun republics had gone far enough. A continuation of destructive warfare would jeopardise prospects for reconstruction and the installation of a new and more amenable civilian administration. In January 1902, convinced that the republicans were all in and that unconditional surrender was imminent, he foresaw 'settlement with a free hand', declaring that the 'advantage of a war ending as it is ending is enormous.'[363]

On this front, Kitchener had his own bearings. He had gone much further than Roberts towards a conclusive military defeat of the enemy, and already had his eye on the plum of an Indian army command. But, first, he wanted to see a sustainable Anglo-Boer settlement.

With the Middelburg talks having come to nothing, the war had already ground on well into the next year, and continued to do so until in April the republican governments came together at Klerksdorp in the Transvaal and re-solved to re-open negotiations with Britain's commander-in-chief. Typified by the figures of Marthinus Steyn and the acting Transvaal president, Schalk Burger, who had been staying out in the field with the fighting ranks, these were emphatically war governments, for whom peace was something to be negotiated by serving belligerents. Their Klerksdorp proposals stuck to the fundamental March 1901 principle of a retention of the republics' independence.

Predictably, Steyn was adamant that if Britain 'did not wish the Republics to remain independent, the struggle must continue'. If the moment to yield had to come, he would not be drawn into making peace terms, preferring instead to 'submit unconditionally' to the British 'for ever'.[364] Through all the taxing months of his command, this is what had always bothered a calculating Kitchener. Unconditional surrender, without terms, would not bring in all the Boers. If anything, it would provide a basis for the most hardened opponents to continue their resistance. Even if they could not get far, Britain would continue to be dragged along at further financial cost, against the background of a public which had grown weary of the conflict.

Provided there was no wrangling over independence rights, Boer leadership offered to make a compromise peace based on several republican concessions. Going along with a general amnesty, the Boer states would undertake to 'demili-tarise' their offensive capacities, extend the vote to Uitlanders, sign a binding treaty of friendship with Britain, and accord the English language equal rights with Dutch. Republican forces by now numbered at most between 15 000 and 17 000 combatants, while Britain had considerably better cards in hand, in the form of around 250 000 troops. London rejected the Klerksdorp terms, and re-sponded, essentially, by dusting off the proposals which the Boers had repudi-ated at Middelburg.

With the relinquishment of national independence as the starting point, the assembled republican leaders were in some difficulty, for negotiations could not go forward without the legitimacy of a mandate from those in the field. In due course, with British consent, a conference of sixty Transvaal and Orange Free State representatives, elected as their delegates by commandos, was convened at Vereeniging to discuss British peace terms and to decide if they were toler-able for ending the war. One of them was Smuts, winkled away from an incon-sequential siege action in the northern Cape and conveyed to Vereeniging under British safe conduct for the more humdrum business of getting through agendas.

With one side as good as defeated, it was inevitable that the negotiations would end in the signing of peace, however impassioned and agonised the discussion and debate between delegates, however painful the exchanges with British peace representatives, and however sunny commandants tried to sound in their reports on 'splendid' and 'strong' Boer combat morale. What that assertion signified was no more than a dignified impotence. The Boer representatives with whom the decision rested had to take realistic stock, and their balance sheet was sombre. Externally, the Cape and its Afrikaner rebellion was a shrunken sideshow, and the Boers seemed to know better than Lloyd George that the war would not bring anti-British foreign intervention.

Internally, Kitchener's pulverising drives showed no sign of slackening and his blockhouses and wire barriers were still in place, while the scale of armed 'joiner' and other kinds of 'unfaithful' collaboration had become deeply troubling to the Boers and a source of immense nationalist bitterness. It was as well that the British did not try to usher in the 'handsupper'and 'joiner' interest as a distinctive peacemaking element at Vereeniging: negotiations would in all likelihood have stalled. While camp conditions had been improved following the high mortality rate towards the end of 1901, the relief programme had become tainted. From December onwards, military authorities had been refusing to pull any more women and children into camps, encumbering worn-out commandos with the daunting job of providing for and protecting dependants in a field with desperately lean pickings.

Lastly, and far from least in importance, was the fatal realisation that the republican order had palpably lost too much ground and too much grip. Forced to abandon large chunks of the Orange River Colony and Transvaal Colony by devastation and the scarcity of grain and livestock, many Boers were becoming rusticated ghosts, beset by 'murders and all sorts of cruelties' perpetrated by the 'Kaffir tribes' who had been egged on by the enemy into 'taking part in the war against us'.[365]

Botha was eloquent on this and, together with Smuts, was also persuasive on another decisive matter. He had to convince fellow delegates that while the Boers could not go back militarily, neither could they go forward. For more radical bittereinders, the Boer cause was not yet sufficiently flattened to have to submit to an unconditional surrender. As a guerrilla nuisance, hostilities might be kept going for who knew how long, perhaps a year, or even more. As long as commandos could escape final, agreed defeat in the field, a negotiated settlement would always remain in sight. This was, clearly, a strategic notion based on a soaring kind of faith.

Smuts had recently spent sufficient time on horseback in the Cape to know all about going on too long and having too little to show for it. He and Botha argued vigorously that the Boers' only chance had already come. If Vereeniging failed and the war sputtered on into 1903 or even beyond, the Boers would be so run down as to lose altogether any sort of treaty bargaining position, which might bring the worst kind of defeat, that of flat capitulation to imperial ultimatum. This argument carried sufficient delegates to move along negotiations, although not without some sulking from the most zealous and ill-at-ease diehards.

Leaders like Steyn, and commanders such as De la Rey and Hertzog, had long been scornful of the progressive wing of the new Afrikaner élite represented by the likes of Botha and Smuts. From that quarter, there had been signs before Vereeniging of dispirited introspection and even a willingness to consider calling off the talks. From some anti-monopoly capitalist spirits, there was brief discussion about a conditional peace through some act of appeasement, such as handing over Johannesburg and its gold mines to Britain as an imperial enclave, in return for the retention of an agrarian-based independence. They can only have been hitting the brandy or forgotten the truth of Kruger's 1899 judgement of what it was that Milner wanted.

The outcome was a prickly republican division. Transvaal delegates were overwhelmingly for halting the war to avoid a national catastrophe. That eventuality was obvious to Smuts, who declared that if, 'humanly speaking', there was 'no reasonable chance to retain our independence as Republics, it clearly becomes our duty to stop the struggle in order that we may not perhaps sacrifice our people and our future for a mere idea which cannot be realised'.[366] Orange Free State representatives were, with few exceptions, unwilling to trade that idea through what amounted to a dictated peace. Taking affairs to a forced unconditional surrender still suited Steyn and his circle well enough - the very prospect that had always bothered Kitchener, for whom 'no terms' implied that the Boers could 'hold themselves absolutely free to begin again when they get a chance and see England in any difficulty'.[367] But, as it had been an alliance war, there could be no separate repudiation of any military consequence. Bloemfontein could not be a check upon Pretoria, and on the making of a final peace agreement.

Milner and Kitchener had never really agreed about Britain's strategic war aims, and were constantly at loggerheads over the terms to be settled with Boer leaders. The high commissioner, in fact, disliked having to enter into *any* peace negotiations with upstart colonial forces who had demonstrated so great a threat to British South Africa. He wanted the Boer leadership left high and dry by defeat, and the influence of republican generals destroyed, thereby opening the way to 'anglicisation'.

If Milner was vindictive and tactless, an aloof and hard-headed Kitchener was scarely a more winning figure. Yet he was an experienced general of no small political judgement, and here he had a calculating sense of the need for magnanimity. Defeating the republicans required the making of a judicious peace. That could only be clinched through a fair measure of conciliation with the Boers, who had to be accepted as an essential co-element of a reconstructed white settler order. This is what underpinned Kitchener's belief, aired before Vereeniging got under way and more than once reiterated, that the Boer leadership be accorded due honour and generosity so that they would not go down in history as traitors who had sold out their countries.[368]

Although the dominant influence on the British side, Milner did not get all that he wanted, nor did Kitchener get agreement on every fine detail that he wished to see as part of peace terms. But the commander-in-chief's influence in the accommodationist direction of those terms is apparent: an open-handed and 'honourable' peace as a platform for treaty-making with the Boer generals. In that sense, 'for Kitchener the military and political aspects were intimately tied together'.[369]

The detailed political and administrative issues and activities in bringing Vereeniging through are generally too tedious to document. Broadly speaking, the war had turned essentially on Boer claims: while cut back severely, they could never be completely excised. Even in Milner's fond – and illusory – vision of a significant British dominance within just a few post-war years, what mattered still was that Afrikaner wishes be reconciled with the imperial enterprise of a new South Africa.

But the problem of the war had first to be resolved. This was achieved in the signing of peace in Pretoria shortly before midnight on 31 May 1902, ending the negotiations which had commenced at Vereeniging on 15 May. By fifty-four votes to six, republican delegates consented to surrender their independence and to recognise the sovereign authority of King Edward VII. The British objective was accomplished, and to be made good it required a non-retributive aftermath.

Many of the now 20 000 or so bittereinders still out were said to be 'shattered' by news of the peace treaty, scarcely believing that they had just become British subjects. In their ranks there were tears, and some declared their loss of faith in God.[370] Britain's troops were relieved that it was all over at last, but were hardly cut up by news of the peace. That was hardly surprising. They had, after all, been fighting a different war.

For their part, the Boers came away with the substance of a negotiated rather than a dictated peace. In return for signing away their independence, they secured arrangements for the repatriation of all prisoners of war and the provision of an almost universal general amnesty; the ratification of economic rights, such as the maintenance of property ownership and non-punitive taxation; the provision of major economic relief and renewal – Britain would meet the bill for the republican war debt for anything up to £3m – and reconstruction funding. There would also be a measure of legal protection for the Dutch language.

The terms also made provision for the eventual introduction of self-government in the two newly annexed colonies, and stipulated that limited Cape franchise rights for blacks would not be extended and pushed down Boer throats. That unwelcome prospect would be left for consideration only after the agreed introduction of responsible government. In any case, the war for South Africa had never been for the rights of its black majority.

Coined as a 'surrender' by a smug Milner (but not by a more circumspect British government), and as a credibly negotiated settlement by Botha, the Treaty of Vereeniging brought to an end the British empire's troublesome Boer republics. The South African War was over, ended by peace talks started in a place with a name which meant, roughly, 'join' or 'unite'. A drab and ugly spot, it was not a promising site in which to sow the seed of a South African New Jerusalem.

A new Liberal British government began to hand back authority to the Orange River Colony and Transvaal Colony Boers in 1905, thereafter granting local self-government some five years after the end of hostilities. Union came in 1910, creating a unified white segregationist state presided over by Louis Botha and

Jan Smuts, now won over securely as the empire's Afrikaner colonial collaborators. Those men who came to constitute the governing nucleus of a new self-
ruling imperial Dominion were drawn from the generals who had made things
so difficult for Britain. Afrikanerdom had not been obliterated and, in that
sense, Milner had lost.

Having made up sufficiently with the right kind of realistic and amenable
Afrikaners, the Liberal government had now gained 'good British subjects, whom
we desire to be loyal,' hoping that there would never again be a need to keep
against them 'an enormous garrison at an enormous expense'.[371] In turn, those
subjects, in the shape of Botha and Smuts, championed the reconciliation of
'white people in this land', as 'one solid, united and strong race'.[372]

Invoking the American Civil War analogy much favoured by well-disposed
British observers, Winston Churchill welcomed the day 'when we can take the
Boers by the hand and say as Grant did to the Confederates at Appomattox, "go
back and plough your fields"'.[373] They did, but, for many, not without a well-
nursed grudge. Among militant nationalists, 'the long history of conflict had
aggravated a strongly anti-British sentiment . . . leaving "the reverberations of
menace"'. Wounding memories of the war 'could not be so easily wished away
by the strategic logic of élites'.[374] Having finished one war, traditionalist republican dissenters would in time be ready for another, a political rather than a
military struggle. The creation of the memory which helped to fuel it lay partly
in how Anglo-Boer opponents had come to see the war, and to view each other
once hostilities had started. As we near the end of this story of the war, we turn
now to that question.

9
PATRIOTISM AND PREJUDICE

S WE HAVE NOTED, BRIEFLY, EARLIER IN THIS BOOK, BRITISH ATTI-
tudes towards republican Boer society in the build-up to war were
often condescending and influenced by racial notions of an inefficient
and backward order in need of civilising improvement. This next chapter ex-
plores British imperial and Boer republican attitudes and beliefs in wartime —
again, here too, on the British side, assumptions about the Boers and feelings
about the war were largely arrogant, uninformed and highly racist. Yet, it is
crucial to keep in mind the manner in which these reflected contemporary sen-
timents about Africa in a climate of steadily hardening European racial beliefs
about which distant colonial societies were backward and which were improv-
able. And it is equally crucial to bear in mind that the actual experience of war
could shape attitudes towards, and relations with, adversaries, in some surprisingly humane ways.

Predictably, perhaps, at the outbreak of hostilities it did not look as if there
would be much showing of humanity. A number of writers have characterised
the period from roughly 1870 to 1914 as a frenetic new epoch of nationalist war
psychology and war culture. In these years, the general attitudes of European
society turned to embrace the increasingly belligerent 'realities of modernity',
one of its more influential notions being an acceptance of war as both desirable
and beneficial, a supreme competitive test of national virility and racial fitness.[375]

In Britain, mounting concerns over the empire's place in the wider world led to
excessive fears of foreign states and nationalities, anxieties which were not helped
by startling national humiliations, such as Majuba and Khartoum. By the end of
the 1890s, these setbacks had led to a great flowering of popular patriotism, bil-

iously hostile to anything perceived to be endangering British power. Whether those threatening it were large, like Russia or France, or small, like the contentious Catholic Irish or the Boers, there was to be no toleration of opponents.

The classic conception of this intoxicating brew of patriotism and militarism was the collective pathology of jingoism. As depicted by radical intellectuals like Charles Masterman and Hobson, this was a warped patriotic sentiment in which national feeling was transmuted into hatred of another nation, feeding into a primitive impulse to destroy its members. In one later summary, Hobson's famous *Psychology of Jingoism* conjured up a cynical imperialist 'world of war, a world contaminated by . . . fanatical masses . . . a Boer War world which . . . unmasks illusions about the "purity" of British national character'. South Africa shattered any liberal imperial notion of a John Bull Britain which favoured a fair fight, instead peeling open its 'darker face', and 'unmasking hidden and disturbing propensities'. Abandoning reason, the whole of British society had embraced a rapacious xenophobia, exulting in the plight of a cornered enemy. For Hobson, this was best exemplified by hysterical public celebration of the lifting of the sieges, 'the saturnalia of Ladysmith and Mafeking Days', other ostentatious displays of war enthusiasm despite 'breaches of . . . civilised warfare', and strident press calls for the slaying of Boers 'with the same ruthlessness which would be shown to a plague-infected rat'.[376]

The strength of this perspective rested on the assumption of a pervasive anti-Boer feeling in British society, partly directed from above by the Conservative and Liberal imperialist war interest, and swelling partly from below through social sectors which eagerly absorbed war propaganda. Ratcheting up hostility towards the enemy was a powerful empire patriotism, inculcated by music hall and theatre, schools, military pressure groups, churches, paramilitary youth bodies like the Boys' Brigade and the Church Lads' Brigade, rough-house jingo mobs who broke up anti-war meetings, and 'yellow' newspapers, periodicals, and books. The more sensational blood cravings which so disturbed Hobson were parodied by the socialist, Robert Blatchford, in his lament over the failure of British 'kindness' in South Africa. 'We have killed some of them with kindness, but we have not killed enough . . . Dispatch more. Those in St Helena and Ceylon might be rendered down into beef extract. It will be too expensive to send them back to South Africa.'[377] Blatchford was pro-war, but not without a touch of heavy irony about the enterprise.

Beginning with the florid picture painted by Hobson and his critical contemporaries, there has long been an established notion of mass war enthusiasm, demonstrated by crowd-based 'mafficking' to celebrate British mettle in the face of difficult odds, the disruption of anti-war gatherings, and the roughing up of prominent pro-Boers and attacks on their property. Once hostilities had got under way, and especially after the fright of early British defeats, anti-war or equivocal Liberal, Labour, trade union and socialist positions split. Minority opposition to the war became ever more muted. And if there continued to be dissenting voices, these were few and diminishing. While the issues of the war may have meant precious little, if anything, to working-class and other ordinary people, its rights or wrongs were quite secondary to the need that it be supported and won.

Thus, where popular attitudes might have differed emphatically over something like Irish Home Rule, war against this distant colonial enemy bridged social divisions, creating a shared cause across classes. Moreover, the war encouraged more than a patriotic consensus: by 1900, the episodes of British advance and set-piece victories provided emotion and dazzle. In this perspective, South Africa was also a winning issue at the polls. On the party political front, in some municipal contests and most notably in the 1900 'khaki election', it conditioned political behaviour. There, the strength of feeling was apparent when an excitable election fought by the government on national loyalty and its running of the war produced a thumping majority, scuppering many pro-Boer Liberal MPs. In this charged atmosphere, working-class men were entreated not to dishonour or to betray the memory of 'murdered' or 'treacherously felled' British soldiers by voting the wrong way. Candidates who argued that political criticism of war motives and of strategy did not mean lack of admiration for soldiering achievements and pride in victory, found that this cut little ice. The war was a patriotic cause to be supported to the hilt.

Yet, that proposition has not gone unchallenged. In a reinterpretion of popular attitudes, some writers have argued that there was not all that much from which to conclude that the political culture and beliefs of the working classes were captivated by war and empire. After all, what counted most in working-class culture was the immediacy of concrete, everyday experience, a consciousness in which great national undertakings would have counted relatively little.[378] Given uncertainty as to what the empire actually meant to the mass of British people, attitudes to its wars were not necessarily unambiguous. While some sense of a common Britishness could be said to have been widely felt in the working-class population, attitudes to the wider world rarely ever rose beyond indifference or blank contempt.[379]

If that were so, the weakness of popular opposition to the war could be explained by more specific domestic factors. At the outset, organised labour leadership had indeed opposed hostilities. But, once war became wartime, it was difficult to sustain a united stance, and traditional pro-war, working-class Tory organisation was able to extend its reach. Moreover, if extra-parliamentary anti-war organisation was weak, it was because of poor, unimaginative leadership and organisational deficiencies. Crucially, too, the Liberals were damagingly divided. The gulf in opinion was wide. It was between those who blamed Britain for forcing the war and those who blamed the Boers for starting it with their provocative ultimatum, those who were instinctively pro-Boer and those who were not, those who sympathised with free pastoral peoples but accepted that Britain could not lose, and those who, like Lloyd George, were 'secretly delighted' by the early spectacle of British noses being bloodied by simple farmers.[380] Thus, it followed that the outcome of the decisive 'khaki' election lay in Liberal weakness and disunity, and in a political culture which was more inert than active. Significantly, 1900 drew a far lower poll than in the preceding 1895 election. In any event, there was usually 'little correlation between imperial appeal and electoral success'.[381]

Nor could the flamboyant occasions of Mafeking and other siege relief be viewed as confirmation of jingoism. 'Mafficking' could be seen as flamboyant, self-indulgent crowd celebration, less an expression of aggressive working-class war sentiment, and more as an instinctive airing of relief at Britain's triumph over adversity and joy at the saving of lives. It was also a festive social opportunity, as victory in South Africa provided an excuse (and the licence) to run music hall onto the streets for a communal knees-up. Granted, the war may have provided ordinary inhabitants with their own satisfactions and views of what it meant, through the consumption of cigarettes, alcohol, disinfectant and other commodities as manufacturers exploited the advertising potential of the conflict, marketing Dettol as proven on the Front or tobacco as a welcome Comrade.[382] Equally, in dockyard and arsenal towns the war was hardly unpopular, even among trade unionists. But this was not the ideological appeal of British intervention in the republics which was lapped up by middle-class readers of *Quarterly Review* or the *Nineteenth Century*. Still less did it amount to the mindless jingoism of Hobson's mob. Arguably, the working class *joined* or attached themselves to celebratory war crowds. Indeed, in the archetypal sense of the jingo crowd as one which deliberately piled into anti-war opponents, workers were in fact not prominent in such vengeful 'mobs'. These tended to be composed heavily of patriotic middle-class and lower-middle-class men and belligerent youths, often no-nonsense Unionist supporters.

Another factor was that army recruitment in the earlier months of the war was disproportionately from the volunteering lower-middle and middle classes. Working-class enrolment, on the other hand, was more sluggish, peaking only in the last few months of the fighting and scarcely spurred by ideological passion. In other words, the war just confirmed the traditional role of the regular army as an institution to mop up the unemployed and the unskilled, as its recruitment patterns moved generally in tandem with the rising level of unemployment in the early 1900s. It was bleak prospects, more than patriotism, which induced working men to fight for the empire in South Africa. On the other hand, whether as volunteering or as pro-war rioting, pro-war fever was more squarely a lower-middle-class phenomenon. Some commentators have even characterised Boer War jingoism as an expression of status anxiety, as an insecure lower middle class licked the adhesive of patriotism and militarism to stick itself to the war of middle-class Unionism and Liberal Imperialism.[383]

Lastly, high levels of domestic interest in the South African fighting were not constant, but fluctuating. They were also transitory. After the intensities of 'Black Week' and the recovering British victories, the war lost some of its opening flush. Thereafter, with hostilities dragging on, there was little to give the conflict a fresh imaginative lease, aside from welcoming home returning veterans like Lord Roberts. Increasingly, concentration camp deaths, executions of republican rebels, and Boer killings of blacks who were consorting with the British were not the sort of thing to lend high tone to a war ostensibly in defence of principles of peace, good government, and the world rights of Britons. Even more, as the conflict dispersed widely into irregular warfare, it became that much more tricky for correspondents to report flatteringly and entertainingly on events. With South Africa less head-turning and 'newsworthy', the press stakes were simply less. Thus, by mid-1900, *The Times* was becoming a little bored with South Africa. In June 1900 the Boxer Rebellion began in China, and this exotic tale of British phlegm in the face of 'barbarous' threats, coupled with the Victorian obsession with the heroism and stoicism of sieges, pushed the now messy Boer War from its position at the forefront of public consciousness.[384] By July, the large British press corps had almost evaporated, its correspondents posted to China or elsewhere.

Gradually, too, as awareness grew that civilian suffering had replaced real fighting, so middle-class pro-Boers were listened to more politely, and skilled working men's clubs and institutes became more tolerant of speakers presenting the moral case against an aggressive war and that of the Boer position on Uitlanders and the franchise. Opponents of the war often argued that it was not being fought for patriotic British interests. Rather, *they* were the real patriots, with war supporters having become the pawns of conniving, warmongering, cosmopolitan financial forces.

But again, in turn, emphasis on anti-war feeling or indifference to the war has been questioned. Therefore, stressing the intimate connection between the late-Victorian military and semi-skilled and unskilled segments of the working class, there is an alternative view that the war actually induced an *excess* of working-class army volunteers above the numbers generated naturally by cyclical growth in unemployment.[385] To add to that, the number of wartime volunteers (just over 200 000) did not reflect solely the number of would-be soldiers who presented themselves. Many working-class men would undoubtedly have been rejected on medical grounds, and officers from 'respectable' Volunteer and Yeomanry forces had a class bias, favouring educated recruits who could ride and shoot.

That aside, the influence of militarist and patriotic traditions among unskilled and semi-skilled male workers suggests that a fair number would have been keen on getting stuck into a Boer enemy seen as 'primitive'. The lure of adventure, and an itchy preparedness for colonial conflict, was an old and powerful enough draw. Against that, the cause of the war was at best secondary or irrelevant. For enthusiastic recruits, some already apprenticed to cruelty and brutal confrontation through gang associations in rough industrial city districts, South African army service promised a new, exotic and institutionalised setting for masculine aggression against 'the Boer – a kwaint littel creetchur'.[386]

At the same time, complementary perspectives have stressed the emergence of a fairly suffocating imperialist patriotism in the last quarter of the nineteenth century. In this atmosphere, whatever the different meanings of patriotism for middle and other classes, by the time of the war it was fundamentally about being loyal to the institutions of the country, and resolute in defence of its honour and interests. Through their wide influence, Victorian youth organisations instilled manly (and womanly) imperial virtues, and the mostly working-class Volunteer Force provided part-time service for young men in the task of defending their country. Even the regular forces, for so long the last resort of the jobless and impoverished, had been promoted ever since the Crimean War as the incarnation of British Christian heroism, and for decades there had been earnest talk from the Conservative party about bridging the divide between the nation and the armed forces. The Boer War 'soldier' became associated with 'strength, virility, health and youth', a martial symbol embraced by 'private and public institutions such as boys' clubs and schools'.[387]

Given the addition to this of more diffuse imperialist attitudes channelled through schools, popular literature, music hall, chapels and both establishment Anglican and free churches, the mass of people cannot be seen as having been 'immunised . . . in any thoroughgoing way from the virus of right-wing patriotism'.[388] In taking that measure of the mood, scholars have underlined that the pull of the empire patriotism of this period was sufficient to create and sustain a semblance of national 'unity across class and party lines'. Its basic articles of faith were traditional Conservatism, expansionist militarism in defence of a fuzzy Imperial Preference, a devoted royalism, the identification and aggrandisement of archetypal Victorian national heroes, and the absorption of the supremacist racial thinking of Social Darwinism.[389]

In some ways, understanding of the hold of the war upon the popular British imagination has come virtually full circle. Perceptions have moved from unquestioned jingoism to scepticism of mass pro-war opinion, to findings which almost take one back to Hobson's Boer War saturnalia. So, when it came to joining in the pro-war chorus against the Boers, even Britain's most natural dissenters, its Nonconformists, sang loudly, backed solidly by their Methodist mission interests in South Africa. War for British supremacy in South Africa 'had a moral and religious purpose' in that victory would 'serve the interests of missionary endeavour and end the power of the Dutch reformed churches', sending Boer ministers, all rebel rascals, packing.[390]

In any rounded picture, empire war patriotism, whether as intellectual doctrine or as rollicking street rhetoric, was no doubt a significant element in British
culture. The South African crisis may, indeed, have been a moment when it was
dominant. Yet, questions about the place of the war in popular consciousness
still remain. It is, for instance, hard to know to what extent anti-Boer imagery
influenced the wartime attitudes of working-class women. For that matter, while
numerous middle-class and aristocratic women declared themselves repelled by
the 'racial degeneracy' and 'polluted stock' of the Boers, others were prepared
to ration their favours with the enemy, collecting humanitarian relief funds and
actively aiding distressed Boer families. There were even those like the West
African explorer and social reformer, Mary Kingsley, niece of the writer, Charles
Kingsley, who nursed Boer prisoners of war. Her belief was only in healing the
war, not in winning it. In a bitter irony, she died on the job, of enteric fever,
the disease which accounted for over sixty per cent of the British army's war
fatalities.

Elsewhere, British attitudes towards the Boers were less charitable. The war
did not create the image of Boer primitives, fated to be conquered by a more
advanced order. That was already being propagated by pro-war elements in the
1890s. Rather, it provided circumstances for this to grow more intense and to
acquire new variations. Take, for example, reaction to a charge levelled by French,
German and other European anti-war critics that Britain was set on a criminal
destruction of the republics. There, the brutal methods of Kitchener, turned
from the Sudan's 'Butcher of Omdurman' to 'The Butcher of the Transvaal', were
causing famine and driving the Boers back to the Stone Age. Far from denying
the war's destructive impact, middle-class organs such as *Quarterly Review* and
The Illustrated London News acclaimed it as a positive achievement, one which
was sweeping away a stagnant agricultural community.

The only problem was that Continental critics, such as Pierre Leroy-Beaulieu,
were failing to grasp this. 'If M. Beaulieu were personally acquainted with South
Africa,' explained a writer in April 1902, 'he would learn that generations of
Boers had lived, or more correctly, squatted on their soil,' and that 'except in
the mining districts' there was an 'utter absence of labour on the part of the
inhabitants'. Conceivably, even if 'the whole Boer population had been swept
away by an epidemic, they would have left no marks of their rule other than the
railways . . . constructed for them by the Uitlanders' mostly 'men of British

birth'. As the objective of the war between a vigorous empire and idle colonists was the establishing of 'an industrial civilisation as the basis of Africa's regeneration, even those among us who oppose the war may take comfort'. For its outcome would resolve the tension between 'higher and lower types of civilisation'.[391]

A logical next step was to portray the Boers as technologically immature and intellectually stunted. The average commando was seen best, in one homely observation, as an Irish peasant: if given a cannon, he would instinctively roll it home for use as a dairy churn. Another familiar view was to ascribe Boer mental and physical torpor to the easy availability of African labour, perpetually on call to meet the 'primitive wants' of growing 'the necessary mealies' and the keeping of 'numerous flocks' which was all that constituted existence. Carrying this to a novel conclusion, one journalist suggested in 1901 that the way to end the war would be to have all labouring Africans in the republican territories rounded up, thereby making Boer life immediately insupportable.[392]

In a related manner, belittling Boer opponents at times involved inflating African talents and vigour. In the early weeks of the war in Natal, a West Yorkshire Regiment officer conceded that while his commando adversaries were showing themselves to be 'marvels of ingenuity and still more of energy', this was assuredly a consequence of their having 'gone native', as 'both qualities come more from the inspired Kaffirs, than from the low Boers themselves'. *Under the Union Jack* assured readers that reports of the enemy use of Africans in Natal fighting lines 'loses its seriousness when it is remembered that it is one of their customs' to have servants to prop up and fuss about every commando, as they lacked proper fighting self-reliance.[393] More passionate, fundamentalist forms of Boer religious practice were derided as 'witchcraft' or 'spirit babble', an African contamination. Influenced by such perceptions, some Australian, New Zealand and Canadian politicians declared this to be a war of 'predestination', to quote a member of the New South Wales legislative assembly, in which the lowest stock of European humanity should be displaced by a better type of European who would remain European, such as efficient British Dominion colonists.[394]

More extreme British commentators reinforced the impression of a sub-civilised enemy by turning to apish or other animalistic imagery to depict the Boers as something less than fully human. Popular weeklies like *Pearson's War Pictures* and *Under the Union Jack,* often resorted to such representation, in which commandos, stripped of humanity, became 'Boer herds' or 'Boer flocks'; civilian camp refugees were 'swarms' or 'droves', dull and ruminant by nature. 'I much disliked their aspect,' wrote Lady Rolleston in 1901, 'their eyes are generally small and dark, and too close together, the nose is short . . . the face is nearly always animal . . . the glance is shifty, and reminds me irresistibly of a visit to the Zoological Gardens at home.' In similar vein, Colonel Hubert Jourdain of the Connaught Rangers recorded that he found Boer captives 'reptilian' in appearance, and 'quite hideous to look on'.[395]

While republican politicians, their European allies, and British pro-Boers were dipping into Christian discourse to condemn the immorality of the concentration camps, some metropolitan observers portrayed the removal of Boer 'undesirables' from the countryside as rather like the rounding up of cattle. Charges of 'methods of barbarism' during 1901 and 1902 by anti-war newspapers such as the *Manchester Guardian* were brushed aside. Dramatic uncovering of abysmal conditions, such as that provided by Emily Hobhouse in her investigative 1902 *Report of a Visit to the Camps of Women and Children in the Cape and Orange River Colonies,* was troubling, but could still be dismissed as sentimental and biased. For the Boers were to blame for their own high death rates. In that callous judgement, the irrationalities, ignorance and superstitions of highveld society were merely cultural symptoms of some clinical disorder. If the camps were a mess, it was because their pre-modern inhabitants were congenitally unclean. Justifying farm burning to an anxious English churchman, Salisbury, rarely one to mince his words, was unapologetic. The ensuing 'horrors of concentration camps' were unavoidable, just as 'the huddling together of so many human beings' could 'not but cause a great mortality; particularly among a people so dirty as the Boers'.[396] The British army was there to fight, not to solve its enemy's sanitation malaise.

In an unusual reversal of conventional Victorian social perceptions, in the Transvaal and Orange Free State it was country, not urban, life which was unhealthy or diseased, and it was rural, not urban fertility which was producing socially irresponsible 'race' stock. Camp inmates were falling victim to 'filth, carelessness, fatalism and a belief in absurd or disgusting remedies'. According to Dr John Welenski, writing in the *British Medical Journal* in November 1901, the 'fecklessness, ignorance and dirtiness' of Boer women 'was so ingrained' that 'decent habitation is a thing of which they would have about as much conception as they would have of the aestheticism of Mr Oscar Wilde or the philosophy of Mr Herbert Spencer'. John Buchan also added his piece. Although conditions were 'distressing', this was because 'mentally and bodily underbred' victims represented 'a class of people who have somehow missed civilisation' and the training in proper 'habits' that provided. If anyone merits the last word here, it is Kitchener. In an irritated comment which has often been repeated, he put down rising child mortality levels to 'the criminal neglect of the mothers', and disclosed that, in his view, the most wilful culprits ought 'to be tried for manslaughter'.[397]

In the legalised slaughter of warfare, the notion of enemy criminality also played a propaganda role at various stages. One controversy was the introduction of uncapped or dum-dum bullets, which expanded on bodily impact to mangle flesh. Here, atrocity charges came from both sides. The background was provided by the earlier 1899 First European Peace Conference at the Hague, in which twenty-six states, including Britain, accepted a convention on the conduct of war which banned dum-dums as too 'inhuman' for use in European theatres. A fundamental premise was the late-nineteenth-century endorsement of a distinction between 'civilised' warfare, or regular war between 'civilised' European nations, and 'savage' warfare, or unorthodox colonial war waged by European armies against non-European tribal opponents.[398] The supposedly innate 'fanaticism' and 'animalistic' strength of 'savage' and 'semi-civilised' colonial enemies made the ferocious stopping power of the dum-dum a technical necessity. This was something that had already proved bad news for the Zulu in the 1870s, and the Sudanese in the 1890s.

Some of the accusations which circulated among British soldiers and in published popular opinion were sensational and wholly imaginary. One recurring story was that commandos were putting poison into soft-nosed Mauser cartridges, or were rolling bullets in faeces to spread infection. Other accounts were rooted in the routine unearthing of Boer arms caches which allegedly held 'split-nosed cartridges which had been dipped in verdigris'. There is no doubting the genuine rage of ordinary soldiers at the capture of stocks of expanding bullets at places like Colenso and Paardeberg. Their use violated that mysterious shared code of a combat culture that was clean. Beyond that, such practice confirmed the debased nature of the enemy. If Kruger could sanction the use of 'immoral' techniques against 'civilised troops', it revealed that he was, in the words of one newspaper, a 'diseased growth from the worse of the criminal classes'.[399] In turn, it confirmed that the war was about subduing a criminal enemy.

The officer corps also voiced paternalistic and protective concerns over the exposure of their men to 'improper' mutilation and suffering. 'Unsporting and intolerable', protested an Imperial Yeomanry captain, who took strong exception to his 'good class' of men being gouged by dum-dums. Within the war, things seemed to be moving in the direction of a class war. The Boers were culturally and temperamentally unsuited to observing the 'rules' of combat with 'infantry of civilised stock, men who are clerks, telegraphists and engineers'.[400] On occasion, another sense of a common humanity could be seen in British outrage at the horrific wounds being inflicted upon their African and Coloured transport drivers and scouts by expanding bullets, with 'pitiful' men left 'hideously mangled' and 'rarely unmaimed'. Medical officers even urged soldiers to hit back on behalf of black victims. A legalistic and liberal view of war by the rules could also be found among some commanding officers, who considered blacks in British army service to be entitled to treatment under 'civilised' war conventions, and Cape auxiliaries to be of 'British' status. Thus, when Carolus Duimpies was caught and executed, a British colonel wrote to the Boers with a warning of reprisals, and declared the shooting not only a 'shameful act against one of our men' but the use of 'barbaric explosive bullets' to be 'against all known rules of war'.[401]

In Britain, socialist militarists like H.M. Hyndman of the Social Democratic Federation concluded that Boer peasants had forfeited any rights to restraint. The lives of British troops were being needlessly endangered by a War Office sentimentality which was denying them the lethal tools to do the job. This call was joined by the Tory voice of *Quarterly Review,* which declared the notion of racial conventions of war to be a 'curious . . . discrimination', when all that mattered was 'stopping power. The enemy, whether civilised or savage, must be stopped in his charge'. Hyndman's *Justice,* which incidentally took the novel and romantic view that the only imperial reason for fighting should be to return the country to noble Africans, proclaimed that the ferocity of Boer armaments had destroyed any pro-Boer mystique of republican virtue and Christian piety. Rounding on anti-war Radical Liberals, it taunted them with the mock assurance that 'explosive devices . . . are simply carried around by brother Boer as engineering curiosities'.[402]

The grip of the dum-dum story may have become one of the war's more tenacious combat atrocity myths, with the Boers for their part claiming British savagery in fire at Spioen Kop. There was also the legend of British beastliness in the shooting of pregnant Boer women with cartridges sufficiently powerful to kill the unborn. In an atmosphere of fiery invasion, these nightmare images fitted with feelings of a demonic war of violation and extermination. At the same time, though, leaving aside wilder implausibilities, the use in combat of doctored ammunition was not entirely a myth. While there may have been no authorisation from Buller, Roberts or Kitchener, British command still turned a blind eye to what by 1902 was being termed a 'stock control' problem in the field. For the honest and upright Boers, according to Ludwig Krause, this British 'want of ordinary humanity' had reluctantly degraded their own fighting practices. 'Such ammunition was unknown amongst the Boers,' he insisted, 'until they found it on the bodies of the English soldiers.' When, 'in spite of our repeated protests the English persisted . . . our men retaliated . . . converted ordinary Mauser bullets . . . then both sides continued its use.' The atrocious nature of imperialist warfare had somehow undone the traditionally charitable side of the Boer way of war.[403]

For younger, educated republican officers, making sense of the war involved more than the belief that their cause of national sovereignty was incontestably just. If God-given national rights of self-determination and liberty were to be successfully defended, that cause had to be upheld through a form of decent fighting, in which European Christian virtues would not be abandoned, and in which Boer warfare would not degenerate into brutalised excesses. During the first year of hostilities, this was an article of faith among many leaders in the field: the enemy was barbarous and fought dirty, while the Boers were civilised Christians who fought more honourably. The Transvaal and republican press elsewhere therefore dismissed as a fabrication persistent British accusations of 'treachery' in the commando use (or misuse) of the white flag to buy time for regrouping or to stage ambushes. This was backed by Britain's pro-Boer publications, which declared white flag charges a shabby invention of the 'jingo imagination' to discredit republican adherence to the rules of civilised war.

Instead, what was morally repugnant was the British use of cavalry wielding the *arme blanche* to terrorise opponents who were not 'natives' but Christian Europeans. Critics fastened on the savagery with which imperial soldiers used lances and even bayonets against hapless farmers, in particular the ruthlessness of cavalry officers, whose evident relish in the 'sport' of 'pig-sticking', 'skewering' or 'gutting' in close combat featured prominently in early issues of war periodicals like *Black and White Budget* and *Shurey's Illustrated*. This helped create a metaphor representing the war in South Africa as the hunt, in which the Boers 'would not stand cold steel', with 'native ignorance of the lance' proving 'a pleasing revelation'. On the republican side it is correspondingly well captured by a Cronjé commando's reaction of panic and disbelief that a white enemy would be so 'deranged' and 'barbarous' as to inflict 'tribal savagery' upon the 'civilised'.[404]

To H.R. Fox-Bourne, a leading figure in the British Aborigines' Protection Society, the very campaign against the Boers meant nothing other than the wrong kind of war. Writing to the *Morning Leader* just over a year into hostilities, he condemned the 'wanton brutality of an imperialist onslaught on a small, white, civilised and Christian community'. Warfare there, he protested, was coming to resemble the routine 'savagery' associated with punitive colonial expeditions against 'black, uncivilised and non-Christian peoples'. Even if on colonial soil, the *Europeanness* of Britain's adversaries called for civilized restraint. Lionel Curtis echoed this: it was, after all, a war in which British soldiers would find that whatever their differences with the enemy, 'hospitality to a white man is a religion with these people'.[405]

Writing as recently as the 1970s, one military historian suggested that a defining feature of the war was the lack of hatred felt by British soldiers towards their opponents. Hostilities were shaped by mutual respect, commitment to a fair fight, and some innate recognition of 'their adversaries as Brother Boer'.[406] Contemporary soldiering perceptions were not altogether short of such sentiment, as in the observation of a Volunteer who found the Boers 'misguided in their resistance' but nevertheless 'splendid fighters and decent fellows led by thorough gentlemen. They are kindness itself to any of our wounded who fall into their hands, and the treatment meted out by the average Boer to the average English prisoner contrasts very favourably with that received by the Boers at the hands of the Tommies'.[407]

The Boer states were, then, not packed with barbarous enemies of empire, like the northwest frontier of India. That meant that if *how* the war should be fought was one issue, its proper resolution and settlement was another. Observers like

Curtis, who would be going on to manage reconstruction as part of Milner's Kindergarten, rolled them together. If hostilities were conducted without meanness, this would ensure an accommodating Anglo-Boer peace. Of course, the Salisbury government position was that it *was* being mindful of the European niceties of civilised war. In fact, if anything, it was drawing back from the tempting expedient of military alliances with African societies, which would have been a cheaper and less wearing way of defeating the Boers. 'It would have been easy,' wrote *The Times* journalist Leopold Amery in 1900, 'for the Imperial Government to have let loose Swazis, Basutos and Bechuanas against their old enemies. Attacked on every side and exposed to the terrors of savage warfare at their very doors, the Boers might have been placed in a terribly difficult situation.'[408]

Leo Amery was not alone in this view, for it represented a strand in military opinion. The reason for not engaging black Southern African levies was not a worry about 'reliability' or 'cowardice', as in earlier nervousness over the performance of Hausa soldiers in Wolseley's West African war against the Ashanti. It was quite the opposite. For Baden-Powell, it was a distasteful exultation in 'slaughter . . . to them, as attractive and entertaining as a bull-fight to a Spaniard or a football match to an Englishman'. The moral risk was a rapacious instinct, as in 'a winning fight' the non-European 'want of discipline' would 'lead them to commit excesses as would be unbecoming in allies of the British'.[409] One timely warning was carried by the *Cardiff Western Mail* in 'The Savage and the Boer', depicting Milner and Chamberlain gamely tethering a blood-curdling Gurkha warrior 'to stop that horror being added to the rest'.

Equally, there were plenty of British observers for whom the war did *not* seem to be so obviously a European business. Prominent among these were those who argued that in South Africa it was difficult to establish where 'barbarism' ended and 'civilisation' began. For Blatchford's *Clarion*, 'the Boer method of fighting is not that of reckless, gallant, untrained peasants. No, it is that of the bandit, the redskin, the Afridi and other savage fanatics.' Not to be outdone, an indignant Kitchener deplored his opponents for not being 'like the Sudanese who stood up to a fair fight. They are always running away on their little ponies.'[410]

Not missing a cue, a section of British Indian opinion became increasingly vocal. Fuming commentators suggested that Salisbury's Cabinet was inadvertently prolonging the war effort and disregarding national interest by sticking to the belief that 'in fighting Boers and other semi-civilised white races we are not to employ any of our Imperial resources'. One or two frustrated writers made a point of the 'animal' or 'devilish' behaviour in South Africa of Irish, Australian, and other 'more ruffianly' white colonial volunteers, declaring them far less disciplined than trained Sikhs and Gurkhas. 'Ill-bred' volunteer colonists were merely taking the conduct of the war downhill.

Overall, though, there was no call for being angelic, as a fight with the Boers did not require 'the usages of civilised war'. In the Commons, Arthur Balfour and Edward Grey trumpeted their regard for 'indigenous' Indian troops, with the pro-Indian *Quarterly Review* and *Nineteenth Century* urging the War Office to take this to heart and to act on it. As 'Her Majesty's troops' the native Indian army should not be allowed to think that it was 'not an integral part of the imperial military system', just as Russia's Cossacks had now become part of 'any of its European conflicts'. All that counted by 1901 was soldiering effectiveness to deal with a serious British 'national emergency'. What had that to do with 'possession of a dark skin?', asked Sir Henry Howorth. The Boers, of course, could be expected to whine and to cause a commotion at the Hague, he noted dismissively, just as 'they have complained of our using balloons and Lyddite shells'.[411]

At the same time, many ordinary British soldiers appeared to have little abstract interest in colour bar conventions. The case for Indian deployment rested on persuasive practical knowledge and experience, especially for those in regiments dispatched from Asia. Thus, when the going got tough in Natal because of heavy rain or dense humidity, Indian combatants would have been 'altogether ideal'. Lieutenant Edward Warr wished that he had had Sikhs, Gurkhas or Punjabis alongside him in the Orange Free State in March 1900; they would surely have been 'fantastically good' against De Wet and his frustrating tactical skill. Had the British been assigned even half a Gurkha company in the first place, Gatacre's problems at Stormberg would have been taken care of, after which 'the splendid little heathens in their grass shoes' could have been set after the Transvaal artillery corps.[412]

As the fighting ground on, so did irritation grow that another available string to the British bow was not being hooked. It made no operational sense to restrict companies of accomplished Bengal and Madras Lancers to menial remount duties which could be performed by local black labour, when what the army desperately needed were more mounted troops to increase its range and to raise its speed. Not only were these 'splendid natural horsemen' more than up to the job of 'cutting up the Boers'. They were 'riders of the finest class' virtually 'just like white men, only their colour is different'. With such calibre, declared *The Statist* in 1901, Buller would swiftly have made the Orange River Colony his, and the war would 'long ago' have been over.[413]

Nor were those to be dismembered always viewed as a white or European enemy. It did not require very much contact with commando prisoners or very poor Boer communities for soldiers to recognise an odd thing about the republics. On one hand, they were states based on rigid white supremacy, places where 'the natives really got bossed about'.[414] On the other, Boers at the bottom of the social pile seemed sometimes to be inhabiting somewhat blurred racial communities. Thus, one lieutenant was puzzled by talk of the Boers 'bossing' and 'enslaving' blacks when some swarthier commandos were themselves virtually as dark as their *agterryers*.

Similarly, Private Arthur Dye had a distasteful encounter with 'dreadful low-class' prisoners, a jumble of men, 'half-Dutch, half-Native', and other 'dubious half-castes . . . black or several shades of it'. Elsewhere, observing how captured burghers and *agterryers* were sharing tents, clothing, food, songs and drink, a Durham Light Infantry intelligence officer concluded sardonically that the Boers would have done well to have had 'proper training' in 'how to behave like white men'.[415] Later, at the end of the war, a Yorkshire infantryman encountered a group of young Boer children who had spent much of the conflict with roving Swazi herders who had been given the responsibility of looking after them and their farm's cattle. A lengthy African custodianship appeared to have left them thoroughly acculturated. 'It would be interesting to know,' he reflected, 'on what basis some of these Boers assemble their fancy notions as to being European overlords.'[416] For men steeped in the more distancing style of British imperialism, such contradictions and other lax encounters with 'going native' showed yet again that the Boers did not always dress for dinner.

What of those who did? Here, just as anti-war factions in Britain were accused of prolonging the war by criticising its conduct and providing moral encouragement for the republican cause, so the pro-republican Cape Boer intelligentsia faced acrimony for war reporting seen as subversive of the imperial effort. Of special concern following the fall of Bloemfontein, Johannesburg and Pretoria, was the role of sympathetic Cape Boer papers such as *Het Zuid-Oosten* and *Ons Land* in peddling accounts of British excesses. Offence lay in 'flooding' Boer territories with 'Cape Dutch organs' which were now circulating among 'unlettered' or semi-literate 'philistines', simple rustics unable to make proper judgments. An isolated class of 'poor farmers' with 'Kitchen-Dutch alone', the northern Boers represented a community of 'unreason', having had none of the rational benefits of the Victorian Sunday School movement. Their mood in Natal amply illustrated this. The ransacking of school buildings in Dundee and Colenso, and the feeding of laager campfires with 'school furniture and scholars' copybooks', rekindled the enemy as the new Goths and Vandals.[417] With commandos' anti-educational bigotry extending to the destruction of mission station property in the Cape, they seemed to be negating the entire British liberal vision of constructing a better and self-improving South Africa.

In their lack of educated 'good sense' and 'comprehension', the Boers were seen to be like exasperating Indian villagers, easily misled and at the mercy of a prejudiced nationalist press. In some quarters, this view was carried in a further direction. Through renegade Cape political journalists, meetings, pamphlets, and other kinds of anti-British agitation, manipulative republican 'scum' were seducing 'responsible' or 'true' peasant Boers from a path of sensible accommodation with empire. For those conspirators who believed that the First Anglo-Boer War had been started, not by the gullible Dutch but by the meddling of shady 'foreign' elements linked to the 'criminal classes of Europe',[418] presumably history seemed to be repeating itself. In this regard, the idea that the Boers were themselves the dupes of a scheming and amoral war element produced a curious mirror image. It was the counterpart of those Liberal, Labour and socialist assertions that the war had been forced upon the British by the hidden hand of mercenary capitalists.

Meanwhile, on the fighting ground, contempt for the Boers was, as we have already observed, far from universal among British troops. Their first-hand view of the enemy would have rested on countless small observations, empirical perceptions, and imaginative suppositions. These led some of the British in South Africa not to dismiss their opponents as inferior people, but to be impressed and even intrigued by their combat capabilities and technical accomplishments. In general, there was grudging admiration for the flexibility of Boer tactics, for their frequent ability to engage unseen, for the planning and skill which went into defence-in-depth systems, for their exceptional mobility, for their camouflaging ability and clever use of river lines and fencing stock, and for their effectively timed use of long-range artillery in the opening movements of the war. Beyond this, there were routinely respectful murmurs about their proficiency in horsemanship, skill in marksmanship on or off the saddle, seasoned ability to treat wounds with herbal applications, and rumoured capacity for stupendous campaign endurance, lasting for weeks 'almost entirely' on 'biltong', the odd 'Boer biscuit', and even 'prickly pears'.

In addition, there was admiration of Boer physiology. This sometimes assumed an apocryphal or folklore quality, such as the 'supernatural' strength of mounted warriors, and a belief that the enemy was endowed biologically with 'superior powers of sight', with miraculous 'magnifying' eyes and 'mysterious' night vision. The legacy of 'untold centuries' of evolution as 'natural hunters' and 'nomads', this made them especially perilous riflemen, 'manly, spirited and deadly country folk'. Snatches of this sense of an uncannily able enemy would have fed the superstitions of more stumbling British soldiers from Dickensian Coke-towns, who found the Boer a gifted and agile countryside foe.[419] News that some commando ranks contained prophetic visionaries or *siener*s also created an unsettling sense that Boer fighters inhabited an impenetrable field of chance and possibility. Tactical intelligence, use of of terrain, and planning by superstition all seemed to coexist mysteriously to sustain them in the field.

Away from the lines there was another type of positive perception. Granted, much anti-war sentiment did not necessarily admire Boer society nor back its republican cause, merely believing that whatever the defects of the Boer states, they did not justify an aggressive and unjust war against them. But there was a romantic edge to some of it. For socialists such as Edward Carpenter, the Boer republics were idolised as a pastoral African Eden, inhabited by a humble, family-loving people who were pious and peaceable underdogs. In the best rhetorical comparison, they were not Johannesburg, 'a hell hole of Jews, financiers, greedy speculators . . . prostitutes . . . and every invention of the devil'.[420]

What these devoted rural Protestants had was now being 'criminally' despoiled by a brutal war. If the Transvaal was perhaps a touch imperfect in its running of affairs, the old-fashioned sobriety and rustic virtue of the yeoman Orange Free State could not but command admiration. While Bloemfontein was not quite Banbury, conceded an Oxfordshire correspondent, its surrounding countryside had its own verdant charm, with more tree plantings and better irrigation than Banbury.[421] Not surprisingly, he had yet to survey this lushness during January or February. In associated efforts to raise the Boer image, sympathisers sought also to domesticate the enemy, turning them into people with an agreeable Anglo-Saxon likeness. Hence, they were not to be seen as some homogenous medieval tribe, but as an improving commercial agricultural society, with customary class divisions into wealthy and poor.

'The average Boer is much like the average Englishman of country birth and agricultural surroundings,' noted one observer; some of them were gentry proprietors like 'middling squires', with poorer agriculturalists resembling 'the Earl of Carnarvon's tenants'. This was so much so that 'any group of the better class Boer farmers might be with difficulty distinguished from a matching group of English farmers'. By the same measure, the Boer landed class were said to be 'just the people you are used to in Hertfordshire and Derbyshire, merely talking another tongue'. As 'virtually all the agricultural progress of South Africa is due to the Dutch' it was no surprise to observe 'the extra-ordinary activity and hardihood of the Boers in war'.[422] The Boers were not lesser men than the British; they were virtually the same. This was probably the highest conceivable wartime compliment, of sorts.

What of the Boers themselves? Here, while republican war propaganda was not short on invective and abuse, there was certainly no counterpart to the Social Darwinist racial dogma which coloured many British perceptions of the enemy. The British problem did not lie in their being, in some evolutionary or scientific sense, an inferior race or nation. What it came down to was their dishonest belligerence against free republics. That showed the true colours of the empire, killing any idea of its liberal Christian decency. Others had seen it exposed before, now it was the turn of the unfortunate Boers. Therefore, for some sympathisers in the Cape middle-class intelligentsia, what the northern Boers were experiencing was that heavy hand so long familiar to the nationalist Irish, and indeed to Jamaican rebels in the 1860s.[423] This threat of an oppressive British servitude was a powerful reality among many under arms across the Orange. Imbued by the religiosity of Boer republican nationalism, for those who stuck it out the struggle became a sacred vocation to preserve a God-given free inheritance. As Dietlof van Warmelo suggested in his sober chronicle, it was their wandering lot to persevere through an affliction of quite Biblical proportions, knowing they would be delivered by grace.[424] Locusts, pestilence and famine had become the British War Office, Kitchener its pale horse of Death.

Others in the republics wondered just how aware British citizens were of the contradictions between the civilising assumptions of their empire and the incendiary inclinations of their military conquerors. Equally distressing was that the British seemed to have no qualms about enlisting blacks to spy, bear arms, provide incriminating court evidence, or in other ways keep tabs on the Boers. This was surely no way for civilised Europeans in Africa to deal with one another.

Elsewhere, officers like Ludwig Krause and Abraham Malan had an unusual military understanding of British behaviour. The war became so punitive and severe because 'the English have never been able to forgive the Boer for having been so ready . . . more ready than they were'. It was unpalatable for Britain to give the Boers 'credit for ordinary foresight and common sense . . . genuine wisdom and cunning'. What would have hurt more than anything was the way in which 'the English boasted' that they would flatten the Boers in a fortnight, only to be pulled up short by the surprise 'of the Boer ready for them'. Predictably, 'they have never been able to forgive his "insolence" for daring to be so'.

Inevitably, Boer society was now having to bear the disproportionate cost of British anger over such impudence. That aside, what still remained hard to take was the haughty imperial assumption that the Boers were too backward or ignorant to have been unable to fathom British purpose. British arrogance, reflected Krause, reminded him of how brotherly colonists must have felt in the American War of Independence. They, too, had been slandered as marauders, murderers, looters, and liars, whereas, with nauseating hypocrisy, 'the same acts committed by themselves the English characterise as "reconnoitring parties, executions, collecting cattle . . . punitive measures, etc."'. That sort of patrician sophistry suited well the 'aristocratic' British approach, which sought to 'justify the war by equally high-sounding names', while in reality it was intended mainly to cloak 'their want of humanity and the non-observance of the civilised rules of warfare'.[425]

A host of stories, rumours and legends about British vengefulness and ferocity proliferated during the conflict. Some were ephemeral, others more enduring. One myth was that the invading army intended to 'debase' the Boers by violating the racial purity of white womanhood. Early in 1900, Dutch Reformed Church clergy in the northern Cape advised male congregants to secure the safety of women, as it was rumoured that rural towns were to be garrisoned by Indian sepoys. Such soldiers, inhabitants were warned, would be coming from an Asian army which had already had a taste of assaulting European women in the 1857 Rising. Another sordid tale was that Africans with British forces would be accorded new freedoms in which war tribute or bounty would include permission to 'enslave' or 'carry into their kraals' defenceless Boer war widows.[426] This was all fairly disconcerting for the standard bearers of a protective white masculinity.

As the conquered republics refused to be pacified, so female beliefs grew that the British were either soft on racial protection or were actually encouraging Africans to rise beyond their station. Such concerns were shared by visiting pro-Boer British women activists. Hobhouse and Jane Cobden Unwin, for example, were alarmed at the exposed position of women both in camps and in female-headed rural homesteads, having to confront the growing 'impertinence' of Africans, including the threat of being manhandled. Panicky communities did not have to be susceptible to lurid stories to be apprehensive about what an advancing British army might bring. Rumours of mistreatment or of rape by 'kharkis' or 'kharkies', ran well ahead of the British push into the Orange Free State, leaving many frantic or terrified.

Invasion of civilian areas would have meant almost invariably the committing of rape by soldiers, even if, in a concealing era of shared Anglo-Boer sexual prudery, incidents of sexual violence hardly ever became explicit in records of emotional desolation. On the British side, one of Stead's pamphlets hinted fairly unambiguously at the plight of 'the outraged woman', the victim of 'horrible and shameful incidents' at the hands of soldiers 'released from all the restraints of civilisation' who had no respect for 'the wives and daughters of the enemy'.[427]

Among Boers, its meaning could be plain enough. Near the Vaal River in May 1900, a patrolling soldier observed 'a look of perpetual alarm' on face after face, and found a huddle of women on a farm 'scared stiff by our presence'. After questioning, an African scout and interpreter told him why they seemed so petrified. They had heard that after burning their homes, British soldiers were turning on women 'as they pleased', and were committing brutal acts, including cutting off fingers to steal rings. Inspired by so monstrous a reputation, some men took a vindictive delight in indulging atrocity myths, warning women of further horrors to come, like the abduction of babies or the confiscation of all food, medicine and clothing, 'to frighten them, as they seem to expect us all to be proper demons'.[428]

Equally, British invaders had no need to behave as the devil incarnate to be feared and loathed by those caught between an advancing enemy and their retreating home armies. Ruffianly conduct and spitefulness under a draconian occupation policy was enough to lose hearts and minds. At the same time, though, not all intruding troops smashed precious family heirlooms or wolfed down the holdings of farm pantries. Nor did all officers give the nod to unauthorised plundering of homesteads, as regimental punishment books reveal.[429] Nor did every roving 'farm party' relish the experience of dynamiting, nor the punitive burning of properties.

Despite intelligence assurances that the only farms targeted for 'doing' were those of men who were 'spies, or snipers or otherwise behaving dangerously', or of commandos who had 'ratted on their oaths' and returned to arms, some sappers and infantrymen still felt queasy. Evicting 'sobbing women and their children' was 'a bit sickening' and 'a loathsome task'.[430] On Majuba Day in 1901, an Oxford student in Britain's volunteer forces grimaced at being on 'the seamy side of war', leaving 'a trail of blazing ruins and a country desolate of cattle. It seems very hard, but what can be done?'[431] In that tempered view, they may not have been typical of occupying soldiers – but then neither were all British troops in South Africa wholly without humanity and conscience.

Again, even if the areas they occupied became a front line of domestic dread, by no means all Boer women were cowed or intimidated. According to one Ayrshire Yeomanry officer, scores of the 'hard' females he encountered were prone to giving 'Tommies looks which would have turned milk sour', while another soldier was scandalised by hectoring abuse. Obvious 'insults in their outlandish tongue sounded shocking . . . whatever it was, anyone could tell it was not the language of refined women'.[432] Kitchener himself had reflected on this. 'Boers,' he sighed once, 'were uncivilised Africander savages with only a thin white veneer . . . The Boer woman in the refugee camp who slaps her protruding belly at you and shouts, "When all our men are gone these little Kharkis will fight you" is a type of savage produced by generations of wild, lonely life'.[433]

These small, scattered illustrations of animosity point to the secretion of a web of female hatred of an enemy which was trampling its way into domestic spaces. At times, this was even expressed through violence. While rummaging around farms, troops were sometimes spat at, or had stones and hot water tossed at them. Edgy soldiers seem also to have been wary of any suspiciously friendly offerings of 'blarstid Dutch skoff', in case it had been poisoned or seasoned with ground glass.[434] These spiky encounters both challenged normal gender relations and reflected a restraining impotency for men. Hostile, combative Boer women continued to enjoy some protective female liberty. Their hostilities and incitement may have been intensely visceral. Yet they were not, after all, recognised combatants, and were neither pushed into swearing neutrality oaths nor forced to relinquish any personally owned rifles.

Captain Fletcher-Vane was but one of those who observed how, after the Paardeberg debacle, wilting commandos 'went home and came back fortified by the example of the heroism shown by the women'.[435] That nationalist war militancy has long been recognised by Afrikaans writers and, more recently, beyond those ranks.[436] In this highveld version of the classic 1902 A.E.W. Mason story, *The Four Feathers*, in which a woman shames a cowardly British officer into restoring his honour by rejoining his regiment in the Sudan, agitated Boer women harried their yellow or beaten men into resuming the fight.

As skirted seconds, they were a match for their own commandos, through whose frailty or irresolution the nationalist war effort was crumbling. This intransigence was impressive, certainly impressing those American, Russian, French, Dutch and Irish nationalist observers who applauded such uncompromising fighting conviction. Yet, at the same time, even though Britain's invasion columns carried war into farmhouses, the gap in enemy experience between male and female was distinct. The middle-class women of cities like Bloemfontein and Pretoria who talked of personally avenging lost husbands, or who were contemptuous of commando shirkers, would have known nothing of a petrifying cavalry charge by French's Dragoons and Lancers, nor of the despair of being confined by blockhouse lines, nor of the anguish of being cornered and massively outnumbered. This may have been a moment in which British men made war on Boer women. But, equally, it was not the war that was made on men.

What emerges from all of this is the extent to which wartime attitudes were often shaped by gender. To a similar degree, they were also not one-dimensional, in the sense that British invaders were not always faced with a brick wall. As times got ever harder, it was scarcely surprising to find the need to survive and to live and let live alongside republican earnestness, especially among those whom nationalist messages had never penetrated much. Far from quarrelling with occupying authority, more compliant camp dwellers and 'lax' poorer *by-woner* women were sometimes to be seen 'frequenting the company of soldiers' and engaging in a range of cordial transactions.[437] Nor, for the republican Boers, was this the only instance of a balancing act, or of a way of simply waiting upon events. Their welcome of the largely anti-Semitic nationalists of the Boer armies' Russian commando unit was also extended to a Russian Jewish Commandant Kaplan and to Josef Segal, scout and special agent of Christiaan de Wet.[438]

As the winning side, it was the British who could end up more charitable about their defeated enemies. However illiberal its prosecution of much of the war, the army was never without one or two thoughtful lights who did not shed all the liberal assumptions of their London drawing rooms when crossing the Orange. Typically, there were even officers who were prepared to put down occasional abuse of the white flag by commandos to their ignorance of modern war conventions. Burghers could be forgiven for being a little underhand now and then, because of a decent larger picture. As Methuen informed Milner of his relationship with the Lichtenburg commando general, Jan Celliers, 'the Boers trust me, and I trust them'. When fighting was done, 'he sends a man to show me where any wounded man may be.'[439]

For such members of Britain's officer class, country-bred Boers were honourable foes and admirably effective combatants, hardier fighters for being free of the 'degenerative' defects and 'ill-bred' weaknesses of their own city-bred recruits from overpopulated slums. Surely, they deserved an honourable peace, rather than what one soldier foresaw in December 1900 as their only choice, that of 'an Inexpiable War'. The fair solution would be 'to give terms. Allow those who wish to do so, lay down their arms, and give safe conduct for the irreconcilables to trek to Damaraland. The Germans would give them the welcome they were unable to extend to Kruger.'[440]

Others who shared this feeling added something else. This was a concern that peace with the Boers should not be one in which their naturally free and outdoor future would be mortgaged to a Johannesburg or, more coarsely, 'Jewhannesburg' or 'Jewburgher' capitalist community.[441] This mix of English gentry romanticism and anti-Semitism was embodied perfectly by General Ian Hamilton. As Kitchener's chief of staff at the war's end, he divulged his war impressions to Winston Churchill. A commander who had found indiscriminate farm burnings distasteful, Hamilton considered the Boers worthy people who deserved generous reconciliation, and merited incorporation into the empire on favourable terms at the earliest opportunity. Far more would be gained thereby for Britain's future, 'than by assimilating a million Johannesburg Jews'. By and large, British soldiers in the field tended to respect and even to admire Boers as opponents, he concluded, adding that the republics' farming yeomanry were often viewed more positively than arrogant imperial politicians like Milner. Politically, it was the high commissioner and his squalid bunch of 'Jewburg' capitalists who seemed intent on a continuing death roll and a vengeful peace. Doubtless, no commando at Elandslaagte in October 1899 would have judged Hamilton restrained in attack. But his sentiment was charitable enough.

The liberal Hamilton was not an entirely lone voice amongst the upper echelons of the officer corps. Others drawn from the Anglo-Irish and Anglo-Indian gentry were instinctively anti-urban capitalist and anti-Semitic. Like the Irish Catholic William Butler in 1899, they, too, ended up despising the 'mercenary' and 'Hebraic' character of the 'fat' Uitlanders. What such individuals found most disagreeable was the idea of fighting purely as the military tool of mammon. The conquest and annexation of the Transvaal looked to be all too much to the benefit of a manipulative plutocracy of Randlords and bought Colonial Office politicians and officials. 'If our motive for going to war with the Dutch is to secure freedom and right, this is hypocritical to a high degree.'[442] That was how a patrician General Hamilton saw it, and on that basis it made for a fairly contemptible war, in which national interest seemed to have become thoroughly corrupted by a shabby sectional interest.

Still, whimsical respect for the enemy ought also not to be overstated. For an appalled and war-weary General Henry Rawlinson, the Boers had also done their bit for the war's degeneracy by plundering the property of neutral black civilians, and in the savagery of numerous reprisals against African and Coloured inhabitants who had been colluding with the British. Neither side in South Africa had been altogether angelic.[443] In a wider picture, these more contemplative commanders were not entirely unlike their earlier nineteenth-century counterparts in the United States army. There, too, in fighting proud and determined Indian warriors on the Great Plains, educated professional soldiers came to despise the political context in which they found themselves, that of government expediency and mendacity, the extremes of settler racialism, and the greed of mining kings and cattle barons.[444] In one curious way, Britain's South African frontier had come to echo that of a North America it had long ago lost.

10

MEMORY AND COMMEMORATION

I N HUMAN COST, OR, FOR THAT MATTER, GEOGRAPHICAL SCALE, THE WAR
for South Africa may well be topped by the pre-colonial *Mfecane* wars
which raged across a swathe of the subcontinent in the late eighteenth and
early nineteenth centuries. This warfare, spreading throughout southeastern
coastal areas and deep inland, pulverised old African worlds and provided the
hammer for building new societies from the rubble. Today, the climactic *Mfecane* ('the crushing') conflict is remembered principally in rural oral tradition,
in popular mythologies about Shaka and the Zulu kingdom, and in scholarly
literature about the Southern African and African past.

Yet, there can be little question that it is the 1899–1902 war which still counts
heavily in national memory, however partial its original place in historical consciousness. It is easy to see why it has counted, and with good reason. South
Africa's 'Great War' has left many of the more enduring residues of early twentieth-century colonial warfare, and not only among Boers and Britons. America's
1904 St Louis World's Fair featured an *Anglo-Boer War Historical Libretto*, in
which visiting veterans re-enacted the battles of Colenso and Paardeberg. A more
conventional war legacy lies in the hundreds of books it has generated, from
early Anglo-Boer spy thrillers like the 1907 The *Secret* of *the Scarlet Letter*, to
more recent war adventures such as Sidney Allinson's 2001 *Kruger's Gold*, to
many major works of older and more recent Afrikaans fiction, including Gustav
Preller's *Oorlogsmag en ander Sketse en Verhale* (1923) and Christoffel Coetzee's
Op soek na Generaal Mannetjies Mentz (1998). With a further store of other
artistic works, not least plays such as J.F.W Grosskopf, *Oorlog is Oorlog* (1927)
and N.P. van Wyk Louw, *Die Pluimsaad Waai Ver* (1966), the war's varied literary

epitaph remains unrivalled locally. If anything, this cultural deposit may make it the South African equivalent of an American Civil War, a British First World War, an Irish Easter Rising, or even a Spanish Civil War.

To some degree, that reflects the extent to which interpreters were drawn to the obvious contrast between the quick war that was imagined, and the more lengthy and costly contest which was actually fought. In part, too, the war's long shadow illustrates the extent to which even – or especially – after 1902, its meaning continued to be fought over between camps of South African empire loyalists and defeated but unreconciled Afrikaner republicans. As in post-Civil War Spain after 1939, a war of arms was to continue as a war of words for those for whom the Anglo-Boer War became a crucial building-block of a nationalist Afrikaner history, 'a myth of national origin'.[445]

For many years, that war of words was of relevance to the balance of white political forces, even into the early post-Second World War era, when the survival of cultivated memories of British imperial conquest and concentration-camp cruelties remained closely connected to the rise and eventual ascendancy of a nationalist Afrikanerdom. As the expression of a subordinate yet combative republican-minded nationality, tilting at the political and economic citadels of a smug English establishment, war commemoration provided a moral legacy of heroic manly struggle and female fortitude and sacrifice. That mobilisation of the mind began in the 1900s. It was then kept on its toes through pilgrimages to grave sites and cemeteries, in the ritual disinterring and reburial of the remains of fallen combatants, and in the creation of war memorials, most imposingly, the 1913 *Vrouemonument* or Women's Monument in Bloemfontein.

As a male-inspired shrine to female sacrifice and martyrdom, it reflected a simple commemorative truth, that 'so powerful and pervasive was the impact of the concentration camp experience that ultimately the dominant Boer symbolic representation of the South African War assumed the form of a women's, and not a men's, memorial'.[446] The erection of the monument was followed in the 1920s by the issuing of commemorative medals to *oudstryders* or war veterans and other modes of remembrance which affirmed ethnic attachment to a war-scarred nation. These and later acts of commemoration came to adorn a larger political and cultural tableau of nationalist aspiration, including the doomed 1914–15 Afrikaner Rebellion, the founding in 1930 of the Bloemfontein *Oorlogs-museum van die Boererepublieke* (War Museum of the Boer Republics) and the

1938 Great Trek Centenary and subsequent dedication in Pretoria of the Voortrekker Monument.

In this litany, the 1899–1902 conflict was not to be simply about the miseries of defeat. As nationalistic war poets like Jan Celliers, Eugene Marais and Totius asserted after 1902, cathartic memories of blood sacrifice could fertilise consciousness of national identity and help to renew dignity and purpose.[447] In that view, it would perhaps not be stretching things too much to see the war enshrined as a defining French Verdun of Afrikaner society, or even as its equivalent of a Tsarist 1905, a perilous moment of near-complete national disaster. Taking that moment, Afrikaner nationalist entrepreneurs worked hard to keep the war a glowing issue within social networks of religion, politics, family and friendship. At its most basic, it was obviously necessary to portray the republican struggle in ways which countered the often offensive caricatures of Boer society peddled in wartime by hostile British writers. In the crudest of these, the Boer combatant was a mean rural simpleton, adopting sly and shifty habits to fight a criminal war against progress.[448] So, these stereotypes became refashioned. The cartoon bearded toad on Lord Roberts' mess table would turn out to be the handsome and dashing Albert Viljoen, a commando cheetah able easily to outwit plodding British Tommies.

At the same time, there was always more to this than mere corrective history. For popular historians like Preller, a former republican war correspondent, accounts of war experience all came to serve one overriding purpose – to awaken the Afrikaner to the truth about their War of Freedom and their National Mission. The inheritance of war would be the core of an immanent Afrikaner 'nationalist spirit', with popular histories reminding readers of the Christian Boer crusade 'against the mighty British Empire, and the suffering of women and children'. The war 'had to serve as a constant reminder of the Afrikaners' bitter fight for freedom. Although they had lost . . . they were exhorted not to sacrifice a common identity as Afrikaners. . . History had to be used in such a way that it enhanced patriotism and national consciousness. . . Contemporary Afrikaners had to complete the historic mission of the Boer diehards – they had to continue the fight for Afrikaner independence in the present.'[449]

The rupturing impact of the conflict did not make it easy going for a bookish, middle-class, nationalist intelligentsia to weave together a sense of the war as simultaneously harrowing *and* positively awakening. The ideological industry of ethnic nationhood was also further hampered by the fragility of an Afrikaans literary culture. But, once the assertion of a standard Afrikaans language became buttressed by official recognition from the 1920s, magic could be worked with war writings. Much of this alchemy was pursued in popular magazines like *Die Brandwag* (The Sentinel) and *Die Huisgenoot* (The Home Companion). By running personal war testimony, they plumbed a rich seam of earthy folk memory of hardship and suffering which appealed widely to republican patriots, particularly rural women, as well as to veterans and their families. In this genre, the war largely ceased to be a disputed and internally divided struggle against imperial domination. Instead, it became resurrected in print as the unity of the Boer nation at war, a tribal defence of hearth and home by a small and virtuous Christian people.

While few Afrikaans books on the war appeared between the 1900s and the end of the 1920s, the ensuing two decades witnessed a surge of popular works, ranging from personal chronicles such as Sara Raal's *Met die Boere in die Veld* (With the Boers in the Field) to spirited historical fiction, like Mikro, *Die Ruiter in die Nag* (The Rider in the Night). Popular writings of this kind helped to consolidate a collective mentality and memory, by creating an exalted sense of national character as wiry, valiant, and persevering. While harping on war memories of bitterness, anguish, and redemptive Christian fortitude, it was equally vital to commemorate superhuman bravado, exemplified by the gritty epic of *bittereinder* resistance and the seemingly clairvoyant genius of the younger Boer generalship. In this mostly masculine legacy, 'the courage and determination of the diehard Boer fighters revealed those character traits supposedly typical of the Afrikaner and deemed worthy to emulate'.[450]

As in the Francoist historiography of post-1936–39 Spain, the overlap between popular and scholarly representations of the war which turned history into a nationalist narrative was marked. Through the 1940s and, for a time, even beyond, much academic writing presented the war above all as a militant and emotive moral covenant of Afrikaner nationalist mobilisation. Such classic studies of the later 1940s as J.H. Breytenbach, *Die Betekenis van die Tweede Vryheidsoorlog* (The Meaning of the Second War of Freedom), depicted a war comprised of godless, underhand British and an upright freeborn Boer people, men of the elect who listened to the Prophets and whose women carried the seed of a republican freedom whose time would come. Integral to the promotion of an Afrikaner *volksgeskiedenis* or people's history, this nationalist gloss on the war became its 'objective-scientific' truthfulness about the past.[451]

Central to that truthfulness was the pervading resonance of a *Vryheidsoorlog* or War of Freedom, first coined in the 1880s, after Majuba. Retrospectively, the 1880–81 conflict became the *Eerste Vryheidsoorlog,* or First War of Freedom, the epic struggle of a tribe of Israel for justice and independence in the promised land. As a parable, this imagery went on to season the second conflict. The confection of a *Tweede Vryheidsoorlog,* or Second War of Freedom, served to affirm the spiritual plateau it occupied in the long upward trek of a republicanist Afrikanerdom.

Not all war messages remained fixed in that traditional mould. Between roughly the end of the 1960s and the later 1980s, they grew less crusading in purpose, reflected not least in the use of more prosaic titles such *as Boereoorlog* (Boer War) and *Anglo-Boereoorlog* (Anglo-Boer War), and in an accompanying less partisan historical approach. In this, the significance of victory or defeat tended generally to matter less than the expression of a wider 'meaning' in the war, as a stricken moment for one white community. Standing less as 'a historical marker in Afrikaner nationalist consciousness'[452], it was becoming comprehensible as national tragedy, a fateful fissure between English and Afrikaner South Africans who shared a common European kinship.

There were good reasons for more strident nationalist reminders of the moral lessons and animosities of the war to weaken appreciably through the post-1945 era. To some extent this was because increasing numbers of Afrikaners found themselves enjoying unprecedented prosperity under National Party rule in the post-1948 decades. 'Once Afrikaner political aspirations had been satisfied' the buoyancy of 'the prosperous economic conditions of the 1960s'[453] helped to ensure that brooding over the old privations of the English War became a more minor strand of nationalist *volk* identity. Whatever the accursed English had done in the past could now be undone through the rising soufflé of a mature Afrikanerdom. And there was a lot of such rising still to be done.

For the nationalist government, there were also other warming factors in white identity politics. One was satisfaction at the eventual achievement of a national South African Republic and its withdrawal from the Commonwealth. At the beginning of the 1960s, in spirit at least, the old Boer Republics could start to waltz again. Another, having weathered the 1960 Sharpeville crisis, was the desirability of bringing English South Africans into a more companionable and inclusive white nationalism. Sure enough, in the 1966 general election, the National Party swallowed a thick slice of the English vote. All of this was accompanied by a judicious thaw in war sentiment, as staunch Afrikaners associated English speakers less and less with the sins of old imperial conquest.

By the early 1970s, memory of the war as some ideological totem had largely migrated to the khaki-shirt, nationalist ultra-right. With its gaze fixed firmly on the past, this mostly lower-middle class and working-class strata kept searing war memories alive on the margins, with festering bitterness about the past fate of Afrikaners informing a broadly anti-liberal English agenda. Here, the currency of remembrance was again one of frontal war solidarities. It meant submerging and forgetting those who had had enough of male sacrifice in war: men who had hidden, surrendered, or became turncoats. In this portrayal, memory of the war's trauma remained inextricable from the demonising of an old imperial enemy.

Britain's concentration camps continued to symbolise wartime atrocity, with the Boer women and children of August 1901 becoming the equivalent of the Belgians of August 1914. As the simplest injunction of war memory, what most to 'remember' or 'te onthou', was that historical experience, something that could knit together a focused will to remember. The camps had also long been a fertile site of historical mythology, as in the early implementation of apartheid when nationalists made it clear that Britain ought not even to 'dare to criticise "race" policies in South Africa when it had earlier attempted genocide against the Afrikaners'.[454]

Aside from past nationalist writers, it is probably fair to assume that in South Africa many people – possibly, most – continue to view the war's concentration camps as a singularly British invention. Its devilish 'methods of barbarism' also lit the path to Germany's concentration camps a few decades later. Under Josef Goebbels, Nazi information credited – or discredited – the British as pioneers of incarceration, so depicted in Germany's 1941 Ministry of Public Enlightenment and Propaganda pro-Boer film, *Ohm Krüger* (Uncle Kruger). Britain, however, had had no inventive monopoly on forced resettlement in war. As a tactic to stop rural guerrilla war becoming indefinite war, such policies had been put into service by Spain in the earlier 1890s Cuban War and before that by the republican Mexican army in the 1870s and by the French general, Thomas-Robert

Bugeaud, in the conquest of Algeria in the 1840s, when women and children were carried off and dumped. Memory of Britain's South African camps has also long been marked by singularity or the assumption of a special path of Afrikaner war ordeal. Only in more recent years has there emerged a wider recognition that the experiences of living and dying as inmates was something shared by segregated African refugees, too, while the fate of 'black people in the "white camps"' continues to be almost 'never thought about'.[455]

Ultimately, what has shaped and defined war memories within Afrikaner political culture is invariably an England of the past. Thus, the creation of unified English-Afrikaner Union Defence Forces in 1912 saw Boer veterans fuming over an anglicisation of military methods, the imposition of khaki, a particularly odious colour given their recent history, and the adoption of the British army's clean-shaven look, forcing men to shed that treasured show of masculine identity, their beards.[456] Another very obvious dimension has been the local position and claims of the British monarchy. Take the 1920s tour of the Prince of Wales when, among some Afrikaner representatives, reconciliatory welcome and lingering war resentment rubbed along rather uneasily. Or, take the 1947 royal visit to South Africa which had, as its Churchillian sub-text, Britain's desire to acknowledge Prime Minister Jan Smuts for having been the War Office's finest Boer general of 1940. Appropriately enough, on a Transvaal leg of their tour, the royal family was escorted to a garden party by a folksy commando, complete with serge suits, slouch hats, republican medals and vintage Mausers, where they met a scraping band of 1899–1902 *oudstryders* or veterans. Parliamentary nationalists, now only within a year of electoral office, were unimpressed by what they considered to be so ignominious a ceremonial.[457]

Just as noteworthy were the pricks felt during the first visit of the Windsors since the 1940s, the 1995 tour of Elizabeth II in the wake of South Africa's recent Commonwealth re-entry after its transition to majority rule. In some sulky quarters, old war words and images were rapidly revived. An incensed Afrikaner *Boerestaat* (Boer State) Party declared the Queen unwelcome in the 'Boerestaat of Transvaal and the Free State'. From 'a dynasty of conquerors', she was 'the great grand-daughter of a cruel queen', whose invading armies had not only 'destroyed our Boers' freedom', but had also committed 'the infamous holocaust in which a sixth of our people were murdered in concentration camps'.[458]

Other Afrikaner responses were less apoplectic, if still chastening. The rambling former ANC parliamentarian, diplomat, ex-party official and fantasist, Carl Niehaus, called upon the Queen to observe a more inclusive act of South African war remembrance by commemorating the Boer dead. 'If she is going to lay wreaths at World War II and World War I graves here,' he declared, 'she ought also to lay wreaths on the graves of the tens of thousands of women and children who died in the camps.'[459] Deep in the grain of that particular attitude lay the country's post-1994 political settlement and the project of national integration for a new post-apartheid ruling political élite. South Africa's experience in two world wars, in its modern colonial war, and in its recent anti-apartheid guerrilla insurgency, were to be pulled closer together through common commemorative rites, with Afrikaner Anglo-Boer War losses becoming acknowledged as the *nation's* war dead.

It was in that sense that Elizabeth II was urged by observers like Niehaus to make a redemptive Boer War gesture in the image of a new South African nation, or in the 'imagined community' of that nation. Far from continuing as a divisive historical legacy, the legacy of the war could become part of the fabric of a fully reconciled and healed new country, affirming shared understanding both between Afrikaner and English and between black and white. Indeed, for some more wide-eyed watchers of the royal visit, the presence of the Queen signified both a final transcendence from Anglo-Boer War bitterness and the ratifying of the 'equal footing' of the three symbolic strands of South African society, 'Bantu, Boer and Briton'.[460]

In this new commemorative reworking of the conflict, its most reverential and enduring symbols, the camp and the commando, now came to be detached from nationalist Afrikaner history, and to be given the fresh language of struggle through which to express a unified national war imagination. In 1996, on the fortieth anniversary of the famous African women's march against apartheid pass laws, the ANC Women's League urged the wives of prominent Afrikaner politicians to stretch 'across the divides', and to join in a commemorative walk to 'cement the unity of South African women'. According to the League's president, what made such female solidarity natural was a shared history of colonial brutality. Just as African women had been victims of merciless racist decrees, so 'we recognise that Afrikaner women suffered and died under the British'.[461]

In an even more striking gesture, an ANC-aligned judge of the Constitutional Court reclaimed idealism and the universal story of freedom as the abiding lesson of the war. Merging the language of the present with that of the past, he asserted his personal 'pride in the heroic struggle of the Boer fighters in the history of the world and in our history'. Any history of a liberal human rights culture in South Africa would have to 'take into account the fate of the women and children in the concentration camps'. Downtrodden Afrikaners had defied the British as 'so much of Afrikaans history is part of the struggle for freedom. That *vryheid* (Freedom), said Judge Albie Sachs, 'has real resonance and meaning'.[462]

On those terms, solemn assimilation of the war to a new South Africanism meant that it be identified and understood emphatically as South African. Therefore, according to one government provincial cultural department in 1996, the purpose of any coming centenary anniversary would be to commemorate not an Anglo-Boer War, but a South African War or, rather, a series of South African wars in 1899-1902 in which 'virtually all ethnic groups' participated, so forging 'the common historic destiny of all South Africans'.[463] In the service of national reconciliation, the war was turning into a version of everyone's war or a people's war, ringed around some military maypole. War experience became constructed as a levelling time for Afrikaners and black people, with suffering and despair shared across the colour divide. At the same time, though, such an approach was bound to entail some difficulty or ambiguity. For, apart from anything else, responsibility for the war, for the running of its operations, and for its objectives, did not rest exactly with the mass of South Africa's people.

In the war's centenary decade, it was awareness of that kind that still made it tricky to achieve a smooth commemorative consensus, even within the ruling party itself. In 1996, for instance, Cape Town ANC councillors denounced any 'celebration of a colonial war which produced a new period of oppression and exploitation of our people'. Having 'just got back our dignity', there was no appetite for remembering 'an insular war which has nothing that unites our people'.[464] Scornful critics, including state officials, increased in number as the centenary year approached. For one government official in 1997, the misery endured by black people for most of the twentieth century had been a direct outcome of the war; for him, there could be no question of official commemoration. For another, as the war represented nothing more than a British-Boer squabble over African land, it was inappropriate for a democratic government to honour the centenary of a squalid episode of colonial expropriation.[465]

Why, in the acerbic view of a leading black journalist, mark a grubby colonial squabble between white men? Writing in *The Weekly Mail and Guardian*, John Matshikiza dismissed calls for the wartime role of blacks to be recognised publicly and for black experience to be absorbed into remembrance rituals. The majority had neither started nor run the war, and nor had the Anglo-Boer conflict been for their interests. Black people were, therefore, not authentic historical participants. 'Any attempt to turn the *Amabhunwnu* or Boer War into our collective history is like calling a spade a sunflower,' he declared, for 'it was a white man's war. . .since neither side asked them to join the fight as equals, there is nothing in this centenary for their descendants to celebrate. . .It's like calling on the Native Americans to celebrate the landing of the *Mayflower*, or to join the re-enactment of the Boston Tea Party'.[466]

In another Africanist version of such sentiment in the centenary month of the outbreak of war, Motsoko Pheko of the Pan-Africanist Congress denounced national commemoration of 'a war between two colonial thieves, fighting over the diamonds, gold and land of the African people,' and called for a focus on commemorating Africans' 'own heroic wars to defend their country against colonial aggression'.[467] Meanwhile, not to be outdone by politicians, a couple of months earlier a squad of scholars had called for an international boycott of centenary war conferences and other acts of remembrance. As public history, the hostilities were continuing to be conveyed in an historically indigestible way, as that of 'a war having been fought between white males on the battlefields'.[468] It was a vintage piece of post-apartheid political correctness, although seemingly little heeded by anyone inclined to be corrected or shamed.

Elsewhere, ground so well-watered by Afrikaner nationalism in earlier decades had also begun to bear a little crop again. Although long past its zenith as a mobilising cult of war remembrance by the 1980s, the embers of 1902 were stoked by the terminal crisis of apartheid, with Afrikaners back on the defensive. In a striking 1993 observation, the quixotic Afrikaner historian, Floors van Jaarsveld, concluded that 'Afrikanerdom has suffered two great defeats in its history'. The first had been a military defeat in the republican war with Britain, and the second, a recent 'political defeat at the hands of Africa.'[469]

Stirred, elements of a *bittereinder* resistance aesthetic took imaginative shape around this long view. British domination became African domination, with ANC president Nelson Mandela its version of an odious high commissioner. For its far right, Afrikanerdom seemed to be facing the prospect of complete deracination in a unitary mongrel state. 'Again,' intoned Ferdi Hartzenberg of the Conservative Party, 'dark days have come to our people'.[470] In turn, further to his right there was a rekindled yearning for a Transvaal and Orange Free State *Boerestaat* or *Volkstaat* (People's State) to secure the blood of ethnic self-determination. In one burst of unvarnished Anglophobia, Robert van Tonder of the Boerestaat Party called for 'Boers' to consecrate a pure 'Boerestaat' as a posthumous revenge upon Queen Victoria, who had seen to it that 'our Boer republics were crushed in 1902 and 14 other "peoples" were forced to live with us in one state'. Inevitably, breaking peace would foment an eventual civil war. But then, as now, civil war could not defeat Afrikaners as, 'after all, it was the Afrikaners who invented it'.[471] The lesson to be drawn from that history remained obvious. The desolate traces of camp sites like Winburg and Brandfort amounted to South Africa's Auschwitz or Dachau, 'a war crime to be neither forgotten nor forgiven'.[472]

In the 1990s, this antique Boer War flank engaged not just against the traditional enemy of Englishness, but against a dawning age of racial equality and majority rule, and against a now despised National Party leadership for capitulating to racial and cultural cosmopolitanism. At one tragicomic pole there was the seizure of Pretoria's Schanskop fort and military museum, a place in thrall to a commando heritage. Under the billowing *Vierkleur* flag of the nineteenth-century Transvaal, a knot of armed vigilantes protested against multi-racial political negotiations, seeing their sole purpose as the selling off of the assets of Afrikaner sovereignty. After their arrest and conviction for illegal armed occupation, their leader, Willem Ratte, wrote from gaol to contest his newspaper depiction as right-wing. Taking the 1880s Transvaal war as his inspiration, Ratte declared in a torrential yet powerful manifesto:

Were the Boers of 1880 called right-wingers, for resisting the imperialist British occupation? Then, as now, you had an alien regime lording it in Pretoria over our people, whose gutless president had betrayed and handed over his sovereign state. Then, as now, the new (neo)colonialist administration pretended to be God's gift to the supposedly 'dirty and dumb Dutchmen' and tried its best to smear the pro-independence party as only a few backward 'Don Quixotes tilting at windmills'. Our struggle has nothing to do with right or left . . . this being incidental, like religion in the Irish-British conflict, but everything to do with a nation having an inherent right to be free, to be able to choose its own representatives and leaders democratically.[473]

At another pole, dismal yet also poignant, an October 1992 Kruger Day commemoration saw a sliver of rough-hewn Englishness regain its lustre in right-wing nationalist Afrikaner life. In a cameo of bonding with the English ultra-right, indefatigable ex-Rhodesians and English-speaking adherents of the Conservative Party splashed into the Vaal to retrieve rocks from a camp memorial reputedly torn down by departing British soldiers in 1903. Under the sombre gaze of a crowd of several thousand, the rock was piled up close to the official Paardekraal camp monument, thus atoning symbolically for past desecration. As 'the greatest conciliatory gesture by English-speaking countrymen since before the Boer Wars' the Conservative Party leader, Andries Treurnicht, announced that 'the time has certainly come for all English-speaking patriots to let bygones be bygones, and to join hands with the Boer to resist the common enemy of black domination'.[474] This, as it happens, was a rather droll gesture from a man who had spent a good portion of his political career railing against English influence in South African life.

Meanwhile, shades of the South African conflict had also remained in nationalist Irish memory. In April 1998, there was Afrikaner appreciation of news of stiff opposition in Listowel, County Kerry, to the raising of a plaque to commemorate Kitchener's birthplace because of his inhumane prosecution of the Anglo-Boer War. One correspondent noted that it would be received 'with great satisfaction by Afrikaners in general, but particularly by descendants of the Boers who fought against Kitchener's barbarism'. Others invoked obvious analogies, condemning the camps as the genocidal work of a 'Hitler', and scorched earth as defoliation, unmistakeably Victorian Britain's own Vietnam War in South Africa.

J.A. Marais, 'son of a Boer father' exiled and imprisoned on St Helena, and 'a mother who was interned in the Klerksdorp concentration camp', urged on the idea of an Irish-Afrikaner 'war crimes tribunal for Kitchener' in 1999, to mark 'commemoration of the centenary of the outbreak of the Boer War'.[475] A symbolic 'war crimes tribunal' was supported by other Afrikaans newspaper correspondents as something sure to produce 'great satisfaction. . . most particularly by the Boers who fought against Kitchener's barbarism'.[476] Something of this mood was caught perfectly when liberal English-language papers joined the

Afrikaans press in calling for Prime Minister Tony Blair to apologise for his country's shameful war record. If Britain could be contrite before the Irish for the nineteenth-century potato famine, and before Indians for the 1919 Amritsar massacre, why should it not be penitent towards injured Afrikaners, asked writers in *Beeld* and in the *Sunday Times*. The reason, snorted one astute Afrikaans journalist in *Rapport*, was plain. 'While there were many Irish and Indian voters in the United Kingdom', there was 'not a single Afrikaner voter'.[477]

This flickering, backward gaze upon the war and its aftermath must surely be seen to be among the last touchy episodes of an old Boer past, dredging up for a self-conscious and ailing minority the nostalgias and resentments of a world with declining points of certainty. For those still attached to an actively *volk* war memory, it might not be too much to say that by the 1990s they were being undone by history. Certainly, in one quarter there was quite a knowing sense of this. Likening African political claims to those of the Uitlanders who had been so unwelcome a blot upon Kruger's republic, in 1995 the Afrikaner-weerstandsbeweging (Afrikaner Resistance Movement) leader, Eugène Terre'Blanche, growled that not to recognise Afrikaner 'freedom' and to grant it a free people's state would be to 'play with fire', as British statesmen had discovered in the late 1890s. Sceptics were referred to Thomas Pakenham's *The Boer War,* a work which, in Terreblanche's view, gave the Boers their due and more. It was as admirable as Shakespeare, and therefore 'not part of any English conspiracy'.[478]

Within the AWB, the coming of black majority rule represented 'a second invasion', needing a national Boer state defence, and increasing inclinations to bob about on horseback in pugnacious displays of commando tradition. Because of the danger to Afrikaners from untrustworthy news editors, slippery politicians and meddling imperialists (now more American than British), the call was for a 'return' of 'the generals'. Historically, nationalist Afrikaners had looked for salvation to their tough military men and gruff irreconcilables, the Koos de la Reys and Christiaan de Wets.

Just how much things turned on warming their ashes could be glimpsed in loose – and impotent – fighting talk. The Conservative Party raised the spectre of an imminent *Derde Vryheidsoorlog* (Third War of Freedom), the AWB and Boerestaat Party used the old Transvaal flag and its anthem, *Ken u die Volk* (Do you know the People), there were glancing gunshots at the British Embassy in Pretoria in 1990, and there was a bomb attack on Melrose House, where Boer leaders had signed their surrender in May 1902. Back where it all started, faded ideologues of national purity demanded the reclamation and renewal of the old Boer Republics. Interestingly, this was not something that had to be created, merely reinstated. For, historically, they had already been fully in legitimate existence, based on a Boer occupation which had 'enjoyed internationally recognised independence until 1902'.[479]

In a further pained war parallel, there was condemnation of reformist National Party leadership as *verraaiers* or traitors for having submitted to parleying with the ANC. Politicians to its right went for the government as 'a lot of traitors', guilty of 'treachery' and 'acts of treason against its own people'.[480] The cry of treachery was atavistic, a replay of the war's closing stages and its fullblown 'handsupper' and bittereinder split between falling over to make peace and holding out under arms. There was no argument over which of those was the present death-wish, and who was being overcome. Here, again, were the more flabby of Boer generals, turning traitor through spineless surrender. The main modern embodiment of this behaviour was, of course, President F.W. de Klerk who, in 1997, let slip tellingly in London that he had bowed to the inevitable need to 'surrender the right to national sovereignty'.[481] By then, in the emotional grammar of nationalist Afrikaner history, 'surrender' had had a long post-war run. Very soon after the end of apartheid, it may have reached its last partisan historical moment.

Memory of the 1899–1902 war experienced another kind of historical moment with the 1999 centenary commemoration. English press calls for its ceremonies and rituals to be used as an opportunity for a 're-examination of South Africa's past by the light of its recently-acquired freedoms', received a public answer of one sort from an Abrie Oosthuizen, descendant of a Boer commando. Bemoaning the apartheid version of war history that had been drummed into his generation of Afrikaners, Oosthuizen reflected that African losses had been ignored, 'so that we did not use the common ground we had with the blacks of this country . . . the common suffering, which is the most important unifying factor between us and the blacks'.[482] Other Afrikaans-speaking commentators joined in, noting the absence of an official memorial to African sacrifice.

A century on, the 1899–1902 war was at last transcending its old laager and becoming 'part of a wider South African heritage'.[483] Lining up again with Afrikaans papers, the English press advised Britain that 'a full apology would do much towards closing this chapter in our history'.[484] The Crown came close to obliging. Prim expressions of sorrow and regret for the loss of life, white and black, came from Queen Elizabeth and the Duke of Kent during their South African visit for the centenary opening. While pointing out that 'sorrow' fell short of an admission of war guilt, the Afrikaans *Beeld* nonetheless welcomed royal 'reconciliation'.[485]

Alongside such gestures, there was centenary interest in healing of another sort. Several rural African communities which had collaborated with British forces appealed to Downing Street or Buckingham Palace to honour post-1902 rewards or bounty that had gone unpaid, or to make good losses. Thus, the Tshidi-Barolong of Mafikeng sought to re-activate an ancient 1903 reparations claim for commandeered livestock, requisitioned goods, and wages unpaid by Baden-Powell. Tribal elders estimated the 1899-1900 losses at the current equivalent of £3.8m. Most war reparations demands emanated from ultra-conservative Afrikaner political bodies and cultural associations. These not only revived a portrayal of the war as a massacre, but gave it a more modern political understanding, as an early descent into 'ethnic cleansing', making South Africa some Bosnian or Rwandan conflagration of the early twentieth-century. British 'war guilt' funds would help to make amends for past destruction of fertile agricultural lands, and for the concentration camp 'holocaust'.[486]

Making good for the wrongs of the war then also took an imaginatively fanciful direction. Several of the country's most virtuous literary figures, including the acclaimed Afrikaans writer, Antjie Krog, latched onto the war as a hinge of national reconciliation, as its historical resonances could inform contemporary understandings of how South Africa had become what it is. For Krog, that involved imagining an alternative white South African history between 1902 and 1910 as a post-Boer War moral parable, in which peace became a lost opportunity with disastrous consequences for the rest of twentieth-century South African life.

What was this great, wasted, alternative version ? It was judicially simple. Had Roberts and Kitchener been obliged to appear before a 'war crimes' ethical tribunal, some 1902–1903 confessional version of South Africa's post-1994 Truth and Reconciliation Commission, subsequent South African history would have been easier and healthier. Why? Because Britain would then have faced up to 'Truth and Justice', acknowledged its shameful conduct, and would have done more to ease the pain of defeated Boers. Last-ditch nationalist fighters might then not have borne home with them as veterans the trauma of near-extinction that would course through their lives and harden their politics of survival through racial domination. Had the British lowered their knees after victory in consolation, and faced a future of forgiveness and healing, radical bittereinders might have been left both less bitter and less extreme. As a consequence, the nature of apartheid could have been less harsh.

We can, of course, never know a history that did not happen, other than to ponder a recent teasing thought on counter-factual history, that 'the most likely alternative outcome is much the same as the one that actually took place'.[487] Given his South African convictions, it is hard to conceive of Lord Salisbury owning up to some small voice of conscience and confessing the error of having left it up to Roberts and Kitchener in front of some Edwardian tribunal on national salvation. Much the same could be said of inquiry into war motives and war conduct today, with Britain's unrepentant ex-Labour prime minister informing his country's Chilcot inquiry into the Iraq war that he would, 'frankly, do it all again'.[488]

But, politically, it is not hard to see why that kind of historical retrospection was attractive to some Afrikaner centenary commentators. The creation and enforcement of apartheid was the defensive action of those who had been the sufferers of total war. Therefore, in some underlying way, ultimately, it was Britain that was culpable.

Its hounding of the Boers had produced Afrikaner nationalism and, in turn, the excesses of apartheid. 'The war was used in the 1930s to awaken Afrikaner nationalism, because of the impoverishment of Afrikaners,' observed 'Dawie', the *Die Burger* columnist. From that fevered climate emerged 'an aggressive and intolerant nationalism that flirted with national socialism and then tried to guarantee its own existence through a massive social engineering program'. A 'chain reaction', it 'had been set in motion by British imperialism'. Now, though, the time had come to let bygones be bygones, 'so that all could live peaceably and easily together in the new South Africa'.[489]

The most assiduous commemorative reworking of all was that undertaken officially by the country's first post-apartheid government. For many decades, the ANC and other black resistance movements had resisted any organisational remembrance of an Anglo-Boer struggle. After all, British imperialism's promise of a better deal for the African majority had been hollow. Afrikaners, true enough, had sacrificed much in a great anti-colonial struggle, but had then gone on to oppress others until the ending of apartheid. The centenary, however, ended ANC indifference. The war was now to become commemorated patriotically as a crucial episode in South Africa's bruising experience of European imperialism. 'For a representative understanding of history,' intoned Deputy President Jacob Zuma on September Heritage Day in 1999, South Africans should reclaim 'their common history' by acknowledging 'the role of black citizens in events like the Anglo-Boer War'.[490]

President Thabo Mbeki launched the commemoration cycle in the small and obscure Free State town of Brandfort, a spot to which, in earlier years, the apartheid authorities had banished Winnie Mandela as an internal political exile. The symbolism may or may not have been incidental to the choice of location. Mbeki laid wreaths on the graves of Boer and British war dead, and at the site of some anonymous African dead chosen by the Ministry of Arts and Culture as Brandfort's black concentration camp victims, even though that historical authenticity was not absolutely certain. Although conservative Afrikaner bodies were aggrieved by the 'unfeeling' omission of even a single 'Afrikaner representative' from the Brandfort invitation list, the president played fair. While calling for the recovery of the 'lost' story of black war involvement, he also paid homage to 'the brave Boers and Boer women' who had 'challenged the British Empire a hundred years ago'. They 'had taken on a Goliath in defence of their freedom,' and 'in struggle, they asserted the right of all colonised people to independence'. That inheritance was 'the common history of all South Africans, whatever their race or colour'.[491]

With the war placed in the longer-term perspective of modern South African history in general, and of its fighting spirit in particular, the way was open for a new nationalism to break bread with an older nationalism based on Afrikaner survival. The Anglo-Boer War was one great part of the epic South African struggle for freedom, just as the anti-apartheid armed struggle was another herculean contribution. And, as envisioned by Judge Sachs, the fallen commando bittereinders of 1902 would find a sacred patriotic place alongside the fallen anti-apartheid comrades of the liberation struggles of recent decades. A new post-colonial kind of historical memory for South African citizens would be fertilised by their common heroism under arms in waging just wars.

Against this background, it was probably predictable that the government would authorise or license a new sanitised name for the war. It had, after all, 'involved more than white-on-white violence,' the deliciously pedantic deputy minister of Arts and Culture, Brigitte Mabandla, informed the nation. To reflect involvement by both white and black, to present 'a balanced picture', and to promote 'nation-building through inclusivity', henceforth it would be The Anglo-Boer South African War. As public history, it would be invested with a war understanding more appropriate to a post-apartheid society. To this end, the government established an official panel of black and white scholars to craft an approved new version of the conflict, and announced the convening of a state-sponsored national conference in August 2000 that would focus on 'the role and suffering of blacks in the War'.[492]

When the first South African nation after 1910 parcelled out the deeper memories of its war, Afrikaners, understandably, got the lion's share. That share became the nationalist message of a war of victimhood, of being turned into a skeletal society by British imperial inhumanity. Alongside, white English-speakers remained subdued, tainted by a suspect Anglo-imperial connection. On the eve of the twenty-first century, the second and inclusive South African nation had found the missing share of its war heritage. In a curious way, its grieving message was almost identical to that conveyed by the mourning associated with concentration camp gardens of remembrance. For Minister Mabandla, like the stricken Boers, Africans were 'victims', misused or cheated by British 'subterfuge', their wartime lot being one of the endurance of suffering or of dying. Yet, as with the range and ambiguities of Boer war experience, that verdict on the story is too partial to be a credible epitaph. True, many Africans were the victims of Britain's scorched-earth tactics, and many died in its camps. But many more black people were not simply pawns of a 'white man's war'. They were also its agents, collaborating with the British, serving the Boers, or intervening independently. Commemoration as a belated bearing of witness to suffering and sacrifice was hiding that from full recognition.

Also being hidden were the historical ironies which always loom so large in wars. In reality, as one scholar has suggested, after 1902 most relieved English-speaking white inhabitants and pacified Afrikaners were willing to let bygones be bygones, provided that they could share the warm bread of Union in 1910, and leave the unfranchised majority a thin crust. Yet, for politicians at its centenary, war memory had come to resemble 'a rather tawdry spectacle of the Olympics of suffering . . . trying to prove who suffered most'.[493] Indeed, for that matter, the early precedessors of those politicians had come down firmly on the side of empire. As Union approached, elite members of South Africa's Native Congresses, from which the African National Congress would later spring, thanked Britain's 'able administrators' for their 'great work' in having 'controlled Native refugees', and 'for all that has been done in protecting, housing and feeding them in the camps'.[494] Leaving aside the war's more awkward shadows, after 1999 government interest in a fresh public history of 1899–1902 largely waned. Three years later, invitations to an official June 2002 commemoration to mark the end of the war did, however, give it a fresh date, 1899–1901.[495] That would surely have been a relief to General Botha and to Field-Marshal Lord Kitchener. As ever, governments are rarely famous for their grasp of history, starting and ending with dates.

Beyond that, what remains is, perhaps, a last question about how the history of this war is recalled and used. What will its place come to be in the imagination, or what may happen to the future of its past? One likelihood is that it will come eventually to be seen as an increasingly remote episode from a vanished European imperial age. As the Johannesburg *Sunday Independent* put it on the centenary of the Jameson Raid, 'with this tumultuous century drawing to a close, hindsight puts the do-or-die battle between Afrikaners and English-speakers into its proper, smaller context. White men were never going to win indefinite control of this African continent.'[496] More particularly, it is even conceivable that with the fading of a distinctive Afrikaner political nation, the war will find another kind of existence, even as entertainment. An instance of this could be seen in a conspicuously youthful – and perhaps ironic – popular politics of Afrikaner identity and culture, flaring up as in Bok van Blerk's fashionable hit song of recent years, 'De la Rey', a hymn to the spirit of General Koos de la Rey, 'Die Leeuw van Wes-Transvaal', 'The Lion of the Western Transvaal'.[497] After all, the war's traditional landscape of memory is no longer quite what it was. The old Orange Free State lost its Dutch 'Orange' stamp in 1994 to become simply the Free State. In 1997, its ANC provincial government decided to swap Afrikaans for English as its official language. And as with the Orange, so with the Vaal. The Transvaal, too, has been dismembered, retitled, and de-marcated as new territorial units with non-colonial African names like Gauteng and Mpumalanga. Post-Boer and cleansed of their trekker heritage, on any war-time map they would be lands from nowhere.

For all that, in our time, let alone in what is to come, the Anglo-Boer War or South African War is certain to retain its quite other commemorative significance. This has little to do with nationalist politics or its legitimising mythologies, and everything to do with the war as a *soldiering* war of empire. Able-bodied admirers of De Wet can take guided hikes along his legendary flying escape route in the old Western Transvaal, the South African version of tripping along Vietnam's Ho Chi Minh Trail. In the Cape Karoo region, war tourists can scramble up to remote rock faces on which resting or hiding Boer commandos scratched poignant personal messages or etched images of fellow burghers. Visitors to a battlefield outside Bloemfontein can get, as it were, a bite of the cherry by firing a Boer rifle at a British dummy. Boer War enthusiasts from Britain and the white Commonwealth may trudge across the battlefields of Modder River or Paardeberg, ponder the Boer trench-lines at Magersfontein, and amble through the Ladysmith siege museum and the War Museum in Bloemfontein. Others with an interest in industrial archaeology can pore over the remains of the eight hundred blockhouses left by British forces. As ever, the sites of major battle or the bolt-holes of guerrilla resistance remain a source through which to imagine an old colonial war.

In other respects, the war that has long ceased to wrack South Africa will probably just touch the memory of ever fewer people. Indeed, it is hard to see how it could be otherwise in a country so limited in its shared national memories. South African's modern war is not, and has never been, an American Civil War in the sense of a 'never-to-be-forgotten moment' in 'the collective consciousness that makes Americans American'.[498] It produced no literary Stephen Crane, mythologising a tragic war as a national rite of passage to manhood in *The Red Badge of Courage*. To whistle up 'Sarie Marais' or 'We are Marching to Pretoria', is not to conjure up a shared war of the kind expressed by 'Marching through Georgia', or 'Dixie'. Unlike the Union Blues and the Confederate Greys of that civil war, most Boer fighters and departing British war veterans were never going to end up in some brotherly, camp-fire reconciliation. Both had too many lingering wounds to lick, be those the loss of independence and betrayal by brothers, or the bruising realisation of declining power.

11

COUNTING THE COSTS

AVING CONSIDERED SOME OF THE WAYS IN WHICH THIS WAR HAS
come to be remembered, we are left with a last intriguing question.
What was the War for South Africa for? Or, to put it another way, what
did all this conflict add up to?

In the first place, it ended a long period of complacent peace for the British
empire. True, for the Victorian army, there had been over forty small colonial
wars or 'punitive expeditions' since the Cardwell reforms of the 1860s and 1870s,
but none of these had represented a significant threat to the position of the empire. Second, there cannot be much doubt that this was a war which did not
succeed in mopping things up cleanly, for all that it left recognisable victors
and vanquished and prepared the ground for the first New South Africa, the
independent white supremacist state of 1910 with a loyal affiliation to the British
empire and its later Commonwealth.

For Britain, snuffing out Boer independence was accomplished eventually, but
there was precious little patriotic glory in it. Too much of the campaigning had
ended up morally troublesome, or haunted by the need to demonstrate improved
performance in the light of humiliating early failures. To be sure, the scale of
British war-weariness or war-aversion ought not to be exaggerated, as public
opinion mostly 'acquiesced to war'.[499] Equally, as with Britain's current expeditionary involvements in Iraq and Afghanistan, 'the South African War was not
a faraway colonial conflict, out of sight and half out of mind'. For speedy communications, widespread press coverage and the presence on the battlefield of
all manner of both regulars and volunteers 'gave the war an unprecedented
immediacy'.[500]

Some part of that immediacy lay in candour about, and distaste for, the manner in which it was being waged, and the sense of disillusion among many of those who were waging it which gave the lie to it all, at times in the most frank and uncensored way. They did well to weep over the scale of inhumanity in the war in which they found themselves. Again, some present parallels are almost ghostly. As a London *Sunday Times* correspondent noted acerbically in 2009, the compensation sum of £9 000 for a British soldier who loses his penis in action in Afghanistan was the same amount that one Conservative MP was claiming annually on expenses for gardening and wood chopping.[501] Signs of such smarting realisation were all around in South Africa, and as early as 1900. Writing to his mother from Lichtenburg in December of that year, Imperial Yeomanryman Alan Corbett reported on rumours of Kitchener's intentions to deal 'more harshly' with the enemy, including the shooting of anyone seized under arms. Fearful of Boer reprisal, 'for such a policy would cut both ways', Corbett made no secret of his feelings about those in charge – 'it's rather sharp practice of the Commander-in-Chief safe and comfortable in Johannesburg to mortgage our lives in such a way. We did not come out here to play Spaniards and Cubans'.[502]

Even longer-suffering officers became heartily sick of affairs, and the lengthening drudgery of occupation did little to endear the annexed republics to their khaki invaders. Relatively few took leave of army service for post-war settlement in 'the white man's country' or 'the country of promises', to help to fulfil Milner's fantasy of a mass influx of British settlement to 'anglicise' the Transvaal. Instead, a small number of semi-skilled ex-soldiers picked up artisan trade in port cities, joined the police service, or married local white and also Coloured women with whom they had made wartime relationships.[503]

In sight and sound and smell, much of the country's rural interior lay blighted by a war of waste. 'A serious crisis,' in the words of the influential Standard Bank, 'the effects of which will doubtless be felt for a long time.'[504] Sure enough, imperial repatriation, resettlement and reconstruction resources assisted Boer territories and the country as a whole to recover from the ravages of the war. But it also took a sustained rural military policing effort after 1902 to restore stability, and to put right Boer dominance over Africans which had been eroded by the conflict, as thousands of members of a newly created South African Constabulary fanned out 'to coerce black workers to return to their prewar employers' and to 'protect the Boers and their property'.[505]

The British created waste not just for their enemy, but also for themselves. South Africa had been another of those wars, even if to be the last, in which a physically ill-prepared and unhealthy imperial army sustained more fatalities from sickness and disease than from enemy fire. Viewed in that light, cavalry horses did even worse. The army lost 347 000 out of 518 000 horses in its campaign, through malnutrition, disease, or relentless exertion.[506] The rigours of life on the open veld, lack of sanitation and other hazards, and an uncertain provisioning service made this a war in which to be British was to be largely unfit and unhealthy, whether on two legs or four. Out of the almost 450 000 troops who had been put in the field by the end of hostilities, deaths amounted to 22 000 men. Over 13 000 of these, or close to two-thirds, were fatalities from disease and illness. Several dozen were killed by lightning, and over 270 soldiers drowned. Unlike the rural Boers, they knew neither how to swim nor which rivers were least treacherous.

The manner of this loss, coupled to the wartime rejection of virtually one-third of army recruits because of poor physical condition, made the 1899–1902 episode a low point in British national health. It brought into sharp relief a proliferation of the unfit amongst the mass urban working class, and an assumed physical deterioration of the 'racial stock' of the population. Unease in the aftermath of 1902 that this might lay at risk the imperial future unleashed a flood of chastening prognostication about the state of military fitness and preparedness, and the gloomy outcome for the maintenance of a strong nation and empire if poverty and destitution were not tackled. The mounting concern of the Edwardian élite with the relationship between imperial power and racial vitality as something to be addressed through national efficiency and advanced eugenics or 'race-improvement', was very much a product of the hard going in South Africa.[507]

On the other hand, the war was a less deflating experience for the empire's settler dominions. White New Zealanders played a tough hand, creating a self-confident national identity in South Africa as fighting 'Kiwis'. While Cape authorities would not permit the landing of Maori soldiers, they bestowed upon departing settler contingents that famous ritual of posturing masculinity, the *haka* warrior dance, as the indubitable mark of New Zealand pride. The role of the war in the construction of national identity was no less the case for Canada. As British North American loyalists, Canadian expeditionary force volunteers with their maple leaf badges provided combat experience to underline nationalist patriotism and self-reliance. Bamboozled by the nature of Boer warfare, British army leadership had made a mess because of its crusty adherence to red tape rules, its lack of innovation, and its upper-class stuffiness. In the Canadian critique, all this was no more than evidence of the imaginative brilliance and courage of their colonist citizen soldiers. Far hardier and more independent than socially deprived and stunted British Tommies, superior prairie troops had made a better go of it in South Africa, and represented an assertive country, ready to control its own future. In helping to create the Canadian archetype of the upright Mountie or lumberjack, the experience of war in South Africa could certainly be put to some use in shaping the national imagination.

No less predictably, the war also brightened the star of the emergent 1901 Australian Federation. Making the best of a bad job by the British, the Australian mounted 'bushman' soldier, proficient in open country and not enfeebled by slum life in Birmingham or Glasgow, brought Australian military 'mateship' galloping to the rescue of empire, creating a new breed of loyal white Gurkhas, old immigrant stock renewed as the very best of British horsemen. This turned the war, the third largest in which Australia has been involved, into an early defining moment in national history and mythology.[508] On the other hand, the war's place in the history of the Irish was somewhat more clouded. Roberts himself was but one of tens of thousands of loyalist Irish who fought for Britain, while across the republican divide, Irish nationalist brigades lined up with the Boers. Here were some unusual and memorable circumstances for Catholic republicans. The Boers were Protestant, yet also anti-imperialist soldiers for freedom. They, too, had had to face Buller, as had the fighting Fenians in Kerry and Clare in the 1880s. And this time it was the ally, not the enemy, which was Orange.

So much for the British world. What of continental Europe, and elsewhere? In stoking anti-British passions, the war had its place in historic Anglo-French antagonisms. Yet, there its testy political impact was ephemeral. It produced perhaps the last round of vintage Anglophobia before French opinion swung around to the view that Britain (and not Russia) would be the most solid ally in any future confrontation with Germany. In turn, Russia found that instability in South Africa turned its eye on high strategy. Intense Russian pro-Boer hysteria in Europe which, as elsewhere, was more rhetorical than material, was directly linked to tension and rivalry with British imperialism over the prickly issue of

Afghanistan. Jonkheer van der Hoeven, secretary of the Transvaal mission in Europe, even got himself invited to the wedding of the Tsar's sister mainly to annoy the British. Only in Japan were attitudes to London nicer. Here, there was popular hostility towards a Boer threat to the British empire at the very moment that Tokyo was snuggling up to London on the grounds of a common interest in blocking Russian expansionism into Manchuria. Indeed, Anglo-Boer War sympathies eased the passage of the 1900s Anglo-Japanese alliance, which hitched the fortunes of the Japanese East Asian empire to British imperialism for decades thereafter.[509] Although this war was never at any point likely to be anything more than a colonial one, the shots first fired south of Mafeking still echoed round a good part of the world.

If the wheel is to come full circle, we need to return to the protagonists and the circumstances of their war. Here, which perspectives stand out most will always depend, obviously, on your point of view or angle of vision. In many ways, the 'English War' or *Engelse Oorlog* represented the lowest point of highveld Boer society as it cleared the decks for imperialism in South Africa. Its real significance lies in what it did to a Boer republican order of little more than 200 000 people, for whom its losses amounted to a kind of historical trauma. The Boer republics had had at most about 70 000 of their burghers available for field service, over 7 000 of whom died. This was a significant proportion of their male soldiering complement. Around 28 000 women and children perished in white concentration camps, with some older men and prisoners of war also falling victim to the war.

Yet, despite the terrible mauling of highveld society, the Boers survived, retaining the basic core of their social cohesion and inscribed cultural traditions, a hankering for independence and political power, and a simmering capacity for limbering up again to achieve it. Less than five decades after the end of the war, nationalist Afrikanerdom, through the institutions of the new apartheid state, was regaining not only most of the ground lost, but quite a lot more. In that respect, the fate of the Boers was not that of troublesome indigenous societies in some other colonial wars, in which military defeat at the hands of superior European power meant that they simply crumbled and disintegrated.[510]

It was far from that, in fact, and in more ways than one. For nationalist ideologues, aside from the shadows cast by Cronjé's surrender at Paardeberg and the

Prinsloo disaster of Brandwater Basin, the Boers had suffered no heavy defeats. Just months before the end of fighting, they had even managed to capture a British general. Their enemy was only able to win eventually through superiority in numbers, financial means, military resources, and the use of inhumane methods of warfare – not through any equal or higher combat efficiency against brave and steely bittereinder warriors. So, the war left a morale-boosting legend of male heroism and patriotic fortitude, tested and not found wanting against despised British Tommies, against the moral cancer of betrayal or the treachery of weak fellow fighters who broke the Boer cause. In what was surely a remarkable Afrikaner nationalist accomplishment, the image of the mythic Boer warrior emerged as a transcendent triumph of Christian fighting perseverance.[511] In that sense, the outcome of the war became the best victory Boer republicanism never had. For the war was lost by the Boers rather than won by the British, and it was lost to some republican defeatism, rather than to a conquering enemy.

A few further closing perspectives take us from the fanciful back to the more factual. To the extent that we now recognise the supportive military role played by perhaps as many as 14 000 African and Coloured commando auxiliaries, and possibly 120 000 African, Coloured, and Indian men in non-combatant or armed imperial army service, it is quite evident that this was never a white war. Even if these estimates may be somewhat overstated,[512] there can be no mistaking the significance of the war's 'non-European' role. Black participants serviced both sides, helped to keep them in the field, augmented their fighting power, and made a distinctive, irregular contribution to the art of the war. Theirs was a war of operational maintenance, transport riding, scouting, guarding, raiding, cattle rustling, spying, interpreting, dispatch running and riding, and armed defence of this or that patch of ground.

On the British side, some auxiliaries found it a profitable time. Wages for army labouring were relatively good, and high for service requiring expertise or skill. One of the persistent grumbles from ordinary soldiers was that of having to perform 'on the cheap', while local black men were being better remunerated. Peasant communities in more protected areas such as the Transkeian Territories also made a killing as Army Service Corps forage, livestock, and remount suppliers. Luckier Africans got something in their pockets from the war, and could withhold their labour from poorly paying mines and farms after 1902, even if that lining of greater economic independence was tenuous and temporary. All this left some sort of positive balance sheet, at least for a time.

But to conclude thus is also to underline the point that one cannot go too far in this direction. Had the Anglo-Boer War's centre of gravity included a frontal collision between white and black combatants, it would have been a very different type of 'racial' colonial war. That it did not become this left it with some peculiar features. If some blacks suddenly regained the right to carry and to use arms, wartime conditions hardly provided temptation or the chance to stir up much trouble. After all, at this moment, 'the whole of South Africa was an armed camp with more white men under arms than ever before'.[513] All the same, both warring sides whined intermittently about each other's irresponsibility in calling on armed black collaborators, while issuing bare-faced claims of innocence. Of course, at the time, the real issue was the damage that had already been done. Towards the end of hostilities, even on a conservative calculation, the number of authorised British auxiliaries in the field may well have exceeded the remaining force of fighting bittereinders. Moreover, a threatening climate of social fear triggered by sporadic independent black attacks became a factor in bringing on Boer surrender. If it was looking ominous in 1902, the ending of the war ensured that it did not become a real disaster for white rural society in the annexed states.

At the same time, rural incineration hit many African peasants as well as Boer landowners. The misery and heavy mortality in the Boer concentration camps was matched by the fate of interned black refugees, either working in white camps or in their segregated camps. Known African camp losses of around 14 000 have been lifted to a provisional estimate of around 20 000 fatalities.[514] Here was a mordantly ironic kind of shared tragedy, if not exactly much appreciated in 1902. Undeniable, too, was the face-to-face social connection between Boer families and their servants and tenants, their heavy dependence upon them for food collection and transport riding, and the entrusting to them of livestock for safe keeping, at times a big wartime risk. In all of that, the war had some slippery social and political elements.

No less striking was the difference between the fighting of this war and that of other Victorian colonial campaigns. Here, neither side made major use of indigenous populations as levies in combat. Nor, as in imperial West Africa, were African lives put at risk or routinely expended as a tactic to economise upon European troops. For both combatants, exploiting available labour and skills was one thing. Acquiring the political encumbrance of negotiated black allies was, however, quite another. Viewed in that sort of light, the essence of the Anglo-Boer War can still be seen for what it really was: a European war fought in Africa over how best to get on with the colonial order, and what the dominant terms of white power ought to be. On that assumption, there is a view in which this war can be passed off as an early twentieth-century anti-colonial African struggle against Great Power imperialism, in which the republicans amounted to another tribal order of armed peasantry. This implies that the warring Boers simply replaced the Zulu as the most intractable people in Southern Africa, or can be regarded perhaps simply as Zulu with horses. Or, for that matter, that their contribution to history is to have been the Iraqis of their day, but with gold instead of oil.

Such similarities, however, do not run too far. In retrospect, republican anti-imperialism tripped over the contradictions of the Boers' own colonising cause. Their independence rested upon the expropriation of African land and the appropriation of African labour. Doubtless, the Pedi or the Venda would have been bemused to hear that the Boer war to defend national soil was an anti-colonial undertaking. Accordingly, as one scholar has suggested, both this and the earlier Anglo-Boer conflict might best be depicted as European wars fought within, and conditioned by, a colonial setting. For, just as the War of American Independence can hardly be viewed as an episode in native American resistance to European invasion, so the Anglo-Boer War cannot really be seen as part of the history of African resistance to imperial incursion.[515]

At another crucial level, it is almost a cliché of South African and British imperial history to point out that the war and its outcome did nothing to solve the 'problem' of the position of Africans, Coloureds, and Indians. On the contrary, the expedient manner of its resolution made the handling of the issue more difficult than ever. Things might have been a little different if Whitehall had pressed home in peace the limited political stand on black civil rights which it had taken in war. In the failed March 1901 peace talks, Chamberlain had obliged a dismayed Milner and Kitchener to include a clause about extending the franchise right of the Cape black élite into the new colonies. Naturally, this was conceived of as a long and lowly apprenticeship in 'civilisation' under the just dominance of English and Afrikaner settlers. But it still implied that the end of the war should bring a small stepping stone rather than a dead end. However flimsy the colonial secretary's occasional claim that an imperial war aim was African protection, his fleeting opposition to an unredeemedly 'shameful peace'[516] still provides a passing wartime moment.

Had an earlier peace come, had a successor political order had its white supremacy slightly diluted by imperial decree, who knows about the possible course of later South African history. But it did not happen. In 1902, peacemaking British and peacemaking Boers had come to the end of a large and damaging war, and Whitehall and the Boer generals had no wish to trade any new blows over the trifle of rights for a small middle-class tributary of 'civilised natives'. Their only interest was in cooperation and reconciliation, which in practice meant a colour-bar concession to the traditionally racist constitution and custom of the defeated Boers.

In classic liberal interpretation, the imperial re-enfranchisement and rehabilitation of its defeated enemy was so magnanimous that it meant that Britain won the war but lost the peace to Afrikaner power over the longer term. Equally, its easy mortgaging of African interests to white preferences and needs represented a deplorable lapse in liberal sensibilities. By the same measure, there is a more hard-nosed assessment of what was at stake in the 1902 settlement. For the political and strategic requirements of British imperial interests, and for the needs of mining capital and finance, the 1910 Union produced by the war was a splendid political achievement.[517] It provided a unified, stable and cohesive national dominion that could rip away those barriers to South African capitalist development which had been the cause of such frustration and crisis before the war. In any longer – or, for that matter, shorter – view, the truth is that neither the British nor the Boer cause in South Africa could be termed righteous. In its larger outcome, this was assuredly not one of those romantically perceived wars in which one cause was worthy, and the other was not.

If not that, what, in the end, defined it? For Britain, it was its location squarely within a period of tangled crises for the later Victorian imperial order, a crisis inching through the 1880s and persisting through to the Great War. Like some wind across the world, the South African crisis blew up anxieties about the wellbeing of empire, declining economic vitality, the deteriorating effects of poverty and unemployment, and defence capability. While the British succeeded in South Africa, for both Unionists and Liberals, South Africa had been discomfiting. Nor, in some other ways, did conquest immediately present all that much benefit. Immigrants hardly sprinted in, and initial investment beyond post-1902 reconstruction requirements was modest.

At the same time, while the considerable significance of the war for South Africa to modern British imperialism is apparent, this is not to say that it should be made to look bigger than it was. Not everything about it was necessarily fundamental in its impact. It is, for instance, conventional wisdom to stress the imposing financial and other costs of the conflict, and the alarm that this caused. Five months into the conflict, that estimated cost had increased from £10m to £68m, virtually the charge of the Crimean War, turning a colonial affray into something of European size. By April 1901, expenditure had risen to £153m, with the final cost to the British Exchequer reaching a whopping £217m. Furthermore, when war ended not a farthing of indemnity was extracted from the Transvaal.

Still, financing the war, and coping with large budget deficits, was not the major cause of any fiscal crisis.[518] War finance became a mundane, if slightly worrying, part of late-Victorian and early Edwardian living. The British state was having to cope with continuously rising national expenditure, and what the war years brought were emergency increases in income tax. In this context, arguably the most significant impact of the conflict was its stimulus to a more general state expansion for national and imperial imperatives. Sobering experience of the veld had confirmed the necessity of beefing up the capabilities of the British state to avoid some real military disaster.[519] Internationally, the borrowing needed to ease strain on the British capital market in funding the war was actually gratifying to Chamberlain. The first substantive British war loan floated in the New York market became a monument to Anglo-American goodwill, assuring the British people that their American friends recognised that their government's war motives and aims were as 'high' and 'unselfish' as those which had roused Washington in the recent Spanish-American conflict.[520]

It is also revealing that, when it came to rethinking imperial defence, the war did not catch on in quite the way which might have been expected. True enough, the performance problems illuminated by the Anglo-Boer War were important in forcing along further reform and reconstruction of the Victorian army. The war, as one authority has stressed, 'was in fact a struggle against two different enemies: the Boers and the changing nature of warfare'.[521] In grappling with the demands of the latter, the experience of the South African colonial campaign was crucial to the reworking of British tactical doctrine before the Great War – greater cultivation of mounted infantry, more dispersed infantry formations, and coordinated artillery fire and infantry movement.[522] There were also other spheres of new attention after 1902, such as training and drill, making soldiers look drabber to improve their survival chances, marksmanship and firepower, and the planning of more effective logistical systems to cope with the burdens of widespread campaigning. As for floundering army medical services, South Africa had been another Crimea, with many more soldiers dying from preventable disease than from enemy fire. This time, reorganisation and reform was on a very much larger scale than the light post-Crimean improvements.[523]

This notwithstanding, the evolving army reforms of influential figures like St John Brodrick and R.B. Haldane, culminating in the formation of a limited General Staff, a home-based British Expeditionary Force, and a non-regular Territorial Force, were not particularly aimed at equipping Britain's army to fight the next threat from armed and defiant colonial nationalism. If anything, it was more the possibility of dealing with a rival expansionist enemy, much more powerful and close to a vital and lucrative sphere of British influence. So, while South Africa gave a modernising push to army and naval thinking, its initial direction was to be prepared for quite another kind of European run-in, like an imperialist tangle in India with a threatening Russia. In that respect, experience of the Orange Free State and the Transvaal did not necessarily leave the army gingered up for better colonial pacification, but, rather, to better mark time for the day when European continental fighting might become unavoidable to preserve the balance of power. Equally, even if there was a more modern army for Continental purposes, it remained largely a pragmatic thing, ready for a crisis but to react in an improvised way, and then only if the crisis became a serious challenge. For, politically, still 'neither the government nor the country was prepared to accept the massive militarisation of society which a continental strategy implied'.[524] This made no sense to alarmist critics such as Erskine Childers, whose 1903 *The Riddle of the Sands* joined other seaborne-invasion literature in urging an unready Britain to prepare to square up to an insidious and aggressive Germany. On that score at least, military reverses in South Africa can be seen to have prepared the ground in the later 1900s for this preoccupation of the popular imagination.[525]

As the Boers fired the first shot, they should probably have the last word of the story. This was their most defining war, and their longest and leanest armed conflict, one which came to rest on scrawny guerrilla fighters fed on the scrawny fruits of pastoralism. A war rich in suffering, exile, and fratricidal internal strife, it left an occupied population lifted from desolation and reinstated on their land only by the reconstruction intervention of their enemy. For all its inequalities and divisions, it was also a pronounced people's war, with a semi-professional and independent-minded civilian character – both a strength and a weakness when it came to the imposition of tactics and discipline. And, at this level, 'people' did not mean only that fighting proportion of the male population, for the impact and implications of the conflict bore down heavily upon women.

Looking back in speculative vein, perhaps the misfortune of the Boers was not so much that they fought on doggedly in a lost cause, earning international respect but not much more. Nor was it the fact that, like the winning side, they, too, were prone to errors, incompetence, and bouts of feuding. That, surely, is a feature of virtually every war. Most of all, it was, perhaps, the fatal delay in choosing guerrilla strategy. Fundamentally, they held the keys to this from the beginning: fine mounted marksmanship and good firearms, skilled auxiliary field support, flexible lower-level command, superior mobility to skip potentially damaging confrontation and to pick fights when and where it suited, and proficiency at small-scale tactics. Had the republicans launched a guerrilla war when they still had a whiff of quick victory in their nostrils, rather than when they were more or less already defeated, the strategic direction of the first phase of the conflict might very well have been more fruitful for them, or at least less lethargic and indecisive.

If the Boers chose war with their eyes open, these were perhaps not wide enough. The weight of the blow which fell on them changed the way many thought, not just about the nature of Britain, but about the shattering nature of modern war itself. The crisis of their 'English War' confirmed the extinction of a Gladstonian Liberal imperialism, with its notion of a negotiating moral empire. It also confirmed empire as the strongest conceivable armed test of national will, whatever the price. For a while, then, the Boers had a taste of the earlier fate of their African counterparts in Southern Africa, such as the Xhosa, whose fields and gardens were deliberately destroyed by Sir Harry Smith in the Eastern Cape frontier or land wars of the early 1850s.

Perhaps the harshness of imperial conquest and occupation was some unforeseen turn of the screw in the course of a Boer trekker history built on Sotho, Tswana, Pedi and other land annexations of its own. Still, the Tswana were certainly never as squashed as the Kurds of Iraq, nor was the lumbering Kruger regime of 1899 'the brutal tyranny of the Ba'ath regime'[526] of Baghdad in more recent times. However suggestive, some colonial war analogies should not be taken *too* far.

As an early chapter carried the view of one of Britain's most popular and opinionated twentieth-century historians, it is appropriate that A.J.P. Taylor should again have some of the last words. Writing on 11 October 1949, his rueful anniversary conclusion was that, 'fifty years afterwards, it is clear that victory has gone to the worst elements of both sides . . . the mining houses and the most narrow-minded Boers have joined hands to oppress and exploit the native peoples who are the overwhelming majority . . . If Milner could see the results of victory, or Campbell-Bannerman the results of Boer self-government, would either have reason to be proud of his handiwork?'[527] A year previously, the apartheid National Party had assumed power, signalling the beginning of the end of the Union of South Africa as a Commonwealth animal, or at least for almost half a century. Twelve years after the war's fiftieth anniversary, South Africa became a national republic and stalked off from Britain's Commonwealth, something that might have made President Marthinus Steyn stir in his grave. It was all, in its way, a late sequel to the war. And if it left a postscript, it was the return of South Africa to the Commonwealth in July 1994. Marking it at Westminster Abbey, Britain's prime minister, John Major, declared that 'The Commonwealth without South Africa' was 'a bit like rice pudding without milk'.[528]

Today, it bears being reminded of another part of that sequel, surely more fundamental and enduring over time than the history of apartheid. The 1899–1902 war, and the 1906–1910 unification process to which it led, are the engines which turned South Africa from a place imagined to an established country. Before 1910, 'South Africa' had no legal meaning and 'neither South African citizens nor subjects could be said to have existed'.[529] The year this book has been published, 2010, is the centenary of the founding of the South African state, whatever the racially segregationist nature of its original basis. This may surprise some, not least Pretoria's current government, who think – or pretend – that what 2010 means mainly for South Africa is its hosting of the FIFA football World Cup.

THE NEW SOUTH AFRICA: UNION 1910

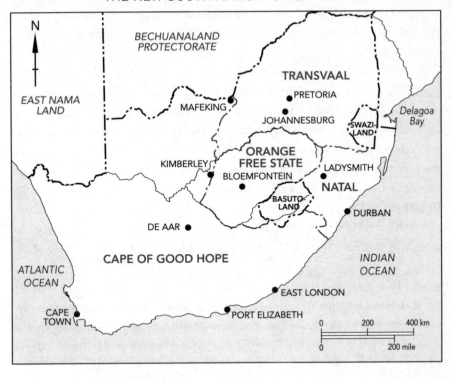

N

BECHUANALAND
PROTECTORATE

EAST NAMA
LAND

TRANSVAAL

MAFEKING

PRETORIA

JOHANNESBURG

SWAZI-
LAND

Delagoa
Bay

KIMBERLEY

ORANGE
FREE STATE

BLOEMFONTEIN

LADYSMITH

NATAL

BASUTO
LAND

DURBAN

DE AAR

CAPE OF GOOD HOPE

INDIAN
OCEAN

ATLANTIC
OCEAN

EAST LONDON

CAPE
TOWN

PORT ELIZABETH

0   200   400 km

0   200 mile

ENDNOTES

INTRODUCTION

1 *Sunday Independent*, 20 April 1997.

2 M. Marix Evans, *Encyclopaedia of the Boer War, 1899-1902* (Oxford, 2000); J.C. (Kay) de Villiers, *Healers, Helpers and Hospitals: A History of Military Medicine in the Anglo-Boer War*, 2 vols. (Pretoria, 2009); R. Greenwall, *Artists and Illustrators of the Anglo-Boer War* (Cape Town, 1992).

3 R. Bester, *Boer Rifles and Carbines of the Anglo-Boer War* (Bloemfontein, 1995); D.R. Maree, *Bicycles During the Boer War* (Johannesburg, 1977); T. Bridgland, *Field Gun Jack Versus the Boers: The Royal Navy in South Africa 1899-1900* (London, 1998).

4 T. Pakenham, *The Boer War* (London, 1979), reissued in abridged and pictorial format as *The Boer War: Illustrated Edition* (Johannesburg and London, 1993); E. Lee, *To The Bitter End: A Photographic History of the Boer War, 1899-1902* (Harmondsworth, 1985); B. Nasson, *The South African War, 1899-1902* (London, 1999).

5 K. Lette, *Foetal Attraction* (London, 1993), p. 96.

6 Quoted in Selborne to Milner, 27 July 1899, in G. Boyce (ed.), *The Crisis of British Power: The Imperial and Naval Papers of the Second Earl of Selborne, 1895-1910* (London, 1990), p. 92.

7 A. Roberts, 'Salisbury: The Empire Builder Who Never Was', *History Today*, 49/10 (1999), p. 51.

8 Nasson, *South African War*, p. ix.

9 G. Wheatcroft, *Yo, Blair!* (London, 2007), p. 52.

10 N. Stone, *World War One: A Short History* (London, 2008), p. 74.

CHAPTER 1

11 D. Denoon, *Settler Capitalism:The Dynamics of Dependent Development in the Southern Hemisphere* (Oxford, 1983), p. 38; T. Keegan, *Colonial South Africa and the Origins of the Racial Order* (Leicester, 1996), p. 196.

12 G.R. Searle, *A New England? Peace and War, 1886-1918* (Oxford, 2004), p. 274.

13 C. Trebilcock, 'War and the failure of industrial mobilization: 1899 and 1914', in J.M. Winter (ed.), *War and Economic Development* (Cambridge, 1975), p. 141.

14 J.F.C. Fuller, *The Last of the Gentlemen's Wars* (London, 1937).

15 P. Warwick, *Black People and the South African War, 1899-1902* (Cambridge, 1983); B. Nasson, *Abraham Esau's War: A Black South African War in the Cape, 1899-1902* (Cambridge, 1991); *Uyadela Wen'Osulapho, Black Participation in the Anglo-Boer War* (Johannesburg, 1999).

16 D. Pick, *War Machine: The Rationalisation of Slaughter in the Modern Age* (New Haven and London, 1993), p. 86.

17 J. Horne, 'Introduction: Mobilizing for "total war", 1914-1918', in *State, Society and Mobilization in Europe During the First World War* (Cambridge, 1997), p. 3.

18 C. Coetzee, *Op Soek na Generaal Mannetjies Mentz* (Johannesburg, 1998).

19 V.G. Kiernan, *The Lords of Human Kind* (Harmondsworth, 1972), p. 235.

20 I.R. Smith, *The Origins of the South African War, 1899-1902* (London, 1996), p. 10.

21 *The Guardian*, 9 November, 2009.

22 B. Bond, *The Pursuit of Victory: From Napoleon to Saddam Hussein* (Oxford, 1998), pp. 97, 99.

23 B. Freund, *The Making of Contemporary Africa: The Development of African Society Since 1800* (Bloomington, Ind., 1984), p. 106; B. Davidson, *The People's Cause: A History of Guerrillas in Africa* (London, 1981), p. 31.

CHAPTER 2

24 A.J.P. Taylor, *Essays in English History* (London, 1976), pp. 184-85.

25 Quoted in B. Porter, *The Lion's Share: A Short History of British Imperialism, 1850-1970* (London, 1975), p. 175.

26 Smith, *South African War*, p. 415.

27 G. Blainey, *The Causes of War* (Melbourne, 1988), p. 141.

28 Quoted in G.H.L. Le May, *British Supremacy in South Africa, 1899-1907* (Oxford, 1965). p. 28.

29 *Cape Colony Hansard (Legislative Assembly Debates)*, 18 Oct. 1898, p. 46; *Sir James Rose Innes: Selected Correspondence, 1884-1902*, ed. H. M. Wright (Cape Town, 1972), p. 200.

30 *The War Memoirs of Commandant Ludwig Krause, 1899-1900*, ed. J. Taitz (Cape Town, 1996), pp. 1-3.

31 A. Porter, 'The South African War (1899-1902): Context and Motive Reconsidered', *Journal of African History*, 31/1 (1990), p. 43.

32 S. Hynes, *The Edwardian Turn of Mind*, (Princeton, 1968) p. 19.

33 B. Semmel, *Imperialism and Social Reform: English Social-Imperial Thought 1895-1914* (New York, 1968), pp. 30, 57; P. Crook, *Darwinism, War and History* (Cambridge, 1994), pp. 80, 89-90.

34 *Justice*, 12 July 1900; *Clarion*, 17 November 1899.

35   Generally, *Marxism and the Science of War*, ed. B. Semmel (Oxford, 1981), pp.13-18.
36   B. Porter, *Critics of Empire: British Radical Attitudes to Colonialism in Africa 1895-1914* (London, 1968), pp.123-30; M. Taylor, '"Imperium et Libertas": Rethinking the radical critique of imperialism during the nineteenth century', *Journal of Imperial and Commonwealth History* 19/1 (1991), p. 16.
37   *Jan Smuts: Memoirs of the Boer War*, eds. S.B. Spies and G. Nattrass (Johannesburg, 1994), p. 130.
38   Quoted in D. Feldman, 'Nationality and ethnicity', in *Twentieth-Century Britain: Economic, Social and Cultural Change*, ed. P. Johnson (London, 1994), p. 157.
39   J. Grigg, 'Lloyd George and the Boer War', in *Edwardian Radicalism, 1900-1914*, ed. A.J.A. Morris (London, 1974), p. 13.
40   L. Thompson, *A History of South Africa* (New Haven and London, 1990), p. 109.
41   S. Marks, 'Scrambling for South Africa', *Journal of African History*, 23/1 (1982), p. 101.
42   Quoted in Bond, 'The South African War, 1880-1', in *Victorian Military Campaigns*, ed. B. Bond (London, 1967), p. 204.
43   J. Laband, *The Transvaal Rebellion: The First Boer War, 1880-1881* (Harlow, 2005), p. 237.
44   J. Lehmann, *The First Boer War* (London, 1972); M. Hugo, 'Wapenstilstand', in *Die Eerste Vryheidsoorlog*, eds. F.A. van Jaarsveld, A.P.J. van Rensburg, and W.A. Stals (Pretoria, 1980), p. 201.
45   Quoted in P. Hayes, *Modern British Foreign Policy: The Twentieth Century, 1880-1939* (London, 1978), p. 19.
46   A. Grundlingh, 'Prelude to the Anglo-Boer War, 1881-1899', in *An Illustrated History of South Africa*, eds. T. Cameron and S.B. Spies (Johannesburg, 1986), p. 184.
47   A. Porter, *European Imperialism, 1860-1914* (London, 1994), p. 70.
48   J.D. Omer-Cooper, *History of Southern Africa* (London, 1987), p. 124.
49   D.M. Schreuder, *Gladstone and Kruger: Liberal Government and Colonial Home Rule, 1880-85* (London, 1969), p. 15.
50   P. Richardson and J-J. Van-Helten, 'The gold mining industry in the Transvaal 1886-99', in *The South African War: The Anglo-Boer War, 1899-1902*, ed. P. Warwick (London, 1980), p. 21.
51   Studies of particular distinction include *Industrialisation and Social Change in South Africa: African Class Formation, Culture and Consciousness, 1870-1930*, eds. S. Marks and R. Rathbone (London, 1982); C. van Onselen, *Studies in the Social and Economic History of the Witwatersrand, 1886-1914*, 2 vols (London, 1982).
52   Porter, *Lion's Share*, p. 98.
53   S. Trapido, 'Reflections on land, office and wealth in the South African Republic, 1850-1900', in *Economy and Society in Pre-industrial South Africa* (London, 1980), eds. S. Marks and A. Atmore (London, 1982), p. 357.
54   T.R.H. Davenport, *South Africa: A Modern History* (London, 1991), p. 85; R. Mendelsohn, *Sammy Marks, The 'Uncrowned King' of the Transvaal* (Cape Town, 1991), p. 93.

55 Smith, *South African War*, p. 83.

56 S. Trapido, 'Imperialism, Settler Identities and Colonial Capitalism: The Hundred Year Origins of the 1899 South African War', *Historia*, 53/1 (2008), p.67.

57 D. Cammack, *The Rand at War 1899-1902: The Witwatersrand and the Anglo-Boer War* (London, 1990), pp. 12-32.

58 R. Mendelsohn, 'Thirty years' debate on the economic origins of the raid', in *The Jameson Raid: A Centennial Perspective* (Johannesburg, 1996), pp. 55-87.

59 N. Parsons, 'The Jameson Road', *Southern African Review of Books*, 8/1 (1996), p. 7.

60 Quoted in J.A. Coetzee, *Die Politieke Groepering in die Wording van die Afrikaner-natie* (Johannesburg, 1941), p. 185.

61 P. Harries, 'Capital, State and Labour on the 19th Century Witwatersrand: A Reassessment', *South African Historical Journal*, 18 (1986), pp. 25-45; E. N. Katz, 'Outcrop and deep-level mining in South Africa before the Anglo-Boer War: re-examining the Blainey thesis', *Economic History Review*, 48 (1995), p. 326.

62 A. H. Jeeves, 'The Consequences of the Raid', in *Jameson Raid*, p. 172.

63 *Selections from the Correspondence of Percy Alport Molteno*, ed. V. Solomon (Cape Town, 1981), p. 185; S. Dubow, 'Colonial nationalism, the Milner kindergarten and the rise of "South Africanism", 1902-10', *History Workshop Journal*, 43 (1997), p. 57.

64 A. Porter, 'Lord Salisbury, Mr Chamberlain and South Africa, 1895-9', *Journal of Imperial and Commonwealth History*, 1/1 (1972), p. 22.

65 Milner to Chamberlain, 23 February 1898, in *The Milner Papers*, ed. C. Headlam (London, 1931), p. 220.

66 Quoted in J. Lee Thompson, *Forgotten Patriot: A Life of Alfred, Viscount Milner of St James's and Cape Town, 1854-1925* (Cranbury, NJ, 2007), p.148.

67 Smuts to Te Water, 4 September 1899, in *Selections from the Smuts Papers*, vol. 1, eds. W.K. Hancock and J. van der Poel (Cambridge, 1966), p. 309.

68 Quoted in Lee Thompson, *Forgotten Patriot*, p.151.

69 J.L. Garvin and Julian Amery, *The Life of Joseph Chamberlain*, vol. 3 (London, 1949), p. 476.

70 *Selections from the Correspondence of John X. Merriman*, vol. 3 (1899-1905), ed. P. Lewsen (Cape Town, 1966), p. 95.

71 D. Reynolds, *Britannia Overruled: British World Power and Decline* (London, 1991), pp. 67-68.

72 M. Tamarkin, *Cecil Rhodes and the Cape Afrikaner: The Imperial Colossus and the Colonial Parish Pump* (London, 1996), p. 181.

73 P.J. Cain, 'British Radicalism, the South African Crisis, and the Origins of the Theory of Financial Imperialism', in *The Impact of the South African War*, ed. D. Omissi and A. Thompson (London, 2002), p.182.

74 E. Hobsbawm, *The Age of Empire, 1975-1914* (London, 1987), p. 66.

75 Porter, 'South African War', pp. 47-48.

76 R. Robinson and J. Gallagher, *Africa and the Victorians: The Official Mind of Imperialism* (London, 1961), pp. 457-61; Smith, *South African War*, pp. 393-413.

77 I. Phimister, 'Africa Partitioned', *Review*, 18/2 (1995), p. 375; 'Unscrambling the Scramble for Southern Africa', *South African Historical Journal*, 28 (1993), pp.216-19; Grundlingh, 'Paul Kruger', in *Jameson Raid*, p. 232; Marks and Trapido, 'Lord Milner and the South African state reconsidered', in *Imperialism, The State and the Third World*, ed. M. Twaddle (London, 1992), p. 84.

78 P. Henshaw, 'The Origins of the Boer War: The Periphery, the Centre and "the Man on the Spot"', in *The International Impact of the Boer War*, ed. K. Wilson (Chesham, 2001), pp.12-18.

79 R. Ovendale, 'Profit or Patriotism: Natal, the Transvaal, and the coming of the Second Anglo-Boer War', *Journal of Imperial and Commonwealth History*, 8/3 (1980), pp. 225-27.

80 J. Bottomley, 'The application of the theory of "economic backwardness" to South Africa's early modern period: the development initiatives of the various governments from the Zuid-Afrikaansche Republiek to the Pact Government of 1924', unpublished South African Economic History Society conference paper, University of Natal, 1992; A. Porter, 'The origins of the South African War', *South African Historical Journal*, 35 (1996), pp. 159-60.

81 A. Gamble, *Britain in Decline: Economic policy, political strategy and the British state* (London, 1990), pp. 55-56.

82 Quoted in Robinson and Gallagher, *Africa and the Victorians*, p. 454.

83 Porter, 'South African War', p. 55; J.M. Mackenzie, *Propaganda and Empire: The Manipulation of British Public Opinion, 1880-1960* (Manchester, 1984), p. 2.

84 R. Ally, *Gold and Empire: The Bank of England and South Africa's Gold Producers, 1886-1926* (Johannesburg, 1994), pp. 24-25, 136-37; D. French, *British Economic and Strategic Planning 1905-1915* (London, 1982), p. 16.

85 P. Cain and A.G. Hopkins, *British Imperialism: Innovation and Expansion, 1688-1914* (London, 1993), p. 360.

86 P. Marsh, *The Discipline of Popular Government: Lord Salisbury's Domestic Statecraft, 1881-1902* (Hassocks, 1978), p. 273; Marsh, *Joseph Chamberlain: Entrepreneur in Politics* (New Haven and London, 1994), p. 420.

87 K. E. Wilburn, 'The climax of railway competition in South Africa, 1886-1899', D. Phil. diss. (University of Oxford, 1982), pp. 148-49; P. Kennedy, *The Realities Behind Diplomacy: Background Influences on British External Policy, 1865-1980* (London, 1981), p. 108.

88 Trapido, 'Settler Identities', p. 71.

89 Taylor, *From the Boer War to the Cold War: Essays on Twentieth-Century Europe* (Harmondsworth, 1996 edn.), p. 39.

90 Quoted in Marsh, *Joseph Chamberlain*, p. 472.

91 Marsh, *Joseph Chamberlain*, p. 471.

CHAPTER 3

92 *Het Zuid-Oosten*, 24 October 1899.

93 Keegan, *Colonial South Africa*, pp. 279-80; Trapido, 'Aspects in the Transition from Slavery to Serfdom: the South African Republic, 1842-1902', *Collected Seminar Papers on the Societies of Southern Africa in the 19th and 20th Centuries* (London University, 1976), pp. 26-28.

94 J.J. Oberholster and M.C.E. van Schoor, *President Steyn aan die Woord* (Bloemfontein, 1953), p. 19.

95 C. Duggan, *The Force of Destiny: A History of Italy since 1796* (London, 2008), pp. 383, 394.

96 M.A. Gronum, *Die Engelse Oorlog, 1899-1902*, vol. 1 (Cape Town, 1971), p. 46; G.J. Schutte, *De Boerenoolog na Honderd Jaar* (Amsterdam, 1997), pp. 25-26.

97 Memorandum, Sept. 1899, in *Smuts Papers*, vol. 1, p. 327.

98 D. Denoon, 'Participation in the "Boer War": People's War, People's Non-War, or Non-People's War', in *War and Society in Africa*, ed. B. A. Ogot (London, 1972), p. 110; Smuts to W.T. Stead, 4 Jan. 1902, in *Smuts Papers*, vol. 1, p. 484.

99 *Further Correspondence Relating to Affairs in South Africa*, Cd.547 (1901), p. 34.

100 D. Cammack, *The Rand at War, 1899-1902: The Witwatersrand and the Anglo-Boer War* (London, 1990), pp. 440-42.

101 Quoted in Smith, *South African War*, p. 368.

102 *Pall Mall Gazette*, Nov. 1898, p. 19.

103 For which, see S. Conway, *The War of American Independence, 1775-1783* (London, 1995), pp. 59-64.

104 M. Maubrey, Les Francais et la "veau d'or": la question sud-africaine (1896-1902)', in *La France et Afrique Du Sud*, ed. D. C. Bach (Paris, 1990), pp. 55-58.

105 As suggested, improbably, by R. B. Mulanax, *The Boer War in American Politics and Diplomacy* (New York, 1994), p. 219; G.D. Scholtz, 'Die Tweede Vryheidsoorlog in Wereldverband', *Historia*, 1/2 (1975), p. 141.

106 *Smuts: Memoirs*, p. 24.

107 S. Mahajan, 'The Defence of India and the End of Isolation: A Study in the Foreign Policy of the Conservative Government, 1900-1905', *Journal of Imperial and Commonwealth History*, 10/2 (1982), pp. 174-76.

108 *Ons Volk*, 7 August 1899; *Ons Land*, 13 September 1899.

109 Smuts to Stead, 4 Jan. 1902, in *Smuts Papers*, vol. 1, pp. 464-92.

110 Smuts to Executive Council, South African Republic, 4 Sept. 1899, in *Smuts Papers*, vol. 1, pp. 322-26.

111 J.H. Breytenbach, *Die Geskiedenis van die Tweede Vryheidsoorlog in Suid Afrika, 1899-1902*, vol. 1 (Pretoria, 1969), p. 157.

112 W. McElwee, *The Art of War: Waterloo to Mons* (London, 1974), p. 217.

113 Pakenham, *Boer War*, p. 42.

114 A. Niemann, *Pieter Marits: Lotgevallen van een Transvaalschen Boerenjongen* (Arnhem, 1885), pp. 82-130.

115 L. Kruger, 'The drama of country and city: tribalization, urbanization and theatre under apartheid', *Journal of Southern African Studies*, 23/4 (1997), p. 569.

116 D. Reitz, *Commando: A Boer Journal of the Boer War* (London, 1931), p. 26.

117 Memorandum, Sept. 1899, in *Smuts Papers*, vol. 1, pp. 322-26.

118 H. Bailes, 'Military aspects of the war', in Warwick, *South African War*, p. 70.

119 Breytenbach, *Geskiedenis*, pp. 77-90.

120 Bailes, 'Military aspects', p. 70; M. Glover, *Warfare from Waterloo to Mons* (London, 1980), p. 209.

121 R. Scales, 'Artillery in small wars: the evolution of British artillery doctrine, 1860-1914', Ph.D. diss. (Duke University, 1976), p. 219.

122 J. Malan, *Die Boere-offisiere van die Tweede Vryheidsoorlog, 1899-1902* (Pretoria, 1990).

123 J.W. Meijer, 'Die Vroeë Militêre Loopbaan van Generaal Ben Viljoen, 1896-1898', *Historia*, 39/2 (1994), pp. 50-51.

124 J. Keegan and A. Wheatcroft, *Who's Who in Military History from 1453 to the Present Day* (London, 1996), pp. 68-69.

125 McElwee, *Waterloo to Mons*, p. 233.

126 R. Sibbald, *The War Correspondents: The Boer War* (London, 1993), p. 22.

127 H. Strachan, *European Armies and the Conduct of War* (London, 1983), p. 77.

128 Sibbald, *Boer War*, p. 22.

129 Trebilcock, 'War and the failure of industrial mobilisation', p. 159.

130 *The Times History of the War in South Africa*, vol. 1 (1899-1900), ed. L. Amery (London, 1900), p. 371.

131 C.M. Bakkes, 'Die Kommandostelsel', in *Die Kultuurontplooing van die Afrikaner*, ed. P.G. Nel (Pretoria, 1949), pp. 64-68.

132 Schutte, *Boerenoorlog*, p. 40.

133 *Commandant Ludwig Krause*, p. 6.

134 B. Viljoen, *My Reminiscences of the Anglo-Boer War* (London, 1903), p. 309.

135 S. S. Swart, 'The rebels of 1914: masculinity, republicanism and the social forces that shaped the Boer rebellion', M.A. diss. (University of Natal, 1997), p. 39.

136 Keegan, *Rural Transformations*, p. 25.

137 J. Keegan, *Warpaths: Travels of a Military Historian in North America* (London, 1996), p. 34.

138 Nasson, 'Blacks who Backed the Boers: Republican Commando Auxiliaries in the Anglo-Boer or South African War, 1899-1902', in *Soldiers and Settlers in Africa, 1850-1918*, ed. S. M. Miller (Leiden, 2009), p.145.

139 F. Pretorius, *Kommandolewe tydens die Anglo-Boereoorlog, 1899-1902* (Cape Town, 1991), p. 316.

140 Warwick, *Black People*, p. 179.

141 A. Davidson and I. Filatova, *The Russians and the Anglo-Boer War, 1899-1902* (Cape Town, 1998), p. 63.

142 D. Judd, *Someone has Blundered: Casualties of the British Army in the Victorian Age* (London, 1973), p. 164.

143 *The Economist*, 15 September 1899; *The Spectator*, 19 August 1899; *Cape Argus*, 19 October 1899.

144 Quoted in H. Kochanski, 'Wolseley and the South African War', in *The Boer War: Direction, Experience and Image*, ed. J. Gooch (London, 2000), p. 57.

145 Marsh, *Lord Salisbury's Domestic Statecraft*, pp. 283-85.

146 George Wyndham to his mother, 6 Oct. 1899, in *Life and Letters of George Wyndham*, eds J.W. Mackail and G. Wyndham (London, 1926), p. 361; Gooch, 'The armed services', in *The First World War in British History*, eds. S. Constantine et. al. (London, 1995), p. 185; Bailes, 'Technology and imperialism: a case study of the Victorian Army in Africa', *Victorian Studies*, 24/1 (1980), p. 86.

147 *Hansard*, Fourth Series, vol. xi, Cols. 915-18, 8 May 1896.

148 *Justice*, 27 September 1899.

149 M. Yakutiel, 'Treasury control and the South African War, 1899-1905', D.Phil. diss. (University of Oxford, 1989), p. 23.

150 Col. C.G. Melville, *The Life of Sir Redvers Buller*, vol. 1 (London, 1923), pp. 2-4.

151 P. Dudgin, *Military Intelligence: The British Story* (London, 1989), p. 32.

152 Quoted in D. Steele, 'Salisbury and the Soldiers', in Gooch, *Boer War*, p.16.

153 K. Surridge, '"All you soldiers are what we call pro-Boer": the military critique of the South African War, 1899-1902', *History*, 82/268 (1997), pp. 588-89.

154 K. Booth, *Strategy and Ethnocentrism* (London, 1979), p. 33; W.S. Hamer, *The British Army: Civil-Military Relations, 1885-1905* (Oxford, 1970), p. 175.

155 Hamer, *British Army*, p. 176.

156 A. H. Page, 'The supply services of the British Army in the South African War, 1899-1902', D.Phil. diss. (University of Oxford, 1976), p. 239.

157 J. Haswell, *British Military Intelligence* (London, 1973), pp. 48-50; Dudgin, *Military Intelligence*, pp. 31-33.

158 T. G. Fergusson, 'The development of a modern intelligence organization: British military intelligence, 1870-1914', Ph.D. diss. (Duke University, 1981), p. 203.

159 I.F.W. Beckett, *The Amateur Military Tradition, 1558-1945* (Manchester, 1991), p. 200.

160 E. Spiers, 'The Late Victorian Army, 1868-1914', in *The Oxford Illustrated History of the British Army*, ed. D. Chandler (Oxford, 1994), p. 193.

161 Beckett, *The Victorians At War* (London, 2006), p. 216.

162 Bailes, 'Technology and Tactics in the British Army, 1866-1900', in *Men, Machines and War*, eds. R. Haycock and K. Nelson (Toronto, 1988), p. 42.

CHAPTER 4

163 Breytenbach, *Tweede Vryheidsoorlog*, pp. 387-90.

164 J. Lambert, *Betrayed Trust: Africans and the State in Colonial Natal* (Pietermaritzburg, 1995), p. 160.

165 *Cape Argus*, 6 November 1899.

166 G. Blaxland, *The Middlesex Regiment* (London, 1977), p. 55.

167 Beckett, 'Buller and the Politics of Command', in Gooch, *Boer War*, p. 47.

168 *Commandant Ludwig Krause*, p. 21.

169 Scales, 'British artillery doctrine', p. 219.

170 *Commandant Ludwig Krause*, p. 21.

171 Keegan and Wheatcroft, *Military History*, p. 106.

172 L. Cooper, *British Regular Cavalry, 1644-1914* (London, 1965), p. 193; G. Powell, *The Green Howards* (London, 1968), p. 72.

173 *Popular Imperialism and the Military, 1850-1950*, ed. J. Mackenzie (Manchester, 1992), p. 20.

174 J. Laffin, *Scotland the Brave: The Story of the Scottish Soldier* (London, 1963), pp. 36-37.

175 *Commandant Ludwig Krause*, p. 31; Pretorius, 'Afrikaner nationalism and the Burgher on Commando', in *Writing a Wider War: Rethinking Gender, Race and Identity in the South African War, 1899-1902*, eds. G. Cuthbertson, A. Grundlingh, and M-L. Suttie (Athens, OH, 2002), p. 77.

176 J. Meintjies, *Anglo-Boer War*, p. 45.

177 Warwick, *Black People*, p. 131.

178 *Commandant Ludwig Krause*, p. 31.

179 M. Langley, *The East Surrey Regiment* (London, 1976), p. 47.

180 B. Willan, 'The Siege of Mafeking', in Warwick, *South African War*, p. 141.

181 *Edward Ross, Diary of the Siege of Mafeking, October 1899 to May 1900*, ed. Willan, p. 50.

182 Quoted in Sibbald, *War Correspondents*, pp. 144-45.

183 M. Parris, *Warrior Nation: Images of War in British Popular Culture, 1850-2000* (London, 2000), p. 104.

184 Judd and Surridge, *The Boer War* (London, 2002), p. 156.

185 *The War Diary of Burgher Jack Lane, 1899-1900*, ed. W. Lane (Cape Town, 2001), p. 68.

186 Sibbald, *War Correspondents*, p. 117.

187 Sibbald, *War Correspondents*, p. 114.

188 *South African News*, 26 February 1900.

189 Pakenham, 'The Anglo-Boer War, 1899-1902', in Spies and Cameron, *Illustrated History*, p. 204.

190 I. Hofmeyr, *We Spend our Years as a Tale that is Told: Oral Historical Narrative in a South African Chiefdom* (Johannesburg, 1993), pp. 109-11.

191 Warwick, *Black People*, p. 116.

192 Nasson, *Abraham Esau's War*, pp. 113-17.

193 Quoted in Nasson, 'Black Communities in Natal and the Cape', in *The Impact of the South African War*, eds. D. Omissi and A. Thompson (London, 2002), p. 53.

194 B. Lugan, *La guerre des Boers, 1899-1902* (Paris, 1998), p. 148.

195 A. Barker, *Battle Honours of the British and Commonwealth Armies* (London, 1986), pp. 92-93.

196 C.J. Barnard, *Generaal Louis Botha op die Natalse Front, 1899-1900* (Kaapstad, 1970), pp. 29-30.

197 Bailes, 'Military aspects', p. 72.

198 *Jan Smuts: Memoirs*, p. 69; J. van Loggerenberg, 'Schalk Willem Burger as Boeregeneraal', *Historia*, 37/1 (1992), p. 43.

199 Pretorius, 'Die Voorsiening van Lewensmiddele aan die Boerkommando's in die Anglo-Boereoorlog, 1899-1902', *Historia*, 35/2 (1990), p. 100.

200 Field Marshal Lord Carver. *The Seven Ages of the British Army* (London, 1984), p. 150.

CHAPTER 5

201 *Ons Land*, 26 October 1899; *Het Zuid-Oosten*, 30 October 1899; *Natal Witness*, 8 November 1899.

202 Glover, *Waterloo to Mons*, p. 208.

203 Quoted in Fergusson, 'British military intelligence, 1870-1914', p. 334.

204 J.M. Grierson, *Scarlet into Khaki: The British Army on the Eve of the Boer War* (London, 1899).

205 *Rifle Brigade Chronicle* (1900), p. 86.

206 Bailes, 'Military aspects of the war', in Warwick, *South African War*, p. 76.

207 Pakenham, *Boer War*, p. 161; B. Farwell, *Eminent Victorian Soldiers* (Harmondsworth, 1986), p. 166.

208 Keegan and Wheatcroft, *Military History*, p. 43; R.J.J. Hills, *The Royal Dragoons* (London, 1972), p. 68.

209 M. Barthrop, *The Northamptonshire Regiment* (London, 1974), pp. 54-55.

210 *Household Brigade Magazine*, 51/3 (1902), p. 115.

211 A.J. Barker, *The West Yorkshire Regiment* (London, 1974), p. 43.

212 H. Wood, *The King's Royal Rifle Corps* (London, 1967), pp. 79-80.

213 N. F. Dixon, *On the Psychology of Military Incompetence* (London, 1979), p. 59.

214 *Cape Mercury*, 23 December 1899.

215 *Rifle Brigade Chronicle* (1901), p. 185.

216 L.B. Oatts, *The Highland Light Infantry* (London, 1969), p. 67.

217 J.M. Brereton, *The British Soldier: A Social History* (London, 1986), p. 103.

218 Wood, *Rifle Corps*, p. 69.

219 H.J.C. Pieterse, *My Tweede Vryheidstryd* (Kaapstad, 1945).

220 Scales, 'British artillery doctrine', p. 211.

221 *St George's Gazette*, 19/203 (1900), p. 29.

222 Quoted in K. Jeffery, 'The Irish Soldier in the Boer War', in Gooch, *Boer War*, p. 143.

223 *Cape Argus*, 24 December 1899.

224 Quoted in Bailes, 'Military aspects', p. 84.

225 Quoted in Pakenham, *Boer War*, p. 244.

226 Hamer, *British Army*, p. 177.

227 Pakenham, *Boer War*, pp. 457-58.

228 R.J.Q. Adams, 'Field-Marshal Lord Roberts: army and empire', in *Edwardian Conservatism: Five Studies in Adaptation* (New York, 1988), pp. 53-54.

229 *Official British History of the War in South Africa, 1899-1902*, eds. Maj.-Gen. Sir F. Maurice and M.H. Grant (London, 1906), vol. 1, p. 282.

230 Beckett, 'Politics of Command', pp.53-54.

231 *Light Bob Gazette*, 2/9 (1901), p. 25.

232 Nasson, 'Spioenkop, 1900', in M. Rayner (ed.), *Battlefields: Exploring the Arenas of War, 1805 – 1945* (London, 2006), pp. 86-91.

233 G. Blaxland, *The Middlesex Regiment* (London, 1977), p. 67; A. Barker, *Battle Honours of the British and Commonwealth Armies* (London, 1986), p. 94.

234 Nasson, 'Black Communities in Natal and the Cape', in *The Impact of the South African War*, eds. D. Omissi and A. Thompson (London, 2002), p. 45.

235 *Oxfordshire Light Infantry Chronicle* (1900), p. 91.

236 *Commandant Ludwig Krause, 1899-1900*, pp. 58-59.

237 J. Beaumont, '*The Times* at War, 1899-1902', in *The South African War Reappraised*, ed. D. Lowry (Manchester, 2000), p.74.

CHAPTER 6

238 L. Scholtz, *Waarom die Boere die Oorlog Verloor Het* (Pretoria, 1999), p. 107.

239 Breytenbach, *Tweede Vryheidsoorlog*, vol. 1, p. 466.

240 Beaumont, 'The British press and censorship during the South African War, 1899-1902', *Rethinking the South African War* conference paper, UNISA, 1998.

241 Judd and Surridge, *Boer War*, p. 172.

242 *The Guardian*, 10 March 1900.

243 Lee, *Bitter End*, pp. 61-62.

244 R.J. Moore-Colyer, 'Horse supply and the British cavalry: a review, 1066-1900', *Journal of the Society of Army Historical Research*, 70/284 (1992), pp. 259-60; S.R. Badsey, 'Fire and sword: the British army and the *arme blanche* controversy, 1871-1921', Ph.D. diss. (University of Cambridge, 1981), p. 135.

245 S. Swart, *Riding High: Horses, Humans and History in South Africa*, (Johannesburg, 2010), Chapter 5.

246 G. Crew, *The Royal Army Service Corps* (London, 1970), pp. 90-93.

247 *Highland Light Infantry Chronicle*, 2/14 (1900), pp.368-69.

248 Farwell, *Victorian Soldiers*, p. 335.

249 A. Wessels, 'Afrikaners at War', in Gooch, *Boer War*, p. 101.

250 H. Bradford, 'Gentlemen and Boers: Afrikaner Nationalism, Gender and Colonial Warfare in the South African War', in *Wider War*, p. 45.

251 Badsey, 'Fire and sword', pp. 78-79; Glover, *Waterloo to Mons*, p. 207.

252 *Het Zuid-Oosten*, 22 February 1900.

253 Bradford, 'Gentlemen and Boers', p.46.

254 *Smuts Memoirs*, p. 39.

255 R.W. Schikkerling, *Commando Courageous* (Johannesburg, 1964), p. 66; Pretorius, 'Afrikaner Nationalism and the Burgher on commando', in *Wider War*, pp. 68-70.

256 Wessels, 'Afrikaners at War', p.86.

257 *Lloyds Weekly Newspaper*, 17 March 1900.

258 *Cape Daily Telegraph*, 7 May 1900; *Green Howards Gazette*, 89/8 (1900), p. 63.

259 Lowry, '"The Boers were the beginning of the end?": The Wider Impact of the South African War', in *War Reappraised*, p. 204.

260 S.F. Malan, 'Die Britse Besetting van Bloemfontein, 13 Maart 1900', *Historia*, 1/1 (1975), pp.41-42; Badsey, 'War Correspondents in the Boer War', in Gooch, *Boer War*, pp. 196-97.

261 Lt.-Col. J.H. Plumridge, *Hospital Ships and Ambulance Trains* (London, 1975), pp. 90-91.

262 *African Review*, 23/387 (1900), pp. 96-98.

263 Cammack, *Rand at War*, p. 102.

264 R.L.V. ffrench-Blake, *The 17th/21st Lancers* (London, 1968), p. 97.

265 *Smuts: Memoirs*, p.45.

266 *Oakleaf*, 1/8 (1900), p. 26.

267 Pakenham, *Boer War*, pp. 381-83; Lee, *Bitter End*, pp. 109-13.

268 Searle, '"National Efficiency" and the "Lessons" of the War', in Omissi and Thompson, *South African War*, p. 207.

269 *Lloyds Weekly Newspaper*, 21 May 1900.

270 A. Lynch, *My Life Story* (London, 1924), p. 194.

271 Cammack, *Rand at War*, p. 107.

272 *Cape Times*, 12 Aug. 1900.

273 Quoted in Nasson, *Abraham Esau*, p. 33.

274 Pakenham, *Boer War*, p. 428.

275 Quoted in Pakenham, *Boer War*, p. 428.

276 D.H. Doolittle, *A Soldier's Hero: General Sir Archibald Hunter* (Rhode Island, 1991), p. 229.

CHAPTER 7

277 *Smuts Memoirs*, pp. 39-41.

278 M.E. Jooste, 'De Boeren hadden Radio-Beheer voor hul Kanonnen', *Historia*, 28/1 (1983), pp. 108-10.

279 *Smuts Memoirs*, pp. 43-44; Breytenbach, *Tweede Vryheidsoorlog*, vol. 5, pp. 298-99.

280 Pretorius, 'Afrikaner Nationalism', in *Wider War*, p. 68.

281 *Smuts: Memoirs*, p. 41; *Commandant Ludwig Krause*, p. 81.

282 Grundlingh, 'Collaborators in Boer society', in Warwick, *South African War*, pp. 258-59.

283 De Wet, *War*, p. 158.

284 R.L. Wallace, *The Australians at the Boer War* (Canberra, 1976), pp. 213-14.

285 De Wet, *War*, p. 164.

286 Bailes, 'Military Aspects', p. 95; F. Myatt, *The British Infantry, 1660-1945*, (Poole, 1983), p. 157.

287 G. van den Bergh, 'The Three British Occupations of Potchefstroom during the Anglo-Boer War 1899-1902', *Scientia Militaria*, 37/1 (2009), p. 101.

288 S.M. Miller, *Lord Methuen and the British Army: Failure and Redemption in South Africa* (London, 1999), p. 206.

289 *Globe and Laurel*, 59/8 (1900), p. 119.

290 *Navy and Army Gazette*, 5 November 1900.

291 Quoted in Pretorius, 'Afrikaner Nationalism', in *Wider War*, p. 79.

292 *Cape Mercury*, 19 October 1901.

293 *Naval and Military Record*, 16 November 1900.

294 Capt. F.P. Fletcher-Vane, *The War One Year After* (Cape Town, 1903), pp. 5-8.

295 Wessels, 'Afrikaners at War', in Gooch, *Boer War*, p. 75.

296 Scholtz, 'Die Strategiese Oogmerke van Genl. C.R. de Wet tydens die Eerste Dryfjag, Juli-Augustus 1900', *Historia*, 22/1 (1977), p. 14.

297 *Smuts: Memoirs*, p. 132.

298 Quoted in Pakenham, *Boer War*, p. 485.

299 *Suffolk Gazette*, 131 (1900), p. 44.

300 P.W. Vorster, 'Generaal J.B.M. Hertzog as Kampvegter vir die Kaapse Rebelle, 1902-1903', *Historia*, 39/2 (1990), p. 116.

301 P. Bateman, *Generals of the Anglo-Boer War* (Cape Town, 1977), p. 14.

302 Nasson, 'Black Communities in Natal and the Cape', p. 42.

303 D. M. Moore, *General Louis Botha's Second Expedition to Natal* (Cape Town, 1979), pp. 96-101.

304 *Oakleaf*, 8/7 (1900), p. 39.

305 Pretorius, *The Great Escape of the Boer Pimpernel, Christiaan de Wet: The Making of a Legend* (Pietermaritzburg, 2001), p. 52; Pretorius, 'Die Eerste Dryfjag op Generaal C.R. de Wet', *Historia*, 17/3 (1972), pp. 201-202; Scholtz, *Generaal Christiaan de Wet as Veldheer* (Pretoria, 2003), p. 245.

306 *Cape Daily Telegraph*, 8 January 1901.

307 Grundlingh, 'Collaborators', p. 263.

308 Pakenham, *Boer War*, pp. 489-91.

309 Beaumont, 'The Making of a War Correspondent: Lionel James of *The Times*', in Lowry, *South African War*, p. 131.

310 Grundlingh, 'Collaborators', p. 264.

311 Stone, *World War One*, p. 130.

312 Pretorius, 'Afrikaner Nationalism', in *Wider War*, p. 71.

313 Dietlof van Warmelo, *On Commando* (Johannesburg, 1977), p. 122.

314 Grundlingh, 'Probing the prophet: the psychology and politics of the Siener van Rensburg phenomenon', *South African Historical Journal*, 34 (1996), pp. 226, 231-32; A.
Snyman, *Siener van Rensburg: Boodskapper van God* (Mosselbaai, 1995), pp. 49-66.

315 Miller, *Lord Methuen*, p. 222.

316 Scholtz, 'Die Slag van Tweebosch, 7 Maart 1902', *Historia*, 24/2 (1979), pp. 53-55.

317 Pretorius, *Op Kommando: Die Lewe in die Veld tydens die Anglo-Boereoorlog* (Pretoria,
2001), p. 73.

CHAPTER 8

318 Quoted in Spies, *Methods of Barbarism?*, p. 237.

319 Fergusson, *British Military Intelligence*, p. 161.

320 J. Keegan and R. Holmes, *Soldiers: A History of Men in Battle* (London, 1985), p. 243;
C. Townshend, *Britain's Civil Wars: Counterinsurgency in the Twentieth Century* (London, 1986), p. 183.

321 Nasson, 'The War for South Africa', in *New History of South Africa*, eds. H. Giliomee and B. Mbenga (Cape Town, 2007), p. 215.

322 C.A.R. Schulenberg, 'Boerekrygsgevangenes van Bermuda', *Historia*, 23/2 (1978),
pp. 83-85.

323 H. Schulze, 'The Boer Prisoners of War in Ceylon and the "Great and Grand Old
Manly Game of Cricket"', in *Empire & Cricket: The South African Experience, 1884-
1914*, eds. B. Murray & G. Vahed (Pretoria, 2009), p. 194.

324 *Globe and Laurel*, 75/8 (1902), p. 74.

325 Quoted in Grundlingh, 'Collaborators' in Boer society', p. 268.

326 Wessels, 'Afrikaners at War', p. 100.

327 J.D. Kestell and D.E. van Velden, *The Peace Negotiations* (London, 1912), pp. 94,
179-82, 195-96.

328 Grundlingh, 'Collaborators', esp. pp. 272-75.

329 K. Macksey, *Technology and War* (London, 1986), p. 46.

330 O.J.O. Ferreira, *Memoirs of General Ben Bouwer* (Pretoria, 1980), p. 95.

331 Archives of the Royal Sussex Regiment, du Moulin Papers, RSR Mss. 1/101, Journal
entry, 15 Dec. 1901.

332 A. Kramer, *Dynamic of Destruction: Culture and Mass Killing in the First World War*
(Oxford, 2007), p.12.

333 West Yorkshire Regimental Museum, Cayley Journals, entry for 27 August 1900;
Spies, 'Women and the War', in Warwick, *South African War*, p. 165.

334 M.A. Gronum, *Die Bittereinders, Junie 1901-Mei 1902* (Kaapstad, 1974).

335 *Morning Post*, 15 January 1902.

336 *The Times*, 18 June 1901.

337 Paula Krebs, '"Last of the Gentlemen's Wars": Women in the Boer War Concentration Camp Controversy', *History Workshop Journal*, 33 (1992), p. 45.

338 L. Stanley, *Mourning Becomes. . .Post/memory, commemoration and the concentration camps of the South African War* (Manchester, 2006), p. 6.

339 *Naval and Military Record*, 11 May 1901.

340 Quoted in Spies, 'Women and the war', p. 168.

341 F.A. van Jaarsveld and F.J. Pretorius, 'Tussen Lewe en Dood: Briewe uit die Bloemfonteinse "Refugee Kamp", 1901-1902', *Historia*, 28/1 (1983), p. 57.

342 Stanley, *Mourning Becomes*, p.77.

343 Quoted in N.O. Goulart, 'Back bencher against war: a rhetorical analysis of the parliamentary speaking of David Lloyd George during the Boer War', Ph.D. diss. (Indiana University, 1982), p. 230; Malcolm MacColl, *Memoirs and Correspondence* (London, 1914), pp. 230-31.

344 Pretorius, 'Reflection', in *Scorched Earth*, ed. Pretorius (Cape Town, 2001), p. 278.

345 P. Zietsman, 'The concentration camps schools – beacons of light in the darkness', in *Scorched Earth*, p.107; Stanley and H. Dampier, 'The Number of the South African War (1899-1902) Concentration Camp Dead: Standard Stories, Superior Stories and a Forgotten Proto-Nationalist Research Investigation', *Sociological Research Online*, 14/5 (2009).

346 L.M. Brady, 'The Wilderness of War: Nature and Strategy in the American Civil War', *Environmental History*, 10/3 (2005), pp. 16-17.

347 Searle, *New England*, p. 281.

348 Pretorius, 'The fate of the Boer women and children', in *Scorched Earth*, p. 44.

349 Castle Museum, York, Records of the Friends South African Relief Fund, memo of committee meeting, 12 May 1902.

350 Bradford, 'Gentlemen and Boers', p. 58.

351 B. Fetter and S. Kessler, 'Scars from a childhood disease: measles in the concentration camps during the Boer War', *Social Science History*, 20/4 (1996), pp. 596-601; Spies, 'Women and the war', pp. 169-71; E. van Heyningen, 'Women and Disease: The Clash of Medical Cultures in the Concentration Camps of the South African War', in *Wider War*, p.196.

352 Kestell and Van Velden, *Peace Negotiations*, p. 175.

353 Kestell and Van Velden, *Peace Negotiations*, p. 85.

354 Nasson, *Abraham Esau's War*, pp. 120-41.

355 M. Legassick, 'The battle of Naroegas: context, historiography, sources and significance', *Kronos: Journal of Cape History*, 21 (1994), pp. 32-60.

356 J. Krikler, *Revolution from Above, Rebellion from Below: The Agrarian Transvaal at the Turn of the Century* (Oxford, 1993).

357 *Household Brigade Magazine*, 49/5 (1902), p. 43; *Oxfordshire Light Infantry Chronicle* (1902), p. 166; Beckett, *Johnnie Gough*, V.C. (London, 1989), p. 82.

358 Townshend, *Britain's Civil Wars*, p. 185.

359 Smuts, *Memoirs*, p.186.

360 Reitz, *Commando*, p. 320.

361 R. Constantine, 'The guerrilla war in the Cape Colony during the South African War of 1899-1902: a case study of the republican and rebel commando movement', M.A. diss. (University of Cape Town, 1996), p. 23.

362 Searle, *New England*, p. 288.

363 Bodleian Library, Oxford, Milner Papers, MP IV/B/221/fols.172-6, Milner to Dawkins, 16 Jan. 1902.

364 *Smuts Papers*, vol. 1, pp. 151-52.

365 Kestell and Van Velden, *Peace Negotiations*, pp. 185-86.

366 Kestell and Van Velden, *Peace Negotiations*, pp. 188-89.

367 G. Arthur, *The Life of Lord Kitchener* (London, 1920), vol. 2, p. 93.

368 Surridge, 'The Politics of War: Lord Kitchener and the Settlement of the South African War, 1901-1902', in *Wider War*, p. 226.

369 Judd and Surridge, *Boer War*, p. 270.

370 Pretorius, 'Waarom het die "Bittereinders" Gedurende die Anglo-Boereoorlog van 1899-1902 op Kommando Gebly?', *Historia*, 35/1 (1990), p. 72.

371 Le May, *British Supremacy*, p. 154.

372 Quoted in L. Thompson, *The Unification of South Africa, 1902-1910* (Oxford, 1960), pp. 30-32.

373 Quoted in Le May, *British Supremacy*, p. 112.

374 A. W. Marx, *Making Race and Nation: A Comparison of the United States, South Africa, and Brazil* (Cambridge, 1998), p. 90.

CHAPTER 9

375 G.R. Wilkinson, '"The Blessings of War": the Depiction of Military Force in Edwardian Newspapers', *Journal of Contemporary History*, 33/1 (1998), pp. 98-104.

376 Hobson, *The Psychology of Jingoism* (London, 1901), pp. 17-19, 31-40; Pick, *War Machine*, pp. 111-13.

377 *Clarion*, 1 September 1900.

378 R. Price, *An Imperial War and the British Working Class: Working Class Reactions to the Boer War: 1899-1902* (London, 1972), pp. 132-77; H. Pelling, *Popular Politics and Society in Late-Victorian Britain* (London, 1968), pp. 82-100; R. McKibbin, *The Ideologies of Class: Social Relations in Britain, 1880-1950* (Oxford, 1991), pp. 23-24.

379 B. Porter, *The Absent-Minded Imperialists: Empire, Society, and Culture in Britain* (Oxford, 2004), pp. 310-11.

380 J. Grigg, 'Lloyd George and the Boer War', in *Edwardian Radicalism, 1900-1914*, ed. A.J.A. Morris (London, 1974), p. 13.

381 Price, *Imperial War*, p. 131.

382 Wilkinson, '"To the Front": British Newspaper Advertising and the Boer War', in Gooch, *Boer War*, p. 210.

383 Price, 'Society, status and jingoism: the social roots of lower middle class patriotism, 1870-1900', in *The Lower Middle Class in Britain, 1870-1914*, ed. G. Crossick (London, 1977), pp. 89-112.

384 Sibbald, *War Correspondents*, p. 177.
385 M.D. Blanch, 'British society and the war', in Warwick, *South African* War, p. 226.
386 Blanch, 'British society and the war', pp. 225-29; *Ladysmith Lyre*, 5 December 1899.
387 Wilkinson, 'Newspaper Advertising', p.206.
388 H. Cunningham, 'The Language of Patriotism, 1750-1914', *History Workshop Journal*, 12 (1981), p. 27.
389 J. Mackenzie, *Propaganda and Empire: The Manipulation of British Public Opinion, 1880-1960* (Manchester, 1984), p. 2.
390 Cuthbertson, 'Pricking the "nonconformist conscience": religion against the South African War', in Lowry, *South African War*, p. 180; 'Preaching Imperialism: Wesleyan Methodism and the War', in Omissi and Thompson, *South African War*, pp. 160-62.
391 *Quarterly Review*, 195 (1902), p. 523.
392 *Quarterly Review*, 193 (1901), p. 239.
393 *Under the Union Jack*, 28 December 1899.
394 B. R. Penny, 'Australia's reactions to the Boer War: a study in colonial imperialism', *Journal of British Studies*, 7/1 (1967), p. 103.
395 *Black and White Budget*, 4/60 (1900); C. E. M. Rolleston *On Yeoman Service*, (London, 1901), p. 58; National Army Museum (NAM), 5603/10/7, Col. H.F.N. Jourdain, Boer War Diary 1901-1902, entry for 29 October 1901.
396 Quoted in A. Roberts, 'They Brought it on Themselves', *The Spectator*, 2 October 1999.
397 J. Buchan, *The African Colony: Studies in the Reconstruction* (Edinburgh, 1903), p. 78; *The New Penny Magazine*, 2/132 (1901), p. 161; Spies, 'Women', p. 171.
398 E. M. Spiers, 'The Use of the Dum-Dum Bullet in Colonial Warfare', *Journal of Imperial and Commonwealth History*, 4/1 (1975), pp. 3-14.
399 *Pearson's War Pictures*, 31 April 1900.
400 *Lloyds Weekly Newspaper*, 25 March 1900.
401 *Oakleaf*, 8/5 (1900), p. 134.
402 *Justice*, 20 July 1901.
403 *Commandant Ludwig Krause, 1899-1900*, p. 16.
404 *Black and White Budget*, 4/59 (1900), p. 232.
405 L. Curtis, *With Milner in South Africa* (Oxford, 1951 ed.), p. 16.
406 E. Belfield, *The Boer War* (London, 1975), p. xxiv.
407 Dichmont Mss., The Boer War Letters and Diary of Alan Frederick Corbett, Corbett to his mother, 25 December 1900.
408 *Times History*, p. 138.
409 R.S.S. Baden-Powell, *The Downfall of Prempeh: A Diary of life with the Native Levy in Ashanti, 1895-96* (London, 1898), p. 177.
410 Quoted in C. Barnett, *Britain and Her Army, 1509-1970* (London, 1970), pp. 171-72.
411 Sir Henry Howorth, 'Our Indian Troops', *Nineteenth Century*, 47 (1900), p. 37; S. Akita, 'The Second Anglo-Boer War and India', *Journal of Osaka University of Foreign Studies*, 8 (1993), p. 122.

412 *The Ladysmith Lyre*, 27 November 1899.

413 NAM, 7208/8, Paterson Letters, Cpl. J. Paterson to his brother, 17 April 1900; *The Statist*, 27 April 1901, p. 762.

414 *Black and White Budget ('Transvaal Special, No. 2')*, November 1900, p. 27.

415 Quoted in Nasson, *Abraham Esau*, p. 99.

416 Castle Museum, York, The Wharfedale Yeomanry, 1901-2, mss. typescript.

417 H.W. Wilson, *With the Flag to Pretoria* (London, 1901), p. 459.

418 NAM, 7305/82, Craig-Brown Diary, 1900-1901, entry for 21 February 1900; *Black and White Budget*, 2/25 (1900), p. 31.

419 Charles James O'Mahony, *A Peep over the Barleycorn* (Dublin, 1911), pp. 191-93; Archives of the West Yorkshire Regiment, 78/1, Lothian Nicholson Diaries, Lnt. A.H. Lothian Nicholson, entry for 22 March 1900.

420 Quoted in Lowry, 'Wider Impact', in Lowry, *South African War*, p. 205.

421 *Morning Leader*, 22 June 1900.

422 A.M.S. Methuen, *Peace or War in South Africa* (London, 1899), p. 140; P. Kaarsholm, 'Pro-Boerism and romantic anti-capitalism on the European continent during the South African War', in *Patriotism: The Making and Unmaking of British National Identity*, ed. Raphael Samuel (London, 1989), vol. 1, p. 113.

423 *De Graaf-Reinetter*, 23 November 1900.

424 Van Warmelo, *Commando*, pp. 115-24.

425 *Commandant Ludwig Krause*, p. 16.

426 *Under the Union Jack*, 1/7 (1899), p. 162.

427 Quoted in Judd and Surridge, *Boer War*, p.12.

428 Archives of the West Yorkshire Regiment, 2nd Battn. Journal, mss. typescript.

429 Royal Sussex Regiment Archives (RSR), Mss. 1/116, Battalion punishment books, vol. 3 (1901).

430 RSR, 1/119, Bidder letterbooks, vol. 5, letter encl. 2 November 1901; J. Selby, *The Boer War: A Study in Cowardice and Courage* (London, 1969), p. 217.

431 Dichmont Mss., The Boer War Diary and Letters of Alan Frederick Corbett, Corbett to his mother, 27 February 1901.

432 *Bugle*, 19/4 (1900), p. 18.

433 Quoted in Spies, *Methods of Barbarism?*, p. 235.

434 Nasson, 'Tommy Atkins in South Africa', in Warwick, *South African War*, p. 133.

435 Captain F.P. Fletcher-Vane, *The War One Year After* (Cape Town, 1903), p. 7.

436 Bradford, 'Gentlemen and Boers', in *Wider War*, pp. 37-66.

437 *All the World*, January 1902, pp. 113-14; Nasson, 'Tommy Atkins', p. 133.

438 A. Davidson and I. Filatova, *The Russians and the Anglo-Boer War* (Cape Town, 1998), pp.51-52.

439 Miller, *Lord Methuen*, p. 221.

440 Dichmont Mss., The Boer War Letters and Diary of Alan Frederick Corbett, Corbett to his mother, 25 December 1900.

441 Surridge, ' "All you soldiers are what we call pro-Boer" ', p. 599.

442 J. Lee, 'Sir Ian Hamilton After the War: A Liberal General Reflects', in *Facing Armageddon: The First World War Experienced*, eds H. Cecil and P. H. Liddle (London, 1996), pp. 880-81.

443 Pakenham, *Boer War*, p. 534.

444 Keegan, *Warpaths*, p. 310.

CHAPTER 10

445 I. Hofmeyr, 'Building a nation from words: Afrikaans language, literature and ethnic identity, 1902-1924', in *The Politics of Race, Class & Nationalism in Twentieth Century South Africa*, eds. Marks and Trapido, p. 109.

446 Grundlingh, 'The National Women's Monument: The Making and Mutation of Meaning in Afrikaner Memory of the South African War,' in *Wider War*, p.19.

447 D. Moodie, *The Rise of Afrikanerdom: Power, Apartheid and the Afrikaner Civil Religion* (Los Angeles, 1975), p. 17.

448 Nasson, 'Race and Civilisation in the Anglo-Boer War of 1899-1902', M.A. diss. (University of York, 1977), pp. 44-50.

449 Grundlingh, 'War, wordsmiths and the "Volk": Afrikaans historical writing on the Anglo-Boer war of 1899-1902 and the war in Afrikaner historical consciousness, 1902-1990', in *Mfecane to Boer War*, eds. E. Lehmann and F. Reckwitz (Essen, 1992), p. 52.

450 Grundlingh, 'War, wordsmiths', pp. 45-46; also Hofmeyr, 'Popularizing History: The Case of Gustav Preller', in *Regions and Repertoires: Topics in South African Politics and Culture*, ed. S. Clingman (Johannesburg, 1991), p. 67.

451 Grundlingh, 'War, wordsmiths', p. 48; Grundlingh 'Politics, principles and problems of a profession: Afrikaner historians and their discipline, c.1920-c.1965', *Perspectives in Education*, 12/1 (1990/91), pp. 6-14.

452 Grundlingh, 'The War in Twentieth-Century Afrikaner Consciousness', in *South African War*, p.29.

453 Grundlingh, '"Are We Afrikaners Getting Too Rich ?" Cornucopia and Change in Afrikanerdom in the 1960s', *Journal of Historical Sociology*, 21/2-3 (2008), p.146.

454 Stanley, *Mourning*, p.7.

455 Stanley, *Mourning*, p.164.

456 Grundlingh & S. Swart, *Radelose Rebellie ? Dinamika van die 1914-1915 Afrikanerrebellie* (Pretoria, 2009), pp. 48-51.

457 *Cape Argus*, 26 March 1947.

458 *Die Burger*, 21 March 1995.

459 *Cape Times*, 21 March 1995.

460 *Cape Times*, 18 March 1995.

461 *Cape Argus*, 8 March 1995.

462 Judge Albie Sachs, cited in Grundlingh, 'War, wordsmiths', p. 54.

463 *Cape Argus*, 1 October 1996; Grundlingh, 'Reflecting Remembrance: The Politics of the Centenary Commemoration of the South African War of 1899-1902', *Journal of Southern African Studies*, 30/2 (2004), p. 359.

464 *Cape Times*, 26 September 1996.

465 *Cape Times*, 8 December 1997.

466 *The Weekly Mail and Guardian*, 15-21 October 1999.

467 *Sunday Times*, 11 October 1999.

468 *Cape Times*, 3 August 1999.

469 *Beeld*, 12 February 1993.

470 *Die Burger*, 17 December 1993; *Rapport*, 20 December 1993.

471 *Die Burger*, 1 March 1995.

472 *Sunday Times*, 5, 19 April 1998.

473 *Sunday Independent*, 31 December 1995.

474 *Weekly Mail*, 16-22 October 1992.

475 *Sunday Times*, 5, 19 April 1998; *Rapport*, 12 April 1996.

476 *Rapport*, 12 April 1998; *Beeld*, 26 April 1998; *Die Burger*, 7 May 1999.

477 *Rapport*, 12 April 1998.

478 *Sunday Independent*, 31 December 1995.

479 J. van Rooyen, *Hard Right: The New White Power in South Africa* (London, 1995), p. 43.

480 *Patriot*, 5 April, 7 June 1991; *House of Assembly Debates*, col.106, 6 February 1990.

481 *Cape Times*, 19 February 1997.

482 *Sunday Times*, 10 October 1999.

483 Grundlingh, 'Afrikaner Consciousness', in *South African War*, p.35.

484 *Cape Times*, 11 October 1899.

485 *Beeld*, 11 November 1999.

486 *Die Volksblad*, 3 November 1999.

487 *What Might Have Been: Imaginary History from Twelve Leading Historians*, ed. A. Roberts (London, 2004), p. 7.

488 *The Week*, 6 February 2010.

489 *Die Burger*, 9 October 1999.

490 *The Citizen*, 24 September 1999.

491 *Rapport*, 10 October 1999; *Beeld*, 12 October 1999; *Cape Times*, 15 October 1999.

492 *Sunday Times*, 16 October 1999; M. Xulu, *International Conference on the Participation of Blacks in the Anglo-Boer War*: Paper Call and Communique, Department of Arts, Culture, Science and Technology, Pretoria, 25 January 2000.

493 Grundlingh, quoted in L. Vergnani, 'Scholars Unearth Evidence of the Boer War's Black Victims', *Chronicle of Higher Education*, January (2000), p. 19.

494 Quoted in *From Protest to Challenge: A Documentary History of African Politics in South Africa, 1882-1921*, Vol.1, eds. T. Karis and G.M. Carter (Stanford, 1972), p. 18.

495 These were reissued, with a line thanking a recipient for having pointed out the

error.

496 *Sunday Independent*, 31 December 1995.

497 *Van Volksmoeder tot Fokofpolisiekar: Kritiese Opstelle oor Afrikaanse Herinnering-splekke*, eds. Grundlingh & S. Huigen (Stellenbosch, 2008), pp. 177 – 87.

498 Noah Andre Trudeau, *Out of the Storm: The End of the Civil War, April-June 1865* (Baton Rouge, 1995), p. 422.

CHAPTER 11

499 P. Laity, 'The British Peace Movement and the War', in Omissi and Thompson, *South African War*, p.153.

500 J. Darwin, 'Afterword: The Imprint of the War', in Omissi and Thompson, *South African War*, p. 293.

501 *The Sunday Times*, 13 December 2009.

502 Dichmont Mss., The Boer War Letters and Diary of A.F. Corbett, Corbett to his mother, 25 December 1900.

503 Nasson, 'Bobbies to Boers: police, people and social control in Cape Town', in *Policing the Empire: Government, Authority and Control, 1830-1940*, eds. D. M. Anderson and D. Killingray (Manchester, 1991), p. 240.

504 *The Confidence of the Whole Country: Standard Bank Reports on Economic Conditions in Southern Africa, 1865-1902*, eds. A. Mabin and B. Conradie (Johannesburg, 1987), p. 494.

505 B. Mbenga, 'The Role of the Bakgatla of the Pilanesberg in the South African War', in *Wider War*, p.104.

506 Keegan, *A History of Warfare* (London, 1993), pp. 187-8, 361.

507 Searle, *The Quest for National Efficiency* (Oxford, 1971).

508 J.A. Williams, *The Politics of the New Zealand Maori: Protest and Cooperation, 1891-1909* (Seattle, 1969), p. 150; C. Miller, 'The Unhappy Warriors: Conflict and Nationality among Canadian Troops during the South African War', *Journal of Imperial and Commonwealth History*, 23/1 (1995), pp. 76-104; Denoon, 'The Isolation of Australian History', *Historical Studies*, 22/87 (1986), p. 255; R. White, *Inventing Australia* (Sydney, 1992), pp. 79-80.

509 R.A. Bradshaw, 'Japan and colonialism in Africa, 1800-1939', Ph.D. diss. (Ohio University, 1992), pp. 156-60.

510 M. Howard, 'Colonial Wars and European Wars', in *Imperialism and War: Essays on Colonial Wars in Asia and Africa*, eds. J.A. de Moor and H.L. Wesseling (Leiden, 1989), p. 221; V.G. Kiernan, *European Empires from Conquest to Collapse, 1815-1960* (London, 1982), p. 36.

511 J.A. du Pisani and L.W.F. Grundlingh, '"Volkshelde": Afrikaner nationalist mobilisation and representations of the Boer warrior', *Rethinking the South African War Conference* paper, University of South Africa, 1998.

512 Wessels, *Die Militêre Rol van Swart Mense, Bruin Mense en Indiërs tydens die Anglo-*

Boereoorlog (1899-1902) (Bloemfontein, 1998), p. 19.

513 Darwin, 'Afterword', p. 292.

514 Warwick, *Black People*, p. 145; S. Kessler, 'The Black and Coloured Concentration Camps', in *Scorched Earth*, p. 148.

515 B. Vandervort, *Wars of Imperial Conquest in Africa, 1830-1914* (London, 1998), p. ix.

516 Pakenham, *Boer War*, p. 491.

517 Compare R. Shannon, *The Crisis of Imperialism, 1865-1915* (London, 1974), p. 337; Freund, *Contemporary Africa*, pp. 173-75.

518 Porter, 'The South African War and Imperial Britain: A Question of Significance?', in *Wider War*, p.296.

519 J. E. Cronin, *The Politics of State Expansion: War, State and Society in Twentieth Century Britain* (London, 1991), pp. 28, 31, 51.

520 Marsh, *Joseph Chamberlain*, p. 495.

521 Miller, *Lord Methuen*, p. 251.

522 H. Strachan, *European Armies and the Conduct of War* (London, 1983), pp. 86-87; T. Travers, 'The Hidden Army: Structural Problems in the British Officer Corps, 1900-1918', *Journal of Contemporary History*, 17/2 (1982), p. 524.

523 A. Summers, *Angels and Citizens: British Women as Military Nurses, 1854-1914* (London, 1988), p. 205; Marks, 'British Nursing and the South African War', in *Wider War*, p.180.

524 G. J. de Groot, *Blighty: British Society in the Era of the Great War* (London, 1996), p. 24.

525 R.J.Q. Adams and P. P. Poirier, *The Conscription Controversy in Great Britain, 1900-18* (London, 1987), pp. 4-5.

526 T. Ali, *The Clash of Fundamentalisms: Crusades, Jihads and Modernity* (London, 2002), p. 148.

527 Taylor, *Boer War*, p. 38.

528 Quoted in R. Hyam and P. Henshaw, *The Lion and the Springbok: Britain and South Africa since the Boer War* (Cambridge, 2003), p.347.

529 S. Dubow, 'Imagining the New South Africa in the Era of Reconstruction', in Omissi and Thompson, *South African War*, p.77.

SELECT BIBLIOGRAPHY

I have not included a full bibliography. Sources for a book of this kind are numerous as well as eclectic. Unsurprisingly, the list of available sources on the 1899–1902 war is longer than the beard of President Marthinus Steyn. It would take at the very least the proverbial lifetime to plough through everything. To compound the task, scholarly literature is available not merely in English and in Afrikaans, but also in many European languages, and even in Japanese. For present purposes, rather than to reproduce my own sources (chapter references will show my indebtedness to the work of others), the short list which follows is intended more as a guide to further perspectives in English for interested readers. It is designed to cite the more accessible literature produced mainly in recent decades, and especially in the last few years since the 1999 war centenary. Many useful older works may be found in *their* bibliographies.

General histories
The fullest single military narrative is provided by Thomas Pakenham, *The Boer War* (London, 1979) and in more condensed form in *The Boer War: Illustrated Edition* (Johannesburg and London, 1993), their chief merit being the meticulous documentation of operations and engaging style; there is another handy version of Pakenham, 'The Anglo-Boer War, 1899–1902', in *An Illustrated History of South Africa*, eds. Trewella Cameron and S.B. Spies (Johannesburg, 1986). Other accomplished pictorial histories are *The Anglo-Boer War, 1899–1902* (Cape Town, 1985), by Fransjohan Pretorius, a leading Afrikaans authority on the conflict, and Emanoel Lee's *To the Bitter End* (Harmondsworth, 1985), which is graphic on civilian trauma. Tabitha Jackson, *The White Man's War* (London, 1999), sees the war as being responsible for apartheid, a rounded view which may be too round. In its own class altogether is Ryno Greenwall's sumptuous *Artists and Illustrators of the Anglo-Boer War* (Cape Town, 1992), which is an outpouring of world-wide images inspired by the conflict. A scholarly yet accessible, nicely illustrated survey of it all is *The South African War: The Anglo-Boer War, 1899-1902*, ed. Peter Warwick (London, 1980), a set of essays which still stands up. Denis Judd and Keith

Surridge, *The Boer War* (London, 2002), is an especially clear big-canvas account, reflective and fair-minded.

There are now several informative essay collections, good on both British and Boer – and South African – sides, each with their own distinguishing mark. *The South African War Reappraised*, ed. Donal Lowry (Manchester, 2000), is strong on the global impact and moral significance of the war, and on its repercussions for the British empire. For the politics and technicalities of command, varied experiences of warfare and contemporary depiction of the conflict, see *The Boer War: Direction, Experience and Image*, ed. John Gooch (London, 2000). *The Impact of the South African War*, eds. David Omissi and Andrew Thompson (London, 2002), is another wide-ranging collection, strong on the conflict's wider impact and consequences, and thoughtful on that theme of all wars, the gap between aspiration and reality.

For the significance of gender, nationalism, memorialisation and local kinds of African experience, *Writing a Wider War: Rethinking Gender, Race, and Identity in the South African War, 1899-1902*, eds. Greg Cuthbertson, Albert Grundlingh, and Mary-Lynn Suttie (Athens, OH & Cape Town, 2002), makes for thought. Complementary scholarly essays can be sampled in the *South African Historical Journal Special Issue: South African War Centennial Perspectives*, 41/1999, eds. Greg Cuthbertson and Alan Jeeves. *A Century is a Short Time: New Perspectives on the Anglo-Boer War* (Pretoria, 2005), is strongly cultural in its approach, and philosophical and literary as well as historical. To supplement these interpretations, very useful reference works are Darrell Hall, *The Hall Handbook of the Anglo-Boer War* (Pietermaritzburg, 1999); B.J. Barker, *A Concise Dictionary of the Boer War* (Cape Town, 1999); Martin Marix Evans, *Encyclopaedia of the Boer War* (Oxford, 2000); and Fransjohan Pretorius, *Historical Dictionary of the Anglo-Boer War* (Lanham, MD, 2009).

The Anglo-Boer crisis and the origins of war

Perhaps the definitive explanation will never be written. This is a tortuous topic, and has long been the cause of contentious debate over both fine detail and wider interpretation. A grand attempt to bring in the jury is Iain R. Smith, *The Origins of the South African War, 1899-1902* (London, 1996), an exhaustive overview which tends perhaps to overstate its case. Andrew Porter, *The Origins of the South African War: Joseph Chamberlain and the Diplomacy of Imperialism, 1895-99* (Manchester, 1980), is informative on high politics and crisis diplomacy. For a more economic view, stressing capitalist forces, there is Shula Marks and Stanley Trapido, 'Lord Milner and the South African State', *History Workshop Journal*, 8 (1979); 'Lord Milner and the South African State Reconsidered', in *Imperialism, the State and the Third World*, ed. Michael Twaddle (London, 1992); Stanley Trapido, 'Imperialism, Settler Identities and Colonial Capitalism: The Hundred Year Origins of the 1899 South African War', *Historia*, 53/1 (2008).

Military operations

Particular campaigns, specific operations and major battles have generated a host of specialised books and essay studies, not least the substantial volume of Afrikaans micro-histories on assorted Boer commandos and their field performance. Fransjohan Pretorius, *Life on Commando during the Anglo-Boer War, 1899-1902* (Pretoria, 1999), is a highly readable and informative portrait of commando experience. Older standard treatments like Johannes Meintjes, *Stormberg: A Lost Opportunity* (Cape Town, 1969), can be augmented by a newer *Anglo-Boer War Battle Book* series, Pam McFadden, *The Battle of Talana* and *The Battle of Elandslaagte*; S.B Bourquin and Gilbert Torlage, *The Battle of Colenso*; Gilbert Torlage, *The Battle of Spioenkop*; Steve Watt, *The Battle of Vaalkrans*; Ken Gillings, *The Battle of Thukela Heights* (all Johannesburg, 1999).

For individual commanders and evaluations of generalship, there is Fransjohan Pretorius, *The Great Escape of the Boer Pimpernel, Christiaan de Wet: The Making of a Legend* (Pietermaritzburg, 2001); Stephen M. Miller, *Lord Methuen and the British Army: Failure and Redemption in South Africa* (London, 1999). Earlier potted portraits are provided by Philip Bateman, *Generals of the Anglo-Boer War* (Cape Town, 1977). Keith Surridge, *Managing the South African War, 1899-1902: Politicians vs. Generals* (Woodbridge, 1998) is a very thorough account of British strategic management and its attendant military-political tensions. On the important issue of Boer collaboration with British forces, Albert Grundlingh, *The Dynamics of Treason: Boer Collaboration in the South African War of 1899-1902* (Pretoria, 2007), is *the* book.

Older works still provide absorbing detail on the atmosphere of the sieges, such as Kenneth Griffiths, *Thank God We Kept the Flag Flying* (London, 1974) and Brian Gardner's *Mafeking: A Victorian Legend* (London, 1966), and *The Lion's Cage* (London, 1969); Steve Watt, *The Siege of Ladysmith* (Johannesburg, 1999), is a more concise and recent evocation. Siege life is recorded in wonderfully resigned – and different – ways by two of those trapped. Making a nice comparison, they are Edward Ross, *Diary of the Siege of Mafeking, October 1899 to May 1900*, ed. Brian Willan (Cape Town, 1980), and *The Boer War Diary of Sol T. Plaatje*, ed. J. L. Comaroff (London, 1973), the latter a classic personal record of an educated African's war experience. Pat Hopkins and Heather Dugmore, *The Boy: Baden-Powell and the Siege of Mafeking* (Johannesburg, 1999), is unromantic and takes a few liberties with the history. For the overall military doings, almost inside-out, there is Martin Marix Evans, *The Boer War* (Oxford, 1999) and David Smurthwaite, *The Boer War: 1899-1902* (London, 1999). *Scorched Earth*, ed. Fransjohan Pretorius (Cape Town, 2001), is a well-informed recounting of the impact and consequences of Britain's rural clearances and its concentration camps. As its title suggests, Owen Coetzer, *Fire in the Sky: The Destruction of the Orange Free State, 1899-1902* (Johannesburg, 2000), is unambiguous and devastating.

Black experience

A shrewd, now classic probe is Donald Denoon, 'Participation in the "Boer War": People's War, People's Non-War or Non-people's War', in *War and Society in Africa*, ed. Bethwell A. Ogot (London, 1972). Peter Warwick, *Black People and the South African War, 1899–1902* (Cambridge, 1983), remains the standard survey of the war's impact upon black societies across the whole region. My *Uyadela Wen'osulapho: Black Participation in the Anglo-Boer War* (Johannesburg, 1999), provides a highly concise, illustrated account. More localised involvement can be seen in my *Abraham Esau's War: A Black South African War in the Cape, 1899–1902* (Cambridge, 1991), and Jeremy Krikler, *Revolution from Above, Rebellion from Below: The Agrarian Transvaal at the Turn of the Century* (Oxford, 1993). On the lives of black commando auxiliaries, see Pieter Labuschagne, *Ghostriders of the Anglo-Boer War (1899- 1902): The Role and Contribution of Agterryers* (Pretoria, 1999), and my 'Blacks Who Backed the Boers: Republican Commando Auxiliaries in the Anglo-Boer or South African War, 1899-1902', in *Soldiers and Settlers in Africa, 1850-1918*, ed. Stephen M. Miller (Leiden, 2009).

British and Boer societies
Although not specifically war-related, there are any number of useful general histories, such as Robert Ross, *A Concise History of South Africa* (Cambridge, 2nd edn., 2008), Hermann Giliomee, *The Afrikaners: Biography of a People* (Cape Town, 2003), Andrew Thompson, *Imperial Britain: The Empire in British Politics, c.1880–1932* (Harlow, 2000), and G. R. Searle, *A New England ? Peace and War, 1886–1918* (Oxford, 2004). On the war itself, an older book that asked key questions about British wartime sentiment is Richard Price, *An Imperial War and the British Working Class* (London, 1972). On domestic war opposition, Preben Kaarsholm, 'Pro-Boerism and Romantic Anti-Capitalism on the European Continent during the South African War', in *Patriotism: The Making and Unmaking of British National Identity*, Vol.1, ed. Raphael Samuel (London, 1989), also deserves mention. Diana Cammack, *The Rand at War, 1899–1902: The Witwatersrand and the Anglo-Boer War* (London, 1990), documents urban war crisis in the Transvaal superbly.

Personal testimonies and first-hand accounts
In general, it is Boer rather than British soldiering memoirs which stand out, the finest of which are, undoubtedly, Deneys Reitz, *Commando: A Boer Journal of the Boer War* (London, 1931), endlessly reprinted, and Jan Smuts, *Memoirs of the Boer War*, eds. Gail Nattrass and S.B. Spies (Johannesburg, 1994). Other records of note include Roland William Schikkerling, *Commando Courageous: A Boer's Diary* (Johannesburg, 1964); Dietlof van Warmelo, *On Commando* (Johannesburg, 1977); and *The War Memoirs of Commandant Ludwig Krause, 1899–1900*, ed. Jerold Taitz (Cape Town, 1996). Sarah Raal, *The Lady Who Fought: A Young Woman's Account of the Anglo-Boer War* (Cape Town, 2000), is a deeply felt and sharp-eyed female account of being caught up in commando campaigning.

For the extraordinary muddle of a pro-British republican citizen commandeered for Boer service, see *The War Diary of Burgher Jack Lane, 1899–1900*, ed. William Lane (Cape Town, 2001). Another English view of things from within the Boer world can be glimpsed in *Letters from a Boer Parsonage: Letters of Margaret Marquard during the Boer War*, ed. Leo Marquard (Cape Town, 1967), while the experience of being overrun by the Boers in the Cape is captured by Edith Jeffreys, *Aliwal North in the Boer War, 1899–1900: A Contemporary Account*, ed. D. R. M. Wilkinson (Groningen, 2009). For war reportage from both sides, Raymond Sibbald, *The War Correspondents: The Boer War* (Johannesburg, 1993), is read best together with J. E. H. Grobler, *The War Reporter: The Anglo-Boer War Through the Eyes of the Burghers* (Johannesburg, 2004). *Witnesses to War: Personal Documents of the Anglo-Boer War from the Collections of the South African Library*, ed. Karel Schoeman (Cape Town, 2000), is a rich collection of accounts, while his volume on the prominent Cape pro-Boer, Olive Schreiner, *Only an Anguish to Live Here: Olive Schreiner and the Anglo-Boer War, 1899-1902* (Cape Town, 1992), is a thorough and imaginative portrait. For moving humanitarian documentation of refugee life and camp conditions, see Lawrence Richardson, *Selected Correspondence (1902–1903)*, ed. Arthur M. Davey (Cape Town, 1977) and *Emily Hobhouse: Boer War Letters*, ed. Rykie van Reenen (Cape Town, 1984).

International dimensions

Contributors to *The International Impact of the Boer War*, ed. Keith Wilson (London, 2001), discuss, variously, the global political and diplomatic impact of the war. Of national accounts, especially informative on empire involvement and European volunteering, are Carman Miller, *Painting the Map Red: Canada and the South African War, 1899–1902* (Kingston, 1993); *One Flag, One Queen, One Tongue: New Zealand, the British Empire and the South African War, 1899–1902*, eds. John Crawford and Ian McGibbon (Auckland, 2003); Craig Wilcox, *Australia's Boer War: The War in South Africa, 1899–1902* (Melbourne, 2002); Donal P. McCracken, *The Irish Pro-Boers, 1877–1902* (Johannesburg, 1989); Appollon Davidson and Irina Filatova, *The Russians and the Anglo-Boer War, 1899-1902* (Cape Town, 1998).

Literature

The war produced a large body of poetry and fiction, much of it partisan and most of it of variable quality. It did, though, engage the imaginative sensibilities of notable British and South African writers; of those, Rudyard Kipling, Thomas Hardy, Olive Schreiner, Sol Plaatje, Herman Charles Bosman, C. Louis Leipoldt and Eugene Marais should be at the top of any author list. For the flavour of contemporary literature, see Malvern van Wyk Smith, *Drummer Hodge: The Poetry of the Anglo-Boer War, 1899–1902* (Oxford, 1978); *A Century of Anglo-Boer War Stories*, eds. Chris N. van der Merwe and Michael Rice (Johannesburg, 1999); *Songs of the Veld and Other Poems*, ed. Marthinus van Baart (Cape Town, 2008), is a loving re-publication of a 1902 London pro-Boer volume.

War memory and commemoration

Finally, there is the question of how the war has come to be remembered or imagined over time. Its key place in Afrikaner historiography is analysed perceptively by Albert Grundlingh, 'War, Wordsmiths and The "Volk": Afrikaans Historical Writing on the Anglo-Boer War of 1899–1902 and the War in Afrikaner Nationalist Consciousness, 1902–1990', in *Mfecane to Boer War*, eds. E. Lehmann and E. Reckwitz (Essen, 1992). The wider – and changing – politics of commemoration is examined in my 'The South African War/Anglo-Boer War, 1899–1902, and Political Memory in South Africa', in *The Politics of War Memory and Commemoration*, eds. T.G. Ashplant, Graham Dawson and Michael Roper (London, 2000), and in 'Commemorating the Anglo-Boer War in Post-apartheid South Africa', in *Memory and the Impact of Political Transformation in Public Space*, eds. Daniel J. Walkowitz and Lisa Maya Knauer (Durham, NC, 2004). My 'The Priest, the Chapel and the Repentant Landowner: Abraham Esau Revisited', *African Affairs*, 93/387 (1994), considers a strand of the legacy of black involvement. On the concentration camps, and how their memory has been constructed, there is Liz Stanley, *Mourning Becomes . . . Post/memory, Commemoration and the Concentration Camps of the South African War* (Johannesburg, 2008).

INDEX

Page numbers in italics indicate maps.

memory 13, 14
and peace initiatives 193
perceptions by British 18, 19, 35, 36, 37, 268–269
pursuit by Roberts and exile 206–210
retreat from Pretoria 200–201, 205
strong position after Jameson Raid 51–52, 53
and Uitlanders 54
Krugersdorp 195, 203, 207, 213, 217
Krupp guns 75, 76, 77, 92, 102, 113, 187, 188

labour force
in Cape 23, 81
during war 109–110, 115, 118, 121, 125, 182, 191, 196, 245
on mines 42, 46, 51, 67, 72, 196, 197
in republics 24, 42, 46, 71, 266
Labour Party 39, 55, 260, 275
Ladysmith
British headquarters 100, 101, 103, 106
connection with Dundee severed 101–102
relief of siege 164–167, 168, 259
sabotage of railway line 98
siege 106–110, 107, 147, 151, 154, 161, 303
Laing's Nek 74, 91, 100, 106, 190, 206
Lansdowne, Lord
on capture of Pretoria 199
communications from Buller 147, 151
confident of swift victory 90
conflict with Wolseley 131–132
expectation of war 62, 63
inadequate preparation for war 88, 89, 92, 94, 147
Lennox Hill 103
Leyds, W.J. 69, 126
Liberal Imperialists 43, 51, 259, 260, 261, 262
Lichtenburg 196, 229, 282, 305

literature 28, 51, 284–285, 286, 287–288, 314
Lloyd George, David 40, 244, 253, 261
Lombard's Nek 106
London Convention (1884) 44, 50
Long, Charles 149–150
Long Tom guns 113
Lyttelton, Neville 133, 162

Machadodorp 202, 205, 218
Mafeking
British relief offensive 168, 191–192
relief of siege 259, 261
sabotage of railway 98
siege 111–115, 178
Mafikeng 112, 113, 298
Magaliesberg 202, 203, 204, 217, 227, 228
Magersfontein 136, 137, 138, 143–147, 146, 149, 170, 172, 303
Mahon, Bryan 192
Majuba 32, 43, 66, 74, 89, 96, 100, 106, 126
Mandela, Nelson 293
Mandela, Winnie 300
mapping 93, 94, 135, 169, 221
Mareuil, George-Henri de Villebois de 189
Marks, Sammy 72, 185
Marxism 38
Mauser rifles 52, 75, 76, 87, 113, 268
Maxim-Nordenfeld guns 76, 97, 227
May telegram 54
medical services 15, 146, 191, 245, 247, 314
memorials 13, 285, 295
Merriman, John X 36, 56, 69
Methuen, Lord Paul
advance towards Kimberley 133, 134–138, 139, 143–147, 146, 153, 172, 191
pursuit of Boers 208, 226, 228–229
surrender by Piet de Wet 223
on trust in Boers 282
Meyer, Lukas 102, 103, 106, 201, 233, 238
Mfengu community 115, 143

Middelburg 223–224, 249, 251
migrant labour 42, 46, 51
military culture
Boer 71, 74, 103, 109, 122
British 268–269, 270–271
Milner, Lord Alfred
arrogance 53, 56, 199, 283
attitude towards Roberts 216
desire for Boer capitulation 33, 35, 37, 91, 231
desire to 'anglicise' Transvaal 254, 255, 305
on fall of Pretoria 199
'forward' policy 15, 19
ill-preparation of troops 62
Jameson Raid 25, 33, 50
and Kimberley siege 119
negotiations over Uitlander grievances 53–54, 55
opposition to Buller's strategy 134
peace negotiations 127, 224, 255, 256, 257, 311
purpose of concentration camps 243–244
mining industry
see also diamonds; gold
and Boers' control 51–52
coalfields 59, 109, 132, 194
motive for war 17, 21, 25, 57–58, 61
Modder River 135, 137–138, 139, 143–144, 170, 171, 173, 176, 177, 303
Molteno 140, 141
Mozambique 41, 44, 58, 59, 168, 209

Naauwpoort 124, 133, 139–140, 170, 221
Namaqualand Scouts 249
Naroegas battle 249
Natal
Boer offensive 98, 100–103, 104, 105–110, 107, 126
British counter-offensive 133–134, 147–151, 152, 153–157, 158, 159–163
early history 23, 24, 40
economics 57, 58, 59
guerrilla struggle 214, 219–220

importance in Boer war plan 74–75
importance of defence 89, 91, 92
importance of ports 41, 44
relief of Ladysmith 164–167
Natal Indian Ambulance Corps 160
nationalism
Afrikaner 31, 43, 245, 285, 286–288, 293–295, 296–297, 299
and English South Africans 289
new South African 300
National Party 288, 289, 294, 297, 316
National Scouts 237, 238, 239
Ndebele people 30, 122
Netherlands 13, 22, 183, 209
Netherlands South African Railway Company 80
New Zealand 27, 92, 133, 306
Nicholson's Nek 106
Nooitgedacht 217–218
Northern Border Scouts 249
North Lancashire Regiment 117

Orange Free State
alliance with Transvaal 51, 52, 55, 56, 70, 100, 254–255
Bloemfontein fall and Boer counter-offensive 179, 179–180, 181, 182, 187–191, 200–201
Boer war ultimatum 35, 37
British strategy 133, 134
independent Boer republic 23–24, 40, 56, 276
name change to Free State 302
support for war 55, 70–71
Orange Free State commandos
see also commando system
artillery 75, 77
at Belmont 135
Cape Colony offensive 123–124, 125, 127